UNIX Internetworking

Second Edition

For a complete listing of *The Artech House Telecommunications Library,*
turn to the back of this book.

UNIX Internetworking

Second Edition

Uday O. Pabrai

Artech House
Boston • London

Library of Congress Cataloging-in-Publication Data
Pabrai, Uday O.
    UNIX internetworking/Uday O. Pabrai. – 2nd ed.
        p.   cm.
    Includes bibliographical references and index.
    ISBN 0-89006-778-3 (alk. paper)
        1. Computer networks. 2. UNIX (Computer file) 3. Internetworking (Telecommunication) I. Title.
TK5105.5.P32   1995   95-40925
004.6–dc20   CIP

British Library Cataloguing in Publication Data
Pabrai, Uday O.
    UNIX Internetworking. – 2Rev. ed.
    I. Title
    004.6

    ISBN 0-89006-778-3

© 1996 ARTECH HOUSE, INC.
685 Canton Street
Norwood, MA 02062

All rights reserved. Printed and bound in the United States of America. No part of this book may be reproduced or utilized in any form or by any means, electronic or mechanical, including photocopying, recording, or by any information storage and retrieval system, without permission in writing from the publisher.
All terms mentioned in this book that are known to be trademarks or service marks have been appropriately capitalized. Artech House cannot attest to the accuracy of this information. Use of a term in this book should not be regarded as affecting the validity of any trademark or service mark.

International Standard Book Number: 0-89006-778-3
Library of Congress Catalog Card Number: 95-40925

10 9 8 7 6 5 4 3 2 1

To my best friend and wife, Tina. To my heartbeats, Natasha and Nathan.

Contents

Preface to the First Edition		xv
Preface to the Second Edition		xvii
Acknowledgments		xix

Chapter 1   UNIX Operating System Environment   1
    1.1   UNIX: Past and Present   2
        1.1.1   History and Growth of UNIX   2
        1.1.2   Flavors of the UNIX Operating System   4
        1.1.3   Windows NT and UNIX   12
    1.2   Key UNIX Concepts   13
        1.2.1   Operating System Versus Kernel   13
        1.2.2   Programs and Processes   14
        1.2.3   Signals   15
        1.2.4   File System   15
        1.2.5   System Calls   16
    1.3   Important System Files   17
        1.3.1   **/etc/passwd**   18
        1.3.2   **/etc/shadow**   18
        1.3.3   **/etc/group**   20
        1.3.4   **/etc/inittab**   21
    1.4   UNIX System Initialization (Start-Up)   21
        1.4.1   Memory Management   23
    1.5   Standards: SVID, POSIX, COSE, OSF, and X/Open   24
    1.6   UNIX and Client/Server Computing   24
        1.6.1   Processor Technology   25
        1.6.2   Client/Server System Strategies   27
        1.6.3   Peripheral Devices   28
    1.7   Summary   29
    References   30
    Select Bibliography   30

Chapter 2		Network Architectures and Technologies	31
	2.1	Network Architectures	31
		2.1.1 OSI/RM	32
		2.1.2 The OSI/RM and the Internet Architecture	33
	2.2	Internet (TCP/IP) Architecture	33
		2.2.1 Layers in the Internet Architecture	36
		2.2.2 Internet Network Addresses	37
		2.2.3 Internet Address Notation	38
		2.2.4 Internet Address Classes	38
		2.2.5 Loopback Address	39
		2.2.6 Subnet Mask	40
		2.2.7 Broadcast Address	41
		2.2.8 Multicast Address	41
	2.3	Network Access Layer	41
		2.3.1 Ethernet	41
		2.3.2 Fast Ethernet (100Base-X)	43
		2.3.3 Ethernet 100VG-Any LAN	44
		2.3.4 Token Ring	45
		2.3.5 Fiber Distributed Data Interface	46
		2.3.6 Frame Relay	46
		2.3.7 ATM	52
		2.3.8 IEEE LAN Standards	63
	2.4	Internet Layer	64
		2.4.1 Address Resolution Protocol (ARP)	65
		2.4.2 Reverse Address Resolution Protocol (RARP)	66
		2.4.3 Internet Protocol (IP)	68
	2.5	Transport Layer	72
		2.5.1 Transmission Control Protocol (TCP)	72
		2.5.2 User Datagram Protocol (UDP)	92
	2.6	Application Layer	94
		2.6.1 Bootstrap Protocol (BOOTP)	94
		2.6.2 Dynamic Host Configuration Protocol (DHCP)	96
	2.7	Summary	98
	References		101
	Select Bibliography		101
	Appendix 2A	Important Network Concepts	101
		2A.1 Transmission Types	101
		2A.2 Data Transmission Modes	101
		2A.3 Baseband and Broadcast Services	102
		2A.4 Switching Virtual LANs	102
		2A.5 Switching	103
		2A.6 Classes of Switching Hubs	104

			Contents ix

	2A.7	Fast Packet Switching, Cell, and Frame Relay	104
	2A.8	T1/T3 Standards	105
Chapter 3		UNIX Network Elements	107
3.1		Network Files on UNIX Systems	107
	3.1.1	**/etc/hosts**	107
	3.1.2	**/etc/protocols**	108
	3.1.3	**/etc/services**	109
	3.1.4	**/etc/ethers**	111
	3.1.5	**/etc/bootptab**	112
	3.1.6	**/etc/netmasks**	113
	3.1.7	**/etc/inetd.conf**	114
3.2		Network Processes on UNIX Systems	118
	3.2.1	*inetd*	120
	3.2.2	*routed*	121
	3.2.3	*rarpd*	121
	3.2.4	*bootpd*	121
	3.2.5	NFS-Related Processess: *nfsd, biod, automount*	122
	3.2.6	NIS Related Processess: *ypserv, ypxfrd, ypbind*	122
	3.2.7	DNS Related Process: *named*	123
	3.2.8	*rpcbind* and *portmap*	123
3.3		Network-Related Commands	124
	3.3.1	**ifconfig**	124
	3.3.2	**netstat**	125
	3.3.3	**arp**	135
	3.3.4	**nslookup**	136
	3.3.5	**hostname**	137
	3.3.6	**domainname**	137
	3.3.7	**rpcinfo**	137
	3.3.8	**uname**	138
	3.3.9	**telnet**	139
	3.3.10	**rlogin**	139
	3.3.11	**ftp**	139
	3.3.12	**rcp**	141
	3.3.13	**rsh**	141
	3.3.14	**snoop**	142
3.4		Internet Resources	144
	3.4.1	ftp anonymous Accounts and Request for Comment (RFC) Documents	145
	3.4.2	User Information Commands	145
3.5		Summary	148
		References	149
		Select Bibliography	149

Chapter 4		Distributed Computing	151
	4.1	Network File System (NFS)	151
		4.1.1 Design and Working	151
		4.1.2 Stateless Protocol	152
		4.1.3 NFS Procedures	153
		4.1.4 BSD UNIX and NFS	153
		4.1.5 SVR4 UNIX and NFS	158
		4.1.6 NFS Server Configuration	163
		4.1.7 NFS Client Configuration	164
		4.1.8 NFS Automounter	165
		4.1.9 NFS: Future Direction	168
	4.2	Network Information Service (NIS or YP)	169
		4.2.1 Motivation for NIS	170
		4.2.2 Terminology	170
		4.2.3 Client/Server Model	171
		4.2.4 NIS Files	171
		4.2.5 NIS Maps	171
		4.2.6 Modifying and Propagating NIS Maps	172
		4.2.7 Configuring an NIS Master Service	173
		4.2.8 Configuring an NIS Slave Server	175
		4.2.9 Configuring an NIS Client	177
		4.2.10 About NIS Password Files	177
		4.2.11 NIS Usage	179
	4.3	NIS+	180
		4.3.1 Definition of Terminology	181
		4.3.2 NIS+ Files	182
		4.3.3 NIS+ Daemons	185
		4.3.4 NIS+ Commands	188
		4.3.5 NIS+ Root Master Server Configuration	191
		4.3.6 NIS+ Client Configuration	195
		4.3.7 NIS+ Replica Configuration	197
		4.3.8 NIS+ Master Server Configuration in a New Domain	199
	4.4	Domain Name Service (DNS)	201
		4.4.1 DNS: Types of Servers	202
		4.4.2 DNS Primary Master Server Configuration	204
		4.4.3 DNS Client Only Configuration	206
		4.4.4 Configuring a DNS Caching Only System	208
		4.4.5 Using the **nslookup** Command	210
	4.5	Summary	211
		References	212
		Select Bibliography	212

Chapter 5	Security		213
5.1	ISO Security Architecture 7498-2		213
	5.1.1	Definition of Security	213
	5.1.2	Motivation for Security	213
	5.1.3	Security Terminology and Abbreviations	214
	5.1.4	Security Threats	214
	5.1.5	Types of Attacks	214
	5.1.6	Security Services	218
	5.1.7	Security Mechanisms	218
	5.1.8	Security Management	220
5.2	UNIX and Security		220
	5.2.1	Super-User Sessions	220
	5.2.2	Passwords	220
	5.2.3	System Accounts	222
	5.2.4	Controlling Account Access	222
	5.2.5	Logging Unsuccessful Logins	223
	5.2.6	Search Path	224
	5.2.7	Restricting Root Access	225
	5.2.8	**umtp** and **wtmp** Files	225
	5.2.9	syslog Facility	226
	5.2.10	The **last** Command	226
	5.2.11	Directory and File Permissions	227
	5.2.12	The **umask** Command	227
	5.2.13	The **chmod** Command	227
	5.2.14	UIDs and GIDs	228
	5.2.15	setuid, setgid, and the Sticky Bit	229
5.3	TCP/IP and Security		229
	5.3.1	**telnet** Versus **rlogin**	229
	5.3.2	Incoming FTP Connections	231
	5.3.3	sendmail, SMTP, and Security	231
	5.3.4	Denying Incoming Network Access	232
	5.3.5	Denying Outgoing Network Access	232
	5.3.6	NFS Security	232
	5.3.7	The Trivial File Transfer Protocol	233
	5.3.8	NIS+ Security	234
5.4	Security-Related Products and Applications		236
	5.4.1	ASET	236
	5.4.2	Computer Oracle Password System (COPS)	239
	5.4.3	TCP Wrapper	247
	5.4.4	Other Security-Related Applications	249
5.5	Kerberos		249
5.6	What Do We Need To Do?		251
5.7	Summary		252

	References		252
	Select Bibliography		252
	Appendix 5A About Anonymous FTP Accounts		252
	5A.1	Anonymous FTP Account Configuration on Solaris 2.x System	253
	5A.2	Anonymous FTP Configuration on a SUNOS 4.1.3 System	255
Chapter 6	Client/Server Applications		259
6.1	Interprocess Communication Mechanisms (IPCs)		260
6.2	Distributed Applications		266
	6.2.1	Berkeley Sockets	267
	6.2.2	Transport Layer Interface (TLI)	267
	6.2.3	Remote Procedure Calls (RPCs)	268
	6.2.4	TCP and UDP Ports	269
6.3	Berkeley Socket System Calls		274
	6.3.1	Iterative and Concurrent Servers	274
	6.3.2	System Calls	275
	6.3.3	Using the *portmapper* Service	278
6.4	Summary		280
	References		280
	Select Bibliography		281
	Appendix 6A Berkeley Socket Client/Server Application		281
	6A.1	Server Application	281
	6A.2	Client Application	285
	Appendix 6B UDP Broadcast Client/Server Application		289
	6B.1	Server Application	289
	6B.2	Client Application	290
Chapter 7	Internetworking		293
7.1	Novell's Netware Architechture		293
	7.1.1	Novell NetWare Protocols	293
	7.1.2	Case Study: Novell System Configuration	300
	7.1.3	Open Data–Link Interface (ODI)	306
	7.1.4	Internetworking Products	307
7.2	UNIX-Macintosh Integration		310
	7.2.1	The AppleTalk Environment	310
	7.2.2	AppleTalk and the OSI/RM	311
	7.2.3	AppleTalk Addressing	311
	7.2.4	AppleTalk Protocols	312
	7.2.5	AppleTalk Network Types	312
	7.2.6	Internetworking Services	313
	7.2.7	Internetworking Software	315

	7.3	X Window System	316
		7.3.1 MIT's Project Athena and X	316
		7.3.2 The X Standard	317
		7.3.3 X Terminology	318
		7.3.4 X Servers and Clients	319
		7.3.5 X Protocol	319
		7.3.6 XDMCP	322
		7.3.7 X and Serial Line Protocols	322
		7.3.8 X Commands and Applications	323
		7.3.9 PCs, UNIX, and the X Window System	325
	7.4	Windows NT	326
		7.4.1 NT and TCP/IP	327
		7.4.2 NT Installation and Configuration	330
	7.5	Summary	336
		Select Bibliography	336
Chapter 8		Managing UNIX Networks	339
	8.1	Communication Devices	339
		8.1.1 Repeaters	339
		8.1.2 Bridges	340
		8.1.3 Routers	340
		8.1.4 Brouters	340
		8.1.5 Gateways and Protocol Converters	341
		8.1.6 Hubs	341
		8.1.7 CSU/DSU	341
	8.2	Routing	342
		8.2.1 RIP	343
		8.2.2 OSPF	345
		8.2.3 EGP	347
		8.2.4 What About OSI's IS-IS?	347
	8.3	Network And System Management	348
		8.3.1 Model for Network Management	348
		8.3.2 ASN.1	349
		8.3.3 SNMP	350
		8.3.4 SNMPv2	365
		8.3.5 System Management	368
		8.3.6 NMS Product: SunNet Manager, Installation and Usage	375
	8.4	ICMP: TCP/IP's Troubleshooting Protocol	381
		8.4.1 ICMP Destination Unreachable Message	383
		8.4.2 ICMP Time Exceeded Message	384
		8.4.3 ICMP Parameter Problem Message	385
		8.4.4 ICMP Source Quench Message	386

		8.4.5	ICMP Redirect Message	386
		8.4.6	ICMP Echo Request Message	388
		8.4.7	ICMP Echo Reply Message	389
		8.4.8	ICMP Timestamp Request Message	390
		8.4.9	ICMP Timestamp Reply Message	391
		8.4.10	ICMP Address Mask Request Message	392
		8.4.11	ICMP Address Mask Reply Message	393
		8.4.12	ICMP Information Request and Reply	394
	8.5	Network Application (**telnet**, **ftp**) Problems		394
	8.6	Network File System (NFS) Problems		395
		8.6.1	File System Errors	395
		8.6.2	Read Only Errors	395
		8.6.3	**mountd** Daemon Problems	396
	8.7	Summary		396
	Select Bibliography			397
Appendix A	RFC 1340			399
Appendix B	Glossary			401
Appendix C	Acronyms			417
Appendix D	Internic Internet Service Providers List			423
Appendix E	Internet Address Application			425
Appendix F	Domain Registration Application			431
Appendix G	IP Version 6			435
About the Author				437
Index				439

Preface to the First Edition

Just as TCP/IP is increasingly being accepted as the common thread to interconnect heterogeneous computer systems and X as the common denominator for graphical user interfaces, we find UNIX is slowly but surely asserting itself as the operating system for commercial organizations. This is despite the fact that the UNIX command interface is cryptic, and system configuration is no easy task.

The UNIX operating system of today supports features that are hard to find in any other operating system, past or present. For example, the flexibility the UNIX provides for client-server configuration of systems is unmatched. You can have UNIX nodes configured without any disk where the operating system is dynamically loaded from the network when the system starts up or you can have hundreds of processor loosely coupled together running UNIX and functioning as a CPU server for others. Most important, support for the TCP/IP protocols stack is built in to the UNIX kernel—it has been for a long time. UNIX. X and TCP/IP are the cornerstones of open system technology.

As we integrate UNIX systems in our environment, we need to understand how to configure a UNIX system on the network and how to configure an internetwork between UNIX and other technologies on the same network. The focus of this text is to take you through critical elements of the UNIX system and describe how they relate to the network, so that not only can we connect UNIX systems to the network, but also understand now to communicate between Novell, VAX/VMS, X, Macintosh, and DOS systems and UNIX host.

We begin by defining system and network protocol fundamentals. Next we examine the key elements of the UNIX system as they relate to networks: files, processes, and commands. Then we take a look at distributed computing technologies: NFS, NIS, and DNS. Chapter 4 turns to open, yet secure networks: there is a neeed to secure transactions on the network—this chapter emphasizes security—both for the operating system and the network. Chapter 5 details how to develop client-server applications—UNIX supports a rich set of interprocess and intersystem communication mechanisms, which this chapter describes. Finally, the last chapter focuses on internetworking: how to communicate between UNIX hosts and any other system in your environment, including Macintosh, DOS, X, and Novell systems.

Preface to the Second Edition

Both the UNIX industry and TCP/IP, the protocol stack that is the basis of the Internet, have grown incredibly in the last few years. When you seriously think about the basic building block for any computing environment, today, more than ever before, UNIX and TCP/IP are the natural choices. Anything else is expensive, proprietary, and not necessarily scaleable.

In a client/server computing environment, no operating system comes close to all of the advantages offered by UNIX. I think of price, performance, support for open industry standards, and most importantly, *flexibility* and *scaleability*. UNIX is it—be it database servers, compute servers, application servers, or communication servers. On the other side, from the smallest businesses to the largest global networks, the network protocol that is increasingly deployed is TCP/IP. TCP/IP is open, simple, and scaleable. Be it two PCs or the global Internet, TCP/IP is the global standard in designing networks.

My *motivation* in writing the second edition was to try and keep pace with the phenomenal changes in the UNIX and TCP/IP industry. My *approach* is to explain concepts and then describe step-by-step what it takes to configure and use specific protocols. The *style* is based on what I have learned from thousands of students nationwide—the style is practical and hands-on. Students who have attended my classes and you, the reader—your time is precious and your interest sincere. Hence, my objective is to be to the point and describe UNIX and network-related technologies in a clear, concise manner, so that you may apply the concepts to improve computing processes around you.

There are eight chapters in this book. Chapter 1 describes the fundamentals of UNIX especially as it relates to networks. Chapter 2 emphasizes network fundamentals with the focus on the TCP/IP protocol stack. Chapter 3 explains critical network related files, daemons (processes) and commands on UNIX systems. When you think of UNIX systems in a client/server computing environment, you think about NFS, NIS, NIS+ and DNS.

Distributed protocols, such as NFS, are emphasized in Chapter 4. Security concepts and terminology are described in Chapter 5, while Chapter 6 explains how to develop client/server applications. Chapter 7 details how to internetwork UNIX hosts with PC DOS, Windows, Novell NetWare, Apple

Macintosh, X Windows, and Windows NT systems. Chapter 8 describes how to effectively troubleshoot and manage UNIX and TCP/IP networks with technologies based on standards such as SNMP. The appendixes include some extremely useful references and UNIX and TCP/IP-related information including applications for Internet addresses and domain names.

All the examples specified in this text have been tested on Sun SPARCstation 2 systems running SunOS (BSD) 4.1.3 and Solaris (SVR4) 2.3.

Acknowledgments

I am grateful to all of my students who attended the NGT 3-day hands-on class on UNIX Internetworking—your never-ending questions helped further enhance my understanding of the subject matter. *Never stop asking questions*—asking questions is a key element in the overall process of learning and understanding.

I am very grateful to many who have assisted me with this project. I would like to thank the people at Fermi National Accelerator Laboratory, a pioneering environment for high energy physics research and its applications. Specifically, I thank Joel Butler, Tom Nash, Judy Nicholls, Bill Lidinsky, Hemant Shah, Frank Koenen, Janet Weber, Chris O'Reilly, and Madi. Special thanks to Vijay Gurbani—thanks for reviewing and assisting with the section on client/server applications. Thanks to Mike Calwas and Ken Cunningham at Teradyne. I will always cherish my discussions with Ed Brady of Teradyne.

Thanks to Serbjeet Kaur for assisting with the many diagrams in this text. Steve Chen and Mike Barbic from the Illinois Mathematics and Science Academy (IMSA) assisted testing many security-related products—special thanks and I wish both of you the very best in college and beyond. Remember, *learning is a continuous process*.

I am also very grateful to the staff at Artech House, especially Mark Walsh, Beverly Cutter, Joanne Crerand, Judi Stone, and Kim Field: thanks for your patience and dedication to this text.

To my sister Jyoti—I wish you the best in academics and thanks for your encouragement and support—I am and will always be very proud of you. To my brother Mohnish, I wish you the very best in all your endeavors. To the best parents that anyone could have—I cannot indicate how thankful I am for the emphasis you placed on academics and learning, Papa and Mummy—thank you very, very much. Mother, Sri Aurobindo, and Ganesh—I am grateful for all your love and spiritual guidance.

To my children, Natasha and Nathan, you make a father proud. Tina, my best friend and companion for life, *this one is for you*. I love you with all my heart.

UNIX Operating System Environment

1

The basics of the UNIX operating system are described in this chapter. The concepts discussed are from the perspective of a stand-alone UNIX system—the network element is introduced in later chapters. It is important to understand operating system fundamentals without the complication of network protocols and processes. Specifically, this chapter emphasizes important UNIX concepts such as:

- Kernel and the operating system;
- Program;
- Processes;
- System calls;
- Signals;
- Partitions and file systems.

Further, we describe important files on UNIX systems, such as:

- **/etc/passwd**;
- **/etc/shadow**;
- **/etc/group**;
- **/etc/inittab**.

To establish the relationship between various concepts introduced in this chapter, we walk through the process of booting a UNIX system. We discuss how various elements of the UNIX operating system are involved in the system initialization process. In our experience, this helps the reader appreciate the relationship between operating system entities. This understanding is important when in later chapters we introduce network protocols and processes on UNIX systems.

Once operating system fundamentals are understood, we describe the various types of client/server architectures that are possible with the UNIX operating system.

The flexibility that UNIX offers in client/server computing is unmatched.

Server nodes may be:

- A single-processor system;
- A multiprocessor (both asymmetric and symmetric multiprocessor) system;
- A farm of processors (possibly, hundreds) loosely coupled together.

Client nodes may be:

- Diskless;
- Dataless;
- Hybrid;
- X terminals.

The flexibility that UNIX offers is that any combination of servers and clients may be deployed to support client/server computing.

Also, in this chapter we study client/server configurations of UNIX systems architected on *complex instruction set computer* (CISC) and *reduced instruction set computer* (RISC) processors. We then investigate the types of peripheral devices attached to UNIX systems.

No other operating system gives you the flexibility that UNIX does in distributing system resources across the network.

1.1 UNIX: PAST AND PRESENT

We examine the past and present status of the UNIX operating system.

1.1.1 History and Growth of UNIX

The UNIX operating system has been around for more than two decades. Ken Thompson developed the first version of the operating system at Bell Laboratories in 1969.

By the late 1970s UNIX was finding its presence in universities and colleges. UNIX was also being used in operating telephone companies because it provided a good environment for software development and network transaction operations services. UNIX was first implemented on a PDP-7 system. In 1971 UNIX was moved to a PDP-11. In 1977, the UNIX operating system was first ported to the Interdata 8/32 system.

Between 1977 and 1982 Bell Laboratories combined several AT&T UNIX variants into a single system that was referred to as UNIX system III. UNIX System V was the result of several features added to UNIX system III. AT&T officially supported System V in January 1983. The major operating systems at this point were System V and Berkeley Software Distribution (BSD).

The University of California at Berkeley was instrumental in integrating network protocols with the UNIX operating system. The Defense Advanced Research Projects Agency (DARPA) funded Bolt Beranek and Newman, Inc. (BBN) to implement the TCP/IP protocols on UNIX systems and funded Berkeley to support TCP/IP with its version of UNIX, referred to as *Berkeley Software Distribution UNIX* (BSD UNIX). Because most computer science departments were running BSD UNIX, DARPA was successful in reaching a large percentage of these universities.

Berkeley's networking implementation supported communication among diverse network facilities that included both local area networks such as Ethernet and token-ring and *wide area networks* (WANs) such as DARPA's Advanced Research Projects Agency Network (ARPANET).

By the mid-1980s, UNIX was installed on tens of thousands of systems worldwide. These systems included machines from several different manufacturers and varied in computing power from microprocessors to mainframes. No other operating system came even close in comparison. A major advantage of UNIX systems today is they can be used as client nodes or server nodes in client/server configurations. Some other factors that contributed to the success of the UNIX operating system include [1]:

- UNIX is a *multiuser, multiprocessor* system. Each user can therefore execute several processes concurrently. Moreover, users have control over the processes they create; thus each user can create several processes, control the execution of these processes, and terminate them.
- The *machine architecture* (to a large extent) *is hidden from the end user*. From the perspective of the software developer it makes it easier to write programs that run on different hardware implementations. A user executing commands typically finds a consistent command interface whether working on a Silicon Graphics IRIX operating system or a SunOS system.
- Because the *operating system is written in C*, it is relatively easier to port UNIX from one hardware architecture to another.
- UNIX supports a *hierarchical file system*.
- UNIX provides a *consistent format for files*, which makes the process of writing application programs easier.
- The operating system provides a *consistent interface to peripheral devices*.

Some of the disadvantages of UNIX are:

- The user interface, although consistent, is cryptic; commands such as **grep, awk, man,** and others make UNIX a difficult operating system to learn.
- The system management issues related to UNIX are complex and vary significantly from one flavor of UNIX to another.

1.1.2 Flavors of the UNIX Operating System

There are many flavors of the UNIX operating system available in the market today. These include SunOS, ULTRIX, AIX, IRIX, BSD, HP-UX, NeXTStep, Coherent, XENIX and SCO UNIX, SVR4, and OSF/1. The UNIX operating system runs on both CISC- and RISC-based systems. For example, if one has an interest in running UNIX on a PC based on an Intel 80486 processor, the choices include:

- Dell SVR4;
- UnixWare;
- Solaris for Intel;
- NeXTStep;
- Coherent;
- Consensys UNIX;
- NetBSD;
- Linux.

1.1.2.1 BSD 4.x

Outside of Bell Laboratories and AT&T, the institute that has had the most influence on the UNIX operating system is the University of California at Berkeley. Bill Joy, Chuck Haley, and Ken Thompson were the key individuals involved with UNIX at the University of California, Berkeley. In 1976 Joy's team introduced a 32-bit BSD UNIX version. All the development work was done on a VAX 11/780 computer.

The first Berkeley work was released in 1979, known as *release 3BSD*. This release supported virtual memory, demand paging, and page replacement. In 1979 DARPA funded the development of an enhanced version of 3BSD, including support for TCP/IP. Later, DARPA funded the University of California to add the following features in 4.1BSD:

- Fast file system;
- Disk quotas;
- TCP/IP socket interface.

There have been a number of BSD releases since 3BSD: 4.0BSD, 4.1BSD, 4.2BSD, 4.3BSD, and 4.3BSD Tahoe. Release 4.3BSD provided support for multiple network protocol families, such as the XEROX Network System (XNS) and TCP/IP. Release 4.3BSD also provided support for TCP/IP subnetting and routing.

Release 4.4BSD includes support for the OSI protocols at a number of layers. Both IBM and the University of Wisconsin contributed implementations of the network layer (CLNS) and the transport layer (TP.0 and TP.4). Release 4.4BSD marked the end of the BSD series of UNIX.

1.1.2.2 SVR4

SVR4 unifies the most popular versions of UNIX: System V Release 3, XENIX, BSD, and SunOS. System V Release 4 (SVR4) was developed by UNIX System Laboratories (USL) under the directive of *UNIX International* (UI). In 1990 AT&T transferred control of the UNIX operating system from the Bell Laboratories research facility to UNIX System Laboratories (USL). USL, a subsidiary of AT&T, was acquired by Novell. UNIX International, a nonprofit, independent organization, was formed to unify the UNIX system market. Its members included:

- Amdahl Corporation;
- Apple;
- Cray Research Corporation;
- Silicon Graphics Computer Systems;
- Solbourne Computer;
- Sony International;
- Sun Microsystems.

SVR4 provides support for real-time processing. To do this, it supports two types of processes: time sharing and real time. New system calls, including several adapted from the BSD system, are used to manage real-time processes. Like BSD, SVR4 offers microsecond resolution for timing to accommodate the scheduling of applications dealing with short time intervals.

Key enhancements have been introduced by SVR4 in the area of networking. Release 4 supports TCP/IP protocols and includes commands for file transfer, remote login, and remote execution. Support is also provided for NFS, RPC, and XDR protocols.

The SVR4 MP (multiple processors) kernel is multithreaded and allows up to 16 processors to operate concurrently. The enhancements by USL to SVR4 include:

- *SVR4 ES*: This release provides security at the B2 level. New security features include prevention of unauthorized access, auditing capability, and capability for controlling resources. SVR4.1 ES (enhanced security) contains features of the *multilevel security* (MLS) package such as multiple access to control methods, trusted paths, and customized audit trails.
- *SVR4 MP (multiprocessing plus)*: This release provides additional features for multiprocessing support via symmetrical shared memory architectures. Plans also include extended graphics user interface support, transaction processing support, and enhanced file management.
- *SVR4 network computing plus:* The primary objective of this release is to provide additional distributed network computing capabilities. New

features include system and network administration enhancements to manage and control resources across heterogeneous networked systems, support for OSI protocols, real-time enhancements, and C++ support.
- *SVR4.2 (Destiny)*: SVR4.2 is based on SVR4.1 enhanced security and is the basis for the SVR4.2 ES/MP (enhanced security–multiprocessing) release. USL hopes that SVR4.2 will be a popular operating system in PC environments. The operating system includes point-and-click graphical user interface; simplified system administration; shrink-wrap packaging; DOS emulation (thus supporting DOS and Windows applications); and support for OSF's application environment specification (AES), a specification for the OSF operating system similar to what System V Interface Definition (SVID) is for System V. The potential competitors to SVR4.2 are Windows NT, Solaris, OS/2, and AIM (Apple–IBM–Motorola consortium).

1.1.2.3 OSF

Key members of the *Open Software Foundation* (OSF) include IBM, Digital, and HP. The operating system available from OSF is OSF/x, where x is the version number. OSF/2, for example, incorporates a microkernel that requires only about 60,000 lines of code and, thus, frees memory for other applications. It is expected to be certified at a B3-level of security because of its trusted computing base.

Elements of the operating system such as those that control processes and provide access to the CPU are in the kernel, whereas other parts of the operating system run just as applications would. This was demonstrated by OSF at Uniforum 1992, where the OSF/1 microkernel (MK) supported DOS, OSF/1, and the BSD operating systems. The OSF/1 kernel was based on Mach 2.5 and Mach 3.0 from Carnegie-Mellon University and includes the POSIX conformant version of BSD4.3. The key feature of the Mach operating system is that it supports concurrent use of threads, which makes it easier to implement symmetric multiprocessing. *Threads* are separable sequences of related instructions. OSF/1 also includes portions of IBM's AIX and Encore Computers' symmetric multiprocessing implementation.

The technologies being offered by OSF include:

- Distributed computing environment (DCE);
- Distributed management environment (DME);
- MOTIF.

OSF's DCE has been completely specified. DCE code has been available to members and nonmembers; various vendors and organizations including USL and IBM have announced support for the DCE specifications. The elements of the DCE include functionality of network layers 4 through 7. The adopted technologies include RPCs from HP Apollo (with some extensions from IBM and Digital), Digital's domain name service, Seimens-Nixdorf's X.500 service, MIT's Kerberos authentication-security service, and Transarc Corporation's Andrew File System (AFS).

1.1.2.4 HP-UX

HP-UX is based on UNIX System V Release 3.0. Hewlett-Packard is a founding member of the Open Software Foundation and supports OSF's Distributed File System (DFS) part of DCE. HP systems are based on the PA-RISC processor architecture. Hewlett-Packard, like some other UNIX vendors, offers NetWare for UNIX. HP-UX 9.0 supports:

- XPG4;
- POSIX 1003.1 and POSIX 1003.2;
- SVID-2;
- OSF AES;
- Logical volume manager;
- Disk mirroring;
- TCP/IP;
- NFS;
- FDDI support;
- X11R5;
- MOTIF v1.2;
- X.400;
- X.500;
- DCE;
- Encina;
- NetWare for UNIX;
- LANManager/U.

HP-UX 10.0, the next major release of the operating system, will support fault resilience and enhanced security and provide support for standards with binary compatibility.

1.1.2.5 Digital's ULTRIX and OSF/1

Digital's previous operating system, ULTRIX, was based on 4.2BSD with enhancements from 4.3BSD. The operating system was compatible at the source code level with AT&T's System V Interface Definition (SVID) Issue 2. Digital was the first company to release a version of UNIX based on the Open Software

Foundation's OSF/1 operating system. Digital supports OSF/1, Windows NT, and OpenVMS on its 64-bit Alpha processor.

1.1.2.6 IBM's AIX

The Advanced Interactive Executive (AIX) is IBM's version of UNIX. It was called AIX to distinguish it from the Personal Computer Interactive Executive (PC/ix, which ran on PC/XT systems) and the Virtual Machine Interactive Executive (VM/ix, which ran in a virtual machine on 370 XA hardware). IBM's AIX operating system is derived from AT&T UNIX SVR1 and includes some SVR2 and SVR3 extensions. AIX for RISC systems, such as the RS/6000, uses the following priorities where conflicts and differences may exist: POSIX, SVID, 4.3BSD, and AIX/RT.

AIX provides support for protocols such as TCP/IP, NFS, NCS, SNA, and the X Window system standard. IBM also offers a version of NetWare for AIX based on NetWare 3.11. IBM's UNIX workstations and servers are based on the Power and PowerPC RISC processors. The RISC System/6000 Model 250 is an example of a system based on the PowerPC processor. AIX Release 3.2.5 works with both the PowerPC and Power2 processor architectures. The Power2 processor was designed by IBM engineers and is used on some IBM systems. A feature of interest in AIX 3.2.5 is that the AIX System Management Interface Tool (SMIT) has been expanded to use remote procedure calls (RPCs) to manage a network of AIX systems–this environment is referred to as distributed SMIT or DSMIT. DSMIT on AIX can also be used to manage HP/UX 9.0 and SunOS 4.1.x systems. Another system administration enhancement is the Visual Systems Management (VSM) tool, which is a graphical drag-and-drop tool to add users, manage devices, and handle security.

IBM's AIX/ESA (Enterprise Systems Architecture) Version 2 Release 2 is based on OSF/1 and is an operating system for System/390 type mainframes. AIX/ESA supports:

- File systems that may be as large as 500 GB;
- X Window System, X11R5;
- POSIX 1003.1 (1990 specification);
- Disk striping and asynchronous I/O, which enables an I/O operation to be initiated before the previous operation may have completed.

Note that the AIX/370 operating system could not run in native mode; it ran as a guest operating system under VM. Another AIX release, AIX PS/2 version 1.3, runs on 386 and 486 PCs and supports:

- MOTIF;
- X11R5;

- TCP/IP;
- NFS;
- Korn Shell;
- POSIX 1003.1;
- Multiple DOS sessions.

AIX/6000 version 4.1 runs on RS/6000 workstations and servers. This version supports:

- POSIX 1003.1;
- SVID;
- XPG4;
- Streams;
- TCP/IP;
- NFS;
- SNMP;
- X11R5;
- MOTIF;
- CDE Desktop;
- Display Postscript;
- Logical volume manager;
- Mirroring;
- Disk striping;
- SMP/Threads;
- C2 Security;
- FDDI;
- SMIT;
- Xstation manager.

1.1.2.7 Sun Microsystem's SunOS and Solaris

The Sun Operating System (SunOS) was developed by Bill Joy. SunOS used 4.2BSD as its foundation and added many features to the operating system, especially in the area of networking. These features included the *Network File System* (NFS), the *Network Information Service* (NIS), *Remote Procedure Calls* (RPC), and *External Data Representation* (XDR). The next generation of operating system technology from Sun is known as Solaris. SunOS version 5.0, more commonly known as *Solaris version 2.0,* is based on System V Release 4 (SVR4). Sun Microsystems has ported the Solaris operating system to an Intel processor (Intel 80 × 86) base. Solaris supports the OpenWindows Graphical User Interface (GUI) and the *Open Network Computing* (ONC) environment. As a part of the Common Open Software Environment (COSE) agreement, Sun today supports OSF's MOTIF GUI. (COSE is an alliance formed by vendors to standardize elements related to UNIX.) Sun's UNIX workstations are based on the SPARC processor. The key differences between SunOS 4.1.x and Solaris version 2.x are:

- *Run levels:* The system may be started at run levels 0 (monitor PROM), 1 (single-user mode), 2 (multiuser mode), and 3 (multiuser mode with services such as NFS, RFS, and NIS).
- *Directories:* Those such as **/etc/rc[0-3].d** now contain the system initialization scripts instead of files such as **/etc/rc**, **/etc/rc.boot**, and **/etc/rc.local**.
- *File systems:* Four are standard with Solaris: **/**, **/usr**, **/export**, **/opt**. The home directories for users are in **/export/home**; the automounter makes possible access to the home directories as **/home/username**.
- **/etc/fstab** *file:* Now **/etc/vfstab**.
- **/etc/exports** *file:* Now called **/etc/dfstab**.
- *Disk partitions:* Instead of disk partitions such as **/dev/sd0a**, you now have disk slices such as **/dev/dsk/c0t0d0s6**.
- *Installation:* Sun recommends that all optical, unbundled software be installed in the directory, **/opt**, hence the **/opt** file system.
- *Optional software:* Now shipped as *packages* and you can use utilities such as **pkgadd** (to add software), **pkginfo** (to inquire about software), and **pkgrm** (to remove software).
- *NIS+:* Solaris supports Network Information Service + (NIS+).

SunSoft has synchronized Solaris releases on Intel and SPARC systems with version 2.4. Solaris also supports:

- POSIX 1003.2;
- Multiprocessing and multithreading;
- Journaled File System;
- C2 Security;
- MOTIF;
- Image and Video Library (XIL);
- Display Postscript;
- Windows Application Binary Interface (WABI);
- RPC;
- SVID;
- PEX;
- TCP/IP;
- IPX/SPX;
- XPG4;

- NIS+;
- ONC;
- X11R4.

In the near future, Solaris will be supported in PowerPC-based systems.

1.1.2.8 XENIX and SCO UNIX

Microsoft in 1980 introduced the XENIX operating system to run on microcomputers. The XENIX operating system was based on the seventh edition with some utilities from 4.1BSD. XENIX release 3.0 included new features from AT&T's UNIX System III. In 1985 the XENIX operating system was moved to a UNIX System V base.

In 1986 XENIX was ported to an Intel 80386–based system by Santa Cruz (SCO). Also, in 1987 Microsoft and AT&T began joint development efforts to merge XENIX with UNIX System V. This was accomplished in UNIX System V Release 3.2.

Although SCO continues to support UNIX, it offers two other operating systems: SCO UNIX SVR3.2 version 4 and SCO Open Desktop Release 2.0. SCO UNIX SVR3.2 version 4 supports automatic kernel configuration and C2-level security. The Open Desktop release includes support for the X Window System, OSF/MOTIF, desktop manager, and the capability to run DOS applications.

1.1.2.9 NeXTStep

NeXTStep is an object-oriented operating system. The NeXT operating system ran on Motorola 68040–based systems. The NeXT operating system is based on Carnegie-Mellon University's Mach version 2.5 operating system. NeXTStep includes:

- *NetWare client support:* Thus the NeXT machine can attach to Novell file servers. The protocol used is Novell's Internetwork Packet Exchange/ Sequenced Packet Exchange (IPX/SPX). NeXT systems can mount NetWare volumes and print to NetWare printers.
- *AppleShare clients:* NeXT systems can mount Macintosh 1.44-MB floppies, Macintosh SCSI disks, and CD-ROM drives. NeXT hosts can print to AppleShare printers. The NeXT operating system supports both AppleTalk Phase 1 and Phase 2 protocols.

Today, NeXTStep runs on Intel 80486–based systems.

1.1.2.10 Coherent

The Coherent operating system is a UNIX-like operating system available from the Mark Williams Company. Coherent supports the Intel 80386 32-bit architecture and includes more than 200 UNIX-like commands, a C compiler, **make**, **lex**, **yacc**, **nroff/troff**, the Korn and Bourne Shells, and implementations of EMACS and Kermit. In the near future, Coherent plans to support TCP/IP, the X Window system, ANSI C, and streams or sockets.

1.1.2.11 UnixWare

UnixWare is an operating system developed by Univel. Univel, backed by Novell and Unix System Laboratories (USL), emphasized the integration of the Novell IPX/SPX protocol stack inside the UnixWare kernel. There are two major UnixWare products: the UnixWare Application Server and the UnixWare Personal Edition. UnixWare supports DOS and Windows 3.1 sessions; thus, you can run Windows 3.1 applications on a UnixWare system. UnixWare runs on Intel 486–based systems.

1.1.3 Windows NT and UNIX

Windows NT is Microsoft's response to UNIX. The Windows NT operating system runs on Intel 486, Pentium, MIPS, and ALPHA processors. The minimal configuration required for NT systems is 8 MB of memory; 70-MB disk, and a 25-MHz 386SX computer. NT is a multithreaded, multitasking operating system. NT supports DOS, Windows, and OS/2 applications. It supports 16-bit Windows and POSIX-based applications. NT comes with IPX/SPX, NetBIOS/NetBEUI, DLC, and TCP/IP protocols such as TCP, UDP, IP, ARP, **telnet**, and **ftp**.

The server version of NT, referred to as Windows NT Server, supports LANManager, centralized administration, and fault tolerance (disk mirroring and stripping); the server can also be set up as an AppleTalk server. The Windows NT Server system supports up to 4 GB of RAM. Further, it supports 2 GB of virtual memory per application. The NT Server uses 64-bit addressing to access the disk drive; thus, it can support up to 408 TB of disk storage.

A key feature built into the NT Server is that it allows users to transparently access all network resources with a single network logon. The operating system includes graphical tools to centrally manage groups of NT servers and desktops. As far as fault tolerance is concerned, the NT Server protects against:

- Application failure;
- Hard disk failure;
- Power failure.

There is a separate protected virtual address space for each application to guard against application or software failure. The operating system elements are protected from each other and from applications. The NT Server protects against hard-disk failure by supporting disk mirroring and striping with parity–RAID 5.

The NT Server system can support DOS, Windows, Windows for Workgroups, NT, OS/2, and Macintosh client systems. The Microsoft SNA Server may be installed on the NT Server to enable client systems to access IBM hosts for 3270 terminal emulation or for APPC applications. The SNA Server also allows one to access IBM AS/400 systems.

As far as client/server applications are concerned, NT includes support for DCE-compatible RPC calls. Thus, the NT systems may be a client or a server to any OSF/1-based system.

1.2 KEY UNIX CONCEPTS

In this section we describe important UNIX operating system concepts. The relationship between the operating system and the kernel, programs and processes, and partitions and file systems are established. Further, we analyze the role of signals on UNIX systems and determine how system calls relate to the operating system.

1.2.1 Operating System Versus Kernel

The *kernel,* in operating system terminology, is the core software that provides only the minimal facilities necessary for implementing additional operating system services. The UNIX kernel supports operating services such as:

- System initialization (start-up);
- Processes;
- File systems;
- Communication facilities.

Applications gain access to system services through system calls. *System calls* are direct entry points into the UNIX kernel. Most UNIX operating systems support between 60 and 200 system calls. A major component of the kernel provides support for these system services. For example, in 4.3BSD, the operating system software is organized according to [2]:

- *Basic kernel facilities:* Time and system clock handling, descriptor management, and process management;
- *Memory management support:* Paging and swapping;

- *Generic system interfaces:* The I/O, control, and multiplexing operations performed on descriptors;
- *The file system:* Files, directories, path name translation, file locking, and I/O buffer management;
- *Terminal handling support:* The terminal-interface driver and terminal line disciplines;
- *Interprocess communication facilities:* Sockets, pipes, shared memory and semaphores;
- *Support for network communication:* Communication protocols and generic network facilities, such as routing.

On SunOS systems, the file **/vmunix** is referred to as the UNIX kernel. This file may be known as **/unix** on other UNIX systems. The operating system includes all software that is installed on the system as part of configuring the system.

The kernel is a subset of the operating system.

The operating system environment includes various file systems such as **/** and **/usr** and shells such as **/bin/csh** and **/bin/ksh** and typically also supports tools for software development.

1.2.2 Programs and Processes

A *program* is an executable file that resides on disk. For example, after you compile and link a file on a system, you create an executable file. If you use the **cc** (C language compiler) command on UNIX, by default, the file created is called **a.out**, which is a program and an executable file that resides on the system disk.

The executing instance of a program is referred to as a *process*. On a UNIX system, associated with each process is a unique numeric identifier known as the *process identifier* (PID). The operating system loads the program into memory using one of the six *exec* functions.

Each task or thread of execution is termed a *process*. A *program* is an executable file that resides on disk. A process is an instance of the program being executed by the operating system. The *context of a process* consists of the user-level state and the kernel-level state (which includes, for example, scheduling parameters, resource controls, and identification information). The kernel creates a process by duplicating the context of another process.

Users can create processes, control the processes' execution, and receive notification of when the processes' execution status changes. Each process is assigned a unique value, known as a *process identifier (PID)*. The kernel uses the PID to identify a process and to report status changes to the user.

1.2.3 Signals

How does one notify a process on a UNIX system that some event or condition has occurred? On a UNIX system that mechanism of process notification in the case of some condition is accomplished using signals. When a process receives a signal it can do one of the following.

- Let the default action take place.
- Ignore the signal.
- Process a signal-handling routine or function, which is then responsible for reacting when a signal is received.

To be able to send a signal one needs to be the owner of the process with which one is communicating. Under UNIX, the **kill** command may be used to generate signals. For example,

kill -HUP 92

This command sends the SIGHUP signal to PID 92. The SIGHUP signal is commonly used to notify the process that it needs to re-read its configuration file.

1.2.4 File System

The file system controls the storage and retrieval of data in user files. Files are organized into file systems, which are treated as *logical devices*. A physical device such as a disk can contain several logical devices, known as *file systems*. *Partitioning* a disk into several file systems makes it easier for system administrators to manage and organize data. For example, the SunOS operating system supports the following partitions: **a, b, c, d, e, f, g, h**. The file systems typically defined on UNIX systems include:

- **/ (root)**;
- **swap**;
- **/usr**;
- **/var**;
- **/home**.

On some systems the **/home** file system is referred to as **/u** or **/usr/people**. The Solaris operating system supports the following file systems.

- **/**;
- **swap**;
- **/usr**;
- **/opt**;
- **/export**.

The **/opt** file system is where unbundled operating system and third-party software resides.

Each file system has a *super block* that describes the structure and contents of the file system, and each file in a file system is described by an *inode* (information node or index node). System calls manipulate files via inodes. Every file has one inode but may have several names, all of which map into the inode. Each name is referred to as a *link*. The following information is maintained in an inode.

- Owner of the file;
- Type and access mode of the file;
- Group associated with the file;
- Size of the file in bytes;
- Number of physical blocks used by the file;
- The time the file was last modified;
- The number of references to the file;
- Time when the inode itself was last updated;
- Time when the file was last accessed.

Under Solaris 2.x the convention for naming disk partitions has changed. The disk partition slice numbers, 0 through 7, correspond to partitions *a* through *h* in the SunOS version of the operating system. The naming convention is

/dev/dsk/cAtBdCsD

where **cA** refers to the slice or partition number, which may vary between 0 and 7; **tB** specifies the drive number—since most SCSI disks have embedded controllers, the drive number will always be 0; **dC** refers to the physical bus target number; and **sD** specifies the logical controller number.

1.2.5 System Calls

The shell that one uses on a UNIX system, **csh**, **sh**, or **ksh**, interacts with the UNIX kernel to execute certain tasks. Interaction with the kernel takes place via system calls. System calls may be viewed as direct entry points into the UNIX kernel.

1.2.5.1 fork()

The *fork()* system call is used to create a new process, which is called the *child process* of the originating *parent* process. It shares all of the parent resources: file descriptors, signal-handling status, and memory layout. The *fork()* system call returns twice: It returns 0 to the child process and to the parent process it returns the process ID of the child. Figure 1.1 illustrates the use of the *fork()* system call in a C program.

The output of the program in Figure 1.1 may be

From child process: Child PID = 769, parent PID = 768
From parent process: Child PID = 769, Parent PID = 768

or

From parent process: Child PID = 769, Parent PID = 768
From child process: Child PID = 769, Parent PID = 768

The results of this program depends on which process (parent or child) gets to its *printf()* statement first. In the example, the variable **id** in the child process is assigned the value 0 if the *fork()* system call is successful. In the parent process, the variable **id** is assigned the process identification of the child process (assuming a successful return from *fork()*). Note that if a process wants to communicate more than a byte of information, it must set up an interprocess communication or use an intermediate file.

1.3 IMPORTANT SYSTEM FILES

In this section we examine important UNIX system files such as:

- /etc/passwd;
- /etc/shadow;
- /etc/group;
- /etc/inittab.

```
/* Example of using the fork() System Call */
#include <stdio.h>
main()
{
int id;
if ((id = fork()) == -1) {
   printf("Unable to create new process\n");
   exit(1);
} else if (id == 0) {   /* Child Process */
   printf("From child process: Child PID = %d, Parent PID = %d\n", getpid(), getppid());
   exit(0);
} else {        /* Parent Process */
   printf("From parent process: Child PID = %d, Parent PID = %d/n", id, getpid());
   exit(0);
   }
} /* End Main Function */
```

Figure 1.1 Example of using the *fork()* system call.

1.3.1 /etc/passwd

All accounts, be they operating system, end user, or those related to applications, are defined in the **/etc/passwd** file. Associated with each entry or account in the **/etc/passwd** file are seven fields. The format for an account defined in the file is:

Account-name:Password:UID:GID:User information:Directory:Program

> *Account-name:* This is the user's login name–the name the user enters in response to the **login:** prompt.
> *Password:* This field may initially be empty (::)–the user, upon logging into the system, would use the **passwd** command to set a password for this account. On Solaris, this field is an "x", signifying that the encrypted password is in the **/etc/shadow** file.
> *UID:* Is a user identifier number whose value may be between 0 and 65535. 0 indicates super-user while 1 to 99 are used for system-related accounts. A UID is associated with each account defined on the system.
> *GID:* Is a group identification number whose value may be between 0 and 65535. It identifies the user as a member of a group.
> *User information:* May contain the user's name and phone number or other related information.
> *Directory:* The absolute pathname of the user's home directory.
> *Program:* The name of the program, typically **/bin/sh** or **/bin/csh** or **/bin/ksh**, that is run after the user logs in.

Figure 1.2 offers an example of the entries in the **/etc/passwd** file. Let us examine the following line in the **/etc/passwd** file.

> **pabrai:x:1003:30:Uday O. Pabrai:/export/home/pabrai:/usr/bin/csh**

In the above example, the account-name is *pabrai*. The second field is the encrypted password. In this example, there is an **x** in the second field since the encrypted password is stored in the **/etc/shadow** file (discussed next in this chapter). Fields three and four provide information on pabrai's UID and GID numbers, respectively. Information about account *pabrai* is specified in the next field–**Uday O. Pabrai**. The login directory for user *pabrai* is **/export/home/pabrai**, while *pabrai*'s default shell is **/usr/bin/csh**.

1.3.2 /etc/shadow

The **/etc/shadow** file stores encrypted passwords associated with accounts defined in the **/etc/passwd** file. Each entry in the shadow file is of the format:

username:password:lastchg:min:max:warning:inactive:expire:flag

username is the user's login name. The **password** field includes either:

- A 13-character encrypted password;
- A lock string (LK) to indicate that the account is not accessible;
- No string to show that there is no password for the account.

lastchg specifies the number of days between January 1, 1970, and the date the password was last modified. **min** is the minimum number of days required between password changes. **max** is the maximum number of days the password is valid. **warn** is the number of days before the password expires that the user is warned. **inactive** refers to the number of days of inactivity allowed for the user. **expire** is the absolute date when the login may no longer be used. **flag** is reserved for future use; its default value is zero.

Password aging is the process of defining some parameters associated with passwords. These parameters are defined in the **/etc/shadow** file and include fields such as *minimum, maximum,* and *warning*.

Figure 1.3 is an example of the **/etc/shadow** file.

For example,

tina:C.UyunD7qlSHk:9092::::::

tina is the name of the account defined on the system. **C.UyunD7qlSHk** is the encrypted password, and **9092** is the UID associated with this account. Since fields such as the *minimum, maximum,* and *warning* have not been

```
root:x:0:1:0000-Admin(0000):/:/bin/ksh
daemon:x:1:1:0000-Admin(0000):/:
bin:x:2:2:0000-Admin(0000):/usr/bin:
sys:x:3:3:0000-Admin(0000):/:
adm:x:4:4:0000-Admin(0000):/var/adm:
lp:x:71:8:0000-lp(0000):/usr/spool/lp:
smtp:x:0:0:mail daemon user:/:
uucp:x:5:5:0000-uucp(0000):/usr/lib/uucp:
nuucp:x:9:9:0000-uucp(0000):/var/spool/uucppublic:/usr/lib/uucp/uucico
listen:x:37:4:Network Admin:/usr/net/nls:
nobody:x:60001:60001:uid no body:/:
noaccess:x:60002:60002:uid no access:/:
rdhawan:x:1001:30::/export/home/rdhawan:/usr/bin/csh
sarunach:x:1002:30::/export/home/sarunach:/usr/bin/csh
pabrai:x:1003:30:Uday O. Pabrai:/export/home/pabrai:/usr/bin/csh
suresh:x:1005:10:Suresh:/export/home/suresh:/bin/ksh
ngtusr:x:1006:10:NGT User:/export/home/ngtusr:/bin/csh
ftp:x:456:10:Anonymous:/opt/ftp:/bin/ksh
```

Figure 1.2 Sample **/etc/passwd** file.

```
root:x6CscGumc89vs:9055:::::::
daemon:NP:6445:::::::
bin:NP:6445:::::::
sys:NP:6445:::::::
adm:NP:6445:::::::
lp:NP:6445:::::::
smtp:NP:6445:::::::
uucp:NP:6445:::::::
nuucp:NP:6445:::::::
listen:*LK*:::::::
nobody:NP:6445:::::::
noaccess:NP:6445:::::::
rdhawan:QZ.dUt36aCFMw:9057:::::::
sarunach:yC9lJLCrYGZHU:9051:::::::
pabrai:SDyFjL8iuALHk:9051:::::::
suresh:C.UyunD7qlSHk:9092:::::::
ftp:*LK*:::::::
```

Figure 1.3 Sample **/etc/shadow** file.

defined, it is implied that we are not using password-aging mechanisms for the *suresh* account.

1.3.3 /etc/group

Groups are a mechanism available under UNIX to organize users on the basis of departments or other functions. We noted that the fourth field in the **/etc/passwd** file was the GID field. This field uniquely identifies the group to which the user belongs. All groups defined in the system are included in the **/etc/group** file. Each entry in the **/etc/group** file has four fields:

Group-name:Password:GID:Account-name-list

The following is a description of each field.

1. *Group-name:* The group name is from 1 to 6 characters (first alphabetic & none are uppercase).
2. *Password:* Group password field is typically not used–generally an "*" is placed in this field.
3. *GID:* Is a group ID number whose value may be between 0 and 65535. This number is defined in the **/etc/passwd** file.
4. *Account-name-list:* This is a list of users who belong to the group.

Figure 1.4 describes entries typically seen in the **/etc/group** file.

root::0:root
other::1:
bin::2:root,bin,daemon
sys::3:root,bin,sys,adm
adm::4:root,adm,daemon
uucp::5:root,uucp
mail::6:root
tty::7:root,tty,adm
lp::8:root,lp,adm
nuucp::9:root,nuucp
staff::10:
daemon::12:root,daemon
nobody::60001:
noaccess::60002:
ngt::30:

Figure 1.4 Sample **/etc/group** file.

Let us examine an entry in the **/etc/group** file.

staff::10:

In the above example, **staff** is an example of a group name defined on the system. The second field is the password field, and there is no password associated with the group names defined. The next field specifies the GID associated with the group name and is 10 for **staff**. The last field provides information on users who belong to the group.

1.3.4 /etc/inittab

The **inittab** file specifies the default initialization (**init**) state for UNIX systems. The **init** state or run level determines what programs run on the UNIX system when it is powered on (booted). The **init** states typically defined are described in Table 1.1.

Figure 1.5 is an example of the **/etc/inittab** file on a Solaris system.

1.4 UNIX SYSTEM INITIALIZATION (START-UP)

Only a small part of the kernel is devoted to initializing the system. The system initialization code is used when the system is bootstrapped into operation and is responsible for setting up the kernel hardware and software environment. Therefore, first the UNIX kernel has to be loaded into the main memory of the

Table 1.1
Typical UNIX System **init** States (or Run Levels)

Run Level	Description
0	Shuts down the system completely, after which one may turn off power. It unmounts all file systems and terminates all processes.
1	Single-user state. Stops all system services and daemons and unmounts all file systems.
2	Normal multiuser operation without NFS file systems exported. It mounts the / and **/usr** file systems, loads the network interfaces, and starts processes. It cleans the **/tmp** and **/var/tmp** directories.
3	Normal multiuser operation of a file server with NFS file systems exported. Starts NFS and RFS services.
4	Alternative multiuser state (not currently used).
5	Software reboot—prompts for a boot device other than the EEPROM default.
6	Reboot run level. Kills all active processes, unmounts file systems, and reboots to the **initdefault** entries in **/etc/inittab**.
S, s	Single-user state. All file systems are mounted and accessible.

```
ap::sysinit:/sbin/autopush    -f    /etc/iu.ap
fs::sysinit:/sbin/rcS                            >/dev/console 2>&1 </dev/console
is:3:initdefault:
p3:s1234:powerfail:/sbin/shutdown  -  >/dev/console 2>&1
y -i0 -g0
s0:0:wait:/sbin/rc0 off                          >/dev/console 2>&1 </dev/console
s1:1:wait:/sbin/shutdown -y -iS -g0              >/dev/console 2>&1 </dev/console
s2:23:wait:/sbin/rc2                             >/dev/console 2>&1 </dev/console
s3:3:wait:/sbin/rc3                              >/dev/console 2>&1 </dev/console
s5:5:wait:/sbin/rc5 ask                          >/dev/console 2>&1 </dev/console
s6:6:wait:/sbin/rc6 reboot                       >/dev/console 2>&1 </dev/console
of:0:wait:/sbin/uadmin 2 0                       >/dev/console 2>&1 </dev/console
fw:5:wait:/sbin/uadmin 2 2                       >/dev/console 2>&1 </dev/console
RB:6:wait:/sbin/sh -c 'echo "\nThe sys-          >/dev/console 2>&1
tem is being restarted."'
rb:6:wait:/sbin/uadmin 2 1                       >/dev/console 2>&1 </dev/console
sc:234:respawn:/usr/lib/saf/sac -t 300
co:234:respawn:/usr/lib/saf/ttymon -g -h -p " 'uname -n' console login:" -T sun -d /dev/console -l console -m ldterm,ttcompat
```

Figure 1.5 Sample **/etc/inittab** file.

processor. After the kernel is loaded, it goes through an initialization phase to set the hardware in a known state.

Next, the kernel is responsible for *auto-configuration,* where a process finds and configures peripherals attached to the processor. Then the system executes in single-user mode, and a start-up script is responsible for the disk checks, accounting, and quota. When the system is in single-user mode, only the **root** file system is mounted. The first two processes started by the operating system are *swapper* and *init.*

The *swapper* process enables UNIX to use the main and secondary memories (support for virtual memory). The *init* process runs as process number 1 and is responsible for running the system start-up scripts in addition to starting a *getty* process for each terminal line connected to the UNIX system. The *init* process is the parent of all login shells that run on the system when the system is in the multiuser mode. A start-up script, such as **/etc/rc**, starts general system services and brings the system to full multiuser operation.

For normal multiuser operation, the *getty* process is responsible for starting the *login* program; the *login* program verifies the login name and the password that a user may have entered by checking the **/etc/passwd** file. It then executes the login shell specified in the **/etc/passwd** file. At this point the user is logged into his or her account and can start applications or execute commands at the shell command prompt.

Note that 4.3BSD assumes that the executable image of the kernel resides in a file named **vmunix** on the file system designated the **root** file system. On System V hosts this file is called **unix** and is in the **root** file system. On a Solaris 2.x system, the UNIX kernel is in a file called, **unix**, in the **/kernel** subdirectory.

1.4.1 Memory Management

Memory management determines when processes should be moved between main memory and secondary memory. The objective of memory management facilities is to optimize the number of runnable processes residing in main memory. Note that each process has its own address space. The address space consists of three logical segments: text, data, and stack. The entire content of a process address space need not be resident for a process to execute.

Context switching refers to switching between the execution of processes. Most of the work involved is in saving and restoring the operating context of a process. Context switching is hardware-dependent. Position-independent addressing enables context switching to be done very quickly.

So what does one mean by paging and swapping? *Paging* refers to the servicing of page faults. Paging systems are characterized by fetch, placement, and replacement policies. *Swapping,* on the other hand, is a memory management policy in which entire processes are moved to or from secondary storage.

1.5 STANDARDS: SVID, POSIX, COSE, OSF, AND X/OPEN

With so many different versions of the UNIX operating system, it is difficult to develop applications that run on a variety of UNIX-based computer systems.

In 1983, AT&T published the *System V Interface Definition* (SVID) to assist vendors in testing their version of UNIX for conformance to System V functionality. Developers could thus build programs guaranteed to run on any machine running a SVID compliant version of UNIX. Further, the SVID specifies features of UNIX that are guaranteed not to change in future releases, thus enabling applications to run on all releases of UNIX System V. So, how do vendors check whether their version of UNIX is SVID compliant? They do so by running the System V Verification Suite developed by AT&T. A new version of SVID has been developed along with SVR4. SVR4 is SVID compliant.

Another standard that is influencing UNIX is the IEEE *Project 1003* (P1003). The standards that various working groups in P1003 are establishing are called the *Portable Operating System Interface for Computer Environments* (POSIX). The POSIX standard specifically covers the areas of system calls, libraries, tools, interfaces, verification and testing, real-time features, and security. The P1003.1 standard is the part of the POSIX standard that defines the system interface. POSIX has been endorsed by the National Institute of Standards and Technology (NIST).

Organizations such as the Common Open Software Environment (COSE), the Open Software Foundation (OSF), and X/Open are working together to standardize the UNIX operating system. For example, X/Open's *Spec 1170* defines a set of common application programming interfaces for the UNIX operating systems and their applications. Thus, all Spec 1170–compliant UNIX flavors will interoperate and any application written to Spec 1170 standards will run on any compliant UNIX flavor without modification. Most of the 1,170 APIs in Spec 1170 are actually based on the 100 most popular UNIX applications across flavors. In the near future any organization that wants to use the name "UNIX" must successfully pass the Spec 1170 conformance tests available through X/Open. X/Open acquired the UNIX trademark from Novell in 1993.

The relationship between OSF and X/Open is important. OSF is committed to use requirements formulated by X/Open's User Council as the starting point.

1.6 UNIX AND CLIENT/SERVER COMPUTING

In this section we cover technologies commonly associated with UNIX systems. These include processors, systems, and peripheral devices such as disk and tape drives. Further, the configuration of UNIX systems as client nodes, be they diskless, dataless, or hybrid, is presented.

Increasingly, a large component of any organization's computing environment consists of distributed systems. Distributed systems are characterized by:

- A client/server architecture;
- The underlying network that is a key element in the system architecture;
- Network protocols that define the extent of the client/server architecture;
- The operating system that may be resident on client systems;
- Peripheral devices that may appear to be centralized but could be configured on different systems;
- Computing MIPs that are not limited to server nodes.

A client/server architecture implies some degree of dependency between nodes on the network. A node may require resources such as that the UNIX operating system be downloaded at boot time. The network is a key component of the system architecture because nodes depend on the network for resources–resources such as files, programs, applications, operating system, and peripheral devices.

If a protocol, such as the network file system (NFS) protocol, is used as the basis to exchange information between the server and the client, then the extent of the client/server architecture is typically the local area network because local area network (LAN) technologies such as Ethernet, token ring, and FDDI have typically provided a higher degree of reliability than wide area network (WAN) protocols, which are generally prone to more errors. This is beginning to change with the advent of emerging standards such as frame relay and asynchronous transfer mode (ATM). Thus, the network protocol defines the extent of the client/server architecture.

If the client node is a diskless or dataless workstation, then the operating system is resident locally. In the case of a diskless workstation, it is downloaded over the network at boot time; whereas for the dataless system, it is resident on the local disk.

Using a protocol such as NFS one can make available peripheral devices configured on different hosts to all nodes on the network. As far as nodes on the network are concerned, the resource appears locally configured (such as a disk and tape drive).

The client nodes may be workstations with processors such as the SPARC, PA-RISC, Intel, MIPS, or POWER–the point being that the CPU is local and thus computing can be done locally. As a matter of fact, a challenge in any environment is to take advantage of client-computing millions of instructions per second (MIPS) so that there are not *wasted* MIPS (resources that may not have been fully utilized). *Craysoft* offers a product called NQS that enables CPUs to work together to process computing tasks/jobs. This section examines the components of distributed systems and describes the system architecture that is typically found in a UNIX-TCP/IP-based environment.

1.6.1 Processor Technology

Until recently, the evolution of computer architectures was dominated by families of increasingly complex processors. Examples of complex instruction set computer (CISC) processors include the Intel 80×86 family, Motorola's 680x0 family and the Digital VAX processor.

The reduced instruction set computer (RISC) processor architecture resulted from the analysis of how software actually uses the resources of a processor. Dynamic measurements of system kernels and object modules generated by optimizing compilers show an overwhelming predominance, even in the code for *complex instruction set computers* (CISC), of the simplest instructions. The complex instructions available in CISC processors are rarely used because microcode rarely provides the precise routines needed to support a variety of high-level language and system environments.

The main emphasis of the RISC architecture is not to reduce or simplify the instruction set—which is actually a side effect of the technique used to obtain the highest performance possible from available technology—rather the push for performance really drives and shapes RISC. Characteristics normally associated with RISC processors are:

- Low number of instructions (less than 100; maximum of 150);
- Low number of addressing modes (1 or 2; maximum of 4);
- Low number of instruction formats, all the same length (1 or 2; maximum of 4);
- Single-cycle execution of all instructions;
- Memory access by LOAD/STORE instructions only;
- Large CPU register file (more than 32 registers) with all operations register to register;
- Hardware control unit;
- Extensive support of high-level language (HLL) operations.

Examples of RISC processors include:

- *Motorola M88000:* For example, Data General UNIX workstations (AViiON series) are based on the Motorola RISC processor.
- *Intel 80860, 80960:* The Intel RISC processors are often used in massively parallel processing forms of computing.
- *SPARC:* The basis for Sun SPARCstations and workstations from Solbourne, Tadpole, and Hyundai.
- *AMD 29000.*
- *MIPS R2000, 3000, 4000, 6000:* The MIPS processor was used by Digital for its DECstation (UNIX) series of workstations. The processor is a Silicon Graphics IRIS workstations.
- *Alpha:* Used by Digital and other vendors. Supports OpenVMS, OSF/1 and Windows NT operating systems.
- *PowerPC.*

1.6.2 Client/Server System Strategies

A number of factors must be taken into account in designing a client/server configuration.

- *Compatibility of the server and client systems:* These include MIPS (compute power), I/O throughput, and memory.
- *Architecture of the network:* This refers to the placement of network elements such as a bridge or a router in relation to a given client/server configuration.
- *Applications:* They are key factors in determining the extent of the client/server configuration and the types of clients and servers required.

1.6.2.1 Server Node

A *server node* makes available resources on the network. These resources may include file systems, applications, and computing capability.

The file systems that may be made available could include the **home** file system and file systems that consist of all or part of the operating system. Application servers include specialized servers such as a database server. The application resides on disks configured on the server system.

The server node need not be an operating system, application, or database server; it can also be a CPU server, where, for example, many UNIX systems are configured as "headless" (no monitor) and their primary function is to make available CPU resources to nodes on the network.

Thus, in general, server nodes accept requests that arrive over the network, perform their service, and return the result to the requester.

1.6.2.2 Client Node

Client systems typically send requests to a server node and wait for a response. Client nodes may contain portions of the operating system. There are basically two types of client systems: dataless and diskless.

1.6.2.3 Dataless Workstation

A *dataless system* requires that executables and the user home area be made available to it by a server host. The file systems available on a dataless system include **/(root)** and **SWAP**. The dataless system mounts the **/usr** and **/home** file systems from the server.

When a dataless system is powered it loads the UNIX kernel from its local disk because the **/(root)** file system is resident locally. Also, all paging or swapping is done on the dataless system because it has space reserved locally for swap. In terms of system administrator resources, a dataless configuration requires more administrator resources, as the operating system is local; thus, each time an operating system is upgraded, configuration work is to be done on each dataless system.

1.6.2.4 Diskless Workstation

If the system has no disk, then it must be configured as a *diskless client.* The resources available to a diskless client are defined by the server system. When a diskless workstation is powered, it asks the server node for an Internet address and the operating system.

A diskless workstation pages or swaps over the network because the swap space reserved for it is resident on the server node. In terms of system administration resources, it is relatively easier to manage a diskless workstation than a dataless system because all configuration work is done centrally on one system, which is the server system. However, a diskless workstation increases the load on the network because paging or swapping and downloading the operating system is over the network.

1.6.2.5 Hybrid Workstation

Some UNIX workstation and operating system vendors give the flexibility to configure a system as a *hybrid,* where the only resource local on the client is a page or swap disk. The operating system and all file systems such as /, **/usr**, and **/home** are available over the network. This configuration may be suitable to organizations that want to manage all resources centrally and also minimize the increase in network load by client hosts. In the "hybrid" configuration, because there is a local page-swap disk, paging and swapping does not take place over the network as we saw in the diskless configuration. The hybrid configuration is one that would be recommended to minimize system administration and network load.

1.6.3 Peripheral Devices

Devices configured with client/server nodes may include disk drives and tape drives. The UNIX kernel, during the system initialization process, determines the address (SCSI) at which peripheral devices such as disk, tape, or CD-ROM drives are configured. It is possible to mount a CD-ROM drive on a system and export (make it available) to all other nodes on the network. A protocol, such as NFS, may be used to make disk drives and other resources available to nodes on the network.

1.6.3.1 Disk Drives

Mass storage devices are characterized as:

- Not being directly addressable;
- Low in cost per bit;
- Nonvolatile;
- Relatively slow to gain access (compared to main memory).

Note that memory devices such as RAMs, ROMs, EPROM, and EEPROMs are directly addressable; that is, any location can be selected by providing the corresponding address.

1.6.3.2 Tape Drives

Tape drives can operate in either a *start-up* mode or a *streaming* mode. Start-up drives, also referred to as *incremental,* can start and stop for each block of data. The data is divided into blocks with identification headers and gaps between them, which allows any block to be selectively located and read or written. Streaming tape devices are designed to read and write using continuous streams of data. The tape drive does not stop between blocks, and no space is wasted on gaps. This mode of operation is efficient for copying the entire contents of a disk for backup purposes. Streaming drives pack more data onto the tape and read and write at higher data rates.

Quarter-inch, 8-mm, and 4-mm tapes are commonly used in UNIX-based environments. *Quarter-inch cartridge* (QIC) tapes have capacities that vary from 20 MB to 150 MB, and 8-mm tape drives that are available in the market today can store up to 25 GB of data on a single tape.

Typically, UNIX systems allow access to tape devices via the **rmt** protocol.

1.7 SUMMARY

The first section in this chapter provided information on the various flavors of the UNIX operating system such as IRIX, ULTRIX, and Solaris. We then discussed what happens when one starts up a UNIX system, that is, the system initialization process and key services provided by the operating system. These services include process and memory management, system initialization, and maintaining file systems.

Then we covered technologies such as processors and peripheral devices that are commonly associated with UNIX systems. A UNIX system may be configured in a number of different ways, and the method chosen for one's environment depends on the network architecture, application requirements, and system administration resources available. It is also not necessary to attach all peripheral devices on a single server node: one can configure all disk drives on one node and the CD-ROM drive on another node, and all nodes in the network can have access to these resources. As far as all nodes in the network are concerned, these resources appear to be local.

REFERENCES

[1] Bach, M. J., *The Design of the UNIX Operating System,* Englewood Cliffs, NJ: Prentice-Hall, 1986.
[2] Quarterman et al., *The Design and Implementation of the 4.3BSD UNIX Operating System,* Reading, MA: Addison-Wesley Publishing Company, 1989.

SELECT BIBLIOGRAPHY

Stallings, W., *Handbook of Computer-Communications Standards,* New York: Macmillan Publishing Company, 1988.
Winsor, J., *Solaris: System Administrators Guide,* Emeryville, CA: Ziff-Davis Press, 1993.

Network Architectures and Technologies 2

Networks: The computing environment is absolutely dependent on the network infrastructure. The objective of this chapter is to examine network architectures and technologies, independent of the UNIX operating system. An understanding of network technologies and terminology is an important factor in successfully connecting systems to the network. For example, to configure the BOOTP protocol on a UNIX system, you need to work with system resources such as **/etc/bootptab** and *bootpd*. The information contained in the **/etc/bootptab** file and the service provided by the *bootpd* daemon are directly based on the specifications of the BOOTP protocol. That is what this chapter is–a discussion of network architectures, layers, protocols, interfaces, and emerging technologies.

UNIX systems of today support the Internet architecture. This architecture is also referred to as the *transmission control protocol/Internet protocol* (TCP/IP). TCP/IP architecture–TCP and IP being the two dominant protocols in the Internet architecture. Increasingly, the trend is to integrate additional protocols such as those in the *open system interconnect/reference model* (OSI/RM) and NetWare's *Internetwork Package Exchange/Sequenced Packet Exchange* (IPX/SPX) in the kernel.

2.1 NETWORK ARCHITECTURES

There are a number of different network architectures used by systems today. These include:

- *System Network Architecture* (SNA) defined by IBM;
- AppleTalk defined by Apple;
- *NetWare* (IPX/SPX) defined by Novell;
- OSI/RM defined by ISO;
- *Digital Network Architecture* (DNA) defined by Digital;
- *Internet* (TCP/IP) defined by the *Internet Architecture Board* (IAB).

The emphasis is on the OSI/RM and the Internet architecture. Novell's IPX/SPX and Apple's AppleTalk are discussed later in *Chapter 7: Internetwork-*

ing. The approach in this chapter is on a layered basis. Each network architecture defines *layers*. Each layer in the architecture may support one or more *protocol*. A protocol specifies how information is exchanged between the same two layers on different systems. Information is also exchanged between layers on the same system–this is referred to as an *interface*. In the section on Internet architecture, we first examine the different types of Internet addresses:

- Loopback address;
- Subnet address;
- Broadcast address;
- Multicast address.

This is important because a UNIX system is identified on the network by its Internet address. *Subnetting* is particularly important since it provides the basis for an organization's Internet architecture. We then look at the lower layers and technologies, such as Ethernet, token ring, FDDI, ATM, and frame relay that work at that layer. Next, higher layer protocols are covered in detail, for example:

- Address resolution protocol (ARP);
- Reverse address resolution protocol (RARP);
- Bootstrap protocol (BOOTP);
- Internet protocol (IP);
- Transmission control protocol (TCP);
- User datagram protocol (UDP).

These protocols provide the basis for a number of network applications on UNIX systems. Toward the end of this chapter we examine enhancements being made to the Internet architecture and protocols–such as *dynamic host configuration protocol* (DHCP). Chapter 8 provides detailed information on the *Internet control messages protocol* (ICMP).

2.1.1 OSI/RM

Many reading this text may already be very familiar with the OSI/RM–in fact, you may very well be tired of authors writing about it. My motivation in briefly discussing the OSI/RM is to provide a basis for comparing the Internet architecture and its many, many protocols. In fact, it has been my experience that if you are very comfortable with the OSI/RM, then it provides an excellent framework with which to compare almost any network product, hardware, or software and have a good feel for the function of that product. Increasingly, network vendors describe their technologies with respect to the OSI/RM.

The OSI/RM was defined by the *International Standards Organization* (ISO) in 1977. The ISO 7498 standard describes the OSI/RM. The OSI/RM provides a framework for information to be exchanged between heterogeneous systems on the network. The intent was that you could have PCs, Macintoshes, servers, and mainframe systems all of which could potentially support the OSI/RM and thereby be able to talk to each other and exchange information. The reference model consists of seven layers. The objective of describing the architecture in layers was to keep things modular; also as technologies change at a given layer, it is possible to switch technolgies at a specific layer without requiring a change in the entire network architecture. Table 2.1 is a summary of the functions of each layer in the OSI/RM.

2.1.2 The OSI/RM and the Internet Architecture

The Internet architecture is commonly referred to as TCP/IP architecture—TCP and IP are two dominant protocols defined in the Internet architecture—but there are many others such as UDP, ARP, RARP, ICMP, and BOOTP. The Internet architecture consists of only four layers, and all Internet protocols work at one of these four layers. Figure 2.1 provides a comparison between the OSI/RM and the TCP/IP architecture.

2.2 INTERNET (TCP/IP) ARCHITECTURE

The Internet is a global web of interconnected computers and computer networks. It is a network of networks—interconnecting schools, libraries, colleges, universities, hospitals, businesses, federal agencies, and other entities into a single, large communication network that spans the globe. The Internet connects thousands of networks, millions of host systems, and between 25 and 50 million users. These numbers are expected to double in 1995.

Funding for the Internet comes from many sources—the United States government funds some of the major Internet backbones (lower level backbone to which public and private networks connect). The *National Science Foundation* (NSF) controls the nationwide backbone for education and research—it does not control the attached networks. The *Internet Architecture Board* (IAB) coordinates the design, engineering, and management of the Internet.

NSF and NREN

The *National Research and Educational Network* (NREN) is the backbone data network of the Internet—it is administered by the NSF. The NREN backbone is connected at T-3 rates (44.736 Mbps).

Table 2.1
A Brief Description of the OSI/RM

Layer	Description
Physical	Concerned with the transmission of unstructured bit stream over a physical link. Responsible for the mechanical, electrical, and procedural characteristics to establish, maintain, and deactivate the physical link. This layer provides the physical connection between a system and the network media to which it is attached.
Data link	Provides for the reliable transfer of data across the physical link. Frames are transmitted with the necessary synchronization, error control, and flow control. An example of the functionality provided by this layer is the typical use of the CRC checksum algorithm to determine if any errors may have occurred in transmission.
Network	Responsible for forwarding and routing packets (sometimes referred to as datagrams at this layer). A router is an example of a communications device that works at the network layer. An example of the functionality of this layer is to determine the best possible route a datagram should take to be sent from the one point on the network to another point.
Transport	Provides reliable, transparent transfer of data between endpoints and supports end-to-end error recovery and flow control. This layer is referred to as the end-to-end layer or the host-to-host layer or the source-to destination layer. It is primarily concerned with end systems and not intermediate connectivity devices such as routers and bridges.
Session	Establishes, manages, and terminates connections (sessions) between cooperating applications. This layer is responsible for negotiating parameters before a "session" is established between two systems. How many bytes (octets) should be sent in a single packet when end systems are exchanging information is an example of the negotiation between the end system–this may be influenced by factors such as the *maximum transmission unit* (MTU) associated with the technology at the lower layers.
Presentation	Responsible for providing useful transformations on data to support a standardized application interface and general communications services. Services such as data compression to reduce the amount of data on the network, data encryption to secure transactions, and EBCDIC-ASCII conversion are typically provided by this layer.
Application	The interface to the end user in an OSI environment–supports file transfer, network management, and other services. The command that the end user executes to initiate any network transaction is a service provided by the application layer.

NREN succeeded NSFnet as the major Internet network for research and education in the United States with the signing of the "High-Performance Computing Act of 1991," which calls for a high-capacity (gigabits per second) network and the coordination of networking efforts among federal organizations. NREN is designed to connect K–12 schools, colleges, universities, libraries,

Network Architectures and Technologies 35

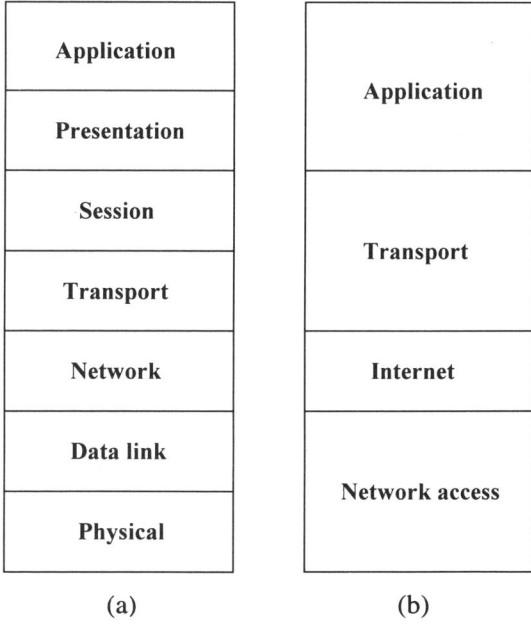

Figure 2.1 A comparison of the OSI/RM and the Internet architectures.

health care industries, business, and manufacturing into a national public network using the Internet.

National Information Infrastructure (NII)

The *National Information Infrastructure* (NII) is also referred to as the "data superhighway." NII is a physical network of fiber-optic lines, switches, and network software that will be constructed, owned, and maintained by private information and service providers–not the U.S. government. The government supports it with research, education, and health care funding. Standards and protocols for accessing data anywhere on the network are defined by the High-Performance and High-Speed Networking Act of 1993.

The network will be built on a combination of fiber-optic cable, copper cable, and microwave systems installed by telephone companies, cable television providers, and other communication service providers. Cable television companies are interested in providing services over their existing coaxial cable systems–long-distance cable systems are in the process of being upgraded to fiber-optic cable–their intent is to provide up to 500 channels (that's all we need!).

The NII is also trying to introduce a digital library infrastructure to the network. The Internet is the model for the NII.

2.2.1 Layers in the Internet Architecture

There are four layers in the Internet (TCP/IP) architecture. The layers are:

- Network access;
- Internet;
- Transport;
- Session.

Let's take a look at the function of each layer in the Internet (TCP/IP) architecture and how it compares to the OSI/RM.

Layer 1: Network Access Layer

This layer corresponds to the physical and data link layers in the OSI/RM. The network access layer accepts high-layer datagrams and transmits them over the network to which the system is attached. For Ethernet-based local area networks, data sent over the media are referred to as Ethernet frames, each of which is between 64 and 1518 bytes.

Layer 2: Internet Layer

The Internet layer corresponds to the network layer in the OSI/RM. This layer handles machine-to-machine communication, where a machine may be a host such as a UNIX workstation or an Internet router. The packet received from the transport layer is encapsulated in an *Internet protocol* (IP) *datagram*. Based on the destination host information, the Internet layer uses a routing algorithm to determine whether to deliver the datagram directly or to send it to the gateway. The datagram is then passed to the network access layer for transmission. For incoming datagrams the Internet layer checks validity, deletes header information, and uses a routing algorithm to determine if the datagram is to be processed on the local system or forwarded. If the datagram is for the local system, the Internet layer software determines which transport layer protocol will next handle the packet. Protocols such as the *address resolution protocol* (ARP) and the *reverse address resolution protocol* (RARP) work at the Internet layer.

Layer 3: Transport Layer

This layer in the Internet corresponds to the functionality provided by the transport and session layers in the OSI/RM. The transport software breaks the data received from the higher layers into small pieces, called *messages*. Each message is passed to the Internet layer. Protocols that work at the transport layer vary in their functionality. For example, the *transmission control protocol* (TCP) regulates the flow of information and is responsible for ensuring that the data arrives without error, in sequence, and without duplication. Another protocol, the *user datagram protocol* (UDP), also works at the transport layer—it is a much simpler protocol that does not provide the guaranteed delivery of TCP. Instead UDP does its best to get the data to the destination as fast as possible. The transport layer is concerned about the two end systems that need to exchange information—the transport layer does not concern itself with how information should be routed from one point on the network to another. Thus, this layer is also known as the *host-to-host layer*, the *end-to-end layer*, or the *source-to-destination layer*.

Layer 4: Application Layer

The application layer in the Internet architecture corresponds to the presentation and application layers in the OSI/RM. Users may invoke application programs such as **telnet**, **ftp**, or **rlogin** to access nodes on the Internet network. The application layer interacts with the transport level protocol to send or receive data. The data, which may be a sequence of messages or a stream of bytes, is passed to the transport layer on the source system. The transport layer may then establish a session and send data to the destination system. The application layer is also referred as the *process layer*, because on UNIX systems application layer protocols are implemented in the form of processes.

Figure 2.2 details the layering model and how information is moved between two systems separated by a router.

2.2.2 Internet Network Addresses

For a host to communicate with a another system on a TCP/IP network, it must know the remote host's Internet address. Each host has its own 32-bit Internet address that uniquely identifies it. Conceptually, each address consists of two parts: the network portion and the host. A common notation for specifying Internet addresses is four fields separated by periods. Each field ranges from 0 to 255 (decimal):

field1.field2.field3.field4

For example, 150.117.19.11 or 14.6.7.19.

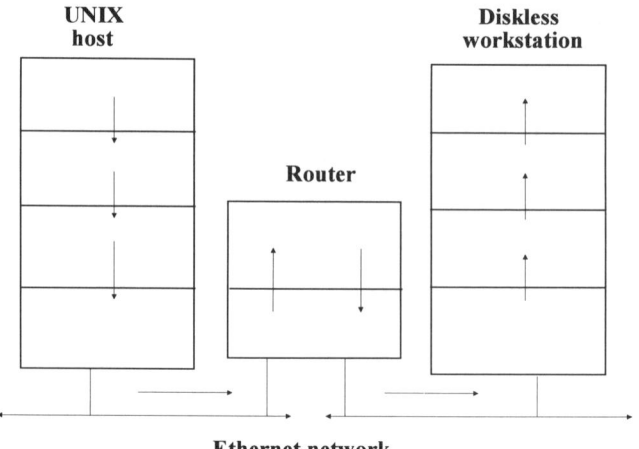

Figure 2.2 Flow of information between two systems and a router on a TCP/IP network.

2.2.3 Internet Address Notation

The 32-bit Internet address is typically written in *dotted decimal notation*. The following is an example of the address notation:

32-bit address: 1000 0011 1110 0010 0000 1000 1100 1000
Dotted decimal: 131.226.8.200
Symbolic form: **jyoti.ngt.com**

Note that this is a Class B address because the first field is between 128 and 191. Also, the address contains four fields, where fields one and two (131.226) refer to the network portion of the address (network) and fields three and four (8.200) refer to the host portion of the address (host).

2.2.4 Internet Address Classes

The network part of the Internet address specifies the network class and the network address. The characteristics of each class follow.

Class A addresses use 8 bits for the network portion and 24 bits for the host part, thereby providing the potential for 128 networks with up to 16 million hosts each. The first field specifies the network number and class. The first field can be from 1 to 127. The first bit of the first field for a Class A network is always 0. An example of a Class A address is 16.4.5.17.

Class B addresses use 16 bits for the network part and 16 bits for the host part, providing the potential for 16,384 networks with up to 64K hosts each. The first two fields specify the network number and class. The first field can be from 128 to 191. The second field can be from 1 to 254. The first two bits of the first field for a Class B network are always 10. 131.117.15.4 is an example of a Class B address.

Class C addresses use 24 bits for the network and 8 bits for the host, providing the potential for 2*1,000,000 networks with up to 256 hosts each. The first three fields specify the network number and class. The first field may vary between 192 and 223. The first three bits of a Class C network are always 110.

Class D addresses enable the use of multicast packets, where a datagram is targeted to a group of hosts. The first four bits of a Class D network are always 1110.

Class E addresses are reserved for future use. The first five bits of a Class E address are 11110.

Note that if you have an Internet address where the middle two fields are 0 in a Class A network, you can obtain an alternate Internet address notation by dropping the two middle fields. Thus, Internet address 92.0.0.1 can be expressed as 92.1. Figure 2.3 illustrates the different Internet address formats.

2.2.5 Loopback Address

When the first field of an Internet address is 127, it is used as the loopback address for the local host. For UNIX systems, this is defined in the **/etc/hosts** file and is, typically, 127.0.0.1.

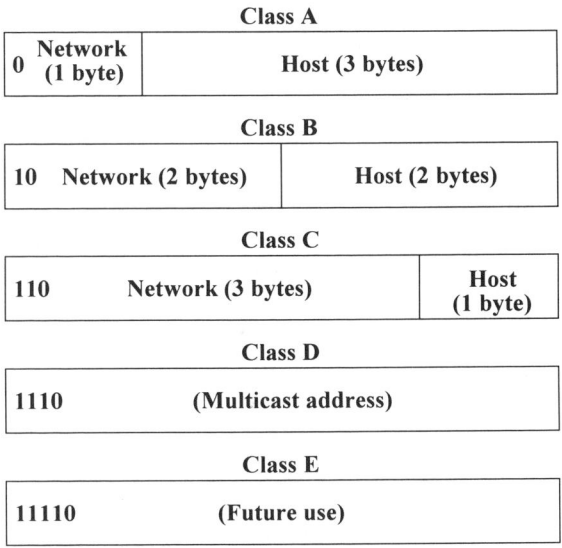

Figure 2.3 Internet address classes.

2.2.6 Subnet Masks

Subnetworks define the architecture of a TCP/IP network.

Subnetworks are a key factor in organizing client/server architectures within any organization. Subnetting is a way to organize hosts within a network into logical groups. *Subnetworks define how your network architecture is partitioned.* Subnet routing allows numerous subnetworks to exist within a given network. The motivation for subnetting is primarily twofold:

1. Reduce congestion;
2. Manage a large network by organizing it into smaller networks.

If subnet routing is utilized, then the bits in the host field (lower order 16 bits for a Class B networks) are divided into two groups: (1) *subnetworks* and (2) *host*. Therefore, the Internet address for subnetted networks consists of the following three fields:

- Network;
- Subnetwork;
- Host.

Because the system does not know which bits in the host field are to be interpreted as the subnetwork part of the Internet address, a *subnet mask* is required. The subnet mask is also referred to as a *netmask*. The subnet mask informs the system which bits of the Internet address are to be interpreted as the network, subnetwork, and host address. A subnet mask is a 32-bit number with one-to-one correspondence between each of the 32 bits in the subnet mask and each of the 32 bits in the Internet address.

In general, the entire 8-bit field is turned on (255) or off (0). The first field of the subnet mask is always 255, so the system can interpret the network number. The fourth field is typically 0, so the system can interpret the host address. The default subnet masks for Internet address classes are

255.0.0.0	Default subnet mask for Class A networks
255.255.0.0	Default subnet mask for Class B networks
255.255.255.0	Default subnet mask for Class C networks

The network portion of an Internet address may be determined by ANDing (Boolean AND operation) the Internet address with the subnet mask. For example, if the Internet address is 131.226.85.1 and the subnet mask is 255.255.255.0, the network portion of the address is 131.226.85.

```
          131.226.85.1
AND       255.255.255.0
          -------------
          131.226.85.0
```

RFC 1219 describes recommended techniques for assigning subnet masks.

2.2.7 Broadcast Address

An Internet broadcast address is used to send messages to all hosts on the network. The default format of the broadcast address consists of the network portion of the address followed by all ones. For example, 131.226.85.255 or 131.107.95.255–here the last byte in the Internet address is all ones.

2.2.8 Multicast Address

A multicast address enables a group of systems within a network to communicate with each other. The Internet Class D address is used for IP multicasting. The set of addresses reserved within Class D for IP multicasting is between 224.0.0.0 and 239.255.255.255. Internet protocol multicast addresses are only used as destination addresses.

2.3 NETWORK ACCESS LAYER

Technologies that work at the network access layer are described in this section. These technologies include:

- Ethernet;
- Fast Ethernet (100Base-X);
- Ethernet 100VG-AnyLAN;
- Token ring;
- FDDI;
- Frame relay;
- ATM.

In this text, special emphasis is placed on standards such as Ethernet, frame relay, and ATM. The IEEE has defined standards for local, metropolitan, and wide area networks. These standards are summarized toward the end of this section.

2.3.1 Ethernet

Ethernet, a 10-Mbps, carrier sense, multiple access/collision detect (CSMA/CD) network, is one of the most successful local area network technologies. The

Ethernet network is an example of systems based on a bus topology. On an Ethernet network all stations have access to the network (*multiple access*). Before transmitting, stations listen for frames on the network (*carrier sense*)–if they sense that no frames are on the network, then a station can transmit a frame. It is possible that two or more stations sense that the channel is idle and transmit frames on the network; in that case collision takes place–transmission ceases and colliding stations are made aware (*collision detect*). The colliding stations then back off for a random period of time before retransmitting the frame.

Ethernet is thus a broadcast system for communication among computing stations. Coordination of network access is completely distributed among contending stations. Any station wishing to transmit must wait if another transmission is already in progress. If no other station is transmitting, the sender can begin immediately.

Note that CSMA/CD is the media access protocol used by Ethernet. It provides the functionality of layer 2 in the OSI/RM, the data link layer function of managing communication over the link. Table 2.2 summarizes some characteristics associated with Ethernet networks [3].

The Ethernet header provides the basis for systems on an Ethernet network to talk to each other. The Ethernet header consists of three fields: destination address, source address, and protocol type. The following is a brief description of each field:

Table 2.2
Ethernet Network Characteristics

Parameter	Description
Transmission medium	Coaxial cable (50 ohm)
Signaling technique	Baseband (Manchester)
Data rate (Mbps)	10
Maximum segment length (m)	500
Network span (m)	2500
Nodes per segment	100
Node spacing (m)	2.5
Cable diameter (mm)	10
Slot time (bit times)	512
Inter frame gap (μs)	9.6
Attempt limit	16
Backoff limit	10
Jam size (bits)	32
Maximum frame size (bytes)	1518
Minimum frame size (bytes)	64

- *Destination address* (6 bytes): Describes the target system's Ethernet address.
- *Source address* (6 bytes): Describes the source system's Ethernet address.
- *Protocol type* (2 bytes): Describes what higher layer protocol is encapsulated in the Ethernet frame. For example, if you see the number 0806 (Hex) in this field, it implies that the ARP protocol is encapsulated in the Ethernet header. Examine RFC 1340 for a list of defined protocol types.

The Institute of Electrical and Electronic Engineers (IEEE) has standardized Ethernet in its specification–the specifications that relate to Ethernet are IEEE 802.2 and IEEE 802.3. There are some differences between the Ethernet version 2 header and the IEEE 802.3 header. Figure 2.4 compares the format of the Ethernet frame with that of the IEEE 802.3. Note that the minimum size of an Ethernet frame is 64 bytes and that the maximum frame size is 1518 bytes. The values defined for the protocol type field in the Ethernet header are always above the maximum frame size on an Ethernet or IEEE 802.3 network.

2.3.2 Fast Ethernet (100Base-X)

Fast Ethernet refers to the IEEE 100Base-X standard originally developed by vendors such as 3Com, Cabletron, SynOptics, Digital, Grand Junction Networks,

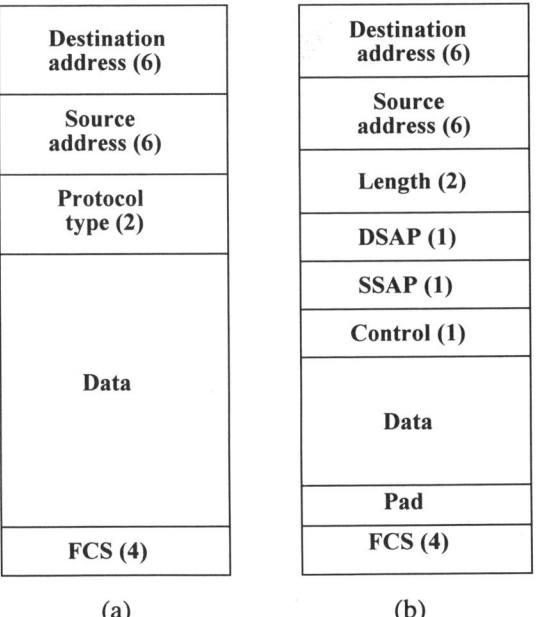

Figure 2.4 Comparing the Ethernet frame to the IEEE 802.3 frame.

and Intel. The IEEE 802.3 committee is responsible for the 100Base-X standard. The major objective of the Fast Ethernet standard is to promote the use of Ethernet at 100 Mbps using CSMA/CD. See Table 2.3 for a side-by-side comparison of Ethernet and Fast Ethernat features.

The Fast Ethernet standard requires the use of EIA/TIA Category 5 twisted pair data-grade wiring to support 100 Mbps. The topology supported by the standard is similar to Ethernet 10Base-T, where a star configuration is used. Vendors will support Ethernet 100Base-X cards that will support both the 10-Mbps and 100-Mbps data rates. While you are limited to a distance of 100m with this standard, it is possible to support longer distances by using fiber-optic cable.

2.3.3 Ethernet 100VG-AnyLAN

The 100VG-AnyLAN proposal was originally developed by AT&T and HP–it is currently being standardized by the IEEE 802.12 committee. While 10BAse-T uses two wire pairs in the cable (one to transmit and one to receive), the 100VG-AnyLAN proposal uses four pairs of Category 3 voice-grade cabling per station, which supports cable distances of 100m.

If you use Category 5 data-grade cable, then the distance supported by the proposed standard is 150m. A key fact to note about 100VG-AnyLAN is that it does not support CSMA/CD, instead it supports a new type of access method referred to as *demand priority*.

Demand Priority

Demand priority is the cable access method used by the 100VG-AnyLAN proposed standard. In demand priority, the hub arbitrates when and how systems

Table 2.3
Ethernet and Fast Ethernet

Description	Ethernet	Fast Ethernet
Speed	Mbps	Mbps
Cost	X	* X
IEEE Standard	IEEE 802.3	IEEE 802.3
Media access protocol	CSMA/CD	CSMA/CD
Topology	Bus/Star	Star
Cable support	Coax/UTP/Fiber	UTP/Fiber
Network diameter (maximum)	meters	meters
UTP link distance (maximum)	meters	meters
Media independent interface	Yes (AUI)	Yes (MII)
Full-duplex capable	Yes	Yes

get access to the network. It supports different levels of priority and, hence, can guarantee that time-sensitive applications such as real-time video get the access time they need to the network. Under this scheme there is basically no contention–since the hub determines which stations get access. If multiple requests for transmissions arrive at the hub, then the transmission with the highest priority is serviced first.

If two stations request the same priority at the same time, then both are serviced by alternating between the two.

100VG-AnyLAN Versus 100Base-X

Both standards require an adapter card replacement. 100VG-AnyLAN is more compatible with existing 10Base-T cable installations. Both standards support fiber-optic cable for longer distances.

While 100Base-X uses the CSMA/CD access method, 100VG-AnyLAN uses demand priority. The demand priority access method may be an advantage to some customers since it provides a way to guarantee priority for some type of LAN traffic. Further, transmissions sent through a hub are not broadcast to other stations–thus preventing the possibility of transmission being monitored by eavesdroppers.

2.3.4 Token Ring

The token-ring standard specifies a maximum data rate of 4 Mbps. An extended version of the token-ring standard operates at 16 Mbps. In a token-ring network one of the nodes is selected as the *ring controller*, which also known as the *active monitor*. The basic operation of a token-ring network is structured around a *token* that circulates around the ring.

A station wishing to transmit must obtain the *free* token. It can then transmit, after changing the token from *free* to *busy*. Other stations must wait. The transmitting station will purge the frame from the ring after the data makes one round trip. When transmission is complete and the *busy* token has returned, the transmitting station will place a new *free* token onto the ring. The process then begins again.

The advantages of token ring include control over network access in that the mechanism used is both efficient and fair especially under heavy load. Disadvantages of token ring are that token maintenance is required and there is some inefficiency under lightly loaded conditions. The ring must be long enough to hold the token (artificial delay may need to be supplied). Thus, the token gives the receiving node permission to send data. Before a packet can be sent, a host has to *capture* the token. The token has a priority associated with it. Each data packet also has a priority associated with it. Error recovery packets, for example, have a higher priority than ordinary data packets.

2.3.5 Fiber Distributed Data Interface

The *fiber distributed data interface* (FDDI) is a standard for a high-speed ring local network developed by the X3T9.5 ANSI Accredited Standards Committee. Like the IEEE 802.5 token ring standard, FDDI employs the token ring algorithm. This standard specifies the *media access control* (MAC) and the physical layers for a counter-rotating, token ring, optical fiber local area network. FDDI supports both synchronous and asynchronous traffic. It uses the IEEE 802.2 *logical link control* (LLC) standard. The standard specifies the use of optical fiber as its primary media. FDDI's transfer rate is 100 Mbps over distances up to 200 km (assuming a single ring) with up to 1,000 stations connected. In a dual-ring topology, each ring is limited to 100 km.

2.3.6 Frame Relay

What is frame relay? Frame relay is a physical and data link layer protocol used to exchange information between communication devices such as routers and switching nodes. It is a protocol used across the WAN, like X.25, and provides a means for statistically multiplexing many virtual circuits over the same transmission link.

The development of the frame relay protocol has come about because of a number of factors:

- The need for better performance across the WAN;
- Substantially increased number of bursty applications;
- General availability of cleaner transmission lines;
- Increased intelligence of endpoint devices.

Frame relay was developed to provide low-error processing, very high throughput, and efficient handling of data bursts. It is the same type of protocol as X.25 but is more streamlined; thus, frame relay has higher performance and greater efficiency. Frame relay has error detection mechanisms but no error correction mechanisms.

Frame relay does not guarantee delivery of data. The network detects, but does not correct, transmission, format, and operational errors. The network does not acknowledge or retransmit frames. Protocols in the user's equipment is responsible for retransmitting data that is lost, misrouted, or discarded by the network because of congestion.

The frame relay protocol only supports data transmission over a connection-oriented path. It enables the transmission of variable-length data units. Frames are transported transparently and are delivered in sequence. The frame relay switch performs three important functions:

1. The frame check sequence is examined, and the frame is discarded if errors are found.
2. The frame address information is read, and the frame is routed to the appropriate link.
3. A congestion check is performed—if congestion is detected, the appropriate congestion notification bits are set or the frame is discarded.

Standards and the Frame Relay Forum

CCITT and ANSI are the two organizations that have a major interest in frame relay standards. The standards committees within the CCITT defined the *additional packet mode bearer service* (within the framework of ISDN); this service, CCITT ISDN I.122, is now known as frame relay. The potential of the I.122 CCITT standards to operate in a stand-alone environment was quickly spotted by vendors.

Vendors felt they couldn't wait for standards to evolve and joined as a group in an attempt to set their own standards. The *Group of Four* vendors (later to become the Frame Relay Forum) consisted of Digital Equipment Corporation, Northern Telecom, Cisco, and Stratacom. Seventeen companies announced in October of 1990 that they were joining the *Group of Four*. In January 1991, after adding even more vendors, the first meeting of the Frame Relay Forum was held; the membership now exceeds 50. Three committees make up the Frame Relay Forum:

- *Technical Committee:* This group is the main technical body within the forum and is also the liaison to the international standards bodies.
- *Marketing Committee:* This group promotes frame relay among the user base.
- *Testing and Interoperability Committee:* This group validates frame relay implementations within a formal framework.

The standards committees and the vendors disagreed on some of the protocol definitions, resulting in two protocols: (1) The user plane protocols are identical but differ on the control plane, the *local management interface* (LMI) procedures; and (2) The two specifications will work together if an appropriate *data link connection identifier* (DLCI) is used and the control plane procedures on each side of the interface are disconnected.

Frame Relay Header

Frame relay is based on the *link access procedures on the D-channel* (LAPD) protocol. The frame relay format merges the *high-level data link control* (HDLC) address and control fields into a single header field (address field). Note that HDLC is the ISO standard for bit-oriented protocols. LAPB, LAPD, LAPF, V.120, and the signaling system No. 7 (SS7) are all based upon HDLC.

All of the following fields along with the *frame check sequence* (FCS) and starting/ending flags must be present in every frame relay frame.

The following is a brief description of fields in the frame relay header (see Figure 2.5):

- *DLCI* (10 bits): The *data link connection identifier* (DLCI) represents a frame relay user address. This is a 10-bit address contained in the six most significant bits of the first octet and the four most significant bits of the

0				7
Flags (8)				
DLCI (6) (MSB)			C/R (1)	EA (1)
DLCI (4) (LSB)	FE (1)	BE (1)	DE (1)	EA (1)
User data				
FCS (8)				
Flags (8)				

Figure 2.5 Frame relay header format.

second octet. It identifies the logical connection that is multiplexed into the physical channel.
- *C/R* (1 bit): This bit is known as the *command/response* indication bit (CR) and is not used by the frame relay protocol. It is passed transparently.
- *FECN* (1 bit): The *forward explicit congestion notification* bit (FECN) is set by the network. It indicates to the user that congestion was experienced in the path from source to destination.
- *BECN* (1 bit): The *backward explicit congestion notification* bit (BECN) is also set by the network. It indicates that congestion is possible in the opposite direction of the frame carrying the BECN–it is set in frames traveling in the opposite direction from frames encountering a congested path. The end systems are under no obligation to heed either the FECN or BECN bits. These bits can be promoted to a higher level protocol that can take flow control action as appropriate.
- *DE* (1 bit): The *discard eligibility* bit (DE) is used to indicate which frames should be discarded first, should congestion arise. The user or the network can set this bit and, once set, can never be reset by the network.
- *EA* (1 bit): The *address extension* bit (EA) is used to extend the header field to support large DLCI addresses. The EA bit indicates whether the current octet is the last octet in the header. If this bit is one, the current octet is the last octet.
- *User Data* (Variable): This field contains user data that is passed unchanged (not processed) across the network. An integral number of octets make up this field; the minimum size is 1 octet and the maximum is network dependent, but the recommended default maximum is 1,600 octets.

Permanent Virtual Circuit and Switched Virtual Circuit

Until recently, frame relay standards primarily addressed *permanent virtual circuits* (PVCs). A PVC is a frame relay connection between two users that is permanently established. PVCs interconnect sites just as a private line would, but bandwidth is shared rather than dedicated solely for the use of that link.

PVCs do not allow users to place frame relay connections on demand. For each pair of endpoint devices, PVCs are predefined, meaning no call setup is necessary and a network path is always ready for the application. In PVC-based frame relay, set up is done once on behalf of the user; that is, a logical connection is set up between end systems prior to exchanging data. PVCs result in faster network access and better response time.

A virtual circuit that is set up dynamically, on a call-by-call basis, is a *switched virtual circuit* (SVC). SVCs gives frame relay much needed flexibility. In the SVC approach, the set-up phase adds some delay to each call but provides dynamic connectivity.

Access Rates, CIR, CBS, and EBS

When you set up a frame relay connection, you have a choice of access speeds and a choice of dedicated or switched access. 56/64-Kbps switched access is provided via Switched-56 service or ISDN; dedicated access is provided by *advanced digital network* (ADN). ISDN and ADN support access at 128 Kbps. 384-Kbps to 1.544-Mbps connection is available through T1 or fractional T1 lines. Routers and *frame relay access devices* (FRAD) connect your network environment to the Frame Relay provider's port.

Frame relay ports are typically connected with PVCs. As mentioned earlier, PVCs are logical links with specific endpoints and service characteristics. PVCs provide logical connections over meshed topologies and provide a way for carriers to specify service characteristics and rates in advance of use. PVCs provide a fast connection between endpoints. Some service characteristics that you define for PVCs when setting up the service with a provider are:

- Access rate;
- Committed information rate (CIR);
- Committed burst size (CBS);
- Excess burst size (EBS).

The *access rate* defines the speed of the line–typical access rates in the United States are 1.544 Mbps (T1) and 56 Kbps. The *committed information rate* (CIR) is the maximum average data rate of a frame relay circuit–it is typically less than the access rate–transmissions can exceed the CIR for short bursts of data. The *committed burst size* (CBS) is the maximum amount of data (in bits) that the network provider agrees to transfer under normal network conditions during a time interval. The *excess burst size* (EBS) is the maximum amount of uncommitted data (in bits) in excess of CBS that the network will attempt to deliver during a time interval; EBS data is treated as discard eligible by the network.

As indicated, the CIR specifies the amount of bandwidth guaranteed as available to the customer at any time, even if the network is congested. The CIR states a maximum bandwidth that can be used within a PVC between two predefined endpoints. Some carriers allow the user to exceed this bandwidth but do not guarantee the delivery of data; others may simply discard data that exceeds the CIR.

Frame relay service providers typically build a greater capacity in their backbone than required and therefore have the capability to offer additional bandwidth on demand with a high probability that bursts above the CIR will pass without appreciable data loss. Each customer is allowed a CBS to pass all traffic if CBS is not exceeded. If the CIR is exceeded by a given value, then the first frames to be discarded are those marked for DE.

Any transmissions whose frames exceed both the CIR and the EBS will be discarded automatically until the level of congestion is brought down to the point where DE set frames are discarded and non-DE frames are passed. *Oversubscription* is the capability to overbook the CIRs coming into a single physical access port. The amount of oversubscription allowed by a frame relay service provider can be an important factor if there are many low-speed-user CIRs contending for a single physical network access port.

Congestion Control

When a frame relay network becomes congested, frames may be arbitrarily discarded or discarded based on customer preference. Customers can designate traffic that is not critical as discard-eligible (DE). Flagging frames with DE is done either by a router or a frame relay switch. Using DE ensures that the most important information makes it through the network while less important information can be retransmitted when the network is less busy.

Management and Services

Frame relay networks support the following management features and services:

- Virtual circuit status messages;
- Multicasting;
- Global addressing.

Virtual circuit status messages provide communication between the network and the customer–it ensures that PVCs exist and reports on deleted PVCs. Multicasting is an optional frame relay service that lets one user send frames to multiple destinations. Global addressing is an optional frame relay service that gives the frame relay network LAN-like capabilities. To manage a frame relay network effectively, some of the following network parameters should be monitored:

- Number of frames sent and received;
- Frames received in error;
- Number of FECNs and BECNs received;
- Number of discarded/nondiscarded DE frames.

Frame Relay Service Providers

Most carriers today offer frame relay services, as do public data network (PDN) providers such as CompuServe. Each carrier has a specific number of places where customers can link into the network points-of-presence. Access to this point is through the LEC or other providers. Examples of some frame relay services are described in Table 2.4.

2.3.7 ATM

What is ATM? ATM is a broadband technology for transmitting voice, video, and data over LANS and WANs. When compared to the OSI/RM, ATM works at the MAC sublayer within the data link layer. It is a *cell relay technology*–data packets have a fixed size.

The switching device is a key element in an ATM network–it provides the capability to relay cells from one node to another or to transmit ATM cells between remote LANs at very high speeds. ATM supports *any-to-any connectivity* and nodes can transmit simultaneously. ATM is an example of a *fast packet technology* like frame relay and SMDS. ATM is certain to be widely deployed in public and private networks–in local and wide area networks. If ATM deployment takes place as expected, it is likely to become the basis for most services in global communications, wherein all forms of traffic are transported over a cell-based switching fabric.

ATM offers the following solutions:

- Large switches for public service networks;
- Medium to small switches/concentrators for private ATM networks;
- Cell-based devices to interconnect Ethernet and token ring LANs, client/server systems within an organization's premises or across a campus area network;
- Interface cards for end-user devices and host and server systems.

Table 2.4
Some Frame Relay Service Providers

Organization	Service	Phone No.
BT North America I	Global Expresslane	(800) 872–7654
CompuServe	Frame-Net Services	(800) 433–0389
MCI	HyperStream Frame Relay	(800) 933–9029
US Sprint	Frame Relay	(800) 877–2000
Williams Telecommunications Group	Wilpak	(918) 588–3210

ATM Standards

ATM was originally defined as part of the *broadband-integrated services digital network* (B-ISDN), which was developed by CCITT in 1988. The ATM standard is described in CCITT Recommendation I.361. The *ATM adaptation layer* (AAL) is described in CCITT I.363.

The *ATM Forum*, not a standards body, is an international consortium formed to accelerate the use of ATM products and services by defining and demonstrating interoperability specifications. ATM Forum specifications include the *User-Network Interface Specifications, Data Exchange Interface* (DXI) *Specification*, and the *B-ISDN Intercarrier Interface* (B-ICI) *Specification*. The ATM Forum may be reached at:

Phone:	(415) 578–6860
Fax:	(415) 525–0182
Fax-on-Demand:	(415) 688–4318
e-mail:	info@atmforum.com
Mailing Address:	3303 Vintage Park, Foster City, CA

The *Internet Engineering Task Force* (IETF) is a group that makes technical and other contributions to the evolution of the Internet and associated technologies; IETF Working Groups have written a number of RFCs that pertain to ATM.

Telecom Industry: Need for ATM

Telephone networks are undergoing a number of changes including *conversion to digital technologies, computerization,* and *deployment of high-capacity fiber.* A single fiber-optic line typically replaces ten or hundreds of copper lines; thus, telephone networks are increasingly multiplexing far more circuits into the same link and at higher bandwidths. However, multiplexing of circuits is difficult and expensive—it is easier at high speeds to multiplex packets than to multiplex mixes of individual bits.

ATM is, in part, a data communication technology being developed by the telecom industry to meet its needs for a flexible transmission technology and to offer new services to users. Table 2.5 summarizes how datacom, telecom, and ATM technologies compare.

ATM networks are designed to be *organized just like the telephone network*—local user equipment is connected to regional ATM providers who in turn are connected to national providers who may be connected to international providers.

ATM is a *connection-oriented service*—a cell is not sent until a channel (connection) is established. Cell transmission is *asynchronous*; thus, ATM can send delay-tolerant traffic such as data intermixed with time-sensitive traffic

Table 2.5
Datacom, Telecom, and ATM Technologies

Feature	Datacom	Telecom	ATM
Traffic type	Data	Voice	Data, voice, video
Transmission length and unit	Variable packet	Fixed frame	Fixed cell
Switching type	Packet	Circuit	Cell
Interval	Bursty	Periodic	Periodic
Timing	Indeterminate	Time-sensitive	Some time-sensitive
Connection type	Connectionless	Connection-oriented	Connection-oriented
Delivery	Best effort	Guaranteed	Defined classes
Media and rate	Defined by protocol	Defined by channel	Scaleable to application
Access to media	Shared	Dedicated	Dedicated

such as voice. Since ATM is connection-oriented, it can specify a guaranteed *quality of service* (QoS) for each connection. Bandwidth is allocated only when an endstation requests a connection—ATM can support a network's aggregate demand by allocating *bandwidth-on-demand* based on immediate user need—the allocation can be accomplished without administrative intervention.

ATM is not tied to a particular transmission rate or physical medium—it is media and rate independent—and can operate at whatever rate is appropriate for whichever physical layer technology is being used. ATM is expected to run mostly over *fiber-optic networks*—a major characteristic of fiber-optic networks is their extremely *low error rate*.

On carrier systems, high-speed ATM implementations, which range from 155 Mbps to 622 Mbps, use the SONET standard. ATM is expected to support *low-cost attachments*. Particularly, as competition for ATM products increases, it is likely that 25-Mbps to 15-Mbps ATM boards will be commonly used in desktop multimedia computer systems.

ATM Network Characteristics

In the ATM world, the user's equipment connects to networks via a *user–network interface* (UNI). The UNI provides an interface to the user equipment that supports multiplexing since it is likely that the user equipment may be multiplexing traffic from various users to the ATM network.

The UNI also protects an ATM provider's network from user equipment that may be misbehaving. Connections between ATM provider networks are made via a *network–network interface* (NNI). The main motivation for the NNI is to provide seamless connectivity between independently operated ATM networks. The ATM backbone networks will typically have only a few high-speed trunk lines connecting each switch to its neighbors—the major routing task here is to determine to which link to forward cells received. Since ATM is connection-oriented, *channel identifiers* are used to establish connections.

The channel identifiers have a hierarchical structure. Each identifier consists of two parts: (1) channel identifier, and (2) path identifier.

At the edges of networks, where transmission links provide connectivity to users' offices and homes, cells are routed based on both the channel and path identifiers. On ATM backbone networks, cells are routed based on the path identifier. On ATM networks, high-priority cells have a *loss rate* that is comparable to that of optical fiber (1 bit error in 10^{12} or better). *Cell reordering* does not take place on ATM networks; thus, ATM attachments and switches can use simpler forms of buffering.

ATM is a *scalable technology* that ranges in speed from less than 12 Mbps to 48 Gbps. While ATM was originally designed to operate over the SONET standard, which specifies single-mode optical fiber, it has been adapted to work with multimode fiber as well as unshielded and shielded twisted pair. ATM has been developed as a *switched-media standard*.

ATM Layers

The B-ISDN/reference model (B-ISDN/RM) defines three layers:

- Physical layer;
- ATM layer;
- ATM adaptation layer.

Figure 2.6 describes the three layers.

The *physical layer* defines electrical, mechanical, and procedural characteristics; line speeds; and interfaces. The *ATM layer* defines the ATM cell format. The *ATM adaptation layer* defines the process of converting information from higher layers into ATM cells.

Physical Layer

ATM supports many different media at the physical layer. Many in the industry are endorsing SONET as the ATM physical transport media for LAN and WAN applications. The ATM Forum recommends the following physical interfaces for ATM:

- FDDI (100 Mbps);
- Fiber channel (155 Mbps);
- OC3 SONET (155 Mbps);
- T3 (45 Mbps).

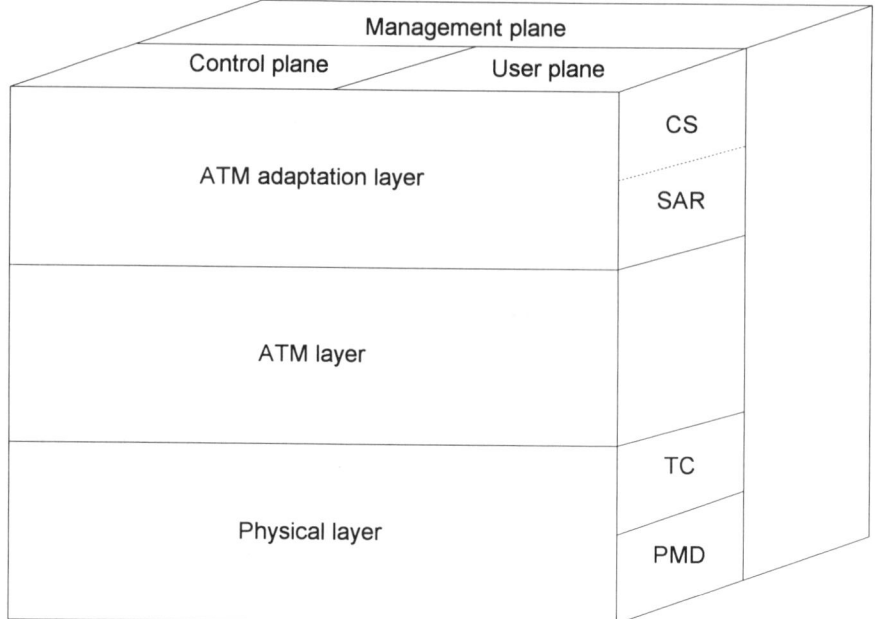

Figure 2.6 B-ISDN (ATM) layers.

The physical layer is divided into the *physical medium–dependent* (PMD) *sublayer* and the *transmission convergence* (TC) *sublayer*. PMD is specific to a particular physical medium and includes definitions for proper cabling as well as bit timing. The TC sublayer performs a convergence function by receiving a bit stream from the PMD and extracting cells using the *header error control* (HER) for cell delineation. *Cell delineation* is the extraction of cells from the bit stream received from the PMD. *Cell rate decoupling* is the adaptation of the speed of the ATM layer cell stream to the cell rate of the physical interface.

TC functions that are common to all the physical layers include:

- Cell delineation;
- Cell rate decoupling;
- HEC generation and checking;
- Various operations and maintenance (OAM) functions.

ATM Layer

The ATM layer defines the format of the ATM cell. The ATM layer is responsible for cell multiplexing, cell header generation or removal, and virtual path identifier/virtual circuit identifier (VPI/VCI) translation. The ATM layer operation varies depending on the type of ATM network device and is responsible for the successful transmission of 53-byte cells.

In the ATM endpoint or endstation, the ATM layer exchanges a cell stream with the physical layer and inserts idle cells if no higher layer information is waiting to trasmit or if empty cells are needed to comply with *quality of service* (QoS) parameters.

ATM Adaptation Layer

The *ATM adaptation layer* (AAL) converges packets from upper layers into ATM cells and provides the ability to support many different types of traffic and applications over an ATM network. The AAL layer is divided into two sublayers: (1) *convergence sublayer* (CS) and (2) *segmentation and reassembly sublayer* (SAR).

Segmentation and reassembly in ATM is the process of segmenting LAN frames into 48-byte information segments, adding an ATM header, and then stripping the header at the destination. Convergence accepts packets from higher layers and passes it to SAR. SAR is responsible for breaking the data into 53-byte ATM cells. If cells are arriving, SAR reassembles the data in the cells and passes it to upper layers.

The *AAL layer* is responsible for adapting higher layer data with different service requirements into cell payloads for the ATM layer and vice versa. Table 2.6 describes the AAL types that have been defined.

Table 2.6
AAL Types

AAL Type	Description
Type 1	Isochronous, constant bit-rate service for audio and video applications–similar to T1 or T3 and supports a variety of data rates
Type 2	Isochronous variable bit-rate application–for example, compressed video–carriers have not implemented this interface
Type 3/4	Supports bursty LAN-type variable bit-rate data–supports Frame Relay and SMDS interfaces
Type 5	Supports a subset of Type 3/4 functions–provides message mode and nonassured operation

ATM Planes

The ATM architecture defines *planes* that operate across all three layers; the planes are:

- User plane;
- Control plane;
- Management plane.

The *user plane* is used for end-to-end data transfer. The *control plane* supports networkwide functions such as signaling used to establish *switched virtual circuits* (SVCs) between endpoints. The *management plane* supports management and control functions for the network and its endpoints.

ATM Service Classes

ATM supports different types of traffic such as voice, video, and data by providing four classes of service, that is, Classes A to D.

The service classes categorize applications based on how bits are transmitted, the required bandwidth, and types of connections required. Class A is a connection-oriented service that provides a constant bit rate—suitable for video and voice applications. Class B is a connection-oriented service and is timed for transmitting variable bit rate voice and video—interface to the AAL is Type 2. Class C is a connection-oriented, variable, bit-rate service without timing—suitable for services such as X.25, Frame Relay, and TCP/IP—interface to the AAL is Type 3/4 or Type 5. Class D is a connectionless service, with variable rate data traffic that does not require timing relationships between end-nodes—interface to the AAL Type 3/4.

Table 2.7 describes ATM service classes.

Table 2.7
ATM Service Classes

Service Class	Timing	Bit Rate	CO vs. CL	AAL Types
A	Required	Constant	Connection-oriented	Type 1
B	Required	Variable	Connection-oriented	Type 2
C	Not required	Variable	Connection-oriented	Type 3/4 Type 5
D	Not required	Variable	Connectionless	Type 3/4

ATM Cells

ATM cells are 53 bytes (octets) in size–the first 5 bytes define the cell header, while the remaining 48 bytes contain cell data. Figure 2.7 describes an ATM cell.

The cell data is formatted in one of the ATM adaptation layer formats. The 48-byte data size was the result of compromise reached by the ATM standards committee–there were some that wanted 128 bytes of data while others insisted on 16 bytes; the two sides then revised their original demand to 64 and 32 bytes of data, eventually compromising by splitting the difference between 64 and 32 bytes of data.

The larger cell size request was to make ATM better suited for data traffic–a cell size of 48 bytes is considered too large for voice–thus, it is likely voice will be sent in partially filled cells. Typically, on telephone providers' backbones, ATM cells will be encapsulated inside SONET frames. The ATM cell header has two formats: cells given to a UNI by an ATM user and cells crossing an NNI. ATM cells are transmitted serially. Figure 2.8 describes the format of the ATM cell header.

The ATM cell header varies for UNI and NNI. The difference between the UNI header and the NNI header is that a part of the VPI field is reserved as a *generic flow control* (GFC). The NNI has a larger range of VPI values (12 bits). The following is a brief description of fields in the ATM cell.

- *GFC* (4 bits): The *generic flow control* (GFC) field is reserved only for the UNI–it is used by the UNI to control traffic flow.
- *VPI* (8/12 bits): The *virtual path identifier* (VPI) identifies virtual paths–in a null or idle cell this field is set to all zeros.
- *VCI* (16 bits): The *virtual circuit identifier* (VCI) identifies virtual circuits–in a null or idle cell this field is set to all zeros.
- *PTI* (2 bits): The *payload type identifier* (PTI) identifies the type of payload carried in the ATM cell.
- *CLP* (2 bits): The *cell loss priority* (CLP) field is set by the AAL and used by the ATM layer throughout the network to determine the relative importance of cells–if this bit is set to 1, then it implies that the cell can be discarded by a switch experiencing congestionp; if this bit is set to 0, then the cell should not be discarded (this may be needed for a a specific QoS).

Header (5 bytes)	Data (payload) (48 bytes)

Figure 2.7 An ATM cell.

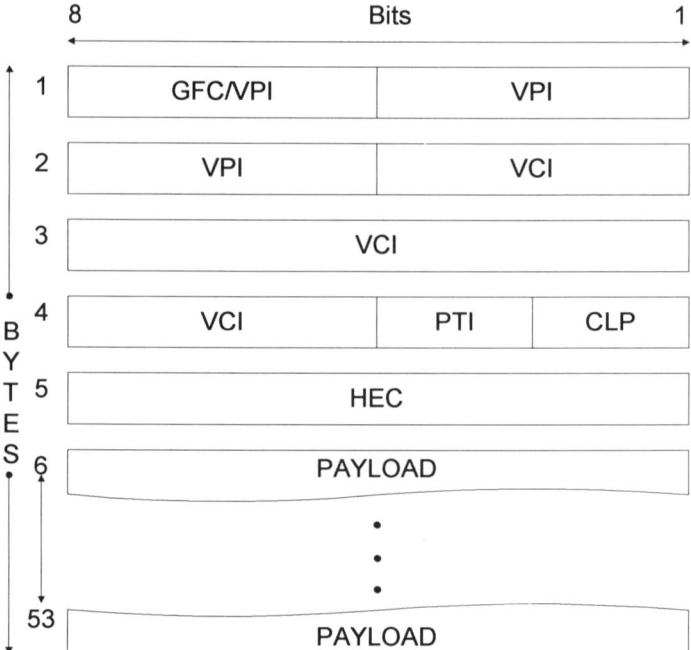

Figure 2.8 ATM cell header format.

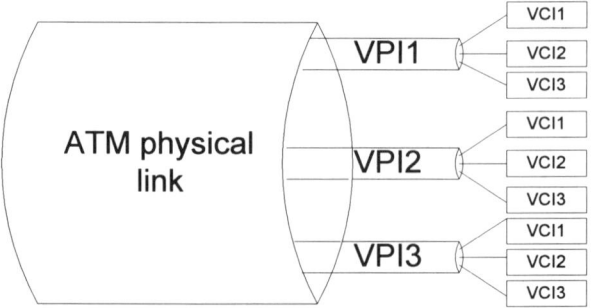

Figure 2.9 Virtual paths and virtual circuits.

This field can also be set by the ATM layer if a connection exceeds the agreed upon QoS parameters during connection setup.
- *HEC* (8 bits): The *header error control* (HEC) field is an 8-bit CRC that is computed only over the ATM cell header–it is capable of detecting all single bit errors and some types of multiple bit errors.

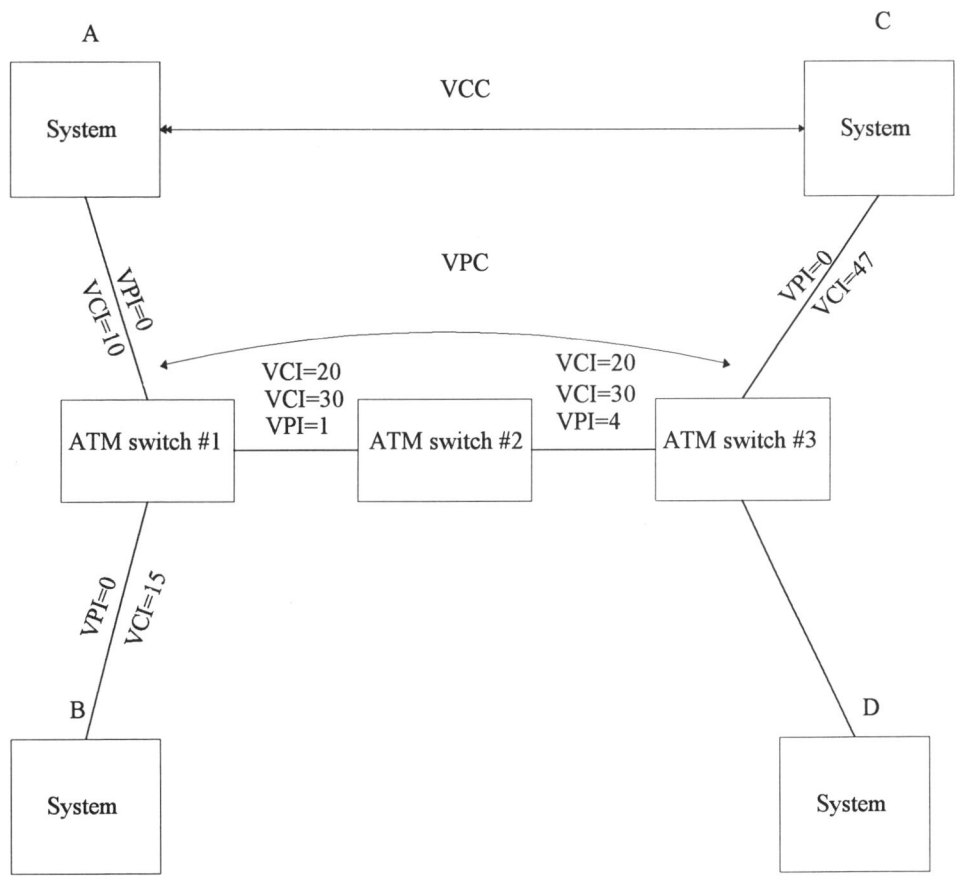

Figure 2.10 ATM switches, VPI, and VCCs.

Virtual Channels and Paths

As mentioned earlier, there are two connection identifiers in the ATM cell header:

1. Virtual path identifier (VPI);
2. Virtual channel identifier (VCI).

A *virtual channel connection* (VCC) is a concatenation of virtual channel links between two ATM points where protocols such as IP are accessed. The cell sequence must be preserved over a VCC. A *virtual path connection* (VPC) is a concatenation of virtual path links between the points where a VCI value is first assigned and the point where that VCI value is either reassigned or terminated. Multiple VCIs can be aggregated into a single VPI. An ATM switch reads an incoming cell's VPI, VCI, or both and determines the output port to which to switch the cell based on its lookup table. The look-up table is updated each time connections are made.

Virtual Channels and Paths

A switch that reads and substitutes new VPI values is referred to as a *virtual path switch* (or *VP Switch*)–a VP switch is analogous to a central office telephone switch in which trunk lines with a number of voice channels are grouped together and switched between several other central offices closer to the destination's voice channel(s). A switch that can read and substitute both VPI and VCI values is referred to as a *virtual channel switch* (or *VC Switch*).

IP, ARP, and ATM

How do protocols in the TCP/IP stack interface with ATM's addressing or connection setup procedures? The IETF has formed a working group to define how protocols such as IP and ARP work on an ATM network. Other working groups within IETF are defining *routing over large clouds* (ROLC) and ATM MIBs.

A technique to use IP and ARP was recently defined in RFC 1577. ATMARP is used to resolve an IP address to an ATM address. IP is used to route PDUs between ATM networks configured as *logical IP subnetworks* (LIS).

ATM at the Desktop?

Consider the following example: A true color, high-resolution, full-motion video flows at the rate of about 24 bits of color × (1024 × 1024 bits (pixels) of resolution) × 30 frames/second = 720 Mbps. Using good compression algorithms for video yields a ratio of 100:1, thus reducing the rate to 7 Mbps; other compression algorithms may yield a ratio of 30:1 or about 22 Mbps. Thus, at 22 Mbps it is possible to send full-motion, very high quality video between desktop systems– typical video signals such as broadcast TV require about 6 or 7 Mbps.

Today, in order to get their products to market as soon as possible, ATM LAN adapter manufacturers are using chipsets intended for FDDI's physical layer–the cost of such ATM LAN adapters that work at 100 Mbps is about $1000 and they require fiber or category 5 unshielded twisted-pair wire. The 100-Mbps ATM LAN adapters are probably a good choice for server systems where throughput is likely to be in the higher data-rate range.

Proposals for cheaper, lower speed ATM solutions for the desktop include a 25-Mbps and 51-Mbps data-rate standard. Vendors such as IBM have strongly been in favor of the 25 Mbps standard. Using existing encoding technology, the 25-Mbps ATM standard can run over any twisted-pair wiring topology that 10BASE-T can use. According to IBM, the 25-Mbps ATM standard can be implemented with one-third the number of chips as required for the 100-Mbps ATM standard (a lower chip count implies the price of 25-Mbps ATM LAN adapters will be cheap and is likely to be integrated in the motherboard of systems).

All of the above factors make it likely that the 25-Mbps ATM standard may be the solution for connectivity at the desktop level–especially, if the applications mostly used are multimedia.

ATM Vendors

The following is a brief list (by no means complete) of ATM vendors:

- 3Com Corporation;
- Ascom Timeplex, Inc.;
- Chipcom Corporation;
- Digital Equipment Corporation;
- Fibermux, Inc.;
- Fore Systems, Inc.;
- General Datacomm;
- Hughes LAN Systems, Inc.;
- IBM;
- Network Equipment Technologies, Inc.;
- Newbridge Networks, Inc.;
- SynOptics Communications, Inc.

The next generation of hubs will most likely use a high-speed ATM switching backplane to provide the basis for bandwidth-on-demand switching in the hub. ATM can deliver between 200 Mbps and 2 Gbps on the backplane, and this is most likely to be used to provide high-speed connection between hubs.

2.3.8 IEEE LAN Standards

The IEEE 802 series of standards specify various LAN and *metropolitan area network* (MAN) technologies. The objective of the various 802 subcommittees was to define comprehensive standards for LANs. For example, the IEEE 802.3 is a media access control standard used with the IEEE 802.2 logical link control to describe a specification based on and very close to the Ethernet standard.

The IEEE 802.4 standard specifies the token bus standard, whereas the IEEE 802.5 standard describes the token ring standard. Figure 2.11 describes how some of the IEEE 802.x standards relate to each other.

Table 2.8 summarizes the various IEEE 802 subcommittees. IEEE 802.1 through IEEE 802.6 are formal International Standards 8802-1 through 8802-6 standards adopted by ISO.

2.4 INTERNET LAYER

The protocols in the TCP/IP architecture that directly use the services of the network access layer include:

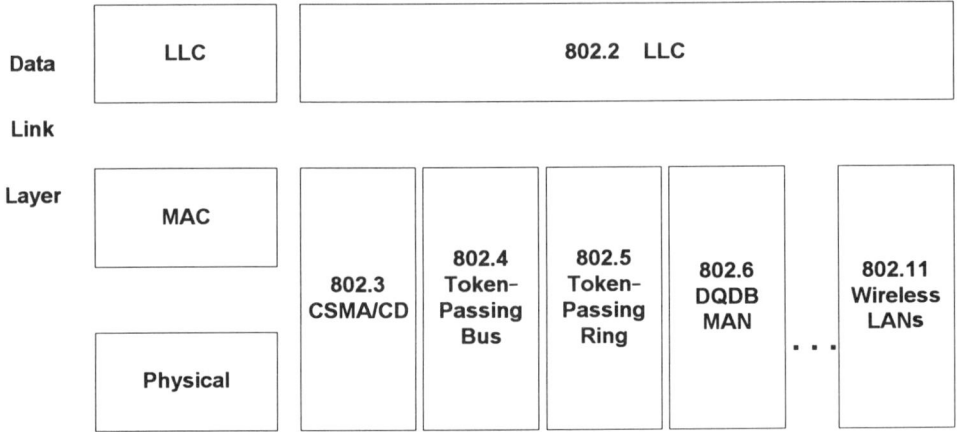

Figure 2.11 IEEE 802 standards and the OSI/RM.

Table 2.8
IEEE 802 Subcommittees

IEEE Subcommittee	Description
802.1	Higher layers and internetworking
802.2	Logical link control
802.3	CSMA/CD LAN
802.4	Token-passing bus LAN
802.5	Token-passing ring LAN
802.6	Distributed queue dual bus LAN
802.7	Broadband Technology Technical Advisory Group
802.8	Fiber Optics Technology Advisory Group
802.9	Integrated voice-data LAN
802.10	Standard for interoperable LAN security

- Address resolution protocol (ARP);
- Reverse address resolution protocol (RARP);
- Internet protocol (IP).

ARP is used by application layer protocols such as **telnet** and **ftp** to determine the destination system's hardware address. RARP is the protocol used by diskless workstations and X terminals to determine their Internet address. IP is used by almost all application layer protocols to exchange data with nodes on the network. IP is used by both TCP and UDP to transport data across the Internet.

2.4.1 Address Resolution Protocol (ARP)

Assume there are two hosts **node1** and **node2** on the network. Host **node1** knows the Internet address for **node2** but does not know the physical hardware address of **node2**. If host **node1** wants to send a packet to host **node2**, how does it translate the Internet adddress to **node2**'s physical address?

The *address resolution protocol* (ARP) is used to translate Internet addresses to physical addresses, such as Ethernet's 48-bit physical address. Dynamic binding or resolution is used with ARP to solve the mapping problem. The following is an example of how dynamic binding with ARP works. When host **node1** needs to resolve the Internet address for host **node2**, it broadcasts a special packet that asks **node2** to respond with its physical address. This message is known as the *ARP request* packet. Although all hosts on the network receive the request, only **node2** recognizes its Internet address and responds with its physical address. This message is referred to as an *ARP reply*.

Hosts that use ARP maintain a cache of recently acquired Internet-to-physical address bindings so that they do not have to use ARP repeatedly. Also the sender's Internet-to-physical address binding is included in every ARP broadcast. Thus, receivers update the Internet-to-physical address binding information in their cache before processing an ARP packet.

An ARP message is encapsulated in an Ethernet frame. Within Ethernet frames, the type field for all ARP packets is set to hexadecimal value 0806. Figure 2.12 illustrates that ARP is encapsulated in an Ethernet frame—note how ARP uses the services of Ethernet directly, that is, there is no IP, TCP, or UDP header in an ARP message.

Figure 2.13 describes the format of the ARP header.
The following is a brief description of fields in the ARP header:

- *Hardware Type* (2 bytes): Specifies the hardware interface type. This field is set to 1 for Ethernet networks. RFC 1340 defines values for this field for various hardware types.

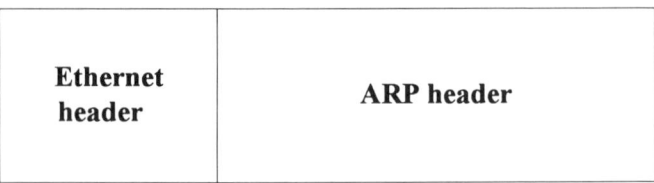

Figure 2.12 Message encapsulated in an Ethernet frame.

- *Protocol Type* (2 bytes): Specifies the protocol used at the higher layer. This field is typically set to 0800 hexadecimal, which implies IP.
- *Hardware Length* (1 byte): Size of the hardware address (in bytes). For example, for Ethernet addresses this field is set to 6.
- *Protocol Length* (1byte): Size of the protocol address (in bytes). For example, for IP addresses, this field is set to 4.
- *Operation* (2 bytes): Specifies the type of ARP operation; that is, 1 implies a ARP Request and 2 implies a ARP Reply.
- *Source Hardware Address* (6 bytes): Hardware address, such as an Ethernet address, of the system sending this message.
- *Source IP Address* (4 bytes): IP address of the system sending this message.
- *Destination Hardware Address* (6 bytes): Hardware address of the target system. In an ARP request message this field is typically set to zero. This is the only field in the ARP request message of which the source system does not know the value.
- *Destination IP Address* (4 bytes): IP address of the target system.

2.4.2 Reverse Address Resolution Protocol (RARP)

Reverse address resolution protocol (RARP) is used by diskless machines and X terminals to find out their Internet address on the network. The diskless system broadcasts its physical hardware address on the network. The RARP message (28 bytes) is encapsulated in the data field portion of the Ethernet frame. Figure 2.14 describes how RARP uses the services of Ethernet. The RARP message allows a machine to determine not only its own Internet address but also that of other systems.

There must be at least one RARP server on the network for RARP to work. Although all machines receive the request, only the RARP server processes the request and sends a reply. Typically, diskless machines and X terminals rely on RARP to boot. Within Ethernet frames the type field for all RARP packets is set to hex value 8035. RARP messages are not forwarded by routers. Figure 2.15 describes the RARP header–it is exactly the same format as the ARP header.

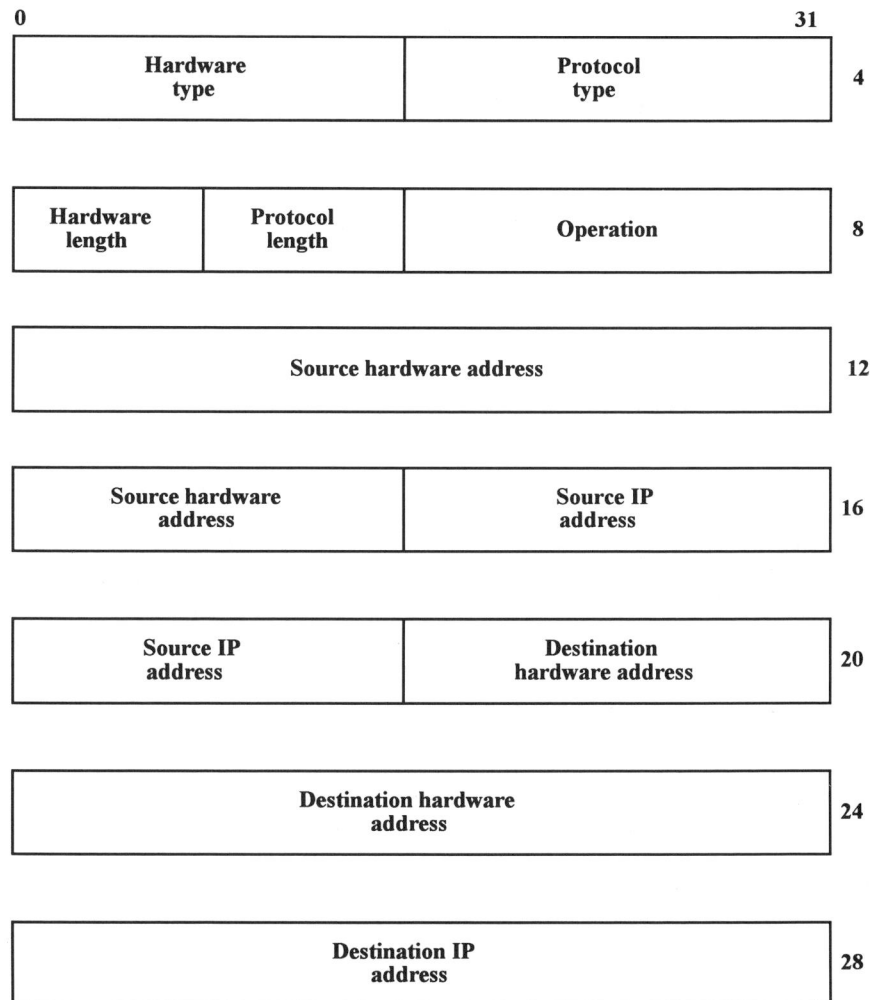

Figure 2.13 ARP header format.

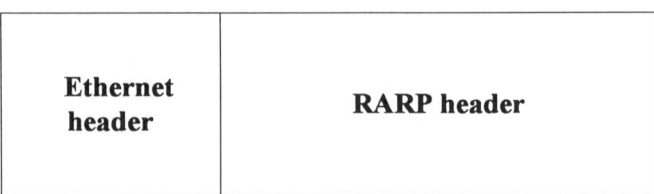

Figure 2.14 RARP message encapsulated in an Ethernet frame.

The following is a brief description of fields in the RARP header:

- *Hardware Type* (2 bytes): Specifies the hardware interface type. This field is set to 1 for Ethernet networks. RFC 1340 defines values for this field for various hardware types.
- *Protocol Type* (2 bytes): Specifies the protocol used at the higher layer. This field is typically set to 0800 hexadecimal, which implies IP.
- *Hardware Length* (1 byte): Size of the hardware address (in bytes). For example, for Ethernet addresses this field is set to 6.
- *Protocol Length* (1byte): Size of the protocol address (in bytes). For example, for IP addresses, this field is set to 4.
- *Operation* (2 bytes): Specifies the type of RARP operation; that is, 3 indicates a RARP request and 4 specifies RARP reply.
- *Source Hardware Address* (6 bytes): Hardware address, such as an Ethernet address, of the system sending this message.
- *Source IP Address* (4 bytes): IP address of the system sending this message. In a RARP request message, the source system typically does know its IP address. Hence this field may be set to zero.
- *Destination Hardware Address* (6 bytes): Hardware address of the target system.
- *Destination IP Address* (4 bytes): IP address of the target system.

2.4.3 Internet Protocol (IP)

The Internet protocol (IP) is a OSI/RM network layer protocol. Internet datagrams may traverse several networks before reaching their destination host. A datagram is a self-contained packet, independent of other packets, that does not require an acknowledgment and carries information sufficient for routing from the originating host to the destination host. Because there is no explicit connection establishment phase, IP is said to be a *connectionless protocol*. The IP datagram is routed transparently, not necessarily reliably, to the destination host. It is the responsibility of the transport or application layers to ensure reliability. Figure 2.16 describes the IP header.

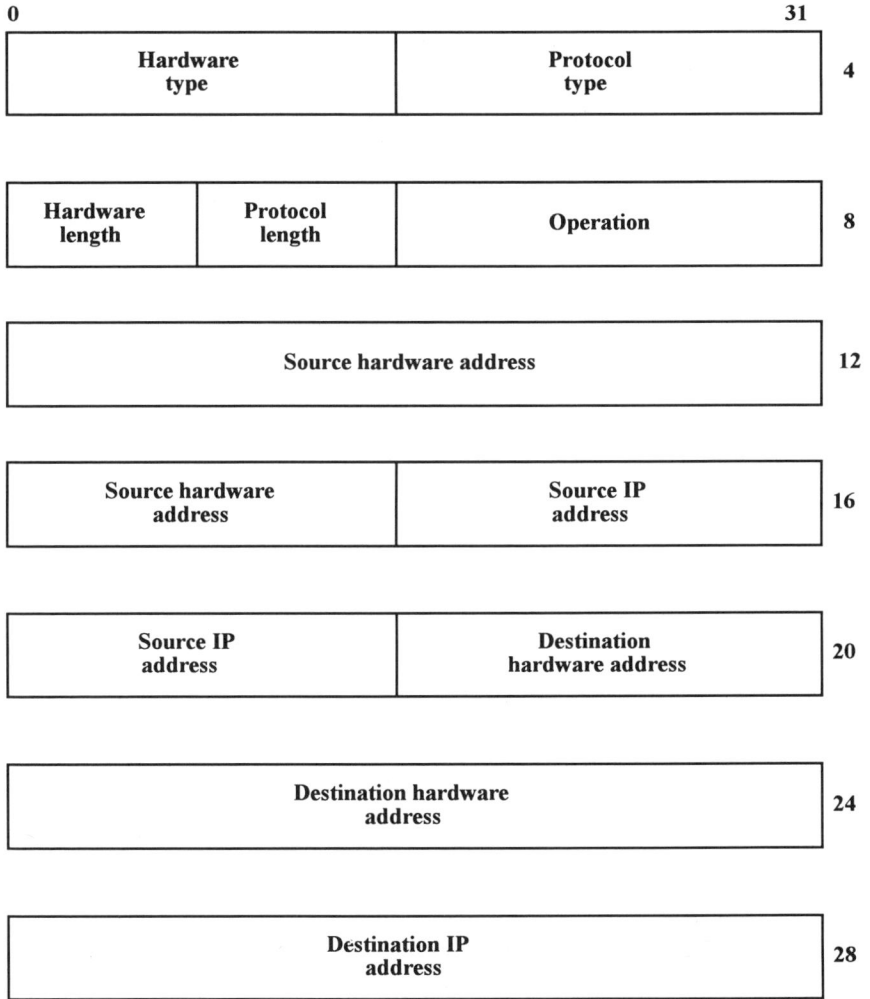

Figure 2.15 RARP header format.

The following is a brief description of each field in the IP header.

- *Version* (4 bits): Specifies the IP protocol version number. This number is currently set to 4.
- *Header Length* (4 bits): Length of the IP header. The IP header can vary in size. The minimum, and typical, size of the IP header is 20 bytes. This field is represented in 32-bit words; so if the IP header is 20 bytes, the number 5 is specified in this field.

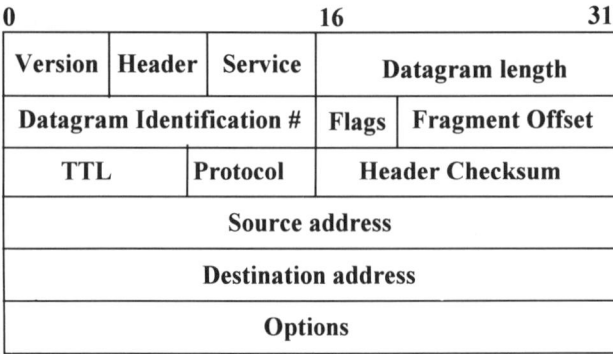

Figure 2.16 The Internet protocol (IP) header.

- *Service* (1 byte): Specifies reliability, precedence delay, and throughput parameters. This field is also known as the *type of service* (TOS) field. RFC 1340, included in the appendix provides further details on this field.
- *Datagram Length* (2 bytes): Total datagram length, including header, in bytes; does not include the header used at the network access layer (e.g., Ethernet header).
- *Datagram ID Number* (2 bytes): This field together with the next two fields, flags and fragment offset, are used by the destination system to reassemble fragmented datagrams.
- *Flags* (3 bits): Used for fragmentation and reassembly.
- *Fragment Offset* (13 bits): Indicates where in the datagram this fragment belongs; the unit of measurement is 64 bits.
- *Time To Live* (1 byte): This field is both a counter and a timer. The maximum value that can be specified in this field is 255. Each time a datagram is received by a router this field is at least decremented by 1. The router also tracks the time it takes to process the datagram (to determine the address of the next hop). This processing time is also subtracted from the TTL field before the datagram is released by the router.
- *Protocol* (1 byte): Indicates the higher layer protocol that is encapsulated in the IP datagram. If the protocol field in the IP packet is 1, it is an ICMP packet; if it is 6, it is a TCP packet; if it is 17, it is an UDP packet.
- *Header Checksum* (2 bytes): Used for error detection.
- *Source Address* (4 bytes): Internet address of the source system (includes network and host portion of the Internet address).
- *Destination Address* (4 bytes): Internet address of the final or destination system (includes both network and host portion of Internet address).
- *Options* (variable): Includes options such as security, loose or strict source routing, error reporting, time stamping, or debugging.

- *Padding* (variable): Used to ensure that the IP header ends on a 32-bit boundary.
- *Data* (variable): Field must be a multiple of 8 bits in length; total length of data field plus header is a maximum of 65,535 bytes.

Fields in the IP datagram are analyzed in the packet in Figure 2.17.

NetMetrix (tm) Packet Report

1) 64 0.000003 000083A21858 000083A21859 TFTP Ack Blk=1
Packet number = 1   Arrival time = 29.820003   Length = 64

——————— DLC Header ———————
DLC: Destination: 0:0:83:a2:18:59
DLC: Source: 0:0:83:a2:18:58
DLC: Protocol: IP

——————— IP Header ———————
IP: Version = 4
IP: Header length = 20
IP: Type of service = Routine(0)
IP: Delay = Normal (0)
IP: Throughput = Normal (0)
IP: Reliability = Normal (0)
IP: Packet length = 32
IP: Id = ea9
IP: Fragment offset = 0
IP: Flags = [Don't Fragment = 0][More = 0]
IP: Time to live = 60
IP: Protocol = UDP (17)
IP: Header checksum = 013E
IP: Source address = 192.136.118.234
IP: Destination address = 192.136.118.235

——————— UDP Header ———————
UDP: Source port = 1055
UDP: Destination port = 1176
UDP: Length = 12
UDP: Checksum = 0

——————— TFTP Header ———————
TFTP: Opcode = Ack (4)
TFTP: Block number = 1

Figure 2.17 IP packet (fields in **bold** relate to IP). *Courtesy: HP NetMetrix.*

Hexadecimal Representation:
```
0000: 00 00 83 A2 18 59 00 00 -   83 A2 18 58 08 00 45 00      .....Y.....X..E.
0010: 00 20 0E A9 00 00 3C 11 -   01 3E C0 88 76 EA C0 88      . ....<..>..v...
0020: 76 EB 04 1F 04 98 00 0C -   00 00 00 04 00 01 4A 08      v..............J.
0030: 00 05 00 90 00 1B 00 90 -   00 22 00 02 00 C4 01 00      .........".....
```

Figure 2.17 continued.

IP Datagram Fragmentation

IP makes its best effort to get the datagram to the destination system as fast as possible. Communication devices such as routers process IP datagrams and determine the route that the datagram traverses to get to the destination system. It is possible that a router may receive a datagram that may be be too large for it to handle, in which case it may break the datagram into smaller pieces, called *fragments*. Reassembly of these fragments is not the responsibility of the router but of the final, destination system. The flags and fragment offset fields in the IP header are used for fragmentation and reassembly functions.

As soon as the destination system receives the first fragment, it starts a timer, referred to as the reassembly timer. The destination system must receive all fragments from the original datagram before the reassembly timer expires. If the reassembly timer expires and the destination system has not received all fragments, an ICMP message is generated and sent to the source system.

2.5 TRANSPORT LAYER

In this section we examine the two transport layer protocols defined in the Internet architecture: TCP and UDP.

2.5.1 Transmission Control Protocol (TCP)

The *transmission control protocol* (TCP) is a transport layer protcol responsible for providing a reliable mechanism for the exchange of data beween processes in different systems. The transport layer is the first *end-to-end layer* or, in other words, a *source-to-destination layer*. Thus, a program on the source system communicates with another program on the destination system. The lower layers, such as network layer and below, communicate between a system and its immediate neighbors (such as routers) and not directly between the source and destination systems.

TCP accepts arbitrarily long messages from higher layers and breaks them into pieces that are less than 64K bytes. Each piece is sent as a separate datagram to the network layer. Because the network layer does not guarantee packet delivery, it is up to TCP to provide reliability. Packets may also be delivered by the network layer out of sequence; TCP is responsible for packet sequencing. The IP module encapsulates TCP segments inside IP packets and routes these packets ultimately to the destination host.

TCP calls the IP module, which in turn calls the network device driver. In general, the services provided by the TCP include:

- Guaranteed delivery of data;
- Data delivered in sequence;
- No duplicate data;
- Management of a session established between the source and destination system.

Figure 2.18 describes how TCP uses the services of IP and Ethernet.

Figure 2.19 details the fields of a TCP header. Note that port numbers are addresses at which a system can access an application. For example, port number 23 is associated with the telnet application.

Ethernet header	IP header	TCP header	Telnet or FTP

Figure 2.18 Telnet or FTP using the services of TCP, IP, and Ethernet.

0		16	31
Source port #		Destination port #	
Sequence number			
Acknowledgment number			
Hdr. Lth.	Resvd. U R G / A C K / P S H / R S T / S Y N / F I N	Window	
Checksum		Urgent pointer	
Opt. kind	Length	Max. segment size	

Figure 2.19 TCP header format.

The following is a brief description of each field in the TCP header:

- *Source Port* (2 bytes): Identifies the source port; may also be viewed as the port number of the client application for the initial connection.
- *Destination Port* (2 bytes): Identifies the destination port; this may also be viewed as the port number of the server application for the initial connection.
- *Sequence Number* (4 bytes): Sequence number of the first data octet in this segment, except when SYN (refers to synchronize sequence numbers) is present; if SYN is present, the sequence number is a randomly selected number.
- *Acknowledgment Number* (4 bytes): A piggybacked acknowledgment that contains the sequence number is a randomly selected number.
- *Header Length* (4 bits): Specifies the number of 32-bit words in the header.
- *Reserved* (6 bits): Reserved for future use.
- *Flags* (6 bits): There are six flag fields, each of which is 1 bit in length.
  - *URG* is the urgent pointer (if there is any urgent data in this packet);
  - *ACK* is acknowledgment (if there is acknowledgment information in this packet);
  - *PSH* is the push function (to force TCP to release data);
  - *RST* is reset connection (to quickly bring down a TCP connection);
  - *SYN* is synchronize the sequence numbers (the first two packets for any connection that uses TCP at the transport layer, this bit is set to 1);
  - *FIN* means no more data from the sender (normal way to bring down a TCP connection).
- *Window* (2 bytes): Flow control credit allocation, in bytes; contains the number of data octets beginning with the one indicated in the acknowledgment field that the sender is willing to accept. If this bit is set to 0, then the destination system is requesting the source system to reduce the rate at which it is generating data. The value of this field can vary during a given TCP connection. This field may be viewed as one way to control the flow of data between systems that use the services of TCP.
- *Checksum* (2 bytes): Used for error detection.
- *Urgent Pointer* (2 bytes): Points to the byte following the urgent data; thus, the receiver can determine how much urgent data is included in the message.
- *Option Type* (1 byte): Currently, only one option is defined, which specifies the maximum segment size that will be accepted; the option number is defined is 2.
- *Option Length* (1 byte): For option number 2 the option length is 4 bytes.
- *Maximum Segment Size* (2 bytes): Also referred to as the MSS field, this field specifies the largest size that the sender can receive for a given connection (if the source and destination have the same network portion of the

Internet address, this number is typically based on the largest frame size at the network access layer). The value contained in this field relates to the *maximum transmission unit* (MTU) of the protocol in use at the network access layer. For example, on an Ethernet network, the value specified in this field is 1460. This is because:
- Maximum Ethernet frame size: 1518 bytes;
- Ethernet header + trailer: 18 bytes;
- IP header: 20 bytes;
- TCP header: 20 bytes.

If you add 18 bytes of the Ethernet header, 20 bytes of the IP header, and 20 bytes of the TCP header, you get 58 bytes. Subtract 58 bytes from 1,518, which is the maximum Ethernet frame size, and you are left with 1,460 bytes. Hence, the value 1,460 is specified in the MSS field.
- *Data* (Variable): Data field is a maximum of 65,535 bytes.

The TCP packet shown in Figure 2.20 describes fields in the TCP header. Fourteen TCP packets are shown in Figures 2.21 to 2.37. The first three packets provide important information on the TCP negotiation process. Packets 4 to 14 detail the **telnet** negotiation process. It is in packet number 14 that the end user is finally able to see the familiar **login**: prompt.

Figure 2.34 summarizes the connection set up, data transfer, and connection termination process associated with any TCP connection.

NetMetrix (tm) Packet Report
---
1) 64 0.000000 000083A21859 Sun2120E1 TCP t1401 -> telnet Flags=S.....
Seq=1150656000   <mss 1460>

Packet number = 1 Arrival time = 16.560000 Length = 64

——————— DLC Header ———————
DLC: Destination: Sun_21:20:E1 (8:0:20:21:20:e1)
DLC: Source: 0:0:83:a2:18:59
DLC: Protocol: IP

——————— IP Header ———————
IP: Version = 4
IP: Header length = 20
IP: Type of service = Routine(0)

Figure 2.20 TCP packet 1/14 (fields in **bold** relate to TCP). *Courtesy: HP NetMetrix.*

IP: Delay = Normal (0)
IP: Throughput = Normal (0)
IP: Reliability = Normal (0)
IP: Packet length = 44
IP: Id = 186b
IP: Fragment offset = 0
IP: Flags = [Don't Fragment = 0][More = 0]
IP: Time to live = 60
IP: Protocol = TCP (6)
IP: Header checksum = F82E
IP: Source address = 192.136.118.235
IP: Destination address = 192.136.118.54

——————— TCP Header ———————
TCP: Source port = 1401
TCP: Destination port = telnet (23)
TCP: Sequence number = 1150656000
TCP: Ack number = 0
TCP: Data offset = 24
TCP: Flags = [URG=0][ACK=0][PUSH=0][RST=0][SYN=1][FIN=0]
TCP: Window = 4096 TCP: Checksum = 31CE
TCP: Urgent pointer = 00000000
TCP: Options = (mss 1460)

Hexadecimal Representation:

```
0000:  08 00 20 21 20 E1 00 00 -   83 A2 18 59 08 00 45 00    .. ! ......Y..E.
0010:  00 2C 18 6B 00 00 3C 06 -   F8 2E C0 88 76 EB C0 88    .,.k..<.....v...
0020:  76 36 05 79 00 17 44 95 -   9E 00 00 00 00 00 60 02    v6.y..D........'.
0030:  10 00 31 CE 00 00 02 04 -   05 B4 00 00 00 00 00 00    ..1.............
```

Figure 2.20 continued.

NetMetrix (tm) Packet Report
———————————————————————————
2) 60 0.000006 Sun2120E1 000083A21859 TCP telnet -> t1401 Flags=S...A.
Seq=1508665344   Ack=1150656001 <mss 1460>

Packet number = 2 Arrival time = 16.560006 Length = 60

——————— DLC Header ———————
DLC: Destination: 0:0:83:a2:18:59
DLC: Source: Sun_21:20:E1 (8:0:20:21:20:e1)
DLC: Protocol: IP

Figure 2.21 TCP packet 2/14 (fields in **bold** relate to TCP). *Courtesy: HP NetMetrix.*

──────── IP Header ────────
IP: Version = 4
IP: Header length = 20
IP: Type of service = Routine(0)
IP: Delay = Normal (0)
IP: Throughput = Normal (0)
IP: Reliability = Normal (0)
IP: Packet length = 44
IP: Id = 3a15
IP: Fragment offset = 0
IP: Flags = [Don't Fragment = 1][More = 0]
IP: Time to live = 255 IP: Protocol = TCP (6)
IP: Header checksum = D383
IP: Source address = 192.136.118.54
IP: Destination address = 192.136.118.235

──────── **TCP Header** ────────
TCP: Source port = telnet (23)
TCP: Destination port = 1401
TCP: Sequence number = 1508665344
TCP: Ack number = 1150656001
TCP: Data offset = 24
TCP: Flags = [URG=0][ACK=1][PUSH=0][RST=0][SYN=1][FIN=0]
TCP: Window = 8760
TCP: Checksum = 5D98
TCP: Urgent pointer = 00000000
TCP: Options = (mss 1460)

Hexadecimal Representation:
0000: 00 00 83 A2 18 59 08 00 -   20 21 20 E1 08 00 45 00   ....Y.. ! ...E.
0010: 00 2C 3A 15 40 00 FF 06 -   D3 83 C0 88 76 36 C0 88   .,:.@.......v6..
0020: 76 EB **00 17 05 79 59 EC** -   **68 00 44 95 9E 01 60 12**   v....yY.h.D...'.
0030: **22 38 5D 98 00 00 02 04** -   **05 B4** 2F 0D   "8]......./.

Figure 2.21 continued.

NetMetrix (tm) Packet Report

3) 64 0.000001 000083A21859 Sun2120E1 TCP t1401 -> telnet Flags=....A.
Ack=1508665345

Packet number = 3   Arrival time = 16.560007   Length = 64

Figure 2.22 TCP packet 3/14 (fields in **bold** relate to TCP). *Courtesy: HP NetMetrix.*

─────── DLC Header ───────
DLC: Destination: Sun_21:20:E1 (8:0:20:21:20:e1)
DLC: Source: 0:0:83:a2:18:59
DLC: Protocol: IP

─────── IP Header ───────
IP: Version = 4
IP: Header length = 20
IP: Type of service = Routine(0)
IP: Delay = Normal (0)
IP: Throughput = Normal (0)
IP: Reliability = Normal (0)
IP: Packet length = 40
IP: Id = 186c
IP: Fragment offset = 0
IP: Flags = [Don't Fragment = 0][More = 0]
IP: Time to live = 60
IP: Protocol = TCP (6)
IP: Header checksum = F831
IP: Source address = 192.136.118.235
IP: Destination address = 192.136.118.54

─────── TCP Header ───────
TCP: Source port = 1401
TCP: Destination port = telnet (23)
TCP: Sequence number = 1150656001
TCP: Ack number = 1508665345
TCP: Data offset = 20
TCP: Flags = [URG=0][ACK=1][PUSH=0][RST=0][SYN=0][FIN=0]
TCP: Window = 4096
TCP: Checksum = 878D
TCP: Urgent pointer = 00000000

Hexadecimal Representation:

0000: 08 00 20 21 20 E1 00 00 -   83 A2 18 59 08 00 45 00   .. ! ......Y..E.
0010: 00 28 18 6C 00 00 3C 06 -   F8 31 C0 88 76 EB C0 88   .(.l.<..1..v...
0020: 76 36 **05 79 00 17 44 95** -   **9E 01 59 EC 68 01 50 10**   v6.y..D...Y.h.P.
0030: **10 00 87 8D 00 00** 02 04 -   05 B4 2F 0D 00 00 00 00   ..../.....

Figure 2.22 continued.

NetMetrix (tm) Packet Report
───────────────────────────

4) 64 0.019993 000083A21859 Sun2120E1 TELNET IAC DO SUPPRESS GO AHEAD

Figure 2.23 TCP packet 4/14 (fields in **bold** relate to TCP). *Courtesy: HP NetMetrix.*

Packet number = 4   Arrival time = 16.580000   Length = 64

──────────── DLC Header ────────────
DLC: Destination: Sun_21:20:E1 (8:0:20:21:20:e1)
DLC: Source: 0:0:83:a2:18:59
DLC: Protocol: IP

──────────── IP Header ────────────
IP: Version = 4
IP: Header length = 20
P: Type of service = Routine(0)
IP: Delay = Normal (0)
IP: Throughput = Normal (0)
IP: Reliability = Normal (0)
IP: Packet length = 46
IP: Id = 186d
IP: Fragment offset = 0
IP: Flags = [Don't Fragment = 0][More = 0]
IP: Time to live = 60   IP: Protocol = TCP (6)
IP: Header checksum = F82A
IP: Source address = 192.136.118.235
IP: Destination address = 192.136.118.54

──────────── TCP Header ────────────
TCP: Source port = 1401
TCP: Destination port = telnet (23)
TCP: Sequence number = 1150656001
TCP: Ack number = 1508665345
TCP: Data offset = 20
TCP: Flags = [URG=0][ACK=1][PUSH=1][RST=0][SYN=0][FIN=0]
TCP: Window = 4096   TCP: Checksum = 8869
TCP: Urgent pointer = 00000000

──────────── TELNET Header ────────────
TELNET: Interpret as Command. (IAC)
TELNET: DO use option SUPPRESS GO AHEAD
TELNET: Interpret as Command. (IAC)
TELNET: WILL use option TERMINAL TYPE

Hexadecimal Representation:

```
0000:  08 00 20 21 20 E1 00 00 -   83 A2 18 59 08 00 45 00    .. ! .....Y..E.
0010:  00 2E 18 6D 00 00 3C 06 -   F8 2A C0 88 76 EB C0 88    ...m..<..*..v...
0020:  76 36 05 79 00 17 44 95 -   9E 01 59 EC 68 01 50 18    v6.y..D...Y.h.P.
0030:  10 00 88 69 00 00 FF FD -   03 FF FB 18 00 00 00 00    ...i............
```

Figure 2.23 continued.

NetMetrix (tm) Packet Report

5) 60 0.040000 Sun2120E1 000083A21859 TCP telnet -> t1401 Flags=....A. Ack= 1150656007

Packet number = 5 Arrival time = 16.620000 Length = 60

──────────── DLC Header ────────────
DLC: Destination: 0:0:83:a2:18:59
DLC: Source: Sun_21:20:E1 (8:0:20:21:20:e1)
DLC: Protocol: IP

──────────── IP Header ────────────
IP: Version = 4
IP: Header length = 20
IP: Type of service = Routine(0)
IP: Delay = Normal (0)
IP: Throughput = Normal (0)
IP: Reliability = Normal (0)
IP: Packet length = 40
IP: Id = 3a16
IP: Fragment offset = 0
IP: Flags = [Don't Fragment = 1][More = 0]
IP: Time to live = 255
IP: Protocol = TCP (6)
IP: Header checksum = D386
IP: Source address = 192.136.118.54
IP: Destination address = 192.136.118.235

──────────── TCP Header ────────────
TCP: Source port = telnet (23)
TCP: Destination port = 1401
TCP: Sequence number = 1508665345
TCP: Ack number = 1150656007
TCP: Data offset = 20
TCP: Flags = [URG=0][ACK=1][PUSH=0][RST=0][SYN=0][FIN=0]
TCP: Window = 8754 TCP: Checksum = 7555
TCP: Urgent pointer = 00000000

Hexadecimal Representation:

```
0000:  00 00 83 A2 18 59 08 00 -   20 21 20 E1 08 00 45 00     .....Y..  ! ...E.
0010:  00 28 3A 16 40 00 FF 06 -   D3 86 C0 88 76 36 C0 88     .(:.@.......v6..
0020:  76 EB 00 17 05 79 59 EC -   68 01 44 95 9E 07 50 10     v....yY.h.D...P.
0030:  22 32 75 55 00 00 02 04 -   05 B4 2F 0D                 "2uU....../.
```

Figure 2.24 TCP packet 5/14 (fields in **bold** relate to TCP). *Courtesy: HP NetMetrix.*

NetMetrix (tm) Packet Report

6) 60 0.800000 Sun2120E1 000083A21859 TELNET IAC DO TERMINAL TYPE
Packet number = 6   Arrival time = 17.420000   Length = 60
——————— DLC Header ———————
DLC: Destination: 0:0:83:a2:18:59
DLC: Source: Sun_21:20:E1 (8:0:20:21:20:e1)
DLC: Protocol: IP
——————— IP Header ———————
IP: Version = 4
IP: Header length = 20
IP: Type of service = Routine(0)
IP: Delay = Normal (0)
IP: Throughput = Normal (0)
IP: Reliability = Normal (0)
IP: Packet length = 43
IP: Id = 3a17
IP: Fragment offset = 0
IP: Flags = [Don't Fragment = 1][More = 0]
IP: Time to live = 255
IP: Protocol = TCP (6)
IP: Header checksum = D382
IP: Source address = 192.136.118.54
IP: Destination address = 192.136.118.235
——————— TCP Header ———————
TCP: Source port = telnet (23)
TCP: Destination port = 1401
TCP: Sequence number = 1508665345
TCP: Ack number = 1150656007
TCP: Data offset = 20
TCP: Flags = [URG=0][ACK=1][PUSH=1][RST=0][SYN=0][FIN=0]
TCP: Window = 8760
TCP: Checksum = 5D46
TCP: Urgent pointer = 00000000
——————— TELNET Header ———————
TELNET: Interpret as Command. (IAC)
TELNET: DO use option TERMINAL TYPE

Hexadecimal Representation:

```
0000:  00 00 83 A2 18 59 08 00 -  20 21 20 E1 08 00 45 00     .....Y.. ! ...E.
0010:  00 2B 3A 17 40 00 FF 06 -  D3 82 C0 88 76 36 C0 88     .+:.@.......v6..
0020:  76 EB 00 17 05 79 59 EC -  68 01 44 95 9E 07 50 18     v....yY.h.D...P.
0030:  22 38 5D 46 00 00 FF FD -  18 00 00 00                 "8]F........
```

Figure 2.25 TCP packet 6/14 (fields in **bold** relate to TCP). *Courtesy: HP NetMetrix.*

NetMetrix (tm) Packet Report

7) 64 0.040000 000083A21859 Sun2120E1 TCP t1401 -> telnet Flags=....A. Ack= 1508665348

Packet number = 7   Arrival time = 17.460000   Length = 64

——————— DLC Header ———————
DLC: Destination: Sun_21:20:E1 (8:0:20:21:20:e1)
DLC: Source: 0:0:83:a2:18:59
DLC: Protocol: IP

——————— IP Header ———————
IP: Version = 4
IP: Header length = 20
IP: Type of service = Routine(0)
IP: Delay = Normal (0)
IP: Throughput = Normal (0)
IP: Reliability = Normal (0)
IP: Packet length = 40
IP: Id = 186e
IP: Fragment offset = 0
IP: Flags = [Don't Fragment = 0][More = 0]
IP: Time to live = 60
IP: Protocol = TCP (6)
IP: Header checksum = F82F
IP: Source address = 192.136.118.235
IP: Destination address = 192.136.118.54

——————— TCP Header ———————
TCP: Source port = 1401
TCP: Destination port = telnet (23)
TCP: Sequence number = 1150656007
TCP: Ack number = 1508665348
TCP: Data offset = 20
TCP: Flags = [URG=0][ACK=1][PUSH=0][RST=0][SYN=0][FIN=0]
TCP: Window = 4096
TCP: Checksum = 8784
TCP: Urgent pointer = 00000000

Hexadecimal Representation:

```
0000:  08 00 20 21 20 E1 00 00 -   83 A2 18 59 08 00 45 00     .. ! ......Y..E.
0010:  00 28 18 6E 00 00 3C 06 -   F8 2F C0 88 76 EB C0 88     .(.n..<../..v...
0020:  76 36 05 79 00 17 44 95 -   9E 07 59 EC 68 04 50 10     v6.y..D...Y.h.P.
0030:  10 00 87 84 00 00 FF FD -   18 70 00 00 00 04 00 80     .........p......
```

Figure 2.26 TCP packet 7/14 (fields in **bold** relate to TCP). *Courtesy: HP NetMetrix.*

NetMetrix (tm) Packet Report

8) 63   0.000001 Sun2120E1   000083A21859 TELNET IAC WILL SUPPRESS GO AHEAD   <FF><FB>

Packet number = 8 Arrival time = 17.460001 Length = 63

─────────── DLC Header ───────────
DLC: Destination: 0:0:83:a2:18:59
DLC: Source: Sun_21:20:E1 (8:0:20:21:20:e1)
DLC: Protocol: IP

─────────── IP Header ───────────
IP: Version = 4
IP: Header length = 20
IP: Type of service = Routine(0)
IP: Delay = Normal (0)
IP: Throughput = Normal (0)
IP: Reliability = Normal (0)
IP: Packet length = 49
IP: Id = 3a18
IP: Fragment offset = 0
IP: Flags = [Don't Fragment = 1][More = 0]
IP: Time to live = 255
IP: Protocol = TCP (6)
IP: Header checksum = D37B
IP: Source address = 192.136.118.54
IP: Destination address = 192.136.118.235

─────────── TCP Header ───────────
TCP: Source port = telnet (23)
TCP: Destination port = 1401
TCP: Sequence number = 1508665348
TCP: Ack number = 1150656007
TCP: Data offset = 20
TCP: Flags = [URG=0][ACK=1][PUSH=1][RST=0][SYN=0][FIN=0]
TCP: Window = 8760
TCP: Checksum = 8527
TCP: Urgent pointer = 00000000

─────────── TELNET Header ───────────
TELNET: Interpret as Command. (IAC)
TELNET: WILL use option SUPPRESS GO AHEAD

Figure 2.27 TCP packet 8/14 (fields in **bold** relate to TCP). *Courtesy: HP NetMetrix.*

84 UNIX Internetworking

TELNET: Interpret as Command. (IAC)
TELNET: SB Interpret TERMINAL TYPE as subnegotiation
TELNET: Interpret as Command. (IAC)
TELNET: End of subnegotiation parameters
TELNET: <FF><FB>

Hexadecimal Representation:

```
0000:  00 00 83 A2 18 59 08 00 -   20 21 20 E1 08 00 45 00    .....Y.. ! ...E.
0010:  00 31 3A 18 40 00 FF 06 -   D3 7B C0 88 76 36 C0 88    .1:.@....{..v6..
0020:  76 EB 00 17 05 79 59 EC -   68 04 44 95 9E 07 50 18    v....yY.h.D...P.
0030:  22 38 85 27 00 00 FF FB -   03 FF FA 18 01 FF F0       "8.'..........
```

Figure 2.27 continued.

NetMetrix (tm) Packet Report

9) 67   0.000001   000083A21859 Sun2120E1   TELNET IAC SB TERMINAL TYPE   <FF><FA><18><00>SUN-C
Packet number = 9 Arrival time = 17.460002 Length = 67

──────────── DLC Header ────────────
DLC: Destination: Sun_21:20:E1 (8:0:20:21:20:e1)
DLC: Source: 0:0:83:a2:18:59
DLC: Protocol: IP

──────────── IP Header ────────────
IP: Version = 4
IP: Header length = 20
IP: Type of service = Routine(0)
IP: Delay = Normal (0)
IP: Throughput = Normal (0)
IP: Reliability = Normal (0)
IP: Packet length = 53
IP: Id = 186f
IP: Fragment offset = 0
IP: Flags = [Don't Fragment = 0][More = 0]
IP: Time to live = 60 IP: Protocol = TCP (6)
IP: Header checksum = F821
IP: Source address = 192.136.118.235
IP: Destination address = 192.136.118.54

──────────── TCP Header ────────────
TCP: Source port = 1401
TCP: Destination port = telnet (23)

Figure 2.28 TCP packet 9/14 (fields in **bold** relate to TCP). *Courtesy: HP NetMetrix.*

TCP: Sequence number = 1150656007
TCP: Ack number = 1508665357
TCP: Data offset = 20
TCP: Flags = [URG=0][ACK=1][PUSH=1][RST=0][SYN=0][FIN=0]
TCP: Window = 4096
TCP: Checksum = 559B
TCP: Urgent pointer = 00000000

───────── TELNET Header ─────────
TELNET: Interpret as Command. (IAC)
TELNET: SB Interpret TERMINAL TYPE as subnegotiation
TELNET: Interpret as Command. (IAC)
TELNET: End of subnegotiation parameters
TELNET: <FF><FA><18><00>SUN-C

Hexadecimal Representation:

```
0000:  08 00 20 21 20 E1 00 00 -   83 A2 18 59 08 00 45 00    .. ! ......Y..E.
0010:  00 35 18 6F 00 00 3C 06 -   F8 21 C0 88 76 EB C0 88    .5.o..<..!..v...
0020:  76 36 05 79 00 17 44 95 -   9E 07 59 EC 68 0D 50 18    v6.y..D...Y.h.P.
0030:  10 00 55 9B 00 00 FF FA -   18 00 53 55 4E 2D 43 4D    ..U.......SUN-CM
0040:  44 FF F0
```

Figure 2.28 continued.

NetMetrix (tm) Packet Report
─────────────────────────────────

10) 110   0.049998 Sun2120E1   000083A21859 TELNET IAC WILL ECHO   <FF><FB-
><01><FF><FD><01><0D><0A><0D><0A>UNIX(r) System V Rel..

Packet number = 10 Arrival time = 17.510000 Length = 110

───────── DLC Header ─────────
DLC: Destination: 0:0:83:a2:18:59
DLC: Source: Sun_21:20:E1 (8:0:20:21:20:e1)
DLC: Protocol: IP

───────── IP Header ─────────
IP: Version = 4
IP: Header length = 20
IP: Type of service = Routine(0)
IP: Delay = Normal (0)

Figure 2.29 TCP packet 10/14 (fields in **bold** relate to TCP). *Courtesy: HP NetMetrix.*

IP: Throughput = Normal (0)
IP: Reliability = Normal (0)
IP: Packet length = 96
IP: Id = 3a19
IP: Fragment offset = 0
IP: Flags = [Don't Fragment = 1][More = 0]
IP: Time to live = 255
IP: Protocol = TCP (6)
IP: Header checksum = D34B
IP: Source address = 192.136.118.54
IP: Destination address = 192.136.118.235

——————— TCP Header ———————
TCP: Source port = telnet (23)
TCP: Destination port = 1401
TCP: Sequence number = 1508665357
TCP: Ack number = 1150656020
TCP: Data offset = 20
TCP: Flags = [URG=0][ACK=1][PUSH=1][RST=0][SYN=0][FIN=0] TCP: Window = 8760
TCP: Checksum = 7A5D
TCP: Urgent pointer = 00000000

——————— TELNET Header ———————
TELNET: Interpret as Command. (IAC)
TELNET: WILL use option ECHO
TELNET: Interpret as Command. (IAC)
TELNET: DO use option ECHO
TELNET: <FF><FB><01><FF><FD><01><0D><0A><0D><0A>UNIX(r) System V Rel..

Hexadecimal Representation:

```
0000: 00 00 83 A2 18 59 08 00 -   20 21 20 E1 08 00 45 00    .....Y.. ! ...E.
0010: 00 60 3A 19 40 00 FF 06 -   D3 4B C0 88 76 36 C0 88    .`:.@....K..v6..
0020: 76 EB 00 17 05 79 59 EC -   68 0D 44 95 9E 14 50 18    v....yY.h.D...P.
0030: 22 38 7A 5D 00 00 FF FB -   01 FF FD 01 0D 0A 0D 0A    "8z]............
0040: 55 4E 49 58 28 72 29 20 -   53 79 73 74 65 6D 20 56    UNIX(r) System V
0050: 20 52 65 6C 65 61 73 65 -   20 34 2E 30 20 28 6E 69    Release 4.0
0060: 72 76 61 6E 61 29 0D 0A -   0D 00 0D 0A 0D 00          (nirvana).....
```

Figure 2.29 continued.

NetMetrix (tm) Packet Report

11)   64   0.010002 000083A21859 Sun2120E1   TELNET IAC DO ECHO

Packet number = 11 Arrival time = 17.520002 Length = 64

Network Architectures and Technologies

──────── DLC Header ────────
DLC: Destination: Sun_21:20:E1 (8:0:20:21:20:e1)
DLC: Source: 0:0:83:a2:18:59
DLC: Protocol: IP

──────── IP Header ────────
IP: Version = 4
IP: Header length = 20
IP: Type of service = Routine(0)
IP: Delay = Normal (0)
IP: Throughput = Normal (0)
IP: Reliability = Normal (0)
IP: Packet length = 46
IP: Id = 1870
IP: Fragment offset = 0
IP: Flags = [Don't Fragment = 0][More = 0]
IP: Time to live = 60
IP: Protocol = TCP (6)
IP: Header checksum = F827
IP: Source address = 192.136.118.235
IP: Destination address = 192.136.118.54

──────── TCP Header ────────
TCP: Source port = 1401
TCP: Destination port = telnet (23)
TCP: Sequence number = 1150656020
TCP: Ack number = 1508665413
TCP: Data offset = 20
TCP: Flags = [URG=0][ACK=1][PUSH=1][RST=0][SYN=0][FIN=0]
TCP: Window = 4096
TCP: Checksum = 8929
TCP: Urgent pointer = 00000000

──────── TELNET Header ────────
TELNET: Interpret as Command. (IAC)
TELNET: DO use option ECHO
TELNET: Interpret as Command. (IAC)
TELNET: WONT use option ECHO

Hexadecimal Representation:

```
0000:  08 00 20 21 20 E1 00 00 -  83 A2 18 59 08 00 45 00   .. ! ......Y..E.
0010:  00 2E 18 70 00 00 3C 06 -  F8 27 C0 88 76 EB C0 88   ...p..<..'..v...
0020:  76 36 05 79 00 17 44 95 -  9E 14 59 EC 68 45 50 18   v6.y..D...Y.hEP.
0030:  10 00 89 29 00 00 FF FD -  01 FF FC 01 0D 0A 0D 0A   ...)............
```

Figure 2.30 TCP packet 11/14 (fields in **bold** relate to TCP). *Courtesy: HP NetMetrix.*

88 UNIX Internetworking

NetMetrix (tm) Packet Report

12) 60   0.009999 Sun2120E1   000083A21859 TELNET IAC DONT ECHO
Packet number = 12 Arrival time = 17.530001 Length = 60

——————— DLC Header ———————
DLC: Destination: 0:0:83:a2:18:59
DLC: Source: Sun_21:20:E1 (8:0:20:21:20:e1)
DLC: Protocol: IP

——————— IP Header ———————
IP: Version = 4
IP: Header length = 20
IP: Type of service = Routine(0)
IP: Delay = Normal (0)
IP: Throughput = Normal (0)
IP: Reliability = Normal (0)
IP: Packet length = 43
IP: Id = 3a1a
IP: Fragment offset = 0
IP: Flags = [Don't Fragment = 1][More = 0]
IP: Time to live = 255
IP: Protocol = TCP (6)
IP: Header checksum = D37F
IP: Source address = 192.136.118.54
IP: Destination address = 192.136.118.235

——————— TCP Header ———————
TCP: Source port = telnet (23)
TCP: Destination port = 1401
TCP: Sequence number = 1508665413
TCP: Ack number = 1150656026
TCP: Data offset = 20
TCP: Flags = [URG=0][ACK=1][PUSH=1][RST=0][SYN=0][FIN=0]
TCP: Window = 8760
TCP: Checksum = 73EE
TCP: Urgent pointer = 00000000

——————— TELNET Header ———————
TELNET: Interpret as Command. (IAC)
TELNET: DONT use option ECHO

Hexadecimal Representation:

```
0000:  00 00 83 A2 18 59 08 00 -  20 21 20 E1 08 00 45 00    .....Y.. ! ...E.
0010:  00 2B 3A 1A 40 00 FF 06 -  D3 7F C0 88 76 36 C0 88    .+:.@.......v6..
0020:  76 EB 00 17 05 79 59 EC -  68 45 44 95 9E 1A 50 18    v....yY.hED...P.
0030:  22 38 73 EE 00 00 FF FE -  01 00 FD 01                "8s.........
```

Figure 2.31 TCP packet 12/14 (fields in **bold** relate to TCP). *Courtesy: HP NetMetrix.*

NetMetrix (tm) Packet Report

13) 64 0.129999 000083A21859 Sun2120E1 TCP t1401 -> telnet Flags=....A.   Ack= 1508665416

Packet number = 13   Arrival time = 17.660000   Length = 64

——————— DLC Header ———————
DLC: Destination: Sun_21:20:E1 (8:0:20:21:20:e1)
DLC: Source: 0:0:83:a2:18:59
DLC: Protocol: IP

——————— IP Header ———————
IP: Version = 4
IP: Header length = 20
IP: Type of service = Routine(0)
IP: Delay = Normal (0)
IP: Throughput = Normal (0)
IP: Reliability = Normal (0)
IP: Packet length = 40
IP: Id = 1871
IP: Fragment offset = 0
IP: Flags = [Don't Fragment = 0][More = 0]
IP: Time to live = 60
IP: Protocol = TCP (6)
IP: Header checksum = F82C
IP: Source address = 192.136.118.235
IP: Destination address = 192.136.118.54

——————— TCP Header ———————
TCP: Source port = 1401
TCP: Destination port = telnet (23)
TCP: Sequence number = 1150656026
TCP: Ack number = 1508665416
TCP: Data offset = 20
TCP: Flags = [URG=0][ACK=1][PUSH=0][RST=0][SYN=0][FIN=0]
TCP: Window = 4096
TCP: Checksum = 872D
TCP: Urgent pointer = 00000000

Hexadecimal Representation:

```
0000:  08 00 20 21 20 E1 00 00  -  83 A2 18 59 08 00 45 00   .. ! .....Y..E.
0010:  00 28 18 71 00 00 3C 06  -  F8 2C C0 88 76 EB C0 88   .(.q..<..,..v...
0020:  76 36 05 79 00 17 44 95  -  9E 1A 59 EC 68 48 50 10   v6.y..D...Y.hHP.
0030:  10 00 87 2D 00 00 FF FB  -  03 FF FA 18 01 FF F0 80   ...-............
```

Figure 2.32 TCP packet 13/14 (fields in **bold** relate to TCP). *Courtesy: HP NetMetrix.*

NetMetrix (tm) Packet Report

14) 61   0.210000 Sun2120E1   000083A21859 TELNET login:

Packet number = 14   Arrival time = 17.870000   Length = 61

————————— DLC Header —————————
DLC: Destination: 0:0:83:a2:18:59
DLC: Source: Sun_21:20:E1 (8:0:20:21:20:e1)
DLC: Protocol: IP

————————— IP Header —————————
IP: Version = 4
IP: Header length = 20
IP: Type of service = Routine(0)
IP: Delay = Normal (0)
IP: Throughput = Normal (0)
IP: Reliability = Normal (0)
IP: Packet length = 47
IP: Id = 3a1b
IP: Fragment offset = 0
IP: Flags = [Don't Fragment = 1][More = 0]
IP: Time to live = 255
IP: Protocol = TCP (6)
IP: Header checksum = D37A
IP: Source address = 192.136.118.54
IP: Destination address = 192.136.118.235

————————— TCP Header —————————
TCP: Source port = telnet (23)
TCP: Destination port = 1401
TCP: Sequence number = 1508665416
TCP: Ack number = 1150656026
TCP: Data offset = 20
TCP: Flags = [URG=0][ACK=1][PUSH=1][RST=0][SYN=0][FIN=0]
TCP: Window = 8760
TCP: Checksum = 12D3
TCP: Urgent pointer = 00000000

————————— TELNET Header —————————
TELNET: login:

Hexadecimal Representation:

```
0000:  00 00 83 A2 18 59 08 00 -    20 21 20 E1 08 00 45 00    .....Y.. ! ...E.
0010:  00 2F 3A 1B 40 00 FF 06 -    D3 7A C0 88 76 36 C0 88    ./:.@....z..v6..
0020:  76 EB 00 17 05 79 59 EC -    68 48 44 95 9E 1A 50 18    v....yY.hHD...P.
0030:  22 38 12 D3 00 00 6C 6F -    67 69 6E 3A 20             "8....login:
```

Figure 2.33 TCP packet 14/14 (fields in **bold** relate to TCP). *Courtesy: HP NetMetrix.*

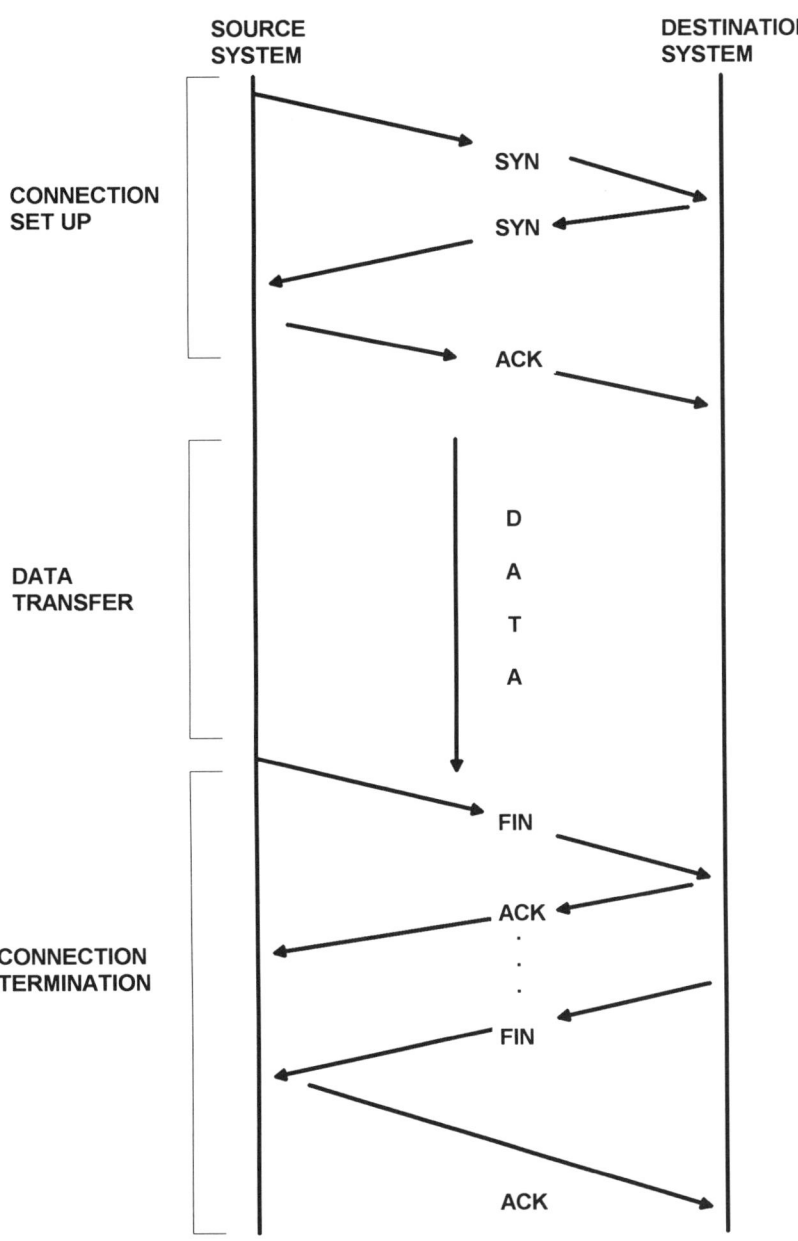

Figure 2.34 TCP connection setup, data transfer, and connection termination.

2.5.2 User Datagram Protocol (UDP)

The *user datagram protocol* (UDP) provides a datagram form of communication at the transport layer. It is a protocol that fits in at layer 4 of the OSI/RM. In contrast to TCP, UDP provides a unreliable stream-oriented service. UDP does not provide congestion control, nor does it use acknowledgements or retransmit lost datagrams. These are functions normally performed at the transport layer. Thus, higher layer protocols, such as the *network file system protocol* (NFS) and the *trivial file transfer protocol* (TFTP), that use UDP must address problems related to congestion control, flow control, and reliability. Figure 2.35 describes how UDP works with protocols such as NFS, SNMP, IP, and Ethernet.

The two mechanisms available to higher layer protocols to access the delivery service of IP are TCP and UDP. Figure 2.36 describes the format of the UDP header.

The following is a brief description of fields in the UDP header:

- *Source Port* (2 bytes): Identifies the source port.
- *Destination Port* (2 bytes): Identifies the destination port.
- *Message Length* (2 bytes): Specifies the number of bytes in the UDP datagram, including the UDP header and application data.
- *Checksum* (2 bytes): This field is optional and may not be used. If the field has a value of zero, it implies that the checksum has not been computed.

Figure 2.37 describes an example UDP packet. This packet was generated as a result of the **tftp** command. The packet was captured by HP NetMetrix's Protocol Analyzer product.

Ethernet header	IP header	UDP header	NFS or SNMP

Figure 2.35 UDP message encapsulated in an Ethernet frame.

Source port number (2)	Destination port number (2)	Message length (2)	Checksum (2)

Figure 2.36 UDP header format.

NetMetrix (tm) Packet Report

1) 64   0.000000   000083A21858 000083A21859 TFTP   Read request

Packet number = 1   Arrival time = 28.830002   Length = 64

——————— DLC Header ———————
DLC: Destination: 0:0:83:a2:18:59
DLC: Source: 0:0:83:a2:18:58
DLC: Protocol: IP

——————— IP Header ———————
IP: Version = 4
IP: Header length = 20
IP: Type of service = Routine(0)
IP: Delay = Normal (0)
IP: Throughput = Normal (0)
IP: Reliability = Normal (0)
IP: Packet length = 44
IP: Id = ea8
IP: Fragment offset = 0
IP: Flags = [Don't Fragment = 0][More = 0]
IP: Time to live = 60
IP: Protocol = UDP (17)
IP: Header checksum = 0133
IP: Source address = 192.136.118.234
IP: Destination address = 192.136.118.235

——————— UDP Header ———————
UDP: Source port = 1055
UDP: Destination port = tftp (69)
UDP: Length = 24
UDP: Checksum = 0

——————— TFTP Header ———————
TFTP: Opcode = Read request (1)
TFTP: Filename = test
TFTP: Mode = netascii

Hexadecimal Representation:

```
0000:  00 00 83 A2 18 59 00 00  -  83 A2 18 58 08 00 45 00    .....Y.....X..E.
0010:  00 2C 0E A8 00 00 3C 11  -  01 33 C0 88 76 EA C0 88    .,....<..3..v...
0020:  76 EB 04 1F 00 45 00 18  -  00 00 00 01 74 65 73 74    v....E......test
0030:  00 6E 65 74 61 73 63 69  -  69 00 00 01 00 01 46 00    .netascii.....F.
```

Figure 2.37 UDP packet format (fields in **bold** relate to UDP). *Courtesy: HP NetMetrix.*

2.6 APPLICATION LAYER

There are many application layer protocols defined in the Internet architecture. These include:

- TELNET;
- File transfer protocol (FTP);
- Trivial file transfer protocol (TFTP);
- Simple network management protocol (SNMP);
- Simple mail transport protocol (SMTP);
- Network file system (NFS);
- Network information service (NIS);
- Domain name system (DNS).

These protocols are discussed in later sections of this book. The application layer protocols that are described in this section are *bootstrap protocol* (BOOTP) and *dynamic host configuration protocol* (DHCP).

BOOTP is a protocol that provides the same function as RARP; however, it supports some additional features. DHCP is an extension of the BOOTP protocol; DHCP supports several mechanisms to allocate addresses. DHCP allows you to manage the allocation of IP addresses from a central location.

2.6.1 Bootstrap Protocol (BOOTP)

An alternative to RARP is the *bootstrap protocol* (BOOTP). It also provides a means for diskless workstations and X terminals to determine their IP address. BOOTP uses UDP to carry messages, which in turn are encapsulated in IP datagrams for delivery. A single BOOTP message specifies many items needed at start-up, including the diskless machine's IP address, the address of a gateway, and the address of the server. BOOTP messages have fixed length fields, and replies have the same format as the request. The BOOTP header is described in Figure 2.38.

The following is a brief description of fields in the BOOTP header.

- *Operation* (1 byte): Specifies whether the message is a BOOTP request (1) or a reply (2).
- *Hardware Type* (1 byte): The type of network hardware interface. This field is set to 1 for Ethernet.
- *Hardware Length* (1 byte): Length of the hardware address. It is 6 for Ethernet.
- *Hops* (1 byte): Initially set to 0. Incremented if the BOOTP message is forwarded by a router.

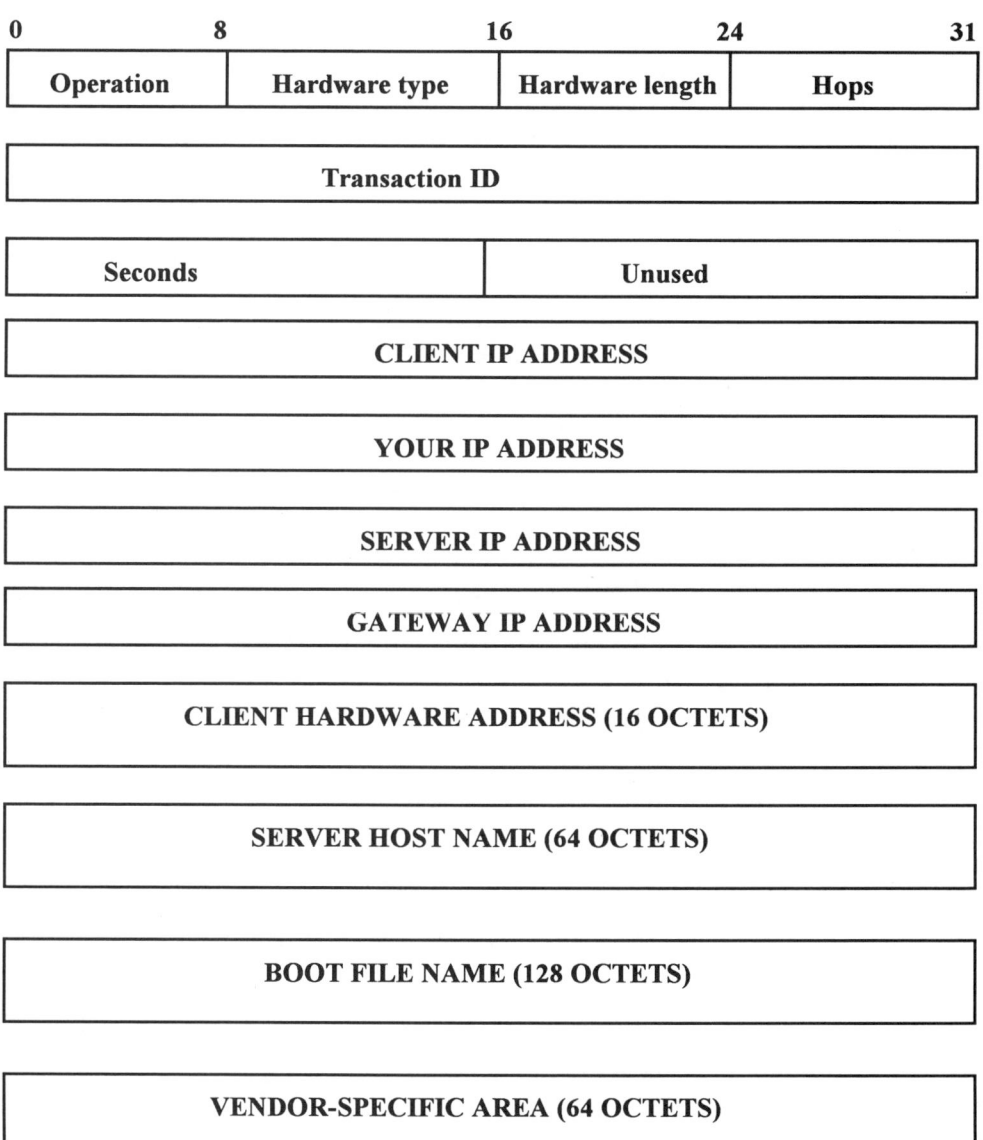

Figure 2.38 BOOTP header format.

- *Transaction ID* (4 bytes): This field is set by the client. It is used by the client to match a BOOTP request message with a BOOTP reply.
- *Seconds* (1 byte): It is set by the client at the time it is starting to boot. It may be used by a secondary BOOTP server to respond after some time, giving the primary BOOTP server a chance to respond first.
- *Client IP Address* (4 bytes): If the client system knows its IP address, it enters it in this field; otherwise, this field is set to zero.
- *Your IP Address* (4 bytes): This field is set by the server and specifies the IP address of the client system.
- *Server IP Address* (4 bytes): IP address of the BOOTP server.
- *Gateway IP Address* (4 bytes): Entered by a proxy server. The proxy server enters its IP address and sends this message to a BOOTP server on the network. The BOOTP server that receives this message sends the response to the proxy system. Note that the address of the proxy system is in this field. The proxy server then forwards the BOOTP reply to the client system.
- *Client Hardware Address* (16 bytes): Hardware; for example, Ethernet address of the system sending the BOOTP request message.
- *Server Host Name* (64 bytes): Symbolic representation of the server's dotted decimal IP address.
- *Boot File Name* (128 bytes): Path name of the file from which the client system needs to boot.
- *Vendor Specific Area* (64 bytes): Contains vendor-specified extensions to BOOTP.

Like other TCP/IP applications, BOOTP is a client/server program wherein the server application runs on the designated BOOTP server system while the client is typically in ROM on X terminals and diskless systems. Most client systems use BOOTP to discover their IP address and then use the trivial file transfer protocol (TFTP) to get the operating system or X server software.

The BOOTP protocol is described in RFC 951.

2.6.2 Dynamic Host Configuration Protocol

The *dynamic host configuration protocol* (DHCP) is a protocol designed to assign Internet dynamically on a TCP/IP network. DHCP is defined in RFCs 1533, 1534, 1541, and 1542. The management of IP addresses and the definition of an enterprise subnet design are two important elements of any TCP/IP-based computing environment. *DHCP is a critical protocol in a client/server configuration of nodes.* With DHCP, client systems do not require manual TCP/IP configuration. A client system gets its TCP/IP configuration parameters dynamically at boot time. Also, if the client system is removed from one subnet and moved to another, it will automatically release its old IP address and be assigned a new one when it is connected to the new segment. The DHCP protocol is based on BOOTP–it has added automatic allocation of reusable network addresses and additional configuration options. DHCP users can communicate with BOOTP systems.

On a TCP/IP network, a key task is the assignment and management of IP addresses. DHCP simplifies the process of centrally managing IP addresses for client nodes on the network.

2.6.2.1 DHCP: How Does It Work?

The client system at boot time sends a DHCP message–refered to as a *discover message*. This is a broadcast message that is processed by all nodes on the local segment and may be forwarded to all DHCP server systems on the private enterprise network. This is known as the *initializing state*.

Each DHCP server who receives this message responds with an *offer message* that contains an IP address and valid configuration information for the specific client that sent the request. Each DHCP server reserves the address it offers so that another client may not be given the same address. Thus, one or more DHCP servers may have *outstanding offers* at this point.

The client system collects all configuration offerings from DHCP servers and enters a *selecting state*. The client chooses one of the configurations and sends a request message that identifies the DHCP server for the selected configuration. This is known as the *requesting state*. Each DHCP server that received the original discover message also receives the request message.

The selected DHCP server sends a DHCP *acknowledgment message*. This message contains the address sent earlier to the client, TCP/IP configuration parameters, and a valid lease for the address. Other DHCP servers return the offered addresses to their free address pools. The client receives the acknowledgment and enters a *bound state*. It can now complete its startup process and communicate with other nodes on the TCP/IP network. The lease includes information expiration date and time.

2.6.2.2 DHCP and TCP/IP Addresses

IP addresses allocated to DHCP servers may be distributed in the following ways:

- Dynamic;
- Automatic;
- Manual.

Dynamic IP Address Allocation

The lease of each address assigned by the DHCP server from its free address pool has an expiration date associated with it. The client must renew the lease if it needs to continue to use the address. The addresses returned to the free address pool can be reused for new DHCP client requests. The administrator may also define a DHCP policy that assigns the same IP address to a client, each time that system boots. Further, addresses returned to the free address pool may be used such that least used addresses are assigned to new client requests.

If a DHCP-enabled system is restarted, it sends a DHCP message with its current configuration to the server. If the server sends a negative response, then the client must go through the initialization stage. A new address may then be assigned to the client system. There is no human intervention required for this transaction.

Note that if a client system has multiple network cards that enable it to connect to multiple networks, then it must request an IP address for each interface.

Automatic IP Address Allocation

Automatic allocation implies that a given client system always receives the same IP address from the DHCP server. A permanent mapping is created, during the initial allocation of the IP address, between the client's unique identifier and its IP address. The DHCP server "remembers" the client's IP address and unique ID mapping so that future requests result in the same address assigned to the client. The address has a permanent lease. IP addresses assigned come from the same address pool as dynamically assigned addresses. However, addresses assigned are not returned to the free address pool.

Manual IP Address Allocation

The administrator assigns a specific IP address and other configuration options for a given client system based on the client's hardware address–this is the client's unique identifier. IP addresses assigned manually cannot be allocated by DHCP servers to other clients using either automatic or dynamic allocation. The manual address assigned has a permanent lease.

2.7 SUMMARY

This chapter provided information on the fundamentals of the TCP/IP network architecture. As we know, TCP/IP is the protocol stack used by UNIX systems to communicate with nodes on the network. Understanding the lower layer protocols such as ARP, RARP, IP, TCP, and UDP gives one a much better understanding of the capabilities and limitations of protocols such as NFS, TFTP, and **telnet**. Figure 2.39 summarizes some of the concepts discussed in this chapter—you can see how data generated by an end user is encapsulated in protocols such as TCP, IP, and Ethernet.

There are two excellent references on the TCP/IP protocol stack and the Internet architecture: (1) Comer's *Internetworking with TCP/IP*, Volume I, Third Edition [1], and (2) Steven's *TCP/IP Illustrated*, Volume I [2].

This chapter also emphasized Internet addresses. These addresses are important to understand because they provide the basis for broadcasting and subnetting. All UNIX hosts on the network are identified by their Internet address. The default size of a packet on the network depends on the network portion of the source and destination addresses; it is therefore important that you feel comfortable with the format of IP addresses and how these addresses may be used to subnet (partition) your network.

Today, a primary factor driving the need for computer networks to become faster is the equipment that is being interconnected has increased significantly in power and performance. Not only is the *bandwidth requirement* increasing but also *distances spanned* between systems are now cross-country if not global. *Fiber optics* is an enabling technology in this evolution, providing longer distances, higher data rates, and improved error rates. The emphasis on today's networks is to communicate files, pictures, and images. The need is not just pictures but presenting computer output data in a movie format, referred to as *visualization*.

The networking requirements of visualization are significant: you need raw speed and noninterference between data streams. If a visualization data stream is interrupted by another packet, it is likely the user will see a glitch. Note that the potential bandwidth of the *human eye-brain system* has been calculated to be on the order of a few gigabits per second; hence, gigabit per second networks (at least from the end user's perspective) are likely to satisfy the individual user's needs for a while.

The network challenge for the 90s and beyond is to provide seemless integration between LANs, supercomputing and high performance system resources available on WANs with the long distance networks used for telecommunications.

In the next chapter, we discuss how application layer protocols on UNIX systems use the services of lower layers.

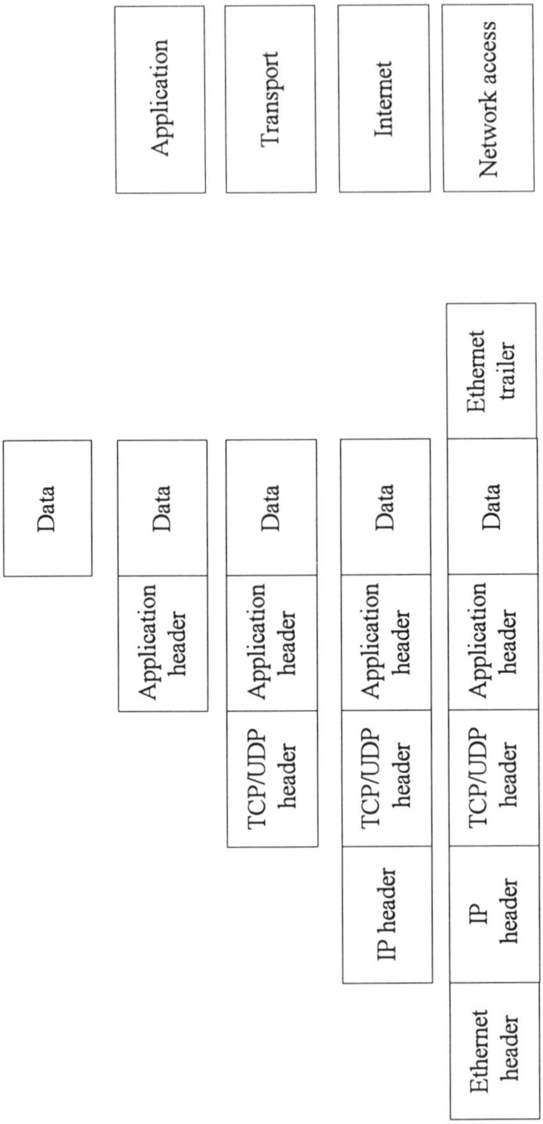

Figure 2.39 TCP/IP architecture and encapsulation of data.

REFERENCES

[1] Comer, D., *Internetworking with TCP/IP, Volume* I, third edition, Englewood Cliffs, NJ: Prentice Hall, 1995.
[2] Stevens, W. R., *TCP/IP Illustrated, Volume* I, Reading, MA: Addison-Wesley, 1994.

SELECT BIBLIOGRAPHY

Flanagan, W., *ATM User's Guide*, Chelsea, MI: Flatiron Publishing, 1994.
Jefferies, R., "ATM to the Desktop: Prospects and Probabilities," *Telecommunications Magazine*, April 1994, pp. 25–32.
McClimans, F. J., "ATM vs. FDDI: Comparing Functionality, Features, and Benefits," *Telecommunications Magazine*, February 1994, pp. 27–33.
Molloy, M., "ATM LANs: A Marketplace Overview," *Telecommunications Magazine*, April 1994, pp. 35–40.
Partridge, C., *Gigabit Networking*, Reading, MA: Addison-Wesley, 1993. "Gigabit Network Testbeds," *IEEE Computer Magazine*, Vol. 23, No. 9, IEEE, September 1990.
Smith, P., *Frame Relay Principles and Applications*, New York: Addison-Wesley, 1993.
Taffel, A., "Frame Relay: Status and Directions," *Telecommunications Magazine*, April 1994, pp. 54–82.

APPENDIX 2A: IMPORTANT NETWORK CONCEPTS

2A.1 Transmission Types

There are three methods of circuit operation: *simplex, half duplex*, and *full duplex*. For voice communication, for example, a *simplex connection* defines a two-wire connection between two points over which voice can travel in both directions but only in one direction at a time. A *half duplex* connection is one where there exists a two-wire connection between two points such that voice can be transmitted in both directions simultaneously. A *full duplex* connection is a four-wire connection between two points over which two simultaneous transmissions can occur on a pair of wires.

2A.2 Data Transmission Modes

Asynchronous and synchronous transmission are the two modes of data transmission. Asynchronous transmission is characterized by the absence of a clock in the transmission media–the access device is not synchronized with the network device–however, the speeds of transmission must be the same. Data, in asynchronous transmission, is transmitted as individual characters; each character is synchronized by information contained in the start (header) and stop (trailer) bits. With synchronous transmission the access device and network device share a common clock and transmission rate–the transmissions are synchronized. Data is exchanged in character streams referred to as message-framed data. Associated with each transmission is a start and stop sequence. The access and network devices need to be synchronized so that the entire message is received in the order transmitted.

Each synchronous transmission message typically starts with two synchronization characters (SYNC) and a start of message (SOM) character–an end of message (EOM) character signals the end of the transmission stream. Examples of asynchronous interfaces include RS232-C and RS232-D and X.21; examples of synchronous interfaces include V.35, RS449/RS442-Balanced, and RS232-C/-D.

2A.3 Baseband and Broadband Services

Baseband refers to a transmission method that uses the full signal spectrum of the cable. *Broadband* transmission is a method where signals from multiple channels are modulated onto separate carrier frequencies–the bandwidth is subdivided into separate communication channels that occupy a specific frequency range. Examples of baseband technologies include Ethernet and LocalTalk; in these technologies, the signal applied to the cable changes the voltage level to indicate a digital value of 0 or 1.

At that point a communication session is established between two systems using the entire bandwidth of the cable–only one system transmits at any point.

The signal placed on baseband transmission system does tend to degrade over distance due to factors such as resistance and capacitance; further, interference from electrical fields can corrupt the signal. The higher the data transmission rate, the higher the probability that the signal will degrade–it is for this reason that standards such as Ethernet specify cable types, cable shielding, and transmission rates. Examples of broadband packet-switching technologies are:

- Frame relay;
- Switched multimegabit data service (SMDS);
- Asynchronous transfer mode (ATM).

These broadband services typically provide data rate at T1 rates (1.544 Mbps) or higher.

2A.4 Switching Virtual LANs

What is a *virtual LAN*? It is an arbitrary grouping of ports (systems) forming a logical LAN segment. Virtual LANS are increasingly being used to support dispersed, temporary task groups that work on specific projects for a limited time. These workgroups need to be attached, detached, and reattached to various LAN segments on an on-going basis–hence, the new generation of switching hubs designed to help network administrators with adds, moves, and changes. Challenges facing virtual LANs include: (1) how and where routing is to be performed and managing security.

2A.5 Switching

The motivation for switching is to increase LAN performance by increasing bandwidth. There are two types of switches: (1) static and (2) dynamic. Some also refer to the two types as *physical layer switching* and *matrix switching* (or MAC layer switching). A *static switch* is one that acts as a light switch–switches occur in minutes, hours, or days apart. A *dynamic switch* may support some or all of the following characteristics:

- Many ports;
- Any port to any port conversation;
- Dedicated bandwidth for each conversation;
- Parallel, simultaneous conversations;
- Scalable bandwidth, switching taking place with each data packet.

2A.5.1 Static Switching

Static switching is also referred to as an *assignment*. There are three types of static switches:

- Module assignment;
- Bank assignment;
- Port assignment.

Module assignment is the ability to assign or configure the connection of a particular Ethernet module to a specific Ethernet segment in the hub's backplane; module switching is handled by network management software. *Bank assignment* is the ability to assign a subset or a bank to specific segments in the hub's backplane; each bank has its own repeater of a module's ports to one of the hub's Ethernet segments. *Port assignment* is the ability to assign each of the module's ports to a specific Ethernet segment.

2A.5.2 Dynamic Switching

There are basically three types of dynamic switches that are being used or will be used in hubs:

- *Ethernet LAN switches* to increase bandwidth to desktops and servers;
- High-speed *traffic switched backplanes* to increase bandwidth and flexibility in backplanes;
- *ATM cell switches* to increase bandwidth and flexibility in hub backplanes and network backbones.

2A.6 Classes of Switching Hubs

There are three classes of switching hubs:

- Backbone switch;
- Departmental switch;
- Workgroup switch.

Backbone switches have the following characteristics:

- 8 to 24 ports;
- Backplane performance of 2+ Gbps;
- Throughput of about 500,000 packets per second;
- Switching architecture is a multiport switch with port-level switching over the backplane.

Departmental switches are characterized by:

- 24 to 120 ports;
- Backplane performance of 1 Gbps to 2 Gbps;
- Throughput of 400,000 packets per second;
- The switching architecture is a multiport bridge/router matrix switch with port and module level switching over backplane.

Workgroup switches typically support the following:

- 8 to 24 ports;
- Backplane performance of 500 Mbps to 1 Gbps;
- Throughput of about 250,000 packets per second;
- The switching architecture is a multiport switch with port-level switching.

2A.7 Fast Packet Switching, Cell, and Frame Relay

Fast switching refers to two different types of transmissions through mesh-type switching networks. Information on the network is typically transferred over telecommunication links provided by local and long-distance carriers. In fast packet switching, tasks such as error correction, packet sequencing, and acknowledgments are not handled by the network—it is the responsibility of end systems—since the network has less overhead associated with the processing of packets, it can move information quickly. Eliminating error correction at the lower layers tremendously improves performance.

Fast packet technology is implemented at the MAC sublayer of the data link layer—in contrast to X.25, a packet-switching technology that is implemented at the network layer. ATM and frame relay are examples of fast packet-switching technologies. Frame relay uses variable-length packets and as the name implies it is a *relay service*—note X.25 is a *packet service*. Frame relay does not extensively support error checking and acknowledgments as X.25 does. Frame relay is said to be an example of fast packet technology. ATM uses fixed-sized cells and is referred to as a *cell relay* technology.

2A.8 T1/T3 Standards

The *T carrier services* provide dedicated and private line services for digital voice and data transmission over LANs and WANs at rates up to 45 Mbps. *T1*, a common digital leased line service, provides a bandwidth of 1.544 Mbps. *Fractional T1*, also referred to as FT1, lets customers lease less than a full T1 line—each T1 line supports 24 channels at 64 Kbps—which yields a data rate of 1.536 Mbps (an additional 64 Kbps is used for overhead). Each of the 24 channels in a T1 circuit can carry voice or data transmission.

To connect a T1 line to your LAN you need the following systems:

- *CSU*: It is the first point of contact for the T1 wires—it diagnoses and prepares the signals on the line for the LAN.
- *DSU*: The DSU connects to the CSU and converts LAN signals to T1 signaling formats.
- *Multiplexor*: Provides a mechanism to load multiple voice and data channels into the digital line.
- *Bridge/Router*: Provides the interface between the LAN and the T1 line.

T2 is not offered to the public—it is an internal carrier specification that is equivalent to 4 T1 lines—6.3 Mbps. *T3* is equivalent to 28 T1 circuits and provides a total bandwidth of 44.736 Mbps. *Fractional T3* allows customers to lease less than the full T3 rate. The *digital signal hierarchy* used in the United States is described in Table 2.9.

Table 2.9
Digital Signal Hierarchy Used in the United States

Service Class	Digital Signal
DS-0	64 Kbps
DS-1	1.544 Mbps
DS-2	6.312 Mbps
DS-3	45 Mbps
DS-4	274 Mbps

UNIX Network Elements   3

In the first chapter, we examined key elements of the UNIX operating system. In Chapter 2, we stepped through important network technologies and terminology. In this chapter, we analyze the ABCs of UNIX networks:

A: Important network-related files on UNIX systems;
B: Critical network-related processes on UNIX systems;
C: Network administrator– and end user–related commands on UNIX systems.

Our objective is to help you understand the relationship between files, processes, and commands, as they relate to networks, on UNIX systems. Just as the file **unix** in the *root* file system is the kernel of the UNIX operating system, the concepts explained in Chapter 3 provide not only the foundation for connecting UNIX systems to the network but also the basis for many network applications.

3.1 NETWORK FILES ON UNIX SYSTEMS

Important network-related files that exist on UNIX systems include:

- /etc/hosts;
- /etc/protocols;
- /etc/ethers;
- /etc/bootptab;
- /etc/services;
- /etc/netmasks;
- /etc/inetd.conf.

The information contained in these files is referenced by network daemons and commands executed by end users or administrators.

3.1.1 /etc/hosts

The **/etc/hosts** file provides a mapping between Internet addresses and host names. This file is referenced by a number of applications and commands to resolve host names (convert symbolic representation of IP addresses into the dotted decimal equivalent). The format of the **/etc/hosts** file is as follows:

Internet-address official-host-name aliases

Internet-address is the symbolic representation of the IP address. *official-host-name* is the dotted decimal Internet address of the system. Figure 3.1 is an example of what this file may look like:

```
#
#    /etc/hosts file
#
127.0.0.1       localhost
#
131.107.15.1    nathan      loghost
131.101.15.2    natasha
```

Figure 3.1 An example of the **/etc/hosts** file on a UNIX system.

The address 127.0.0.1 is known as a *loopback address* for the local host. The Class A address, 127, is reserved as a loopback address. The *localhost* is an alias for the host name of the local system (in this case, *nathan*). The entry *loghost* is also used by daemons such as *syslogd* to send information to your system (system messages).

3.1.2 /etc/protocols

Each line in the **/etc/protocols** file describes a protocol used on the network. The format of the **/etc/protocols** file is as follows:

> **official-protocol-name   protocol-#   aliases**

Fields in this file are separated by blanks spaces or tabs. A number symbol (#) indicates the start of a comment line. *official-protocol-name* is the name of the protocol associated with the *protocol-#* field. The value specified in the *protocol-#* field relates to the 8-bit protocol field in the IP header. If you've developed our own protocol that uses the raw socket interface, it will have to be listed in the **/etc/protocols** file: *inetd* requires this file to process incoming network connections. An example of the **/etc/protocols** file is provided in Figure 3.2.

```
#ident     "@(#)protocols    1.2    90/02/03 SMI"    /* SVr4.0 1.1    */
#
# Internet (IP) protocols
#
ip          0           IP           # internet protocol, pseudo protocol number
```

Figure 3.2 An example of the **/etc/protocols** file on a UNIX system.

icmp	1	ICMP	# internet control message protocol
ggp	3	GGP	# gateway-gateway protocol
tcp	6	TCP	# transmission control protocol
egp	8	EGP	# exterior gateway protocol
pup	12	PUP	# PARC universal packet protocol
udp	17	UDP	# user datagram protocol
hmp	20	HMP	# host monitoring protocol
xns-idp	22	XNS-IDP	# Xerox NS IDP
rdp	27	RDP	# "reliable datagram" protocol

Figure 3.2 continued.

3.1.3 /etc/services

All services specified in the **/etc/inetd.conf** file must be in the **/etc/services** file. This file is a registry of programs and well-known port numbers. Services such as **telnet**, **ftp**, and **tftp** are defined in this file; by examining this file you can determine the port numbers at which these services are available. Any program or application that wants to reserve a port number must specify it in the **/etc/services** file. The **etc/services** file is referenced by the *inetd* daemon process. The format of this file is as follows:

    service-name   **port/protocol**   **aliases**

service-name is the name of the network service associated with the information specified in the *port* field. The *port* field identifies the port number of the network application. The *protocol* field may be TCP or UDP–it identifies the transport layer protocol used for this network service. Figure 3.3 is an example of the **/etc/services** file:

```
#ident      "@(#)services   1.8     93/08/27 SMI"   /*SVr4.0 1.8    */
#
# Network services, Internet style
#
tcpmux      1/tcp
echo        7/tcp
echo        7/udp
discard     9/tcp           sink null
discard     9/udp           sink null
systat      11/tcp          users
daytime     13/tcp
daytime     13/udp
netstat     15/tcp
chargen     19/tcp          ttytst source
```

Figure 3.3 An example of the **/etc/services** file on a UNIX system.

```
chargen        19/udp      ttytst source
ftp-data       20/tcp
ftp            21/tcp
telnet         23/tcp
smtp           25/tcp      mail
time           37/tcp      timserver
time           37/udp      timserver
name           42/udp      nameserver
whois          43/tcp      nicname          # usually to sri-nic
domain         53/udp
domain         53/tcp
hostnames      101/tcp     hostname         # usually to sri-nic
sunrpc         111/udp     rpcbind
sunrpc         111/tcp     rpcbind
#
# Host specific functions
#
tftp           69/udp
rje            77/tcp
finger         79/tcp
link           87/tcp      ttylink
supdup         95/tcp
iso-tsap       102/tcp
x400           103/tcp                      # ISO Mail
x400-snd       104/tcp
csnet-ns       105/tcp
pop-2          109/tcp                      # Post Office
uucp-path      117/tcp
nntp           119/tcp     usenet           # Network News Transfer
ntp            123/tcp                      # Network Time Protocol
ntp            123/udp                      # Network Time Protocol
NeWS           144/tcp     news             # Window System
#
# UNIX specific services
#
# these are NOT officially assigned
#
exec           512/tcp
login          513/tcp
shell          514/tcp     cmd              # no passwords used
printer        515/tcp     spooler          # line printer spooler
courier        530/tcp     rpc              # experimental
uucp           540/tcp     uucpd            # uucp daemon
biff           512/udp     comsat
who            513/udp     whod
```

Figure 3.3 continued.

```
syslog          514/udp
talk            517/udp
route           520/udp       router routed
new-rwho        550/udp       new-who         # experimental
rmonitor        560/udp       rmonitord       # experimental
monitor         561/udp                       # experimental
pcserver        600/tcp                       # ECD Integrated PC board srvr
kerberos        750/udp       kdc             # Kerberos key server
kerberos        750/tcp       kdc             # Kerberos key server
ingreslock      1524/tcp
listen          2766/tcp                      # System V listener port
nfsd            2049/udp      nfs             # NFS server daemon
lockd           4045/udp                      # NFS lock daemon/manager
lockd           4045/tcp
#
# Added by Bridgeway for EventIX
#
nvixsp          7112/tcp
nvixspc         7113/tcp
nvixcr          7114/tcp
nvixfts         7115/tcp
nvixclb         7116/tcp
nvixacm         7111/tcp
evxSnmpd        7117/tcp
bsnmpd-snmp     38/udp
bsnmpd-trap     40/udp
bwysnmpd        7120/udp
snmp            161/udp                       # Simple Network Mgmt Protocol (SNMP)
snmp-trap       162/udp       snmptrap        # SNMP trap (event) messages
```

Figure 3.3 continued.

3.1.4 /etc/ethers

The file **/etc/ethers** lists the Ethernet address and host names of systems such as diskless workstations and X terminals on the local network. It is used by the RARP daemon, *rarpd*, to map Ethernet addresses into Internet (IP) addresses. The format of this file is as follows:

Ethernet-address host-name

The *Ethernet-address* is specified in hexadecimal; each byte in the Ethernet address is separated by a colin. *host-name* is the symbolic representation of the Internet address; the value specified in this field must match the corresponding value in the **/etc/hosts file**.

For example, the **/etc/ethers** file may contain the following line:

112   UNIX Internetworking

      8:0:20:f:aa:d9   ganesh

You can determine the Ethernet address of your system in the following ways:

- At boot time (it is displayed on the system console);
- Use the **dmesg** command;
- Execute the **ifconfig** command with **-a** command (need to be logged in as **root** for the Ethernet address to be displayed).

3.1.5 /etc/bootptab

The **/etc/bootptab** file is read by the *bootpd* daemon upon startup. The parameters specified in this file are separated by colons (:). The general command format is:

bootp-client:tag =

bootp-client is the actual name of the bootp client. *tag* is a two character tag symbol. The currently recognized tags are:

bf	Boot file
bs	Boot file size in 512 byte blocks
cs	Cookie server address list
ds	Domain name server address list
gw	Gateway address list
ha	Host hardware address
hd	Boot file home directory
hn	Send host name
ht	Host hardware type
im	Impress server address list
ip	Host IP address
lg	Log server address list
lp	LPR server address list
ns	IEN-116 name server list
rl	Resource location protocol server address list
sm	Host subnet mask
tc	Table continuation
to	Time offset in seconds from UTC
ts	Time server address list
vm	Vendor magic cookie selector

Figure 3.4 is a sample **bootptab** file.

```
# @(#) $Header: bootptab,v 2.0
# Example /etc/bootptab: database for bootp server (/etc/bootpd).
# Blank lines and lines beginning with '#' are ignored.
#
# Legend:
#
#       first field — hostname
#               (may be full domain name)
#
#       hd —    home directory
#       bf —    bootfile
#       cs —    cookie servers
#       ds —    domain name servers
#       gw —    gateways
#       ha —    hardware address
#       ht —    hardware type
#       im —    impress servers
#       ip —    host IP address
#       lg —    log servers
#       lp —    LPR servers
#       ns —    IEN-116 name servers
#       rl —    resource location protocol servers
#       sm —    subnet mask
#       tc —    template host (points to similar host entry)
#       to —    time offset (seconds)
#       ts —    time servers
#
# Be careful about including backslashes where they're needed.
#
#shiva:\
#       :hn:ht=ether:vm=rfc1048:\
#       :ha=08000553233F:\
#       :ip=192.136.118.236:\
#       :sm=255.255.255.0:\
#       :gw=192.136.118.254:\
#       :lg=190.40.101.3:\
#       :T144="/boot/diskless.cfg":
```

Figure 3.4 A sample **/etc/bootptab** file.

3.1.6 /etc/netmasks

The */etc/netmasks* file contains network masks used to implement IP subnetting. For each network that is subnetted, a single line should exist in this file with the network number followed by the network mask to be used on that network. If you are running NIS on your system, then this file is the basis for the **netmasks.byaddr** map. See Figure 3.5 for an example of an **/etc/netmasks** file.

In this example, the Class B network 131.107 is using a subnet mask of 255.255.255.0; thus, eight bits are used to extend the network portion of the address. As far as the network 131.108 is concerned, nine bits are used to extend the network portion of the Internet address.

```
#
# Network masks database
#
# only non default subnet masks need to be defined here
#
#Network      netmask
131.107.0.0   255.255.255.0
131.108.0.0   255.255.255.128
```

Figure 3.5 An example of the **/etc/netmasks** file on a UNIX system.

3.1.7 /etc/inetd.conf

The *inetd* daemon manages network service daemons according to information contained in the **/etc/inetd.conf** file. Each line in this file contains the information required to manage a particular network service process [1]. Table 3.1 describes fields associated with each entry in the **/etc/inetd.conf** file.

Each field in this file may be separated by blank spaces or tables. Comment lines begin with a # symbol. The entry *inetd* performs a few services itself. If it does so, the server program is indicated by internal.

Figure 3.6 is an example of the **/etc/inetd.conf** file:

By examining this file, we know that the *inetd* daemon services all incoming **ftp**, **telnet**, and **tftp** connection requests. A new process is started by *inetd* for each connection.

```
#
#ident     "@(#)inetd.conf    1.15    93/08/27 SMI"    /*SVr4.0 1.5    */
#
#
# Configuration file for inetd(1M). See inetd.conf(4).
#
# To re-configure the running inetd process, edit this file, then
# send the inetd process a SIGHUP.
#
```

Figure 3.6 Sample **/etc/inetd.conf** file.

Table 3.1
Fields in the **/etc/inetd.conf** File

Field Name	Description
Service name	Name of a valid service listed in the file **/etc/services**. For RPC services, this field consists of the RPC service name or program number, followed by a '/' (slash) and either a version number or a range of version numbers (for example, rstatd/2-4).
Socket type	May be: *stream* for a stream socket; *dgram* for a datagram socket; *raw* for a raw socket; *seqpacket* for a sequenced packet socket; *tli* for TLI endpoints.
Protocol	Must be a recognized protocol listed in the **/etc/protocols** file. For RPC services, this field consists of the string *rpc* followed by a '/' (slash) and either a '*' (asterisk), one or more net-types, one or more net-ids, or a combination of net-types and net-ids.
Wait status	*nowait* for all but single-threaded datagram servers that do not release a socket until a timeout occurs.
User	The user identification (UID) under which the server should run. Servers can thus run with access privileges other than those for **root**.
Server program	Either the pathname of a server program to be invoked by *inetd* to perform the requested service, or the value *internal* if *inetd* itself provides the service.
Server arguments	If a server is invoked with command line arguments, then the entire command line, including argument 0, must appear in this field.

```
# Syntax for socket-based Internet services:

# <service_name> <socket_type> <proto> <flags> <user> <server_pathname> <args>
#
# Syntax for TLI-based Internet services:
#
# <service_name> tli <proto> <flags> <user> <server_pathname> <args>
#
# Ftp and telnet are standard Internet services.
#
ftp       stream    tcp    nowait    root    /usr/sbin/in.ftpd       in.ftpd
telnet    stream    tcp    nowait    root    /usr/sbin/in.telnetd    in.telnetd
#
```

Figure 3.6 continued.

Tnamed serves the obsolete IEN-116 name server protocol.
#
name   dgram   udp   wait   root   /usr/sbin/in.tnamed   in.tnamed
#
Shell, login, exec, comsat and talk are BSD protocols.
#
shell   stream   tcp   nowait root   /usr/sbin/in.rshd   in.rshd
login   stream   tcp   nowait root   /usr/sbin/in.rlogind in.rlogind
exec   stream   tcp   nowait root   /usr/sbin/in.rexecd   in.rexecd
comsat   dgram   udp   wait   root   /usr/sbin/in.comsat   in.comsat
talk   dgram   udp   wait   root   /usr/sbin/in.talkd   in.talkd
#
Must run as root (to read /etc/shadow); "-n" turns off logging in utmp/wtmp.
#
uucp   stream   tcp   nowait root   /usr/sbin/in.uucpd   in.uucpd
#
Tftp service is provided primarily for booting. Most sites run this
only on machines acting as "boot servers."
#
tftp   dgram   udp   wait   root   /usr/sbin/in.tftpd   in.tftpd -s /tftpboot
#
Finger, systat and netstat give out user information which may be
valuable to potential "system crackers." Many sites choose to disable
some or all of these services to improve security.
#
finger   stream   tcp   nowait nobody /usr/sbin/in.fingerd in.fingerd
#systat   stream   tcp   nowait root   /usr/bin/ps   ps -ef
#netstat   stream   tcp   nowait root   /usr/bin/netstat   netstat -f inet
#
Time service is used for clock synchronization.
#
time   stream   tcp   nowait root   internal
time   dgram   udp   wait   root   internal
#
Echo, discard, daytime, and chargen are usedprimarily for testing.
#
echo   stream   tcp   nowait root   internal
echo   dgram   udp   wait   root   internal
discard   stream   tcp   nowait root   internal
discard   dgram   udp   wait   root   internal
daytime   stream   tcp   nowait root   internal
daytime   dgram   udp   wait   root   internal
chargen   stream   tcp   nowait root   internal
chargen   dgram   udp   wait   root   internal
#

Figure 3.6 continued.

```
#
# RPC services syntax:
# <rpc_prog>/<vers> <endpoint-type> rpc/<proto> <flags> <user> \
# <pathname> <args>
#
# <endpoint-type> can be either "tli" or "stream" or "dgram".
# For "stream" and "dgram" assume that the endpoint is a socket descriptor.
# For example:
# dummy/1      tli    rpc/circuit_v,udp    wait    root    /tmp/test_svc    test_svc
#
# System and network administration class agent server
#
# This is referenced by number because the admind agent is needed for the
# initial installation of the system. However, on some preinstalled systems
# the SNAG packages may not be present. Referencing the service by number
# prevents error messages in this case.
#
100087/10    tli    rpc/udp             wait    root    /usr/sbin/admind    admind
#
# Rquotad supports UFS disk quotas for NFS clients
#
rquotad/1    tli    rpc/datagram_v      wait    root    /usr/lib/nfs/rquotad rquota
#
# The rusers service gives out user information. Sites concerned
# with security may choose to disable it.
#
rusersd/2-3  tli    rpc/datagram_v      wait    root /usr/lib/netsvc/rusers/rpc.rusersd
rpc.rusersd
#
# The spray server is used primarily for testing.
# sprayd/1   tli    rpc/datagram_v      wait    root    /usr/lib/netsvc/spray/rpc.sprayd
# rpc.sprayd
#
# The rwall server allows others to post messages to users on this machine.
# walld/1    tli    rpc/datagram_v      wait    root    /usr/lib/netsvc/rwall/rpc.rwalld
# rpc.rwalld
#
# Rstatd is used by programs such as perfmeter.
#
rstatd/2-4   tli    rpc/datagram_v      wait    root    /usr/lib/netsvc/rstat/rpc.rstatd
rpc.rstatd
#
# The rexd server provides only minimal authentication and is often not run
#
#rexd/1      tli    rpc/tcp             wait    root    /usr/sbin/rpc.rexd rpc.rexd
```

Figure 3.6 continued.

```
#
# rpc.cmsd is a data base daemon which manages calendar data backed
# by files in /var/spool/calendar
#
100068/2-4    dgram    rpc/udp         wait   root   /usr/openwin/bin/rpc.cmsd
                                                     rpc.cmsd
#
# Sun ToolTalk Database Server
#
100083/1      stream rpc/tcp           wait   root /usr/openwin/bin/rpc.ttdbserverd
rpc.ttdbserverd
#
#Core SunNet Manager 2.2 Agents
#
na.activity/10      tli rpc/udp wait   root   /opt/SUNWconn/snm/   na.activity agents/na.activity
na.diskinfo/10      tli rpc/udp wait   root   /opt/SUNWconn/snm/   na.diskinfo agents/na.diskinfo
na.etherif2/10      tli rpc/udp wait   root   /opt/SUNWconn/snm/   na.etherif2 agents/na.etherif2
na.event/10         tli rpc/udp wait   root   /opt/SUNWconn/snm/   na.event agents/na.event
na.event/10         tli rpc/tcp wait   root   /opt/SUNWconn/snm/   na.event agents/na.event
na.hostif/10        tli rpc/udp wait   root   /opt/SUNWconn/snm/   na.hostif agents/na.hostif
na.hostmem2/10      tli rpc/udp wait   root   /opt/SUNWconn/snm/   na.hostmem2 agents/na.hostmem2
na.hostperf/10      tli rpc/udp wait   root   /opt/SUNWconn/snm/   na.hostperf agents/na.hostperf
na.iostat2/10       tli rpc/udp wait   root   /opt/SUNWconn/snm/   na.iostat2 agents/na.iostat2
na.ippath/10        tli rpc/udp wait   root   /opt/SUNWconn/snm/   na.ippath agents/na.ippath
na.iproutes/10      tli rpc/udp wait   root   /opt/SUNWconn/snm/   na.iproutes agents/na.iproutes
na.layers2/10       tli rpc/udp wait   root   /opt/SUNWconn/snm/   na.layers2 agents/na.layers2
#na.logger/10       tli rpc/udp wait   root   /opt/SUNWconn/snm/   na.logger agents/na.logger
na.lpstat/10        tli rpc/udp wait   root   /opt/SUNWconn/snm/   na.lpstat agents/na.lpstat
na.ping/10          tli rpc/udp wait   root   /opt/SUNWconn/snm/   na.ping agents/na.ping
na.rpcnfs/10        tli rpc/udp wait   root   /opt/SUNWconn/snm/   na.rpcnfs agents/na.rpcnfs
na.snmp/10          tli rpc/udp wait   root   /opt/SUNWconn/snm/   na.snmp agents/na.snmp
na.snmpv2/10        tli rpc/udp wait   root   /opt/SUNWconn/snm/   na.snmpv2 agents/na.snmpv2
snmp-trap           dgram udp wait     root   /opt/SUNWconn/snm/   na.snmp-trap agents/na.snmp-trap
na.traffic/10       tli rpc/udp wait   root   /opt/SUNWconn/snm/   na.traffic agents/na.traffic
```

Figure 3.6 continued.

3.2 NETWORK PROCESSES ON UNIX SYSTEMS

The previous section emphasized key network files on UNIX systems. This section discusses processes that reference some of those files. These processes include:

- *inetd*;
- *routed*;
- *rarpd*;
- *bootpd*;

- *nfsd, biod, statd, lockd, mountd;*
- *ypser, ypxfrd, ypbind;*
- *named;*
- *rpcbind* and *portmap.*

These processes are critical to the operation of your UNIX system on the network. Figure 3.7 is a listing of processes running on a UNIX SVR4 system.

ps -ef

UID	PID	PPID	C	STIME	TTY	TIME	COMD
root	0	0	80	Nov 18	?	0:02	sched
root	1	0	191	Nov 18	?	1:39	/etc/init -r
root	2	0	27	Nov 18	?	0:00	pageout
root	3	0	80	Nov 18	?	9:13	fsflush
root	336	1	80	Nov 18	?	0:03	/usr/lib/saf/sac -t 300
root	1426	1	67	Nov 21	console	0:01	vkbd -nopopup
root	295	287	22	Nov 18	?	0:00	lpNet
root	243	1	194	Nov 18	?	0:02	/usr/sbin/inetd -s
root	224	1	80	Nov 18	?	0:02	/usr/sbin/rpcbind
root	216	1	80	Nov 18	?	1:06	/usr/sbin/in.routed -q
root	226	1	2	Nov 18	?	0:00	/usr/sbin/keyserv
root	239	1	6	Nov 18	?	0:00	/usr/sbin/in.named
root	232	1	29	Nov 18	?	0:00	/usr/sbin/kerbd
root	250	1	32	Nov 18	?	0:00	/usr/lib/autofs/automountd
root	254	1	42	Nov 18	?	0:00	/usr/lib/nfs/statd
root	256	1	80	Nov 18	?	0:01	/usr/lib/nfs/lockd
root	267	1	75	Nov 18	?	0:01	/usr/sbin/syslogd
root	287	1	68	Nov 18	?	0:00	/usr/lib/lpsched
root	277	1	80	Nov 18	?	0:07	/usr/sbin/cron
root	339	336	80	Nov 18	?	0:03	/usr/lib/saf/ttymon
root	296	1	80	Nov 18	?	0:00	/usr/lib/sendmail -bd -q1h
root	337	1	80	Nov 18	console	0:01	-ksh
root	1432	1415	169	Nov 21	console	0:02	olwm -syncpid 1431
root	1413	1409	22	Nov 21	console	0:00	/usr/openwin/bin/xinit —/usr/openwin/bin/X :0 - auth //.xsun.nirvana:0
root	1429	1	80	Nov 21	console	0:01	ttsession -s
root	1415	1413	19	Nov 21	console	0:00	sh /usr/openwin/lib/Xinitrc
root	1409	337	80	Nov 21	console	0:00	/bin/sh /usr/openwin/bin/openwin
root	1414	1413	80	Nov 21	console	0:44	/usr/openwin/bin/X :0 -auth//.xsun.nirvana:0

Figure 3.7 Listing of processes running on a UNIX SVR4 system.

root	1420	1	38	Nov 21 console	0:00	fbconsole
root	2323	1432	80	07:34:38 ?	0:01	/usr/openwin/bin/cmdtool
root	1433	243	47	Nov 21 ?	0:00	rpc.ttdbserverd
root	1434	1432	51	Nov 21 console	0:01	olwmslave
root	2326	1453	10	07:34:57 pts/2	0:00	script ps-file
root	1438	1	80	Nov 21 console	0:01	/usr/openwin/bin/cmdtool -Wp0 0 -Ws 590 77 -C
root	1440	1438	20	Nov 21 pts/1	0:00	/bin/ksh
root	1453	1451	245	Nov 21 pts/2	0:00	/bin/ksh
root	1451	1432	80	Nov 21 ?	0:04	/usr/openwin/bin/cmdtool
root	2325	2323	19	07:34:41 pts/3	0:00	/bin/ksh
root	2330	2328	40	07:35:07 pts/4	0:00	ps -ef
root	2327	2326	8	07:34:57 pts/2	0:00	script ps-file
root	2328	2327	31	07:34:57 pts/4	0:00	sh -i

\#

Figure 3.7 continued.

3.2.1 inetd

In version 4.2 BSD the network daemons used a lot of resources. With 4.3 BSD, a super daemon was introduced that was responsible for managing other network daemons to improve performance. The *inetd* daemon manages all the network services daemons according to the instructions in the **/etc/inetd.conf** configuration file. The **/etc/inetd.conf** file is read by *inetd* when it is first started, typically at boot time, and in response to the *hangup* signal.

If *inetd* receives an incoming connection request from a connection-oriented application such as **telnet** and **ftp**, it creates a new process to handle the communication. The new process executes the connection-oriented application (**telnet, ftp**) and then does a *getpeername()* to determine the sources host name and source port number.

As far as connectionless services are concerned, *inetd* creates a new process when it receives a datagram. The datagram server can then connect to its peer and thus free the original socket for *inetd* to receive further datagrams or use the existing socket to process new datagrams and time out when done.

The former is an example of a *multithreaded server*, and the latter is said to be *single-threaded*. Thus, in a single-threaded server, *inetd* waits for the server process to exit before starting a second server process.

The *inetd* process listens for connections on well-known ports and starts the appropriate daemons if a connection is requested. *Remote procedure call* (RPC) services can also be started by *inetd*. The *inetd* process simplifies daemon start-up procedures, and that improves performance. It is possible for users to develop their own network service that they could run as *inetd* clients. To do this they would need to modify the configuration file as appropriate and send *inetd* a HUP signal: The HUP signal forces *inetd* to re-read its configuration file.

```
% ps -ax | grep inetd      /*   for PID information   */
% kill -HUP PID            /*   to signal inetd       */
```

The *inetd* daemon must always be running on your system.

3.2.2 routed

The *routed* process is the daemon process that implements the *routing information protocol* (RIP). The process *routed* provides the ability to build routing tables dynamically. It listens on UDP port number 520 for routing information packets. If the host is an internetwork router, it periodically sends copies of its routing table to directly connected hosts and networks.

3.2.3 rarpd

The *reverse address resolution protocol* (RARP) daemon, *rarpd*, runs on a system and listens to RARP request messages. RARP is the protocol used to map a hardware address into an Internet address. RARP is used by diskless workstations and X terminals at boot time to discover their Internet address. The booting system provides its Ethernet address in an RARP request message. The server system responds by looking at the **/etc/hosts** and **/etc/ethers** files to determine the Internet address of the diskless system. The *rarpd* process sends no reply when it fails to locate an IP address.

3.2.4 bootpd

bootpd is the BOOTP server process. It supports the BOOTP protocol defined in RFCs 951 and 1048. Typically, the **/etc/inetd.conf** file includes the following line:

    bootps   dgram   udp   wait   root   /etc/bootpd   bootpd

The *bootpd* command format is

    /etc/bootpd   [-s -t -d]

Thus, the daemon is started only when a boot request is received. If *bootpd* does not receive another boot request within fifteen minutes of the last request received, it will exit to conserve system resources. The **-t** option may be used to specify a different timeout value in minutes (for example **-t30**). A timeout value of zero implies forever.

If the *bootpd* daemon is started with the **-s** option, it runs in stand-alone mode. The daemon should be started with **-s** if there are many BOOTP client machines on the network. The **-d** option is used for debugging. Upon startup, the *bootpd* daemon first reads its configuration file, **/etc/bootptab**, and then listens for BOOTP request packets.

3.2.5 NFS-Related Processes: *nfsd, biod, automount*

Network file system (NFS) servers run both the *nfsd* and *rpc.mountd* daemons. The *nfsd* daemon runs on the NFS server and accepts RPC calls from clients. The *rpc.mountd* daemon is used to handle file system mount requests and some path name translation. NFS servers also run the *rpc.statd* and *rpc.lockd* daemons. These daemons are for file locking and lock recovery.

Running multiple copies of the *nfsd* daemon lets a server start multiple-disk operations at the same time and handle quick turnaround requests such as *getattr*() and *lookup*() while disk-bound requests are in progress.

On an NFS client system you need to have the *biod, rpc.lockd*, and the *rpc.statd* daemons running to use NFS. These daemons are usually started at boot time. The block I/O daemon, *biod*, performs block I/O operations for NFS clients, executing some simple read-ahead and write-behind performance optimization. You can run multiple copies of *biod* so that each client process can have multiple NFS requests outstanding at any time.

For write requests, the buffer cache on a client system batches data until a full NFS buffer has been written. Once a full buffer is ready to be sent to the server, a *biod* daemon picks up the buffer and performs the write RPC request. The *biod* daemons group consecutive pages together to form a single NFS buffer. This process is referred to as *dirty page clustering*.

The *rpc.lockd* and *rpc.statd* daemons handle file locking and lock recovery on the client. These locking daemons also run on the NFS server, and the client-side daemons coordinate file locking on the NFS server through their server-side counterparts [2].

The *automount* is a daemon that automatically mounts the NFS file system when it is referenced and unmounts it when no longer needed. The automounter is included in SunOS, ULTRIX, and AIX systems. A public domain version called *amd* is available from **ftp.uu.net**. It runs on almost any UNIX system. The *automount* process accepts connections on port number 724.

3.2.6 NIS-Related Processes: *ypserv, ypxfrd, ypbind*

The *network information service* (NIS) or *yellow pages* (YP) uses a number of processes to manage system and network information centrally.

These processes include *yperv*, *ypbind*, and *ypxfrd*. The *ypserv* process enables a host to function as a NIS server system. It runs on the NIS master and slave server systems. The *ypbind* daemon is responsible for locating NIS servers and maintaining bindings of domain names to servers. Whenever any system is running ypbind, it is an NIS client. When *ypbind* is invoked, it finds a server for the hosts default domain. The process of locating a server is called *binding the domain*. Under SunOS, a master server daemon, called *ypxfrd*, is used to speed up NIS map transfer operations.

3.2.7 DNS-Related Process: *named*

The *named* process is the name server daemon for the domain-style Internet naming scheme. It is responsible for mapping host names into network addresses. The domain name system and the name server dynamically provide host-to-address lookups. Bind is a tool distributed with 4.3 BSD to help maintain a distributed database of host-name-to-IP-address mappings. Each name server needs to know how to supply information about the host name address mappings in its domain of authority and how to pass on requests for information outside its domain.

BIND consists of a name daemon, *named*, and a resolver, **/usr/lib/resolv.a**. The *named* process responds to resolver queries, queries other name servers, and caches information from previous queries. If *named* is running, all programs that execute the *gethostent()* system call are sent to *named* for resolution [3]. The *named* process can run as a primary master server, secondary master server, or a caching only server. The *named* daemon reads the file, **/etc/named.boot**, for any initial data.

3.2.8 rpcbind and portmap

The *rpcbind* process runs on Solaris (SVR4) systems. It provides the same function as the *portmap* process on SunOS (BSD) systems. *rpcbind* is a universal addresses (port numbers) to the RPC program number mapper.

rpcbind must be started before any other RPC service on the machine. An RPC service, when started, tells *rpcbind* the address to which it is listening and the RPC program numbers it is prepared to serve. The client process first communicates with *rpcbind* on the server system to determine the address of the RPC server process to which it needs to talk.

The process */usr/etc/portmap* is a server process that converts TCP/IP port numbers into RPC program numbers. This process must be running on the system to make RPC calls. When an RPC server process is started on a BSD system, it first informs the *portmap* process to which port number it is listening and what RPC program numbers it will be serving. When a client process wishes to make an RPC call to a given program number, it will first contact the *portmap* process on the server machine to determine the port number where RPC packets should be sent.

Typically, RPC servers are started by the inetd daemon; therefore, the *portmap* must be started before *inetd* is invoked. Note that, if the *portmap* crashes, then all server processes must be restarted.

3.3 NETWORK-RELATED COMMANDS

The focus of this section is on commands that may be used to configure you UNIX system on the network. These commands include:

- **ifconfig**;
- **netstat**;
- **arp**;
- **nslookup**;
- **hostname**;
- **domainname**;
- **rpcinfo**.

We then examine commands that you can execute on UNIX systems to access other nodes on the local and wide area networks. These commands include:

- **telnet**;
- **rlogin**;
- **ftp**;
- **rcp**;
- **rsh**;
- **finger**;
- **who**.

Details are then provided on **ftp anonymous** accounts and how to access *requests for comments* (RFCs) on the Internet.

3.3.1 ifconfig

The **ifconfig** command is used to assign an Internet address to a network interface such as Ethernet. Typically, this is specified in the file **/etc/rc.boot**. The **ifconfig** command format is:

/usr/etc/ifconfig   <interface> | -a | -au | -ad
    [<af>] [<address> [<dest_addr>]] [up] [down]

[auto-revarp]
[netmask <mask>] [broadcast <broad_addr>]
[metric <n>]
[mtu <n>]
[trailers | -trailers] [private | -private]
[arp | -arp]
[plumb]

The **ifconfig** command is used to turn an Ethernet interface on and off from a software point of view. If **root** executes the **ifconfig** command, it reports the Ethernet address of the system. The **ifconfig** command may be used to change the net mask or broadcast address. Figure 3.8 illustrates some examples of using the **ifconfig** command.

shiva#

shiva# ifconfig -a

lo0: flags=849<UP,LOOPBACK,RUNNING,MULTICAST> mtu 8232
    inet 127.0.0.1 netmask ff000000
le0: flags=863<UP,BROADCAST,NOTRAILERS,RUNNING,MULTICAST> mtu 1500
    inet 192.136.118.54 netmask ffffff00 broadcast 192.136.118.255
    ether 8:0:20:21:20:e1

ganesh#

ganesh# ifconfig le0

le0: flags=62<UP,BROADCAST,NOTRAILERS,RUNNING>
    inet 131.107.20.1 netmask ffffff00 broadcast 131.107.20.0
    ether 8:0:20:f:aa:d9

lakshmi#

**lakshmi# ifconfig le0   131.107.20.5   netmask   255.255.255.128   broadcast \
131.107.20.255**

Figure 3.8 Using the **ifconfig** command.

3.3.2 netstat

The **netstat** command displays the contents of various network-related data structures in various formats; it may be thought of as a command that displays information about packets processed by your system on the network. The format of the **netstat** command is

netstat [-adgimnprsMv] [-I interface] [interval] [system] [core]

The **netstat** command with the **-a** option shows the state of all sockets. Typically, with the **-a** option, sockets used by server processes are not shown. The **-i** option shows the state of interfaces that have been autoconfigured. **-n** shows network addresses in a dotted decimal format. The **-n** option is commonly used with the **-r** option. The **-r** option displays routing tables; **-s** shows per-protocol, such as IP, TCP, and ICMP, statistics. The **-s** option when used with the **-r** option displays network statistics.

The display for each socket shows the local and remote addresses, the send and receive queue sizes (in bytes), the protocol, and the internal state of the protocol. Figures 3.9 to 3.11 illustrate information received using the **-a**, **-d**, and **-g** options, respectively. Note that TCP sockets may be in one of the following states:

CLOSED	The socket is not being used.
LISTEN	Listening for incoming connections.
SYN_SENT	Actively trying to establish a connection.
SYN_RECEIVED	Initial synchronization of connection underway.
ESTABLISHED	Connection has been established.
CLOSE_WAIT	Remote shutdown; waiting for the socket to close.
FIN_WAIT_1	Socket closed. Shutting down connection.
CLOSING	Closed; then remote shutdown–awaiting acknowledgment.
LAST_ACK	Remote shut down, then closed–awaiting acknowledgment.
FIN_WAIT_2	Socket closed, waiting for shutdown from remote.
TIME_WAIT	Wait for close for remote shutdown retransmission.

A commonly used option with the **netstat** command is **-i**. This option shows the state of the interfaces that have been autoconfigured and an example is given in Figure 3.12.

The **-m** option provides information on buffers used for packets, as can be seen in the example of Figure 3.13.

The **-n** option reports Internet addresses as numbers and not symbols. See Figure 3.14 for an example. Figure 3.15 gives sample information using the **-p** option.

The **-r** option displays the system's routing tables. See Figure 3.16 for an example.

The **-s** option provides information on packets processed by your system. Figures 3.17 and 3.18 describe example of using the **-s** and **-v** options, respectively, with the **netstat** command.

```
#
# netstat  -a
UDP
Local Address          State
```

Local Address	State
*.route	Idle
.	Unbound
*.sunrpc	Idle
.	Unbound
*.32771	Idle
localhost.domain	Idle
nirvana.domain	Idle
*.domain	Idle
*.name	Idle
*.biff	Idle
*.talk	Idle
*.time	Idle
*.echo	Idle
*.32772	Idle
*.discard	Idle
*.daytime	Idle
*.32773	Idle
*.chargen	Idle
*.32774	Idle
*.32775	Idle
*.32776	Idle
nirvana.syslog	Idle
*.32777	Idle
*.32778	Idle
*.32785	Idle
*.lockd	Idle
*.32780	Idle
*.32781	Idle
*.32782	Idle
.	Unbound
*.761	Idle
.	Unbound

TCP

Local Address	Remote Address	Swind	Send-Q	Rwind	Recv-Q	State
.	*.*	0	0	8576	0	IDLE
*.sunrpc	*.*	0	0	8576	0	LISTEN
*.32780	*.*	0	0	8576	0	IDLE
*.domain	*.*	0	0	8576	0	LISTEN

Figure 3.9 Command example, **netstat -a**.

*.ftp	*.*	0	0	8576	0	LISTEN
*.telnet	*.*	0	0	8576	0	LISTEN
*.shell	*.*	0	0	8576	0	LISTEN
*.login	*.*	0	0	8576	0	LISTEN
*.exec	*.*	0	0	8576	0	LISTEN
*.uucp	*.*	0	0	8576	0	LISTEN
*.finger	*.*	0	0	8576	0	LISTEN
*.time	*.*	0	0	8576	0	LISTEN
*.echo	*.*	0	0	8576	0	LISTEN
*.discard	*.*	0	0	8576		LISTEN
*.daytime	*.*	0	0	8576	0	LISTEN
*.chargen	*.*	0	0	8576	0	LISTEN
*.32771	*.*	0	0	8576	0	LISTEN
*.32772	*.*	0	0	8576	0	LISTEN
*.lockd	*.*	0	0	8576	0	BOUND
*.32773	*.*	0	0	8576	0	LISTEN
*.smtp	*.*	0	0	8576	0	LISTEN
*.6000	*.*	0	0	8576	0	LISTEN
*.32774	*.*	0	0	8576	0	LISTEN
localhost.32776		16340	0	16384	0	FIN_WAIT_2
localhost.32773						
localhost.32773		16384	0	16340	0	CLOSE_WAIT
localhost.32776						
*.762	*.*	0	0	8576	0	LISTEN
.	*.*	0	0	8576	0	IDLE

Active UNIX domain sockets

Address	Type	Vnode	Conn Addr	
fc371400	stream-ord	0	fc36f600	/tmp/.X11-unix/X0
fc36f600	stream-ord	0	fc371400	
fc358e00	stream-ord	0	fc366100	/tmp/.X11-unix/X0
fc366100	stream-ord	0	fc358e00	
fc359300	stream-ord	0	fc359a00	/tmp/.X11-unix/X0
fc359a00	stream-ord	0	fc359300	
fc357700	stream-ord	0	fc357f00	/tmp/.X11-unix/X0
fc357f00	stream-ord	0	fc357700	
fc354900	stream-ord	0	fc352200	/tmp/.X11-unix/X0
fc352200	stream-ord	0	fc354900	
fc34f100	stream-ord	0	fc34f400	/tmp/.X11-unix/X0
fc34f400	stream-ord	0	fc34f100	
fc351500	stream-ord	0	fc351c00	/tmp/.X11-unix/X0
fc351c00	stream-ord	0	fc351500	
fc34d400	stream-ord	0	fc34ed00	/tmp/.X11-unix/X0

Figure 3.9 continued.

```
fc34ed00      stream-ord      0        fc34d400
fc346100      stream-ord      0        fc342200 /tmp/.X11-unix/X0
fc342200      stream-ord      0        fc346100
fc342900      stream-ord      5 0      /tmp/.X11-unix/X0
```

Figure 3.9 continued.

```
#
# netstat -d

msg 1:     group = 263     mib_id = 0      length = 16
msg 2:     group = 263     mib_id = 5      length = 384
msg 3:     group = 262     mib_id = 0      length = 192
msg 4:     group = 262     mib_id = 13     length = 1512
msg 5:     group = 260     mib_id = 0      length = 128
msg 6:     group = 261     mib_id = 0      length = 132
msg 7:     group = 1025    mib_id = 0      length = 36
msg 8:     group = 1026    mib_id = 0      length = 44
msg 9:     group = 260     mib_id = 20     length = 144
msg 10:    group = 260     mib_id = 100    length = 88
msg 11:    group = 1026    mib_id = 1      length = 0
msg 12:    group = 1026    mib_id = 2      length = 0
msg 13:    group = 260     mib_id = 21     length = 1344
msg 14:    group = 260     mib_id = 22     length = 240

mibgetgetmsg() 15 returned EOD (level 0, name 0)

---- Entry 1 ----
Group = 263, mib_id = 0, length = 16, valp = 0x27d58
0 records for tcpConnEntryTable:

---- Entry 2 ----
Group = 263, mib_id = 5, length = 384, valp = 0x28d00
6 records for tcpConnEntryTable:

---- Entry 3 ----
Group = 262, mib_id = 0, length = 192, valp = 0x28e88
3 records for tcpConnEntryTable:

---- Entry 4 ----
Group = 262, mib_id = 13, length = 1512, valp = 0x39358
27 records for tcpConnEntryTable:
```

Figure 3.10 Command example, **netstat -d**.

TCP

Local Address	Remote Address	Swind	Send-Q	Rwind	Recv-Q	State
localhost.32776	localhost.32773	16340	0	16384	0	FIN_WAIT_2
localhost.32773	localhost.32776	16384	0	16340	0	CLOSE_WAIT

Active UNIX domain sockets

Address	Type	Vnode	Conn Addr	
fc384e00	stream-ord	0	fc371500	/tmp/.X11-unix/X0
fc371500	stream-ord	0	fc384e00	
fc358e00	stream-ord	0	fc366100	/tmp/.X11-unix/X0
fc366100	stream-ord	0	fc358e00	
fc359300	stream-ord	0	fc359a00	/tmp/.X11-unix/X0
fc359a00	stream-ord	0	fc359300	
fc357700	stream-ord	0	fc357f00	/tmp/.X11-unix/X0
fc357f00	stream-ord	0	fc357700	
fc354900	stream-ord	0	fc352200	/tmp/.X11-unix/X0
fc352200	stream-ord	0	fc354900	
fc34f100	stream-ord	0	fc34f400	/tmp/.X11-unix/X0
fc34f400	stream-ord	0	fc34f100	
fc351500	stream-ord	0	fc351c00	/tmp/.X11-unix/X0
fc351c00	stream-ord	0	fc351500	
fc34d400	stream-ord	0	fc34ed00	/tmp/.X11-unix/X0
fc34ed00	stream-ord	0	fc34d400	
fc346100	stream-or	0	fc342200	/tmp/.X11-unix/X0
fc342200	stream-ord	0	fc346100	
fc342900	stream-ord	50	/tmp/.X11-unix/X0	

Figure 3.10 continued.

\#
\# netstat -g

Group Meberships

Interface	Group	RefCnt
lo0	224.0.0.1	1
le0	224.0.0.1	1

Figure 3.11 Command example, **netstat -g**.

netstat -i

Name	Mtu	Net/Dest	Address	Ipkts	Ierrs	Opkts	Oerrs	Collis	Queue
lo0	8232	loopback	localhost	172	0	172	0	0	0
le0	1500	192.136.118.0	nirvana	7080	0	150	7	0	0

Figure 3.12: Command example, netstat -i.

#

netstat -m

streams allocation:

	current	cumulative allocation		failures	
		maximum	total		
streams	156	160		1150	0
queues	948	960		4802	0
msg	152	279		244177	0
linkblk	6	6		6	0
strevent	6	6		6	0
strcallbparam	0	0		0	0

145 Kbytes allocated for streams msgs

Figure 3.13 Command example, **netstat -m**.

#

netstat -n

TCP

Local address	Remote Address	Swind	Send-Q	Rwind	Recv-Q	State
127.0.0.1.32776	127.0.0.1.32773	16340	0	16384	0	FIN_WAIT_2
127.0.0.1.32773	127.0.0.1.32776	16384	0	16340	0	CLOSE_WAIT

Active UNIX domain sockets

Address	Type	Vnode	Conn Addr	
fc384e00	stream-ord	0	fc371500	/tmp/.X11-unix/X0
fc371500	stream-ord	0	fc384e00	

Figure 3.14 Command example, **netstat -n**.

```
fc358e00     stream-ord    0        fc366100 /tmp/.X11-unix/X0
fc366100     stream-ord    0        fc358e00
fc359300     stream-ord    0        fc359a00 /tmp/.X11-unix/X0
fc359a00     stream-ord    0        fc359300
fc357700     stream-ord    0        fc357f00 /tmp/.X11-unix/X0
fc357f00     stream-ord    0        fc357700
fc354900     stream-ord    0        fc352200 /tmp/.X11-unix/X0
fc352200     stream-ord    0        fc354900
fc34f100     stream-ord    0        fc34f400 /tmp/.X11-unix/X0
fc34f400     stream-ord    0        fc34f100
fc351500     stream-ord    0        fc351c00 /tmp/.X11-unix/X0
fc351c00     stream-ord    0        fc351500
fc34d400     stream-ord    0        fc34ed00 /tmp/.X11-unix/X0
fc34ed00     stream-ord    0        fc34d400
fc346100     stream-ord    0        fc342200 /tmp/.X11-unix/X0
fc342200     stream-ord    0        fc346100
fc342900     stream-ord    5        0 /tmp/.X11-unix/X0
```

Figure 3.14 continued.

\#

\# netstat -p

Net to Media Table

Device	IP Address	Mask	Flags	Phys Addr
le0	nirvana	255.255.255.255	SP	08:00:20:21:20:e1
le0	224.0.0.0	240.0.0.0	SM	01:00:5e:00:00:00

Figure 3.15 Command example, netstat -p.

\#

\# netstat -r

Routing Table:

Destination	Gateway	Flags	Ref	Use	Interface
localhost	localhost	UH	0	57	lo0
192.136.118.0	nirvana	U	3	4	le0
224.0.0.0	nirvana	U	3	0	le0

Figure 3.16 Command example, netstat -r.

\#

\# netstat -s

UDP

        udpInDatagrams = 28   udpInErrors = 0
        udpOutDatagrams = 44

TCP

        tcpRtoAlgorithm = 4   tcpRtoMin = 200
        tcpRtoMax = 60000   tcpMaxConn = −1
        tcpActiveOpens = 5   tcpPassiveOpens = 5
        tcpAttemptFails = 1   tcpEstabResets = 6
        tcpCurrEstab = 1   tcpOutSegs = 231
        tcpOutDataSegs = 190   tcpOutDataBytes = 13178
        tcpRetransSegs = 10   tcpRetransBytes = 65
        tcpOutAck = 41   tcpOutAckDelayed = 28
        tcpOutUrg = 0   tcpOutWinUpdate = 0
        tcpOutWinProbe = 0   tcpOutControl = 19
        tcpOutRsts = 1   tcpOutFastRetrans = 0
        tcpInSegs = 309
        tcpInAckSegs = 195   tcpInAckBytes = 13186
        tcpInDupAck = 10   tcpInAckUnsent = 0
        tcpInInorderSegs = 186   tcpInInorderBytes = 12530
        tcpInUnorderSegs = 0   tcpInUnorderBytes = 0
        tcpInDupSegs = 0   tcpInDupBytes = 0
        tcpInPartDupSegs = 0   tcpInPartDupBytes = 0
        tcpInPastWinSegs = 0   tcpInPastWinBytes = 0
        tcpInWinProbe = 0   tcpInWinUpdate = 88
        tcpInClosed = 0   tcpRttNoUpdate = 5
        tcpRttUpdate = 184   tcpTimRetrans = 22
        tcpTimRetransDrop = 0   tcpTimKeepalive = 58
        tcpTimKeepaliveProbe = 0   tcpTimKeepaliveDrop = 0

IP   ipForwarding = 2   ipDefaultTTL = 255
        ipInReceives = 425   ipInHdrErrors = 0
        ipInAddrErrors = 0   ipInCksumErrs = 0
        ipForwDatagrams = 0   ipForwProhibits = 0
        ipInUnknownProtos = 0   ipInDiscards = 0
        ipInDelivers = 329   ipOutRequests = 150
        ipOutDiscards = 0   ipOutNoRoutes = 0
        ipReasmTimeout = 60   ipReasmReqds = 0
        ipReasmOKs = 0   ipReasmFails = 0

Figure 3.17 Command example, **netstat -s**.

```
                ipReasmDuplicates = 0           ipReasmPartDups = 0
                ipFragOKs = 0                   ipFragFails = 0
                ipFragCreates = 0               ipRoutingDiscards = 0
                tcpInErrs = 0                   udpNoPorts = 234
                udpInCksumErrs = 0              udpInOverflows = 0
                rawipInOverflows = 0

ICMP            icmpInMsgs = 19                 icmpInErrors = 0
                icmpInCksumErrs = 0             icmpInUnknowns = 0
                icmpInDestUnreachs = 16         icmpInTimeExcds = 0
                icmpInParmProbs = 0             icmpInSrcQuenchs = 0
                icmpInRedirects = 0             icmpInBadRedirects = 0
                icmpInEchos = 2                 icmpInEchoReps = 1
                icmpInTimestamps = 0            icmpInTimestampReps = 0
                icmpInAddrMasks = 0             icmpInAddrMaskReps = 0
                icmpInFragNeeded = 0            icmpOutMsgs = 18
                icmpOutDrops = 0                icmpOutErrors = 0
                icmpOutDestUnreachs = 16        icmpOutTimeExcds = 0
                icmpOutParmProbs = 0            icmpOutSrcQuenchs = 0
                icmpOutRedirects = 0            icmpOutEchos = 0
                icmpOutEchoReps = 2             icmpOutTimestamps = 0
                icmpOutTimestampReps = 0        icmpOutAddrMasks = 0
                icmpOutAddrMaskReps = 0         icmpOutFragNeeded = 0
                icmpInOverflows = 0

IGMP:
        0 messages received
        0 messages received with too few bytes
        0 messages received with bad checksum
        0 membership queries received
        0 membership queries received with invalid field(s)
        0 membership reports received
        0 membership reports received with invalid field(s)
        0 membership reports received for groups to which we belong
        0 membership reports sent
```

Figure 3.17 continued.

\#

\# **netstat -v**

TC
Local/Remote
Address   Swind   Snext   Suna   Rwind   Rnext   Rack   Rto   Mss State

---

Figure 3.18 Command example, **netstat -v**.

localhost.32776 localhost.32773 16340 9992cc2e 9992cc2e 16384 9993c601 9993c601 200 8192 FIN_WAIT_2
localhost.32773 localhost.32776 16384 9993c601 9993c601 16340 9992cc2e 9992cc2e 512   8192 CLOSE_WAIT
Active UNIX domain sockets

Address	Type	Vnode	Conn Addr
fc384e00	stream-ord	0	fc371500 /tmp/.X11-unix/X0
fc371500	stream-ord	0	fc384e00
fc358e00	stream-ord	0	fc366100 /tmp/.X11-unix/X0
fc366100	stream-ord	0	fc358e00
fc359300	stream-ord	0	fc359a00 /tmp/.X11-unix/X0
fc359a00	stream-ord	0	fc359300
fc357700	stream-ord	0	fc357f00 /tmp/.X11-unix/X0
fc357f00	stream-ord	0	fc357700
fc354900	stream-ord	0	fc352200 /tmp/.X11-unix/X0
fc352200	stream-ord	0	fc354900
fc34f100	stream-ord	0	fc34f400 /tmp/.X11-unix/X0
fc34f400	stream-ord	0 1	fc34f100
fc351500	stream-ord	0	fc351c00 /tmp/.X11-unix/X0
fc351c00	stream-ord	0	fc351500
fc34d400	stream-ord	0	fc34ed00 /tmp/.X11-unix/X0
fc34ed00	stream-ord	0	fc34d400
fc346100	stream-ord	0	fc342200 /tmp/.X11-unix/X0
fc342200	stream-ord	0	fc346100
fc342900	stream-ord	5 0	/tmp/.X11-unix/X0

Figure 3.18 continued.

3.3.3 arp

The **arp** command displays and modifies the Internet-to-Ethernet address translation tables used by the address resolution protocol. The format of the **arp** command is

>**arp hostname**
>arp -a
>arp -d hostname
>arp -s hostname ether_addr [temp] [pub] [trail]
>arp -f filename

Figure 3.19 is an example of executing the **arp** command with the **-a** option:
   To delete an entry from the arp cache, enter

shiva# arp -d ngt.com

ngtui{pabrai}: **arp -a**

Net to Media Table

Device	IP Address	Mask	Flags	Phys Addr
le0	nirvana	255.255.255.255	SP	08:00:20:21:20:e1
le0	224.0.0.0	240.0.0.0	SM	01:00:5e:00:00:00

Figure 3.19 Command example, **arp -a**.

3.3.4 nslookup

The **nslookup** command is an interactive program used to query Internet domain name servers. The user has the option of requesting a specific name server to provide information about a given host or get a list of all hosts in a given domain. The **nslookup** command format is

nslookup [-l] [address]

The **-l** option specifies that the local host's name server should be used instead of the servers in **/etc/resolv.conf**. Figure 3.20 presents a few examples using the **nslookup** command.

% nslookup nathan

Server:	ngtui.ngt.com
Address:	200.101.201

Name:	nathan.ngt.com
Address:	200.101.20.2

To get a list of all nodes in a given domain, execute the following sequence of commands:

% **nslookup**
> **ls ngt.com > ngtdomain.lis**
> **exit**
%

To determine the host name associated with a given Internet address, enter:

Figure 3.20 Using the **nslookup** command.

```
% nslookup
> set query=ptr
> 2.20.101.200.in-addr.arpa

Server:              ngtui.ngt.com
Address:             200.101.20.1

2.20.101.200.in-addr.arpa host name = nathan.ngt.com
>
```

Figure 3.20 continued.

3.3.5 hostname

The **hostname** command prints the name of the current host, as given before the system "login" prompt. The host name is typically determined when the **/etc/rc.local** file is executed. The information on the host name is maintained in the file **/etc/hostname.xx0**, where *xx0* refers to the interface type. The Ethernet interface for Sun workstations is typically *le0*, whereas for Tadople SPARCbook computer it is *ni0*. Execute the **netstat** command with the **-i** option to determine the Ethernet device type for your system. For example,

/usr/ucb/hostname nirvana

3.3.6 domainname

The **domainname** command may be used to set or display the name of the current network information service domain. The command syntax is

    domainname [name-of-domain]

If used without an argument, **domainname** displays the name of the current domain. The information about the domain name is maintained in the file **/etc/defaultdomain**. For example,

    % **domainname**
    ngt.com

3.3.7 rpcinfo

The **rpcinfo** command reports RPC-related information. **rpcinfo** executes an RPC call to communicate with the RPC server–the information received is then reported. The command format is

rpcinfo   [-m] [-s] host
           [-p] host

The [-m] [-s] **host** format results in a listing of all services that have registered with the *rpcbind* process on the **host** system. The [-s] option displays information in a concise format.

The command format **rpcinfo -p [host]** lists all RPC services registered with *rpcbind*, version 2. For examples using the **rpcinfo** command see Figure 3.21.

% rpcinfo
  displays all RPC services registered on the local host.

% rpcinfo ganesh
  displays all RPC services registered with *rpcbind* on node **ganesh**.

% rpcinfo -s ganesh

  displays information in a concise format - information is organized according to the following columns:

  * program
  * version (s)
  * netid (s)
  * service
  * owner

  To get a listing of all RPC services registered with version 2 of the *rpcbind* protocol on the local system, enter:

% rpcinfo -p

Figure 3.21 Using the rpcinfo command.

3.3.8 uname

The **uname** format command is

  uname [-snrvmap]
  uname [-S system name]

For example,

$ uname -a
SunOS nirvana 5.3 Generic_101674-01 sun4m sparc

3.3.9 telnet

The **telnet** command allows you to log on to another node on the network—the node may be on a LAN or a WAN, it does not matter. The command format is

telnet [host]

If you execute the **telnet** command with no options it enters the command mode. In this mode it accepts and executes a number of different commands. Some of these commands are **open host**, **close**, and **status**. An example of using the **telnet** command is

% **telnet shiva.ngt.com**

If you just enter **telnet**, you are at the **telnet** command prompt. At this point you may enter **open node-name** to connect to a system on your network. To return to the **telnet** command prompt, enter the escape character (which is, typically, ^]). At the **telnet** command prompt you can enter **z** to return to the local system. To reconnect to the remote system, enter **fg**. The command **telnet** uses TCP as the transport protocol. The well-known port associated with the **telnet** command is port number 23.

3.3.10 rlogin

The command **rlogin** is the BSD remote login command, and it provides the ability to log in to a remote system without specifying a password. It authenticates the login request by checking, on the remote system, the **/etc/hosts.equiv** and **~/.rhosts** files. If the host name of the system requesting the connection is not in these files, then **rlogin** will prompt the user to enter a password. Otherwise **rlogin** continues with the login request and connects the user to the remote system. The **rlogin** command format is

rlogin [-l username] hostname

The **-l username** option is used when the user name associated with the system requesting the connection and the user name on the remote system are not the same. For example, if user *uday* on **node1** is executing the **rlogin** command to connect to **node2** and the account on **node2** is not *uday* but *pabrai*, then in this case the command executed may look like

% **rlogin -l pabrai node2**

The command **rlogin** uses the services of TCP at the transport layer. The port number associated with **rlogin** is 513.

3.3.11 ftp

The *file transfer protocol* (FTP) is used to exchange files between systems on a TCP/IP network. The command **ftp** also provides access to directories and files of local and remote hosts. In addition, FTP can convert among character representations such as EBCDIC and ASCII. The **ftp** command syntax is

ftp [-dgomtv] [hostname]

Figure 3.22 is an example of an **ftp** session.

Commands that are typically executed in a **ftp** session are:

get	to receive a file from the remote system;
put	to send a file to the remote system;
mget	to receive multiple files from the remote system;
mput	to transfer multiple files to the remote system;
type	to indicate whether the file about to be transferred is ASCII or binary.

The command **ftp** uses the services of TCP at the transport layer. The port numbers associated with **ftp** are 20 and 21. Port number 21 is used to transfer command information, and port number 20 is for data transfer. If you need to view a file, before transferring it from one system to another, use the **get** command. For example,

ftp> **get**   README.TXT   -

This will result in the file, README.TXT, displayed on your system.

```
ganesh{pabrai} 1:ftp nathan
Connected to nathan.ngt.com
220 nathan FTP server (SunOS 4.1) ready.
Name (nathan:pabrai):
331 Password required for pabrai
Password:
230 User pabrai logged in.
ftp> ?
Commands may be abbreviated; they are:
!              cr            macdef         proxy         send
$              delete        mdelete        sendport      status
account        debug         mdir           put           status
append         dir           mget           pwd           sunique
ascii          disconn       mkdir          quit          tenex
bell           form          mls            quote         trace
binary         get           mode           recv          type
bye            glob          mput           remotehelp    user
case           hash          nmap           rename        verbose
cd             help          ntrans         reset         ?
cdup           lcd           open           rmdir         close
ls             prompt        runique
```

Figure 3.22 An FTP session.

```
ftp> pwd
257"/home/pabrai" is current directory.
ftp> lcd
Local directory now /home0/pabrai
ftp> type ascii
200 Type set to A.
ftp> get .login login.nathan
200 PORT command successful.
150 ASCII data connection for .login
(131.101.20.1,1040) (2768 bytes).
226 ASCII Transfer complete.
local: login.nathan remote: .login
2879 bytes received in 0.054 seconds (52 Kbytes/s)
ftp> quit
```

Figure 3.22 continued.

3.3.12 rcp

The **rcp** command is similar to the UNIX **cp** command, except that **rcp** is used to transfer files between two systems. The basic file transfer syntax is

    rcp   from-file   to-file

The syntax for the **rcp** command may vary from one machine to another. The **rcp** command works like the **rlogin** and **rsh** commands: it checks on the remote system files, **/etc/hosts.equiv** and **.rhosts** (in the user's home directory). If the host name of the local system is specified in those files it proceeds with the execution of the command. Note that, with the **ftp** command, the user has to enter the user name and password associated with their remote account. With **rcp**, authentication is based on the **/etc/hosts.equiv** or the **.rhosts** files.

The following is an example of transferring a file, **sysnodelist.txt**, to the **network** subdirectory on the remote system **natasha**:

    % rcp sysnodelist.txt natasha:~/network

3.3.13 Command Execution: rsh

The **rsh** command may be used to execute commands on a remote system, without logging onto that system first.

The **rsh** or *remote shell* command connects to the specified host name and executes the command requested. As with **rcp** and **rlogin**, **rsh** expects to find the name of the local system listed in the **/etc/hosts.equiv** or **.rhosts** files. The **rsh** command format is

    rsh hostname [-l username] [-n] [command]

The **-l username** option is used if the remote user name is different from the local user name. The **-n** option is used if you need to redirect the input of **rsh** to **/dev/null**. You sometimes need to do this to avoid interaction between **rsh** and the shell that invokes the command. An example of using the **rsh** command is

% **rsh natasha ls -l /home/swprj**

In this example, the user is interested in getting a listing of files in the **/home/swprj** directory on the remote node **natasha**. Note that if you execute the **rsh** command without specifying a command to be executed on the remote node, **rsh** logs you in the remote system (similar to the case with **rlogin**).

3.3.14 snoop

The **snoop** command may be executed on Sun systems to capture packets off the network. The command format is

```
snoop
        [ -a ]                  # Listen to packets on audio (/dev/audio).
        [ -d device ]           # settable to le?, ie?, bf?, tr?
        [ -s snaplen ]          # Truncate packets.
        [ -c count ]            # Quit after count packets.
        [ -P ]                  # Turn OFF promiscuous mode. Only broadcast,
                                # multicast or packets addressed to the host
                                # system are captured.
        [ -D ]                  # Report dropped packets.
        [ -S ]                  # Report packet size.
        [ -i file ]             # Read previously captured packets.
        [ -o file ]             # Capture packets in file specified.
        [ -n file ]             # Load addr-to-name table from file.
        [ -N ]                  # Create addr-to-name table.
        [ -t [ r|a|d ] ]        # Time: Relative, Absolute or Delta.
        [ -v ]                  # Verbose packet display.
        [ -V ]                  # Show all summary lines.
        [ -p first[,last] ]     # Select packet(s) to display.
        [ -x offset[,length] ]  # Hex dump from offset for length.
        [ -C ]                  # Print packet filter code.
```

   [filter expression]

Figure 3.23 describes examples using the **snoop** command.

Thus, **snoop** captures packets and displays their contents. Captured packets may be displayed as they are received or saved to a file for later inspection.

Let us look at some more examples. To capture and display packets as they are received, enter:

snoop

To capture packets with host **shiva** as either the source or destination and display them as they are received, enter:

snoop shiva

To look at a specific packet (say packet 11) in detail, enter (note that the packet was previously captured in file, **packet.txt**)

snoop   -i   packet.txt   -v   -p11

#

snoop -d le0

Using device le0 (promiscuous mode)

(PING packets captured by snoop)

    nirvana -> 192.136.118.207   ICMP Echo request
192.136.118.207 -> nirvana   ICMP Echo reply

(FTP Packets captured by snoop).

192.136.118.207 -> nirvana   FTP C port=2318
    nirvana -> 192.136.118.207   FTP R port=2318
192.136.118.207 -> nirvana   FTP C port=2318
    nirvana -> 192.136.118.207   FTP R port=2318 220 nirvana FTP serv
192.136.118.207 -> nirvana   FTP C port=2318
192.136.118.207 -> nirvana   FTP C port=2318 USER suresh\r\n
    nirvana -> 192.136.118.207   FTP R port=2318 331 Password require
    nirvana -> 192.136.118.207   FTP R port=2318 331 Password require
192.136.118.207 -> nirvana   FTP C port=2318
    ? -> (broadcast) ETHER   Type=FFFF (Unknown), size = 60 bytes
192.136.118.207 -> nirvana   FTP C port=2318 PASS tamilarasi\r\n
    nirvana -> 192.136.118.207   FTP R port=2318
    nirvana -> 192.136.118.207   FTP R port=2318 230 User suresh logg
192.136.118.207 -> nirvana   FTP C port=2318

Figure 3.23 Using the **snoop** command.

```
192.136.118.207 -> nirvana          FTP C port=2318 QUIT\r\n
    nirvana -> 192.136.118.207      FTP R port=2318 221 Goodbye.\r\n
192.136.118.207 -> nirvana          FTP C port=2318
    nirvana -> 192.136.118.207      FTP R port=2318
    nirvana -> 192.136.118.207      FTP R port=2318
192.136.118.207 -> nirvana          FTP C port=2318
    ? -> *      ETHER Type=0001 (LLC/802.3), size = 60 bytes
    ? -> *      ETHER Type=587B (Unknown), size = 60 bytes
```

Figure 3.23 continued.

3.4 INTERNET RESOURCES

As discussed earlier, the Internet network interconnects thousands of local area, wide area, and national networks. SRI International's *Network Information Systems Center* (NISC) provides information on Internet access.

A book titled *Internet: Getting Started* is available from NISC. It describes in detail information on dial-up access and procedures. SRI NISC may be reached at 415-859-6387 or at nis@nisc.sri.com. You can also obtain information on Internet access from the *NSFNET Network Service Center* (NNSC) at 617-873-3400 or at **nnsc@nnsc.nsf.net**.

The Internet provides access to electronic bulletin boards covering a large number of subjects. Today, there are several thousand news groups. Each group is organized in a hierarchical manner, wherein the root of each tree is focused on a major topic. The major roots are:

- alt;
- comp;
- gnu;
- misc;
- news;
- rec;
- sci;
- soc;
- talk.

Many programs are available to provide an interface to the new groups. These include **rn**, **nn**, **xrn**, and **trn**. The bulletin boards can also be accessed by non-UNIX systems such as PCs, VAX/VMS systems, and Macintoshes.

The *Commercial Internet Exchange* (CIX) consortium is an organization that includes several midlevel and commercial network providers whose objective is to offer unrestricted, unlimited access to the Internet. CIX may be reached at 703-204-8000 or at **info@cix.org**. Today, sites interested in having access to the Internet must choose from competing providers such as PSI, UUnet Technologies, and Netcom. Refer to the appendix section of this text, for a more detailed listing of Internet service providers. Table 3.2 summarizes resources that are widely used on the Internet.

3.4.1 ftp anonymous Accounts and Request For Comment (RFC) Documents

ftp anonymous accounts are typically maintained by sites that wish to make information available to users. This information may include public domain software and documentation. For access to an **anonymous ftp** account, enter

% **ftp node-name**
FTP>**user anonymous**
FTP>password: *******

Enter your e-mail address as the password (for example, pabrai@ngt.com). The host, **nis.nsf.net**, is an example of a **ftp anonymous** account.

Information on the Internet such as architecture, protocols, or current developments can be found in a series of reports referred to as *request for comments* (RFCs). Each RFC has a number associated with it. Once an RFC is assigned a number and made available to the public, its contents do not change. Future RFCs may and frequently do contain revisions and updates to RFCs written earlier. At present, more than 1,700 RFCs describe network protocols such as TCP, UDP, IP, RIP, SNMP, and emerging new technologies. RFCs that may be of interest to new users of the Internet are:

- *RFC 1175*: A Bibliography of Internetworking Information;
- *RFC 1180*: A TCP/IP Tutorial;
- *RFC 1206*: Answers to Commonly Asked "New Internet User" Questions;
- *RFC 1208*: A Glossary of Networking Terms.

A hard copy of each RFC may be obtained from SRI International's NISC at 415-859-6387 (approximate cost, $12 per RFC). You can also get a SRI TCP/IP CD that includes all RFCs and associated source code for software for about $195. If you would like to receive information on new RFCs, you can request to be added to the RFC announcement distribution list by sending e-mail to **rfc-request@nic.ddn.mil**.

You can get copies of RFCs on-line by logging into an **ftp anonymous** account such as **nic.ddn.mil** and then **cd** to the rfc directory (**cd rfc**).

3.4.2 User Information Commands

On UNIX systems, the two commands typically used to provide some information about users are **finger** and **who**.

Table 3.2
Internet Resources

Internet Resources	Description
ftp anonymous Accounts	ftp anonymous accounts are typically maintained by sites that need to make information available to users. This information may include public domain software and documentation. *To access an ftp anonymous account*, use ftp client software on your system.

Archie	Archie servers help you *find ftp anonymous sites that have a file or directory of interest to you*. Typically, the Archie service is used before accessing ftp anonymous accounts. There are approximately 25 Archie servers world-wide. *You can access Archie in the following ways*:
	    * TELNET in to an Archie server
	    * Use Archie client software on your system

Gopher	Gopher is a *menu-driven utility for searching text information* on the Internet. There are over 5,000 Gopher servers - each one is administered locally. You can access Gopher in the following ways:
	    * TELNET in to a Gopher server system.
	    * Specify the GOPHER URL via Mosaic. For example, **gopher://gopher.micro.umn.edu.**

Veronica	Veronica is a tool designed to *track menus maintained by all Gopher servers world-wide*. Veronica may be used to search for keywords on menus on all Gopher servers. The result is a custom menu based on the keyword specified. In January 1995, over 5050 gopher servers were indexed - over 15 million items were indexed. *Veronica is accessed through Gopher client software.*
Jughead	Jughead, like Veronica, also tracks menus from Gopher servers - however, Jughead *narrows the search to a small area of gopherspace*.
Wide Area Information Service (WAIS)	WAIS is a *document indexing system* that is extremely useful for accessing large collections of text. The *user specifies key words for a search and indicates the sources* over which the search should be performed. To access WAIS, you can: * Use WAIS client software on your system
World Wide Web (WWW)	Referred to as the Web or W3 is a *hypertext-based tool* that enables you to access and display data based on keyword searches. The data may be text, graphics, audio, or video. Hypertext, is the key element, since it supports links to other documents. To access WWW, use Mosaic and specify a WWW URL.

finger

The **finger** command displays information about users, such as login name, full name, terminal name, idle time, login time, and location. The command format is

finger [options] name

The **finger** command reads the ~/.**plan** and ~/.**project** files to provide more information about the user. Figure 3.24 is an example of the use of the **finger** command.

% finger smith

Login name:smith   In real life: Tom Smith
Directory: /home/smith   Shell:/bin/csh
On since Feb 28 13:58:23 on ttyp2

No unread mail
No Plan.
%

Figure 3.24 Using the **finger** command.

who

The **who** command, if used without arguments, lists the login name, terminal name, and login time for each user. The command **who** gets this information from the **/etc/utmp** file. If a filename argument is specified, then **who** examines that file to provide information. The command syntax is

who [who-file] [am i]

The **who am i** command indicates who you are logged in as; it displays your host name, login name, terminal name, and login item. The following are some examples of the **who** command:

whoami
root

who am i
nathan!pabrai ttypl Feb 28 12:38

who
pabrai console Feb 228 12:38

3.5 SUMMARY

In this chapter, we examined critical elements necessary to connect a UNIX system to the network. These elements included:

- Files;
- Processes (daemons);
- Commands.

It is important for the system or network administrator to be comfortable with the format and content of files such as:

- /etc/hosts;
- /etc/protocols;
- /etc/ethers;
- /etc/bootptab;
- /etc/services;
- /etc/netmasks;
- /etc/inetd.conf.

Access to UNIX systems on the network is controlled, to a large extent, by entries in these files. These files are looked at by various network-related processes. Each process performs a certain function; for example, the *routed* process implements the *routing information protocol* (RIP). UNIX systems provide support for TCP/IP application layer protocols in the form of processes.

We then examined various network-related commands. These commands can be very useful when you are troubleshooting problems on the network. For example, if you need to determine the Ethernet address of a system and know the Internet address, you can use a combination of the **ping** and **arp** commands to figure out the Internet–Ethernet address mappings. We further discussed the various ways in which you can gain access to UNIX host on the network. Commands such as **telnet** and **rlogin** may be used to log in to UNIX systems, and commands such as **ftp** and **rcp** may be executed to transfer files between UNIX nodes.

Since UNIX provides built-in support for the TCP/IP protocol stack, if you have access to the Internet, it is relatively easy to use your system to access resources on the global network.

UNIX is Internet ready. It has been for a long time.

For example, you can access **ftp anonymous** accounts on the Internet. These accounts are a repository of valuable information: RFCs, public domain software, and documentation. You can use your Mosaic browser to work with applications such as WAIS, gopher and WWW. Finally, commands such as **finger** and **who** provide information about users accessing your UNIX system.

REFERENCES

[1] Nemeth et al., *UNIX System Administration Handbook*, Englewood Cliffs, NJ: Prentice-Hall, 1989.
[2] Pabrai et al., *Understanding and Using Computer Networks*, second edition, Fermilab, Computing Division Document GG0009, September 1991.

SELECT BIBLIOGRAPHY

Stern, H., *Managing NFS and NIS*, Sebastopol, CA: O'Reilly & Associates, 1991.

Distributed Computing   4

Application layer technologies such as the *network file system* (NFS), *network information service* (NIS), NIS+, and the *domain name service* (DNS) are key to successfully share resources in a client/server computing environment. While NFS enables systems on the network to share resources such as disk drives and CD-Rom drives, NIS and NIS+ are used to centralize the management of UNIX system administration files such as **/etc/passwd** and **/etc/ethers**. NIS+ is the new version of NIS and includes several new features such as hierarchical namespace and enhanced security. The primary purpose of DNS is to centralize the management and distribution of Internet addresses. An understanding of NFS, NIS, NIS+, and DNS is important in order to manage and maintain UNIX systems on a TCP/IP network. That is the emphasis of this chapter.

Figure 4.1 illustrates the environments that support protocols such as NFS, NIS, NIS+, and DNS.

While NFS has been implemented on just about very operating system that is available on the market, NIS and NIS+ run mostly on UNIX hosts. DNS is supported on most systems that support TCP/IP.

4.1 NETWORK FILE SYSTEM (NFS)

This section details the specifics associated with the network file system (NFS) protocol. First the protocol is related to the OSI/RM. Next, a summary of NFS procedures is provided, which describes all the things that one can do with the NFS protocol. We address the question: What are the critical files, processes, and commands with which one needs to work to configure a UNIX system as a NFS server or a client? and take a look at changes expected in the new release of NFS–NFS Version 3.

4.1.1 Design and Working

NFS, designed and developed by Sun Microsystems, was introduced in 1984. It enables computer systems to *export* (make available) and *import* (gain access to) file systems and peripheral devices. Thus, file systems of remote hosts

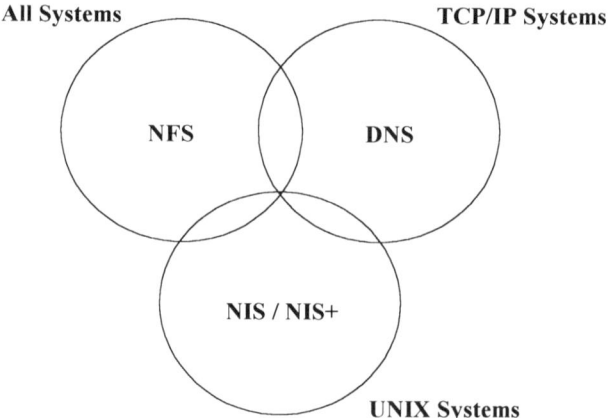

Figure 4.1 NFS, NIS, NIS+, and DNS and systems supported.

appear as though they are attached to the local system. With NFS it is possible for several systems to share the same set of files and directories. The underlying protocols used by NFS are *remote procedures calls* (RPC) and external data representation. Although XDR corresponds to the presentation layer of the OSI/RM, RPC provides the functionality of the session layer. Figure 4.2 describes the relationship between NFS, RPC, XDR, and the OSI/RM.

Today, NFS may be used on almost any computer system including the IBM MVS and VM and Digital's VMS and OSF (UNIX) and in MAC and PC environments. NFS should be viewed as a facility for sharing files in a heterogeneous environment of processors, operating systems, and networks [1].

NFS is designed in terms of a set of procedures, arguments, and their results and effects. It uses the RPC mechanisms to implement remote services. The underlying protocols used by NFS include UDP at the transport layer and IP at the network layer.

4.1.2 Stateless Protocol

NFS is referred to as a *stateless protocol*. A stateless protocol does not keep track of past requests. Thus, each procedure call contains all the information necessary to complete the call. The server does not *remember* past requests. If the server crashes, the client system repeats NFS requests until a response is received. The server does not do any crash recovery. If the client crashes, no recovery is necessary for either the client or the server. Complex recovery transactions between the server and the client systems are thus avoided. Note that the client cannot tell the difference between a server that has crashed and recovered and a slow server.

Application	FTP / Telnet / NFS / NIS
Presentation	XDR
Session	RPC
Transport	TCP / UDP
Network	Internet Protocol (IP)
Data link	Ethernet / Token Ring / FDDI
Physical	Ethernet / Token Ring / FDDI

Figure 4.2 NFS, XDR, RPC, and the OSI/RM.

4.1.3 NFS Procedures

A user may perform a number of different actions on an exported file system, which may include functions such as directory lookup, reading a file, or writing a file. NFS implements these requests in the form of procedures. Because NFS protocol is a stateless protocol, most of the complexity resides in the client software. Note that files are represented by file handles. In other words, for a NFS client to request a NFS server to perform some operation, it needs to tell the server the file handle associated with the file. The NFS server supplies the client the file handle in the first place–clients remember file handles. Table 4.1 summarizes NFS procedures defined in NFS version 2.

4.1.4 BSD UNIX and NFS

We examine the key files, daemons, and commands associated with NFS- on BSD-based UNIX systems, such as SunOS 4.1.3 or ULTRIX systems.

Table 4.1
NFS Procedures

NFS Procedure	Description
null()	Ping server and measure round trip time
lookup()	Returns a new file handle for the named file in a directory
create()	Creates a new file and returns its file handle and attributes
remove()	Removes a file from the directory
getattr()	Returns file attributes
setattr()	Sets the mode, UID, GID, size, access time, and modify time of a file
read()	Returns data from a file; returns file attributes
write()	Writes data to a file; returns file attributes
rename()	Changes name of (moves) a file
link()	Creates a link to a file on the remote host
symlink()	Creates a symbolic link to a file on the remote host
readlink()	Returns the string that is associated with the symbolic link file
mkdir()	Creates a directory on the remote host and returns the new file handle attributes
rmdir()	Removes the empty directory from the parent directory
readdir()	Reads the contents of a directory on the remote host
fsstat()	Returns file system information such as block size and number of free blocks

Critical Files

/etc/fstab

This file describes which file systems are available to be remotely mounted. The file **/etc/fstab** is used at boot time to make available file systems specified in this file. The file **/etc/rc.boot** usually contains the **mount** command with the **-a** option, and this causes the operating system to mount all devices and files specified in **/etc/fstab**.

/etc/mtab

This file contains a list of file systems currently mounted on the local system.

/etc/exports

This file contains a list of file systems on the local system that are to be exported to remote systems using NFS. This file determines if the local system is a NFS server.

/etc/xtab

This files contains the list of currently exported file systems for the local host. Information is placed in the **/etc/xtab** file by the **exportfs** command when it is executed.

/etc/host

This files contains the list of host names and their corresponding Internet addresses. The **exportfs** command checks the **/etc/hosts** or **/etc/netgroup** file to determine the Internet addresses named in the **/etc/exports** file.

/etc/netgroups

This file contains the list of network groups. The information in the file is used for remote mount permission checking.

Critical Daemons

The following are key daemon processes in an NFS environment. Daemons are processes that typically run in the background and are owned by **root**.

/usr/etc/nfsd

The command */usr/etc/nfsd* 8 starts up eight copies of the NFS daemon on the NFS server host to service client file system access requests.

/usr/etc/biod

The command */usr/etc/biod* 4 starts four copies of the asynchronous block I/O daemon, biod, on a NFS client. The *biod* daemon enables a client to make read-ahead and write-behind requests to a remote file system. These requests are buffered to improve NFS performance.

/usr/etc/rpc.mountd

This daemon responds to requests from remote computer systems to mount a local file system. The daemon checks the **/etc/xtab** file to determine what files are available for mounting; if available, it allows NFS access requests and then provides information on file systems via the **showmount** command. The *rpc.mountd* daemon must be running on a NFS server system for the client mount request to succeed.

Critical Commands

Commands such as **exportfs, mount, showmount,** and **nfsstat** are typically used for NFS resources on BSD-based UNIX systems.

/usr/etc/exportfs

This command is typically run at boot time by the **rc.local** script. It is used to export or make available, for mounting, a set of local file systems. **rc.local** reads the **/etc/exports** file and places a list of file systems to be exported in the **/etc/xtab** file. The format of the command is

/usr/etc/exportfs   [options]   directory-name

If the **-a** option is used, then it implies that all directories listed in the **/etc/exports** file are to be exported. The **-u** option is used to "unexport" specified directories. The **-o** option may be used to specify options that you can also execute in the **/etc/exports** file (options such as **ro**, **rw**, and **access**). To *unexport* all file systems or directories previously exported, enter **exportfs -ua**.

/usr/etc/mount

The **mount** command is used to attach a remote file system to a local directory. The **mount** command may be used to mount a local disk drive as well as NFS file systems. A list of mounted file systems is maintained in **/etc/mtab**. The command format is

/usr/etc/mount   [switches]   [-t type]   [-o options]   filesystem   dir

Executing the **mount** command without any parameters will display a list of mounted file systems. The command **mount -a** results in an attempt to mount all file systems listed in **/etc/fstab**. The following example provides information on all mounted file systems on host *natasha* (note that node *nathan* is the server and *natasha* is the client system).

   % **mount**

   nathan:/export/root/natasha on / type nfs (rw)
   nathan:/export/exec/sun4.sunos.4.1.1 on / usr type nfs (ro)
   nathan:/export/exec/kvm/sun4c.sunos.4.1.1 on /usr/kvm type nfs (ro)
   /dev/sd0g on /home1 type 4.2 (rw,noquota)

nathan:/export/share/sunos.4.1.1 on /usr/share type nfs (rw)
nathan:/usr/products on /usr/products type nfs (rw)

/usr/etc/showmount

The **showmount** command is used to determine which system has mounted a file system from a given host. The format of this command is

/usr/etc/showmount [-ade] [server-node]

The default for host is the host name for the local system. The command **showmount -a** displays all file systems that have been mounted from the server node. The command **showmount -e** displays the list of all exported file systems. The following example provides information on all the file systems exported by host *nathan*.

% **showmount -e nathan**

export list for nathan:

/home0	(everyone)
/usr	(everyone)
/home	(everyone)
/export/root/natasha	natasha
/export/swap/natasha	natasha
/usr/products	natasha
/var/macnfs	(everyone)

/usr/etc/nfsstat

The **nfsstat** command is used to obtain usage statistics for NFS and RPC interfaces to the kernel on the local host. The command provides information on how efficient the local system has been in servicing requests. Figure 4.3 is an example of the output of **nfsstat**.

Server rpc:

calls	badcalls	nullrecv	badlen	xdrcall
0	0	0	0	0

Server nfs:

calls	badcalls
0	0

Figure 4.3 Using the nfsstat command.

null	getattr	setattr	root	lookup	readlink	read
0 0%	0 0%	0 0%	0 0%	0 0%	0 0%	0 0%
wrcache	write	create	remove	rename	link	symlink
0 0%	0 0%	0 0%	0 0%	0 0%	0 0%	0 0%
mkdir	rmdir	readdir	fsstat			
0 0%	0 0%	0 0%	0 0%			

Client rpc:

calls	badcalls	retrans	badxid	timeout	wait	newcred	timers
14248	0	3	0	3	0	0	60

Client nfs:

calls	badcalls	nclget	nclsleep
14244	0	14244	0

null	getattr	setattr	root	lookup	readlink	read
0 0%	4459 31%	385 2%	0 0%	5463 38%	644 4%	2072 14%
wrcache	write	create	remove	rename	link	symlink
0 0%	221 1 %	157 1%	94 0%	25 0%	15 0%	0 0%
mkdir	rmdir	readdir	fsstat			
16 0%	0 0%	686 4%	7 0%			

Figure 4.3 continued.

4.1.5 SVR4 UNIX and NFS

The UNIX SVR4 operating system supports the NFS standard. The file with which one needs to work to export file systems and directories is **/etc/dfs/dfstab**. When the system is rebooted and enters run level 3 it reads the **dfstab** file and makes available file systems or directories to nodes on the network. As far as client nodes are concerned, you can specify in the **/etc/vfstab** file the file systems to be mounted at boot time (including NFS file systems).

Typically, to start and stop NFS on SVR4 systems, enter at the command prompt

sh   /sbin/init.d/nfs start

or

sh   /sbin/init.d/nfs stop

In the following section we examine critical NFS files, daemons, and commands on a Solaris 2.x system. Solaris 2.x is UNIX SVR4 compliant.

Critical Files

/etc/init.d/nfs.client

This file contains the necessary shell scripts to start up an NFS client on a Solaris system. The arguments *start* and *stop* can be used to start and stop an NFS client. A typical command line is

sh /etc/init.d/nfs.client start (to start the NFS client)
sh /etc/init.d/nfs.client stop (to stop the NFS client)

NFS servers and clients may also be started during system start-up time by having appropriate entries in the **/etc/rc*** scripts. Typically these get done during the installation of the software itself. On SVR4 systems, there is a single file, **/etc/init.d/nfs**, that is used to start both an NFS server and a client.

/etc/vfstab

The command **mountall** executed during the start-up time of an NFS client (by the **/etc/init.d/nfs.client** procedure) reads the file and mounts all file systems specified in this file. An example **vfstab** file is

nathan:/home   -   /home   nfs   -   yes   -
nathan:/var/spool/mail   -   /var/mail   nfs   -   yes   -

The first field of the **/etc/vfstab** file specifies the device (file system) to be mounted. If the file system is an NFS file system it will assume the form <*machine_name*>:<*file_system_name*>. The second field describes the device on which to perform **fsck** (file system check). This field is applicable only to local file systems and is typically represented by a '-'. The next field indicates the local directory on which to mount the remote file system. The fourth field specifies the file system type. Note that the **/etc/vfstab** file can be used to mount other types of file systems as well (for example, **ufs**). The fifth field is used for **fsck** purposes–it is not relevant for NFS-related file systems. The sixth field specifies whether the file system should be mounted at boot time. A "yes" in this field will indicate to **mountall** to mount the remote file system; a "no" implies that the file system will not be mounted at boot time. The next field is for options to be used with the **mount** command.

/etc/init.d/nfs.server

This file contains the necessary shell scripts to start up an NFS server on a Solaris system. The arguments "start" and "stop" can be used to start and stop an NFS server.

sh /etc/init.d/nfs.server start   (to start the NFS client)
sh /etc/init.d/nfs.server stop   (to stop the NFS client)

/etc/dfs/dfstab

Entries specified in the **/etc/dfs/dfstab** file are shared (exported) automatically whenever NFS operation is started. The **dfstab** file lists all the resources that the server shares with its clients and controls which clients may mount a resource. Each time the system enters run level 3, the system reads the **dfstab** file to determine which resources are shared automatically.

Each entry in the **dfstab** file contains a **share** command that signifies a file system to be shared with remote systems. The **shareall** command that gets executed from the server start-up script (**/etc/init.d/nfs.server**) reads the above file and exports all the entries listed in the file. The format of entries in the **dfstab** file is

share   [-F fstype] [-o options]   [-d "<text"> <path name>   [resource]

For example,

share -F   nfs -o rw -f   "home directories"   /d0

The commands **unmountall** and **unshareall** serve as complements to the **mountall** and "**shareall**" described mentioned above. The **mount** and **umount** commands may be used to manually mount and unmount remote file systems. Super-user privileges are required to use the commands.

/etc/mnttab

This file system contains a list of file systems currently mounted on the local system.

/etc/dfs/fstypes

The **fstypes** file registers the distributed file system packages you have installed on your system. It allows you to define one as a default.

/etc/dfs/sharetab

The **sharetab** file logs the resources currently shared on your system. This file is created by the **share** command.

Critical Daemons

/usr/lib/nfs/nfsd

The command */usr/lib/nfs/nfsd* 8 starts up eight copies of the NFS daemon on the NFS server host to service client file system access requests.

/usr/lib/nfs/mountd

This daemon responds to requests from remote computer systems to mount a local file system. The *mountd* daemon must be running on the server system for the client mount request to succeed.

Critical Commands

/usr/sbin/share

The **share** command allows you to make a resource available for mounting by clients. This command may also be used to display a list of resources that are currently shared on the system. For example,

share   -F   nfs   -o   ro   /opt/metrix

/usr/sbin/unshare

This command enables you to unexport a previously exported resource. For example,

unshare   -F   nfs   /opt/metrix

/usr/bin/shareall

The **shareall** command executes a script that shares a predetermined set of resources. For example,

cat > nfs.test
share -F nfs -o, rw=engr-group /opt/tcpip
share -F nfs /export/home/nathan
^D

shareall nfs.test

This results in both resources, **/opt/tcpip** and **/export/home/nathan**, being exported to nodes on the network.

/usr/sbin/mount

The **mount** command allows you to mount a remote resource on your system. This command is executed on the system that is to be set up as an NFS client host. You can also use the **mount** command to display a list of resources, local and remote, that are currently mounted. The **mount** synopsis is

mount [-F nfs] [-r] [-m] [-o specific_options] [-O] resource | mount_point

The options commonly used are specified important ones and are detailed in the following list. Option lists can be specified by separating individual options with commas.

- **rw | ro**: The file system is mounted read-write or read-only. The default is read-write.
- **rsize=n**: set the read buffer size to "n" bytes.
- **wsize=n**: set the write buffer size to "n" bytes.

For example,

mount -F nfs nathan:/opt /opt/nathan

/usr/sbin/umount

This command allows you to unmount a previously mounted file system.

umount /opt/nathan

/usr/sbin/mountall

The **mountall** command executes a script that mounts a predetermined set of resources. If you create a file on the NFS client that specifies the file systems to be mounted, then you could mount all those resources by using the **mountall** command.

mountall -F nfs filename

The filename is the name of the script that specifies which file systems are to be mounted.

/usr/sbin/umountall

This command executes a script that unmounts all currently mounted resources.

umountall -k

The **-k** option indicates that all processes with files open when the **umountall** command is executed are to be killed.

/usr/sbin/dfshares

The **dfshares** command displays a list of remote resources that are available to you, as well as a list of local resources that are currently shared.

dfshares -F nfs natasha

/usr/sbin/dfmounts

This command gives you a list of which local resources are mounted on a client basis.

dfmounts -F nfs natasha

This gives you a listing of systems that are mounting the server's NFS resources.

4.1.6 NFS Server Configuration

To configure a system as an NFS server, you need to work with NFS files, processes, and commands. First, the processes that must be running on the server include *nfs, mountd, lockd,* and *statd*. Second, you need to create or modify NFS server configuration files such as **/etc/exports** on a BSD system or **dfstab** on a SVR4 platform. And third, the command that you execute is **exportfs** with the **-a** option on a BSD system or the **shareall** command on a SVR4 host, which exports all file systems specified in the NFS server file.

The *mountd* daemon is designed to handle the bootstrap problem, where the client system notifies the server that it will be using files and the sever in turn authenticates the client request. The server returns to the client a *file handle*. A *file handle* may be viewed to be a piece of data that the client will present on future requests so that the server knows which file is being referenced.

The NFS daemon, *nfsd,* handles all incoming NFS requests and responds. Typically, an NFS server system may have up to eight daemons running; therefore, up to eight simultaneous NFS operations can be processed.

4.1.6.1 Export Rules and Regulations

The following four rules apply to an NFS server system [2].

- If a file system is exported then none of its subdirectories can be exported, unless the subdirectory exists on a different partition.

- Any file system or a proper subset of a file system can be exported from a server. A proper subset of a file system is a file or directory tree that exists below the mount point of the file system.
- Only local file systems can be exported.
- The parent directory of a file system cannot be exported unless the parent is on a different partition.

An Example: Exporting File Systems

BSD UNIX System. The following is an example of an entry in the **/etc/exports** file

/home   -access=natasha, root=natasha

In this example, the client nodes *natasha* can mount the **/home** file system. The **access** option specifies what systems are authorized to mount the file system. The **root** option indicates that the super-user privilege for that file system is given only to the node specified. To export all file systems specified in the **/etc/exports** file, execute the **exportfs** command with the **-a** option.

SVR4 UNIX System. The **dfstab** file lists all the resources that the server shares with its clients and controls which clients may mount a resource. For example,

share -F nfs -o rw -f "home directories" /export/home

After the **dfstab** file has been modified, you can execute the **shareall** command to have the file systems available to nodes on the network. For example,

shareall -F nfs

4.1.7 NFS Client Configuration

To configure a BSD UNIX system as an NFS client, you need to modify the **/etc/fstab** file. Specify in the **/etc/fstab** file, the file systems or directories that the client is to mount. Next, mount points need to be defined on the client host. On a SVR4 UNIX system, you will work with the **/etc/vfstab** file.

An Example: Importing File Systems

BSD UNIX System. The following is an example of an entry in the **/etc/fstab** file on the client system:

nathan:/home /home nfs rw 0 0

After this file is executed at boot time, the server's home file system is mounted on the mount point **/home** (on the client system). To create a mount point for a client file system, use the **mkdir** command; for example, **mkdir /home**.

SVR4 UNIX System. To configure a system as a NFS client, you need to modify the **/etc/vfstab** file on a SVR4 UNIX host. An example **vfstab** file is shown below.

natasha:/home   - /home   nfs - yes -
natasha:/var/spool/mail   - /var/mail nfs - yes -

4.1.8 NFS Automounter

The automounter is a daemon that allows users to access remote file systems by mounting required file systems on a need basis.

How Does it Work?

automount can be started from the command line or the system initialization file. It forks a daemon to serve the mount points specified in the automount maps. The daemon sleeps until a request is made by the user to access a file. The daemon intercepts user requests and mounts appropriate directories. The mount points for the newly mounted file systems are always under **/tmp_mnt**. Note that the **/tmp_mnt** directory gets created by the automounter if it does not exist. After a pre-determined amount of idle time (the default is five minutes), the automounter unmounts the remote file system.

Automounter Maps

The automounter, unlike the **mountall** command, does not use the **/etc/vfstab** file. Instead, it uses a set of files called *maps* that contain information about remote file systems. However, an entry is made in the **/etc/mnttab** file every time a remote file system is mounted or unmounted. Maps are of three different kinds:

- Master maps;
- Direct maps;
- Indirect maps.

Besides these, there is a special map called *hosts*. Master maps contain information about direct and indirect maps. Each entry in the master map file contains a direct or indirect map name, its path, and its mount options. A direct map closely resembles the **/etc/vfstab** file. The special mount point "/-" is specified in the master map when specifying an entry for a direct map as a directive not to associate entries in the direct map with any directory. The mount points are fully specified in the direct map itself.

As mentioned earlier, the automounter can be started either on the command line or with an entry in the **/etc/init.d/nfs.client** file. If a file name representing the master map is not specified on the command line, the automounter looks for the file **/etc/auto_master** to read entries for direct and indirect maps. If such a file does not exist, the automounter quits without taking any action.

Automounter Files

The automounter does not require any special files on the server side. The *mount* daemon does not care whether the request came from the automounter or from the **mount** command itself. Note that all the files mentioned below are required only at the client side.

/etc/auto_master

The automounter looks for the file **/etc/auto_master** to read entries for direct and indirect maps. A typical **/etc/auto_master** file is presented in Figure 4.4.

In the file of Figure 4.4 **/etc/auto_direct** is a reference to a direct map, **/etc/auto_home** is a reference to an indirect map, and **-hosts** is a reference to the hosts map. It is not necessary that a **/etc/auto_master** file contain all the above entries. Entries that are not required may be commented out. The mount point "/-" was discussed earlier. The mount point **/home** is the directory under which the entries listed in /etc/auto_home are to be mounted. Note that the automounter mounts all directories under **/tmp_mnt** (unless, otherwise specified). Therefore, for a user *shiva,* a link will be made from **/home/shiva** to **/tmp_mnt/home/shiva.**

We mentioned earlier that **hosts** is a special map. Consider the following: if on a machine, say *machine1,* a user types the command **cd /net/machine2,** the automounter checks to see if *machine2* is in the hosts database (**/etc/hosts**) and, if so, mounts all the file systems exported by *machine2*. This will put the user in the **root** directory of *machine2*. Again, note that the file systems will

```
# auto master file showing entries for direct, indirect, and host map files.

/-           /etc/auto_direct   -ro
/home/etc/auto_home             -rw, secure
/net         -hosts
```

Figure 4.4 An example **/etc/auto_master** file.

be actually mounted in **/tmp_mnt**, but a link will be made from **/net**. No special files are needed to specify this map as the **hosts** database is used

/etc/auto_direct

An example of a typical direct map file is shown in Figure 4.5. As mentioned already, direct map files have close resemblance to the **/etc/vfstab** file. However, the number of fields per entry is not the same as in **/etc/vfstab** because of the fact that automounter mounts only NFS file systems. A typical **/etc/auto_direct** file may look like that in Figure 4.5.

If there are any mount options to be specified, the file will assume the form

\# example /etc/auto_direct file with mount options

/home   -ro   nathan:/home

Figure 4.6 is an example of a typical indirect map.

If user "nathan's" home directory is **/home/nathan**, whenever, he logs in, the directory **/export/home/nathan** from *ruby* will be mounted as **/tmp_mnt/home/nathan** and a link will be made from **/home/nathan** to it. The ampersand character used in Figure 4.6 is used to replace the key ("key" is a path name of the mount point in a direct map and is a simple name in an indirect map) where ever it appears. Without the ampersand, the entries would have assumed the form

    natasha   ruby:/export/home/nathasha
    nathan   -rw   ruby:/export/home/uday

As can be seen from prior discussion, the automounter is an excellent utility to mount remote file systems on a need basis. The only obvious problem is that when we use the **hosts** map file to mount remote file systems, all exported files

\# example /etc/auto_direct file.

/home   nathan:/home
/var/mail   nathan:/var/spool/mail

Figure 4.5 An example **/etc/auto_direct** file.

\# example /etc/auto_home file on host nathan
natasha   ruby:/export/home/&
nathan   -rw   ruby:/export/home/&

Figure 4.6 An example **/etc/auto_home** file.

on the remote file system are mounted. The automounter has no way of knowing which particular file system the user wishes to access. This can be better illustrated with an example.

Assume that on host *ruby* the following file systems are exported **/d0**, **/d1**, **/d2**, and **/d3**. If on the machine *nathan,* a user types **cd /net/nathan**, *nathan*'s automount program mounts **/d0**, **/d1**, **/d2**, and **/d3** while the user may be wishing to access only files in the **/d0** file system.

automount Command

Options that can be used with the **automount** command are

automount [-t duration] -v

The **-v** option implies verbose output. Using the **-t** option, the default idle time can be altered.

4.1.9 NFS: Future Direction

In the very near future, NFS version 3 will be supported on most systems. Important features of NFS version 3 include:

- Improved performance;
- Supports safe asynchronous writes—allowing for asynchronous write operations improves performance;
- Support for new file types.

There are 22 procedures that are defined as a part of NFS. Table 4.2 describes all procedures that are a part of NFS version 3; new NFS version 3 procedures are in bold text.

New procedures that are a part of NFS version 3 provide the following additional capabilities:

- Check access permissions;
- Create a special device;
- Extended read from directory (*readdirplus()*): This procedure gets additional information that a normal *readdir()* call would not return;
- Get dynamic file system information—lets you determine information such as the number of free blocks in a file system;
- Get static file system information—let's you determine the size of the file system;
- Retrieve POSIX information;

Table 4.2
NFS Version 3 Procedures

NFS Procedure	Description
null()	Ping server and measure round trip time
lookup()	Returns a new file handle for the named file in a directory
create()	Creates a new file and returns its file handle and attributes
remove()	Removes a file from the directory
getattr()	Returns file attributes
setattr()	Sets the mode, UID, GID, size, access time, and modify time of a file
read()	Returns data from a file; returns file attributes
write()	Writes data to a file; returns file attributes
rename()	Changes name of (moves) a file
link()	Creates a link to a file on the remote host
symlink()	Creates a symbolic link to a file on the remote host
readlink()	Returns the string that is associated with the symbolic link file
mkdir()	Creates a directory on the remote host and returns the new file handle attributes
rmdir()	Removes the empty directory from the parent directory
readdir()	Reads the contents of a directory on the remote host
fsstat()	Returns file system information such as block size and number of free blocks
access()	Check access permission
mknod()	Create a special device
readdirplus()	Extended read from directory
fsinfo()	Get static file system information
pathconf()	Retrieve POSIX information
commit()	Commit cached data on a server to stable storage

- Commit cached data on a server to stable storage. This function works in conjunction with the *write*() operation–if the write operation specifies an asynchronous operation, the server need not commit the data to stable storage before returning. The commit operation enables the client to direct the server to commit data to stable storage.

4.2 NETWORK INFORMATION SERVICE (NIS OR YP)

In this section we take a look at the network information service (NIS). NIS is an extremely useful protocol, at the application layer, to manage client/server configurations of UNIX systems. NIS+ is an enhancement made to NIS primarily to handle large client/server system configurations. We examine key NIS files, processes, and commands and understand how to set up NIS and NIS+ server and client systems.

4.2.1 Motivation for NIS

The *Network Information Service,* formerly known as *yellow pages,* is a distributed database system that provides a uniform storage and retrieval method for various objects and resources on the network. Instead of managing files such as **/etc/hosts**, **/etc/passwd**, **/etc/group**, and **/etc/ethers**, NIS provides the ability to maintain one database for each file on a central server.

By running the NIS service, the system manager can distribute administrative databases among a variety of hosts and update those databases from a centralized location in an automatic and reliable manner, thus ensuring that all clients share the same databases consistently throughout the network.

The NIS services make the process of updating network databases much simpler. Therefore, if you add a new system to the network, only one file on the central server needs to be modified. The information from this file is then propagated to the rest of the network.

4.2.2 Terminology

NIS domain	An NIS domain shares a common set of NIS maps. Each domain has a domainname. Each host belongs to a domain; machines belonging to the same domain share the same maps.
NIS server	An NIS server is a machine with a disk storing a set of NIS maps that it makes available to network hosts.
Master server	The master server contains a set of maps that are updated by the system manager as necessary.
Slave server	A slave server has a copy of the master's set of NIS maps. Whenever the master server's maps are updated, it propagates the updates among the slave servers. The existence of slave servers enables the system manager to evenly distribute the load implied in answering NIS requests. The NIS master and slave servers are also referred to as *NIS servers.*
NIS clients	NIS clients run processes that request data from maps on the servers.
NIS maps	All NIS maps are located in a separate distinct directory, **/var/yp/domainname**, on the server. Thus, if the domain name is *engineering,* the maps for the master server system would be located in **/var/yp/ engineering**.

Note that the master server system is responsible for all map maintenance and distribution to the slave server.

4.2.3 Client/Server Model

The network information service is based on a client/server model. NIS clients and servers are processes that run on multiple systems. The information distributed by NIS is stored in sets of database files referred to as *maps*. A set of NIS maps is used for each NIS domain. An NIS *domain* describes a set of systems that have access to the same NIS master server and share the same set of NIS maps. A NIS domain is different from an Internet domain name, system domain, or the Sendmail domain.

Each domain can have only one master server. The **domainname** command indicates the name of the NIS domain. The *getdomainname()* system call returns the name of the domain to the program that called it.

For DEC ULTRIX systems the **/etc/svc.conf** file defines the order in which name services are queried by the system; that is, it defines whether the name server, NIS hosts map, or the **/etc/hosts** file is referenced to resolve a host name. The key components of NIS are:

- Domains;
- Maps;
- Daemons (processes);
- Utilities;
- Maintenance commands.

4.2.4 NIS Files

After an NIS master server is configured, the following files are replaced in whole or in part by NIS maps:

- **/etc/hosts**;
- **/etc/passwd**;
- **/etc/group**;
- **/etc/networks**;
- **/etc/netmasks**;
- **/etc/ethers**;
- **/etc/services**;
- **/etc/aliases**;
- **/etc/protocol**.

4.2.5 NIS Maps

In the **/var/yp** directory of the NIS master server, exists a **makefile**. This file calls the *makedbm* utility to create NIS maps. The utility *makedbm* creates two files: (1) var/yp/domainname/mapname.dir and (2) /var/yp/domainname/mapname.pag.

The *.dir* map specifies an index file, and the *.pag* file describes a data file. Table 4.3 provides a description of NIS maps that typically exist on a master server system.

4.2.6 Modifying and Propagating NIS Maps

The following steps must be followed in order to make changes to files such as **/etc/hosts** or **/etc/passwd**.

Table 4.3
NIS Maps on a Master Server System

Map Name	*Description*
bootparams	Path names of files that client systems need to boot (e.g., root and swap); appends to **/etc/bootparams**
ethers.byaddr	Ethernet addresses and names; replaces **/etc/ethers**
ethers.byname	Same as **ethers.byaddr** except index is by machine name
group.bygid	Group information wth GID as key; appends to **etc/group**
group.byname	Group information with group name as index
hosts.byaddr	Host name and IP address is key; replaces **/etc/hosts**
hosts.byname	Host name is key
mail.aliases	Aliases and mail addresses. Aliases is used as key; appends to **/etc/aliases**
mail.byaddr	Mail address is used as the key
netgroup.byhost	Contains information on group name, user name, and host name; host name is used as key; replaces **/etc/netgroup**
netgroup.byuser	User name is used as key
netgroup	Group is the key
netid.byname	Used for UNIX style authentication; contains a machine name and mail address
netmasks.byaddr	network mask used with IP subnetting; replaces **/etc/netmask**
networks.byaddr	Names and IP addresses; replaces **/etc/networks**
networks.byname	network name is the key
passwd.byname	User name is the key; appends to **/etc/passwd**
passwd.byuid	UID is the key
protocols.byname	Network protocols known; replaces **/etc/protocols**
protocols.bynumber	Protocol number is key
publickey.byname	Used for secure RPC; replaces **/etc/publickey**
rpc.bynumber	RPC program numbers and names; replaces **/etc/rpc**
services.byname	Internet services available on system; replaces **/etc/services**

Step 1

Become a superuser on the master server.

Step 2

Edit the input file for the map that needs changing.

Step 3

Enter the following:

cd /var/yp
make

The **ypxfr** command will transfer updated maps from the NIS master server to slave systems. The command **ypxfr** handles map transfer in tandem with the *yppush* program. The **Makefile** in the **/var/yp** directory automatically runs *yppush*. The **ypxfr** command daemon on the NIS master server transfers the map only if the master copy is more recent than the local copy.

4.2.7 Configuring an NIS Master Server

The following steps describe the process of configuring a UNIX system as a NIS master server system.

Step 1

Establish the domain for your machines.

domainname research.ngt.com
domainname
research.ngt.com

The information for the NIS domain name is maintained in the file **/etc/defaultdomain**. Enter

cat > /etc/defaultdomain
research.ngt.com
CTRL/D
#

Step 2

Prepare files on the NIS master server.

- **/etc/hosts**: Should include the Internet address and host names of all systems that are a part of the NIS domain.
- **/etc/passwd**: If all user account information is stored in the **/etc/passwd** file, then the entry:
  +::0:0::
  is not required. If you would like to leave this entry in the **/etc/passed** file, then insert an asterisk (*) in the password field. Thus, the entry would look like:
  +:*:0:0::
- **/etc/group**: If an NIS marker entry +:*:* is inserted as the last line in the **/etc/group** file, then the system reads the global group database (map) after processing the local **/ect/group** file.
- **/etc/ethers**: Ascertain that the Ethernet addresses of all diskless and dataless nodes are in this file.
- **/etc/bootparams**: Contains a list of client entries that diskless clients use for booting. A client entry in the **/etc/bootparams** file supersedes an entry in the corresponding NIS map. Adding a + as the last line of the files tells the system to read the global NIS bootparams database (map) after it has finished processing the local **bootparams** file.

Step 3

Use the *ypinit* utility to initialize the master server. This converts all the input files into the dbm format that the NIS service expects.

cd /var/yp
(Create this directory if it does not exist.)
cp /usr/lib/NIS.Makefile /var/yp/Makefile
make
/usr/etc/yp/ypinit -m

The **ypinit** utility will then prompt for other hosts to become NIS servers. Note that there should be only one master server per NIS domain.

Step 4

Ascertain that the following lines are in the **/etc/rc.local** file.

**if [-f /usr/etc/ypserv -a -d /var/yp/'domainname']; then
   ypserv echo -n ' ypserv'
fi**

The *ypserv* process initiates the process of providing NIS service. To start the *ypserv* process immediately, enter

/usr/etc/ypserv

Step 5

Next, in the **/etc/rc.local** file, uncomment the line

ypxfrd; echo -n ' ypxfrd'

The *ypxfrd* daemon reacts to the **ypxfr** command that handles NIS map transfers. To start the NIS transfer daemon at the command prompt, enter

/usr/etc/ypxfrd

Step 6

In the **/etc/rc.local** file, remove the comment lines for *ypbind*. The entry should look like

if [-f /etc/security/passwd.adjunct]; then
   ypbind -s; echo -n ' ypbind'
else
   ypbind; echo -n ' ypbind'
fi

To start *ypbind* manually, enter

/usr/etc/ypbind

Step 7

Add the following lines to the **/etc/rc.local** file.

if [-f /usr/ect/rpc.yppasswdd -a -d /var/yp/'domainname']; then
   /usr/etc/rpc.yppasswdd /etc/passwd -m passwd
   echo -n ' yppasswdd'
fi

This starts the */etc/rpc.yppasswdd* process at boot time. To manually start this daemon, enter,

/usr/etc/rpc.yppasswdd /etc/passwd -m passwd

4.2.8 Configuring an NIS Slave Server

This subsection describes all the steps required to configure your system as a NIS slave server system.

Step 1

Establish the domain for your machines (it must be same as specified on the NIS master server system).

domainname research.ngt.com
domainname
research.ngt.com

Step 2

Use the *ypinit* utility to initialize the slave server. This converts all the input files into the dbm format that the NIS service expects.

cd /var/yp
/usr/etc/yp/ypinit -s master-server-name

Step 3

Ascertain that the following lines are in the **/etc/rc.local** file.

if [-f /usr/etc/ypserv -a -d /var/yp/'domainname']; then
   ypserv; echo -n ' ypserv'
fi

The *ypserv* process initiates the process of providing NIS service. To start the ypserv process immediately, enter

/usr/etc/ypserv

Step 4

Again, in the **/etc/rc.local** file, remove the comment lines for *ypbind*. The entry should look like

if [-f /etc/security/passwd.adjunct] ; then
   ypbind -s; echo -n ' ypbind'
else
   ypbind; echo -n ' ypbind'
fi

To start *ypbind* at the command prompt, enter

/usr/etc/ypbind

Note that when the new slave server is initialized, it transfers data from the master server's map files and builds its own copies of the maps; therefore make sure that any data in the NIS slave server's configuration files (**/etc/passwd**, **/etc/hosts**, ...) are in the NIS master server's database.

4.2.9 Configuring an NIS Client

This subsection describes all the steps necessary to configure your system as an NIS client.

Step 1

Establish the domain for your machines (it must be the same as specified on the NIS master server system).

domainname research.ngt.com
domainname
research.ngt.com

Step 2

Ascertain that the configuration files on the client (**/etc/passwd**, **/etc/hosts**, ...) include NIS "marker" entries (e.g., +:*:0:0::: for **etc/passwd**, +:*:* for **/etc/group**) so that the NIS map information will be added to the local client files.

Step 3

In the **/etc/rc.local** file, remove the comment lines for *ypbind*. The entry should look like

if [-f /etc/security/passwd.adjunct] ; then
   ypbind -s; echo -n ' ypbind'
else
   ypbind; echo -n ' ypbind'
fi

To start *ypbind* immediately, enter

/usr/etc/ypbind

4.2.10 About NIS Password Files

The purpose of the NIS service is to allow the system administrator to update files from one location. It is a good idea to keep the master password file separate from the NIS master server's local **/etc/passwd** file. Create another password file in the **/var/etc** directory, for example. The **/var/etc/passwd** file should have no entries for any of the system accounts (such as **root, bin, uucp**). It should contain only entries for user accounts. The **/var/etc/passwd** file is the global password file used to make the NIS password map.

The following is an example of the **/var/etc/passwd** file on the server node, **aurobindo**.

guruji:NjrOXdaeWbDLQ:106:100:NGuruji:/home/guruji:/bin/csh
ra:9MWyR1dh6bBcc:111:100:BRao:/home/rao:/bin/csh
.
.
.
dharma:FymnlNBfhdgs16:152:100ADharma:/home/dharma:bin/csh
pabrai:ZEXHHFgBqIEE.:170:30:UPabrai:/home/pabrai:/bin/sch

Note that the file **/var/yp/Makefile** must be modified to contain the following definition near the top:

PWDIR=/var/etc

Then every reference to (DIR)/passwd must be replaced with (PWDIR)/passwd.

Restricting Access

Whenever a user attempts to log onto a system, that machine's local **/etc/passwd** file is consulted first. A + entry as the last entry of the local **/etc/passwd** file indicates that the global NIS password map should be searched if no entry has been found for the user up to this point. Without the + entry as the last entry, the search will stop with the local **/etc/passwd** file.

Restricting access to clients or servers is a relatively easy task. Every machine has a local **/etc/passwd** file. Every user should have an entry in the global password file (**/var/etc/passwd** on the master server). To restrict access, do the following.

1. In the machine's local **/etc/passwd** file put only those user entries belonging to users who are authorized to have access to that particular system. They will still have entries in the global NIS password map (**/var/etc/passwd** on the master server).

2. Begin these entries with a + and blank the password field. The + indicates that the global NIS password map should be consulted for this particular user entry. It also causes the commands **passwd** and **yppasswd** to functionally do the same thing. The **passwd** command changes the local **/etc/passwd** file. If an entry begins with a +, the **passwd** command will

change the NIS password, which is what the command **yppasswd** does. Note that if a + begins an entry, then the password field should be blank.
3. Remove the + entry as the last entry in that machine's local **/etc/passwd** file.

Once these steps have been implemented, only users in that machine's local **/etc/passwd** file can log into that particular machine. The password information is taken from global NIS maps.

Let us consider the case where the local **/etc/passwd** file on a system includes the following entries.

+paramveer::1111:2222:User 1:/home/paramveer:/bin/csh
+karanveer::1112:2223:User 2:/home/karanveer:/bin/csh
+jaswinder::1113:2224:User 3:/home/jaswinder:/bin/csh

In this example, access is restricted. Only **paramveer**, **karanveer**, and **jaswinder** are allowed access to the local machine. Their password information is taken from the global NIS password map in **/var/etc/passwd** on the master server (assuming there is no + entry as the last entry in the local **/etc/passwd** file).

Unrestricted Access

To allow all users in the NIS global password map access to a particular machine, include the + entry as the last entry in that machine's local **/etc/passwd** file.

4.2.11 NIS Usage

The NIS service is transparent for the most part to the end user. There are a few commands that the user can execute to query NIS for information.

ypwhich Command

To find out which NIS server is currently providing service to a client, use the **ypwhich** command as follows:

$ **ypwhich [hostname]**

ypcat Command

To display values in a map use the **ypcat** command.

$ **ypcat ethers**

The above command displays the contents of the *e*thers NIS map.

$ **ypcat passwd**

This command displays the contents of the *passwd* map.

$ **ypcat hosts**

The above command lists the contents of the *hosts* map.

yppasswd Command

To modify your password use the **yppasswd** command. It behaves just like the **passwd** command, but it modifies the NIS *passwd* map.

$ **yppasswd**

(Changing NIS password for *natasha* on **aurobindo**.)
Old password:
New password:
Retype new password:
NIS entry changed on **aurobindo**.

The **passwd** command will behave exactly the same as the **yppasswd** command if your user name entry is included in the NIS global password maps and the local password files have been set up correctly by the system manager with a + as the first character of each entry. Otherwise, **passwd** will affect your local password only on the node you log into.

4.3 NIS+

NIS+ was designed to replace NIS. The main use of NIS+ is to help manage a large configuration of UNIX client/server systems. Information in the **hosts**, **passwd**, **group**, **ethers**, and other files can be managed by NIS+. NIS+ delegates administration of domains downward–similar to DNS. Unlike NIS, NIS+ accepts incremental updates to *replica systems*. Replica systems are backups to the master NIS+ server system. Once changes are made on the master server they are automatically propagated to replica servers and made available to the entire namespace.

NIS+ supports 16 predefined system tables. NIS+ tables can be accessed by any column–not just the first column; thus, you do not have duplicate tables (as in NIS). As far as security is concerned, every component in the namespace specifies the type of operation that it will accept and from whom (*authorization*)–further, every request is *authenticated*.

4.3.1 Definition of Terminology

We examine new terms introduced with NIS+ in this section. Terms discussed are:

- NIS+ namespace;
- NIS+ directories;
- NIS+ domains;
- NIS+ tables;
- Name service switch (switch);
- NIS+ server:
  - Master;
  - Replica;
- NIS+ clients.

NIS+ Namespace

The *NIS+ namespace* is a collection of network information. The namespace is hierarchical as opposed to the flat NIS namespace. The NIS+ namespace can be organized in a number of ways to meet organizational needs. The structural components of the namespace include:

- Directories;
- Tables;
- Groups.

These components are referred to as *NIS+ objects*. The objects can be arranged in a UNIX file, systemlike hierarchy. The objects in the NIS+ namespace are tables and groups. You can administer the namespace only with NIS+ administration commands. The names of objects in the NIS+ namespace are separated by dots.

NIS+ Directories

NIS+ directories hold NIS+ objects, including other directories, tables, and groups. The topmost directory in a namespace is the *root directory*. The directory objects below the root directory are just referred to as directories. A namespace may have several levels of directories. The directory below is called the *child directory*, while the one above is the *parent directory*. NIS+ directories that store NIS+ groups have the name *groups_dir*. Directories that store NIS+ tables have the name *org_dir*.

NIS+ Domains

NIS+ directories, tables, and groups in a namespace are arranged in a configuration known as *domains*. An NIS+ domain consists of the *groups_dir* directory and the *org_dir* directory. Thus, a given organization may have a marketing domain (Mktg.Netguru.Com.), engineering domain (Engr.Netguru.Com.), and a root domain (Netguru.Com.) There may be several NIS+ domains in an organization's namespace.

NIS+ Tables

NIS+ stores the network information in tables. The tables are different from the test files or NIS maps. They have column-entry, they have search path, and they can be linked with each other. *NIS+ tables* are stored in **/var/nis/hostname/table_name.org_dir** files. There are 16 preconfigured tables. They are described in Table 4.4.

4.3.2 NIS+ Files

/etc/defaultdomain

The **defaultdomain** file contains the NIS+ domain name. This file is used to set the domain name of the system during system startup. To add the domain to the file, type the following commands:

domainname ngt.com
domainname > /etc/defaultdomain

/etc/nsswitch.conf

The **nsswitch.conf** file contains the default switch configurations used by the NIS+ services, NIS services, and local files. Table 4.5 lists the three alternate files available on a Solaris system.

You can copy any one of these files to the **/etc/nsswitch.conf** file, or you can create your own customized file. Figure 4.7 gives an example of what the **/etc/nsswitch.nisplus** file looks like.

If the system does not have the **nsswitch.conf** you will be able to add entries to the table or look at the entries in the table but you will notbe able to use the NIS+ services. For example, users defined in NIS+ *passwd* table will not be able to login to the system.

Table 4.4
NIS+ Predefined Tables

Table	Description
Hosts	Contains IP address and name of all the workstation in the domain (**/etc/hosts** file).
Bootparams	Contains the information of the root and the swap partition of all the diskless clients in the domain (**/etc/bootparams** file).
Password	Contains information about all the users in the domain (**/etc/passwd** file).
Group	Contains information about group id, group name, and the members of all the groups in the domain (**/etc/group** file).
Ethers	Contains information about Ethernet address and hostname of workstations in the domain (**/etc/ethers** file).
Services	Contains information about the TCP/IP services used in the domain (**/etc/services** file).
Protocols	Contains information about IP protocols used in the domain (**/etc/protocols** file).
RPC	Contains information about RPC services used in the domain (**/etc/rpc** file).
Aliases	Contains information about the mail aliases used in the domain (**/etc/aliases** file).
Timezone	Contains information about the time zone of all the workstation in the domain (**/etc/timezone** file).
Networks	Contains information about all the networks in the domain and their canonical names (**/etc/networks** file).
Netmasks	Contains information about the netmasks used by the networks in the domain (**/etc/netmasks** file).
Auto_Home	Contains information about the home directories of all the users in the domain (**/etc/auto_home** file).
Auto_Master	Contains information about the automounter map (**/etc/auto_master** file).
Netgroup	Contains information about netgroups to which users and workstations in the domain may belong (**/etc/netgroup** file).
Cred	Contains NIS+ credentials for all the principals in the domain.

Table 4.5
nsswitch.conf Alternate Files

Alternate File	Description
/etc/nsswitch.nisplus	Switch file for NIS+ services
/etc/nsswitch.nis	Switch file for NIS services
/etc/nsswitch.files	Switch file for local files

```
#
# /etc/nsswitch.file:
#
# An example file that could be copied over to /etc/nsswitch.conf; it
# does not use any naming service. "hosts:" and "services:" in this file
# are used only if the /etc/netconfig file contains "switch.so" as a nametoaddr library
# for "inet" transports.

passwd:         files
group:          files
hosts:          files
networks:       files
protocols:      files
rpc:            files
ethers:         files
netmasks:       files
bootparams:     files
publickey:      files
#
# At present there isn't a 'files' backend for netgroup;  the system will figure it out pretty quickly, and
# won't use netgroups at all.
#
netgroup:       files
automount:      files
aliases:        files
services:       files
```

Figure 4.7 An example of the **etc/nsswitch.nisplus** file.

/etc/.rootkey

The **.rootkey** file stores the secret key for root. This is useful during system reboot when on one is around to enter the password. This file is read by *keyserv* daemon.

/var/nis/NIS_COLDSTART

NIS_COLDSTART file contains NIS+ directory objects. These objects are loaded NIS+ cache at startup by **nis_cachemgr** command. This file is created by the **nisinit** command.

/var/nis/NIS_SHARED_DIRCACHE

NIS_SHARED_DIRCACHE file contains the current cache of NIS+ directory objects maintained by **nis_cachemgr**. This cache is shared by all NIS+ processes.

On startup, **nis_cachemgr** initializes the cache from the **NIS_COLDSTART** file and stores it in the **NIS_SHARED_DIRCACHE** file. The cache can be viewed by the **nisshowcache** command.

/var/nis/hostname.log

The *hostname.log* file contains a transaction log for NIS+ services. The changes to the NIS+ tables are stored in this file. The **nisping** command will update the tables from the log file. This file contains holes; thus the apparent size of the file may be lot higher than the actual size. The contents of the log file may be viewed by **nislog** command. There is only one transaction log file per server.

/var/nis/hostname.dict

This is a dictionary file used by NIS+ database to locate its files.

/var/nis/hostname/root.object

This file is created by the **nisinit** command on the root server. It contains a directory object that describes the root of the name space.

/var/nis/hostname/table_name.log

The *table_name.log* file contains the state of individual transaction made to the table *table_name*. When the table is checkpointed via the **nisping** command, this file will have zero length.

/var/nis/hostname/groups_dir

The **groups_dir** directory contains the objects for authorizing the group access to the NIS+ services.

4.3.3 NIS+ Daemons

/usr/sbin/rpc.nisd

The *rpc.nisd* daemon implements the NIS+ services using ONC RPC. This daemon must run on all NIS+ servers. It is usually started from the system startup files. Table 4.6 describes options that *rpc.nisd* accepts.

Table 4.6
rpc.nisd Options

Option	Description
-r	This option tells the daemon that it is running as a root master server. This option is only used on the root master server system.
-v	This option will cause the daemon to run in verbose mode. All the output is sent to the syslog daemon (**syslogd**). This option is useful for debugging purposes.
-c *seconds*	This option sets the number of seconds between the checks for the updates to the namespace. The default timeout period is 120 seconds.
-Y	This option will put the server in NIS (YP) compatibility mode. Since YP protocol is not authenticated, only the items with read access to **nobody** will be visible to NIS clients.
-l	This option will force the server to use only the loopback interface. It will not use the network interface. This option is used to test the NIS+ configuration. This option should not be used during normal operation.
-f	This option forces the daemon to perform a checkpoint of the database when it starts up. It will remove the updates from the transaction log that have been propagated to the replica servers.
-L *load*	This option specifies the amount of load the **rpc.nisd** is allowed to put on the system. The load is specified in terms of number of child processes that the daemon may create. The default value is 128.
-S *level*	This option will set the authentication level. Level **0** means no authentication is performed. Level **1** means it will accept **AUTH_SYS** and **AUTH_DES** credentials from the clients. Level **1** is not a secure method since it is easy to forge **AUTH_SYS** credentials. Level **2** means it will only accept **AUTH_DES** credentials. The default security level is **2**.

For example, to start the NIS+ daemon on the root master server system with NIS compatibility, type

/usr/sbin/rpc.nisd -rY

/usr/sbin/nis_cachemgr

The *nis_cachemgr* daemons caches the NIS+ directory objects. *nis_cachemgr* improves the performance of NIS+, but it is not required to run the *nis_cachemgr* to use NIS+ services. It caches the information necessary to contact the NIS+ servers for the NIS+ domain. The cache contains the following:

- Information needed to authenticate the servers;
- Time-to-live field: the information on how long the information should be cached;
- The port numbers of the servers.

The security credentials for the host should be added to the **cred.org_dir** table before running the *nis_cachemgr* daemon. If the security credentials are not added to the table and *nis_cachemgr* is started without **-n** option, then NIS+ performance may degrade significantly. *nis_cachemgr* maintains the cache in a file that is memory-mapped. *nis_cachemgr* initializes the cache from the **/var/nis/NIS_COLDSTART** file and preserves the unexpired entries in the **/var/nis/NIS_SHARED_DIRCACHE** file. Thus it can maintain the cache entries even after system reboot. *nis_cachemgr* sends the error messages and warnings to the *syslogd* daemon. Table 4.7 describes options supported by *nis_cachemgr*.

keyserv

The *keyserv* daemon stores the encryption keys for each user logged into the system. These keys are used to access secure network services such as NIS+ and secure NFS. *keyserv* will read the root's key from the **/etc/.rootkey** file when the daemon is started. This is useful during system reboot when no one is around to enter the password. If the client does not have a secret key, *keyserv* will use the key for **nobody** as a default key. Table 4.8 describes options accepted by *keyserv*.

Table 4.7
nis_cachemgr Options

Option	Description
-i	Ignore the previous cache file and initializes the cache from cold start file. By default it will initialize itself from the cold start file and old cache file.
-n	Run the daemon in insecure mode.
-v	Run the daemon in verbose mode.

Table 4.8
keyserv Options

Option	Description
-d	Do not use the default key.
-D	Run in debugging mode.
-n	Do not read the **root**'s key from the **/etc/.rootkey** file. Instead, prompt for **root** password to decrypt the **root**'s key stored in **/usr/publickey** database. It will then store the key in the **/etc/.rootkey** file for future use. This option is useful if the **.rootkey** file gets corrupted.

4.3.4 NIS+ Commands

nisaddcred

The **nisaddcred** command is used to create security credentials for NIS+ principal. These credentials provide authentication for various NIS+ services. The NIS+ credentials are stored in **cred.org_dir** table. The structure of the **cred.org_dir** table is as follows:

cname auth_type auth_name public_data private_data

The **cred.org_dir** table fields are described in Table 4.9.

For example:

shah.ngt.com.   LOCAL   2990   10,102,44
shah.ngt.com.   DES   unix.2990@ngt.com   098...819   3b8...ab2

If the client does not have local credentials in a domain, it will not be able to acquire DES credentials. If the NIS+ service is running at security level 2, it will consider such users unauthenticated and assign them the user name **nobody** for access rights. To add entry to the NIS+ credential table for a user with UID 1000 in *ngt.com.* domain, type

nisaddcred -p 1000 -P ngt.com. local
nisaddcred -p unix.1000@ngt.com -P ngt.com. des

To add an entry for a host *ws100* in *ngt.com.* domain, type

nisaddcred -p unix.ws100@ngt.com -P ngt.com. des

Table 4.9
NIS+ **cred.org_dir** Table Fields

Field Name	Description
cname	This column contains the NIS+ principal name. The principal name is the login name, to hostname followed by the NIS+ domain name.
auth_type	There are two types of authentications in NIS+, LOCAL, and DES. Only users can have LOCAL authentication type. The LOCAL type authentication is a UID that is valid only in domains containing the **cred.org_dir** table. The DES authentication is a Secure RPC netname. Users of NIS+ clients must have both types of authentication in their domain.
public_data	The public data for the LOCAL credentials contains list of GIDs for which the user is a member. For DES credentials the public data contains the public key for the principal.
private_data	There is no private data associated with LOCAL authentication. For DES authentication it contains private key of the principal encrypted by the principal's network password.

nischmod

The **nischmod** command is used to change the access rights of NIS+ objects. This command may be used to give permissions. The syntax for the mode is

rights [,rights] .....

rights has the syntax

[who] op permission [op permission]......

who is a combination of

n	Nobody
o	Owner
g	Group
w	World
a or **owg**	All

The following syntax is used with the *op* option.

+	Grant permission
-	Remove permission
=	Explicitly set permission

permission is a combination of

r	Read
m	Modify
c	Create
d	Destroy

For example, to give all *permission* to group, enter

nischmod g=rcmd ngt.com.

Note: The NIS_GROUP environment variable must be set to the domain's *admin* group.

nischttl

The **nischttl** command is used to change the time-to-live value of NIS+ objects. Time to live is used to expire the objects stored in the NIS+ cache. When the object is stored in cache, the time-to-live field, in seconds, is added to the current time to calculate the expire time. When time to live expires, the object is flushed from the cache. For example,

nischttl 3600 passwd.org_dir

The high value of the time-to-live value will cause the object to stay in cache for a longer period of time. This will improve the NIS+ performance. But the changes made to the objects will not be visible to long time.

niserror

The **niserror** command is used to print the NIS+ error message associated with the error code. It is used to convert the NIS+ error code into a descriptive message. For example,

$ niserror 20
Not Found, no such name

nisping

The **nisping** command sends a "ping" to all replica servers in the domain. The replica will then check with the master server for updates. The **nisping** command can also be used to checkpoint the servers. When the servers are checkpointed, they will update the tables from the transaction log file. For example,

 # nisping -C ngt.com.

nisshowcache

The **nisshowcacche** command is used to look at the NIS+ cache shared by all the NIS+ processes. The shared cache is maintained in the **NIS_SHARED_DIRCACHE** file byr *niscachemgr* process. For example,

 # nisshowcache

nistest

The **nistest** command provides shell scripts and other programs to test the existence of the NIS+ objects. It will check the type and allow access rights to the NIS+ objects. For example, to check if the current process has the desired permission (read) on the *passwd* table, enter

$ nistest -a r passwd.org_dir

4.3.5 NIS+ Root Master Server Configuration

This section describes the steps required to set up the root domain.

Step 1

Set the root master server's domain name.

ngt# **domainname ngt.com**
ngt# **domainname > /etc/defaultdomain**

Step 2

Verify that the root master server is using the NIS+ version of the **/etc/nsswitch.conf** file, ensuring that the first sources of information for the root master server are the NIS+ tables.

ngt# **cp /etc/nsswitch.nisplus /etc/nsswitch.conf**

Edit the **/etc/nsswitch.nisplus** file so that NIS+ first looks at the local **hosts** table or the **/etc/hosts** file before sending a request to the DNS system.

ngt# **ps -ef | grep keyserv** (get daemon PID)
ngt# **kill *PID***
ngt# **rm -f /etc/.rootkey**
ngt# **keyserv**

Step 3

Set the environment variable NIS_GROUP to the name of the root domain's *admin* group, NIS_PATH to the search path. This step ensures that the root domain's *org_dir* directory object, *groups_dir* directory object, and all of its table objects are assigned the proper default group.

ngt# **setenv NIS_GROUP admin.ngt.com.**
ngt# **setenv NIS_PATH 'org_dir.$:$'**

Step 4

Now create the root directory and initialize the system as the root master server.

ngt# **nisinit -r**
This machine is in ngt.com. NIS+ domain
Setting up root server...
All done

Step 5

At this point start the NIS+ daemon, *rpc.nisd*.

ngt# **rpc.nisd -r -S 0**

The **-r** option runs the root domain's version of a master server–this is different from a nonroot domain's version. The **-S 0** option sets the server's security level to 0–this is required at this point for bootstrapping. Thus, the root directory now exists and *rpc.nisd* is responsible for serving it. Also, in the **/var/nis** directory you will now find the master server's **NIS_COLD_START** file.

Step 6

Create the "org_dir" and "groups_dir" directories and NIS+ tables below the root directory object.

ngt# **/usr/lib/nis/nissetup ngt.com.**

Objects such as *org_dir.ngt.com.* and *groups_dir.ngt.com.* are created.

Step 7

You now need to create DES credentials for the root master server. This enables the root master server to authenticate its own requests.

ngt# **nisaddcred des**
DES Principal Name : unix.ws100@ngt.com
Adding key pair for unix.ws100@(ws100.ngt.com.).
Enter super-user's login password :

The system displays the DES principal name created. At that point, a key pair will be added for *unix.ws100@ngt.com*. Next, you will be prompted for your login password (enter **root**'s password). The root server's private and public keys are stored in the root domain's *Cred table,* that is, *cred.org_dir.ngt.com,* while the secret key is stored in the **/etc/.rootkey** file.

Step 8

Change the ownership and permissions on tables. Use the **nischgrp** command to change the group of the table. Use the **nischmod** command to change the access rights that the root directory object grants its group from Read to *rmcd* (read, modify, create, and destroy).

ngt# **cd /var/nis/ngt**
ngt# **nischgrp admin.ngt.com. ngt.com.**
ngt# **nischgrp admin.ngt.com. *.org_dir**
ngt# **nischmod g+rmcd ngt.com.**

Step 9

Now, use the **nisgrpadm** command to add the root master server to the root domain's *admin* group. But first create the *admin.ngt.com.* group using the **-c** option with **nisgrpadm** command.

ngt# **nisgrpadm -c admin.ngt.com.**
ngt# **nisgrpadm -a admin.ngt.com. ngt.ngt.com.**

The first argument is the name of the group, while the second is the host name of the root master server.

Step 10

We now need to propagate the root master server's public key from the root domain's *Cred table* to three directory objects:

root;
org_dir;
groups_dir.

ngt# **/usr/lib/nis/nisupdkeys   ngt.com.**
ngt# **/usr/lib/nis/nisupdkeys   org_dir.ngt.com.**
ngt# **/usr/lib/nis/nisupdkeys   groups_dir.ngt.com.**

Step 11

Next, start the NIS+ cache manager. The cache manager takes information from the coldstart file and downloads it into the **/var/nis/NIS_SHARED_DIRCACHE** file.

ngt# **nis_cachemgr**

Step 12

Restart the NIS+ daemon, *rpc.nisd,* with security level 2.

ngt# **ps -ef | grep rpc.nisd**   (get the daemon's PID #)
ngt# **kill PID**
ngt# **rpc.nisd -r**

Note that security level 2 is the default.

Step 13

Use the **nisaddcred** command with the **-p** and **-P** flags to add your LOCAL credentials to the root domain. You need to first create (if one already does not exist) an account for the NIS+ administrator. The account entry must exist in the **/etc/passwd** file.

ngt# **nisaddcred -p 5656 -P nisadm.ngt.com. local**

5656 is the UID of the administrator, while *nisadm.ngt.com.* is the NIS+ principal name.

Step 14

Use the **nisaddcred** command to add DES credentials to the root domain.

ngt# **nisaddcred -p unix.5656@ngt.com -P nisadm.ngt.com. des**

Step 15

Add LOCAL and DES credentials for all other administrators. This step is not necessary if there are no other NIS+ administrators.

ngt# **nisaddcred -p 9292 -P chris.ngt.com. local**
ngt# **nisaddcred -p unix.9292@ngt.com -P chris.ngt.com. des**

You will be prompted to enter the login password for the NIS+ principal.

Step 16

Use the **nisgrpadm** command to add yourself and other administrators to the root domain's *admin* group.

ngt# **nisgrpadm -a admin.ngt.com. nisadm.ngt.com.**

Step 17

Next, modify your search path variable to add **/var/lib/nis**.

ngt# **setenv $PATH /usr/lib/nis:$PATH**

Step 18

Execute the **nisaddent** command to transfer information from files to NIS+ tables.

ngt# **nisaddent -m -f /etc/hosts hosts**
ngt# **nisaddent -m -f /etc/passwd passwd**
.
.
.
ngt# **nisaddent -m -f /etc/services services**

The **-m** specifies the contents of the source are merged with the contents of the table. The **-f** option is followed by a filename. You need to create NIS+ tables for all 16 NIS+ related system files.

4.3.6 NIS+ Client Configuration

This section describes the process of configuring an NIS+ client.

Step 1

Logon to the domain's master server system as super-user.

Step 2

Use the **nisaddcred** command to create credentials for the new client workstation. In this example, *nathan* is the host name of the NIS+ client system.

ngt# **nisaddcred -p unix.nathan@ngt.com -P nathan.ngt.com. des**

You will be prompted to enter the client workstation's **root** password.

Step 3

Logon as super-user on the client system.

Step 4

Specify the domain name on the client system.

nathan# **domainname ngt.com**
nathan# **domainname > /etc/defaultdomain**

Step 5

Next, verify that the client system is using the NIS+ version of the **/etc/nsswitch.conf** file. Modify the file so that local tables and files are checked before a request is sent on the network (e.g., **hosts** table or file is checked before a DNS request is generated).

Step 6

Remove any files that may exist in the **/var/nis** subdirectory.

nathan# **rm -rf /var/nis/***

Step 7

Initialize the client system. The client may be initialized by:

- Broadcast;
- Hostname;
- Cold start file.

For example, to initialize the client by hostname, enter

nathan# **nisinit -c -H ngt**

The **nisinit** command checks the **/etc/hosts** file for the rootmaster server's Internet address. It then initializes the client and creates a **NIS_COLD_START** file in the **/var/nis** directory.

Step 8

You now need to kill and restart the *keyserv* daemon. Restarting the *keyserv* daemon also results in updating the key server's Switch information about the client.

nathan# **ps -e | grep keyserv**   (get PID of process)
nathan# **kill PID**
nathan# **rm -f /etc/.rootkey**
nathan# **keyserv**

Step 9

In this step, we will start the *keylogin* process. This stores the client's secret key with the keyserver.

nathan# **keylogin -r**

You will be prompted for the client node's super-user password.

Step 10

Reboot the client.

4.3.7 NIS+ Replica Configuration

Let's examine how to configure an NIS+ root replica or a nonroot replica system. We assume that the root domain has previously been set up. The system to be configured as a root replica, nonroot replica, and nonroot master system must first be initialized as an NIS+ client.

Step 1

Login as **root** on the master server.

Step 2

Add credentials for the replica server.

ngt# **nisaddcred -p unix.*replica-host*@ngt.com -P *replica-host*.ngt.com. des**

Step 3

Execute the **nismkdir** command to create the NIS+ directory. The **-s** option is followed by the host name of the replica system.

ngt# **nismkdir   -s   natasha.ngt.com.   ngt.com.**
ngt# **nismkdir   -s   natasha.ngt.com.   org_dir.ngt.com.**
ngt# **nismkdir   -s   natasha.ngt.com.   groups_dir.ngt.com.**

Step 4

Login as **root** on the replica server.

Step 5

Set the domain name.

natasha# **domainname ngt.com**
natasha# **domainname > /etc/defaultdomain**

Step 6

Copy the appropriate switch file.

natasha# **cp /etc/nsswitch.nisplus /etc/nsswitch.conf**

Step 7

Add the root master server to the **/etc/hosts** file.

Step 8

Transfer the cold start file.

natasha# **nisinit -c -H ngt**

Step 9

Restart the *keyserv* process.

natasha# **ps -ef | grep keyserv**
natasha# **kill PID**
natasha# **keyserv**

Step 10

Enter the credentials for the host.

natasha# **keylogin -r**

You will be prompted for the **root** password. Enter the **root** password.

Step 11

Start the NIS+ daemon, *rpc.nisd*.

natasha# **rpc.nisd**

Step 12

Verify that the NIS+ directories have been created.

natasha# **ls -F /var/nis**

Step 13

Set the environment variable NIS_GROUP to the name of the root domain's *admin* group, NIS_PATH to the search path. This step ensures that the root domain's *org_dir* directory object, *groups_dir* directory object, and all of its table objects are assigned the proper default groups.

natasha# **setenv NIS_GROUP admin.ngt.com.**
natasha# **setenv NIS_PATH 'org_dir.$:$'**

Step 14

Log in as root on the master server.

Step 15

This step sends a message to the new replica system, telling it to ask the master server for an update.

ngt# **/usr/lib/nis/nisping   ngt.com.**
ngt# **/usr/lib/nis/nisping   org_dir.ngt.com.**
ngt# **/usr/lib/nis/nisping   groups_dir.ngt.com.**

Step 16

Add replica server to the *admin.ngt.com.* group.

ngt# **nisgrpadm -a admin.ngt.com. natasha.ngt.com.**
ngt# **nisgrpadm -l admin.ngt.com.**

4.3.8 NIS+ Master Server Configuration in a New Domain

We now examine the steps required to configure a Sun system as a master server in a new domain. We assume that the root master server is already set up. Also, the system to be defined as a master server must first be initialized as a NIS+ client system.

Step 1

Logon as super-user on the system to be configured as a master server. Let's assume in this example that the master server's host name is *ganesh*.

Step 2

Define the NIS_GROUP environment variable.

tina# **setenv NIS_GROUP admin.branch1.ngt.com.**

Step 3

Run the NIS+ daemon, *rpc.nisd*.

tina# **rpc.nisd**

Step 4

Create the domain's *branch1.ngt.com.* directory and specify its server system(s).

tina# **nismkdir -m ganesh branch1.ngt.com.**

Step 5

Create the domain's subdirectories and tables.

tina# **/usr/lib/nis/nissetup branch1.ngt.com.**

This step adds the *org_dir, groups_dir,* and NIS+ tables below the new directory object.

Step 6

Create the *branch1.ngt.com.* domain's *admin* group.

tina# **nisgrpadm -c admin.branch1.ngt.com.**

Step 7

Assign full group rights to the directory object created.

tina# **nischmod g+rmcd branch1.ngt.com.**

Step 8

Add the servers to the domain's *admin* group.

tina# **nisgrpadm -a admin.branch1.ngt.com. ganesh.ngt.com.**

In this step we added the master server system to the domain's *admin* group.

Step 9

Add credentials for administrators who will be working with NIS+ in this domain.

tina# **nisaddcred -p 7000 -P nisadm.ngt.com. local**

This assumes that **nisadm** already has DES credentials in another domain.

Step 10

Add the administrator to the domain's *admin* group.

tina# **nisgrpadm -a admin.branch1.ngt.com. nisadm.ngt.com.**

4.4 DOMAIN NAME SERVICE (DNS)

The motivation for the *domain name service* (DNS) is to centrally manage and maintain Internet addresses and host names. DNS in the near future will provide support for a number of services besides the host name-to-address translation. After a description of the key components of the DNS is provided, we focus on how to configure UNIX systems as a primary master server, client, or caching only server system.

Systems on the Internet (TCP/IP) network may maintain the host name-to-Internet-address translation information in the **/etc/hosts** file. However, in an environment where new TCP/IP nodes are constantly being added, the process of updating the **/etc/hosts** file on every system is a tedious task. The domain name service is a host name and address lookup service for the Internet network. It enables DNS client systems to obtain host names and addresses from DNS server systems.

A daemon process, in.named, is responsible for implementing DNS. The *in.named* daemon is also sometimes referred to as the *Berkeley Internet name domain service*. The DNS service is based on the client/server model and consists of two parts: server and client software interface.

Servers maintain databases of host names and their associated addresses. Client systems query the servers for information. Systems that run the *in.named* daemon are referred to as name servers. The software interface is called the resolver, which consists of a group of routines that reside in the C library, /usr/lib/libc.a.

DNS servers may be of the following types.

- Root;
- Master (primary or secondary);
- Caching;
- Forwarding;
- Slave.

If a primary name server and a secondary name server are configured in your environment, then your UNIX system can be set up as a DNS client or a DNS caching only server. DNS clients do not run the *in.named* process. Instead, they use the resolver file, **/etc/resolv.conf**, to determine the IP address of the DNS server that can service the client's DNS requests.

The DNS service breaks the Internet network into a hierarchy of *domains*. Each domain is given a label. The name of the domain is a concatenation of all the labels of the domain, listed from right to left and separated by dots. Domains may be further subdivided into *zones*. Each *zone* is an area of authority for which a master server is responsible. Typically, zones represent administrative boundaries. The seven top-level domains in the United States are summarized in Table 4.10.

The top-level names may be specified geographically or organizationally; for example, the U.S. domain is divided into a second-level domain per state: **il.us**

Your organization can decide how to register its name with the Internet authorities; for example, the National Research Initiatives is registered as **nri.reston.va.us**

or, you could register on the basis of the type of organization, for example, **ngt.com**.

4.4.1 DNS: Types of Servers

Let's take a look at the different types of DNS server systems.

Root Servers

Root servers know about all top-level domains on the Internet. If a client requests information about a host in another domain, any server (except the slave server)

Table 4.10
Top-Level DNS Domains in the United States

Domain Name	Description
ARPA	ARPANET domain (now obsolete) except for in-addr.arpa
COM	Commercial organizations
EDU	Educational institution
GOV	Government institution
MIL	Military groups
NET	Network support centers
ORG	Other organizations
INT	International organization
country-code	Geographic code for each country

can communicate the request to the root server. Some root servers in the United States are:

- ns.nasa.gov.;
- nic.ddn.mil.;
- a.isi.edu.;
- gunter-adam.af.mil.;
- terp.umd.edu.;
- c.nyser.net.

Note that the period at the end of each root server name specifies that this is the absolute domain name; without the period, the server name is relative to the current domain. The *Network Information Center* (NIC) determines what systems are root servers.

Root servers know about name servers authoritative for all top-level domains. Root name servers can respond with names and addresses of name servers authoritative for the top-level domain in which the domain name is located. To get the list of root name servers from the Internet, you can use the *ftp anonymous* account on **nic.ddn.mil** and get the file **root-servers.txt** from the **netinfo** subdirectory.

Master Server

The *master server* is the authority for the current domain and maintains the DNS databases for its zone. A server can be a master server for multiple domains: as the primary server for some domains and a secondary server for others.

Primary and Secondary Servers

A server can be a master server for several domains, being a *primary server* for some domains and a *secondary server* for others. A primary server loads its database from a file on disk. The primary server can also delegate to other servers in its zone the authority to answer queries for its domain space. A secondary server receives its authority and database from the primary server. The secondary server periodically checks with the primary server to see if any data base information has changed. Typically, the secondary server polls the primary server periodically to verify that its database information is current.

If the primary master server is *ganesh.ngt.com* (Internet address: 131.107.15.1), then node *ganesh* is the authority for the domain space *ngt.com*.

Caching and Caching Only Server

All servers cache the information they receive until the time specified in the *time-to-live field* expires. *Caching servers* store the IPaddress-to-hostname translation information until the data expires. A *caching only server* is not authoritative for any zone; instead the server handles queries received by asking other servers for the information needed.

Forwarding Servers

Also referred to as *forwarders,* these servers process recursive requests that slave servers cannot resolve locally. A forwarder has access to the Internet. A forwarder can be a primary, secondary, or caching server. The configuration files on the slave servers specifies which systems the slaves have access to as forwarders. Without forwarders your system has no access to the root servers on the Internet.

Slave Servers

Slave servers have no access to the Internet and thus cannot interact directly with root servers to get information that is not in their local cache. Slave servers do not receive complete zones from primary servers, like secondary servers, but instead accumulate data on a per request basis.

4.4.2 DNS Primary Master Server Configuration

Let us step through and examine how to configure your computer as a DNS primary master server. The files you will be working with are:

- /etc/named.boot;
- /var/named/named.hosts;
- /var/named/named.rev;
- /var/named/named.ca;
- /var/named/named.local.

/etc/named.boot File

The **named.boot** file specifies the domain name and the directory in which DNS files are located. This file is read by the **named** daemon. Figue 4.8 gives an example of the **named.boot** file configured for NGT's primary master server.

/var/named/named.local File

The **named.local** file is used to specify the local loopback interface for the primary domain name server. See Figure 4.9 for an example.

```
;
; DNS - /etc/named.boot file
;
domain          ngt.com
directory       /var/named
;
primary         ngt.com                      named.hosts
primary         244.246.198.IN-ADDR.ARPA     rev.named.hosts
primary         0.0.127.IN-ADDR.ARPA         named.local
cache                                        named.ca
```

Figure 4.8 /etc/named.boot DNS file.

The *SOA record* specifies the start of the zone. The term *ganesh.ngt.com.* is the name of the host where this data file resides. *Serial* is the serial number of this file, and it should be updated each time this file is modified. *Refresh* is the frequency in seconds that the secondary name servers should query the primary name server. *Retry* is the time in seconds that the secondary name server should wait for the primary to reply when requesting a refresh. *Expire* is the total time, in seconds, for a secondary server to continue without a refresh before removing (or disregarding) its database. *Minimum* is the default number of seconds to be used for the time-to-live field on resource records that have no TTL specified. The *NS record* specified the name of the name server responsible for a given domain. The *1* in the last line is short for 1.0.0.127; the reverse version of the local host address 127.0.0.1.

```
;
; Contains the "localhost" named information
; Created: 10/27/94  UOP
; Last modified:
;
@    IN    SOA    ganesh.ngt.com.    root.ganesh.ngt.com. (
                 94102701            ; serial #
                 36000               ; refresh time
                 3600                ; retry after 1 hour
                 3600000             ; expire after 1000 hours
                 36000               ; default ttl is 10 hours
                 )
     IN    NS     ganesh.ngt.com.
1    IN    PTR    localhost.
```

Figure 4.9 /var/named/named.local DNS file.

/var/named/named.ca File

The **named.ca** file provides information on DNS root servers. Figure 4.10 specifies a sample **named.ca** file.

```
;
; Specifies name servers for the root domain
;
; Created: 10/27/94
;
.                        99999999    IN    NS    ns.internic.net.
.                        99999999    IN    NS    kava.nisc.sri.com.
.                        99999999    IN    NS    aos.arl.army.mil.
.                        99999999    IN    NS    ns.nic.ddn.mil.
.                        99999999    IN    NS    nic.nordu.net.
.                        99999999    IN    NS    terp.umd.edu.
.                        99999999    IN    NS    c.nyser.net.
.                        99999999    IN    NS    ns.nasa.gov.
ns.internic.net.         99999999    IN    A     198.41.0.4
kava.nisc.sri.com.       99999999    IN    A     192.33.33.24
aos.arl.army.mil.        99999999    IN    A     128.63.4.82
ns.nic.ddn.mil.          99999999    IN    A     192.112.36.4
nic.nordu.net.           99999999    IN    A     192.36.148.17
terp.umd.edu.            99999999    IN    A     128.8.10.90
c.nyser.net.             99999999    IN    A     192.33.4.12
ns.nasa.gov.             99999999    IN    A     128.102.16.10
```

Figure 4.10 /var/named/named.ca DNS file.

/var/named/ngt.hosts File

The **ngt.hosts** file is a summary of all systems and their associated IP addresses in the *ngt.com* DNS domain. Figure 4.11 describes a simple **ngt.hosts** file.

/var/named/rev.ngt.com File

Figure 4.12 describes an example DNS reverse file.

Next, check the **hosts** entry in the file **/etc/nsswitch.conf**. The entry for **dns** should appear first in the search path. Then, the last step is to start the *in.named* daemon.

in.named

4.4.3 DNS Client Only Configuration

To configure your UNIX workstation as a DNS *client only system,* create the client resolver file, **/etc/resolv.conf**. SunOS (BSD) systems must typically be configured as a NIS client system for the DNS client configuration to work. Solaris systems do not need to be set up as a NIS or NIS+ system for DNS to be functional. Figure 4.13 describes an example **/etc/resolv.conf** file.

```
;
; MASTER hosts information for domain 'ngt.com'
; Created: 5/6/94
;
@         IN        SOA       ganesh.ngt.com.      root.ganesh.ngt.com. (
                              93110202             ; serial #
                              36000                ; refresh time
                              3600                 ; retry after 1 hour
                              3600000              ; expire after 1000 hours
                              36000                ; default ttl is 10 hours
                              )
          IN        NS                             ganesh.ngt.com.
ganesh    IN        A                              198.246.244.54
mailhost  IN        CNAME .                        ganesh
lakshmi   IN        A                              198.246.244.55
vishnu    IN        A                              198.246.244.56
ram       IN        A                              198.246.244.57
smtpgtwy  IN        A                              198.246.244.58
```

Figure 4.11 /var/named/ngt.hosts DNS file.

```
;
; MASTER REVERSED hosts information for domain 'ngt.com'
;
; Created: 10/27/94
;
@         IN        SOA       ganesh.ngt.com.      root.ngt.com. (
                              94102701             ; serial #
                              36000                ; refresh time
                              3600                 ; retry after 1 hour
                              3600000              ; expire after 1000 hours
                              36000                ; default ttl is 10 hours
                              )
          IN        NS                             ganesh.ngt.com.
54        IN        PTR                            ganesh.ngt.com.
55        IN        PTR                            lakshmi.ngt.com.
56        IN        PTR                            vishnu.ngt.com.
57        IN        PTR                            ram.ngt.com.
58        IN        PTR                            smtpgtwy.ngt.com.
```

Figure 4.12 /var/named/rev.ngt.hosts DNS file.

```
;
; /etc/resolv.conf file
;
domain              ngt.com
nameserver          198.246.244.54
nameserver          198.246.244.55
```

Figure 4.13 /etc/resolv.conf DNS file.

Note that a DNS client does not run the *in.named* daemon. Instead it consults the **/etc/resolv.conf** file to determine who it should send DNS queries to. Check the **hosts** entry in the file, **/etc/nsswitch.conf**. The **dns** entry should appear first in the search path.

In this example, for the *ngt.com* domain, the address of the primary name server is 198.246.244.54, and that of the secondary is 198.246.244.55. Note that a DNS client does not run the *in.named* daemon. Instead, it consults the **/etc/resolv.conf** file to determine to whom it should send DNS queries. If your UNIX system uses DNS service frequently, it is best to configure the system as a DNS caching only system.

4.4.4 Configuring a DNS Caching Only System

A DNS client only system does not remember past requests. If you use the DNS service frequently, then it is best to configure your UNIX system as a DNS caching only server. A *caching only server* stores (caches) the host name-to-address information it learns from the primary or secondary server, so that the next time there is a request and your system knows the Internet address it will not communicate with the name server. In addition to reducing network traffic, it keeps the primary and the secondary servers less busy because they process fewer requests if UNIX systems are set up as caching only servers.

DNS files required for configuring caching only system are **named.boot** and **named.ca**.

The following steps outline the process of configuring your UNIX system as a DNS caching only system (Steps 1 and 2 are identical to the DNS client only configuration).

Step 1

Log in as **root**.

Step 2

Modify the local **/etc/hosts** file to include entries only for *localhost, loghost,* and all dependent diskless and dataless nodes. The following is an example of the **/etc/hosts** file.

```
#
# Host Database
#
127.0.0.1          localhost
#
198.246.244.65     nathan loghost
198.246.244.66     natasha
```

Step 3

cd to the **/etc** directory.

Step 4

Create the file, **/etc/named.boot**. The following is an example of the **/etc/named.boot** file.

```
;
; /etc/named.boot file for nathan
;
directory               /var/named
cache                   named.ca
```

The **/etc/named.boot** file is read when the *in.named* process is started from the **/etc/rc.local** file. This file indicates to the system what type of server it is and where to get its initial data. The line *directory /var/named* designates the directory in which you want the name server to run. This also allows for the use of relative path names for the files mentioned in the boot file. The *in.named* core dumps will also be put in this directory. The line *cache . named.ca* tells the server to look in the file **/var/named/root.cache** for the location of the authoritative name servers. Note that other file names used for **named.ca** include **root.cache** and **named.root**.

Step 5

Create the file **/var/named/named.ca**. The following is an example of the file **/var/named/named.ca**.

/var/named/named.ca File

```
;
; Specifies name servers for the root domain
;
; Created: 10/27/94
;
.                 99999999    IN    NS    ganesh.ngt.com.
ganesh.ngt.com    99999999    IN    A     198.246.244.54
```

Step 6

If you are running NIS (YP) on your system, you must update NIS maps. On a Sun system, edit the **/var/yp/Makefile** file and modify the following lines.

```
#B=-b
B=
```

to

```
B=-b
#B=
```

Step 7

To start the *in.named* daemon to be started at boot time, on a BSD system, ensure that the following lines exist in the **/etc/rc.local** file.

```
if [ -f /usr/etc/in.named -a -f /etc/named.boot ]; then
    in.named; echo -n ' Starting internet domain name server'
fi
```

On a SVR4 system such as Sun's Solaris operating system, verify that the following lines exist in the **/etc/rc2.d/S72inetsvc** file.

```
if [ -f /usr/sbin/in.named -a -f /etc/named.boot ]; then
    /usr/sbin/in.named; echo -n ' Starting internet domain name server'
fi
```

Step 8

Reboot your system.

 # shutdown -r now

Once the system is up, check if the *in.named* process is running. You can now use commands such as **telnet** or **ftp** and specify a host name. The system would then use the services of DNS to determine the Internet address of the remote host.

4.4.5 Using the nslookup Command

You can use the **nslookup** command to determine the Internet address of a remote host. For example, to determine the Intenet address of host **lakshmi**, enter

% **nslookup lakshmi**
Server: ganesh.ngt.com
Address: 198.246.244.54
Name: lakshmi.ngt.com
Address: 198.246.244.55

If you know the Internet address and need to know the host name associated with that Internet address, enter

% **nslookup**
Default Server: ganesh.ngt.com
Address: 198.246.244.54
>**set query=ptr**
>**54.244.246.198.in-addr.arpa**
Server: ganesh.ngt.com
Address: 198.246.244.54
55.244.246.198.in-addr.arpa   host name =**lakshmi.ngt.com**
>

To get a listing of all nodes in the *ngt.com* domain, enter

% **nslookup**
> **ls ngt.com**

4.5 SUMMARY

NFS is a protocol that enables systems to share file systems and directories. We examined how to configure NFS on UNIX server and client systems. The process consists of working with files such as **dfstab**, processes such as *nfsd* and *mountd*, and commands like **share** and **mount.** Further, we looked at examples to demonstrate how to configure NFS servers and clients.

Next, we analyzed the importance of NIS and NIS+ in client/server systems. NIS and NIS+ enable you to manage important system files such as **/etc/hosts** and **/etc/passwd** for a client/server configuration of UNIX systems. We investigated how to set up NIS master, slave, and client systems. We then compared the differences between NIS and NIS+ and determined how to establish an NIS+ namespace with root master server and client systems.

Any environment that is using TCP/IP is strongly encouraged to implement DNS.

One of the most common problems on the TCP/IP network is the assignment of duplicate IP addresses. This problem can be avoided to a large extent by using the services provided by DNS. DNS is an example of a client/server application—the client side resides on end user systems, while the DNS server is typically administered by the individual or group responsible for assigning IP addresses. We examined the various types of DNS servers and the key differences between them. The DNS client may be set up as a client only system or a caching only system. As mentioned earlier, the caching system caches previous DNS transactions, thereby reducing the load on the network and expediting the connection process.

REFERENCES

[1] Sun Microsystems, Inc., *System and Network Administration Manual,* Part No. 800.3805.10, March 1990.
[2] Stern, H., *Managing NFS and NIS,* Sebastopol, CA: O'Reilly & Associates, 1991.

SELECT BIBLIOGRAPHY

Kochan, S. G., and P. H. Wood, *UNIX Networking,* Indianapolis: Hayden Books, 1989.

Security 5

We are in the midst of a period in which global voice and data networks are being designed and developed and there is a conscious effort to bring connectivity to every computing resource. It is imperative that, as we as a society increase our dependence on networked computers, we have security mechanisms in place to prevent various types of threats. This chapter describes the security architecture used as a basis to define security services, mechanisms, and protocols. Further, we define terminology used in computer and network security and elaborate on the motivation to secure computer networks. The information provided in this chapter is based on the ISO 7498-2 security architecture [1].

5.1 ISO SECURITY ARCHITECTURE 7498-2

The *International Standards Organization* (ISO) 7498 describes the reference model for open systems interconnection. ISO 7498-2 extends the OSI/RM to cover security aspects that are general architectural elements of communication protocols, but are not discussed in the OSI/RM. The definition of computer and network terminology in this section is based on the ISO 7498-2 security architecture. The ISO 7498-2 security architecture (1) provides a general description of security services and related mechanisms that may be provided by the OSI/RM and (2) defines the positions (layers) within the OSI/RM where the services and mechanism may be provided.

5.1.1 Definition of Security

ISO defines *security* in the sense of minimizing the vulnerability of assets and resources. An *asset* is defined as anything of value. *Vulnerability* is any weakness that could be exploited to violate a system or the information it contains. A *threat* is a potential violation of security.

5.1.2 Motivation for Security

As dependence on networked computers is increased, we need to protect against various threats. Increasingly, organizations are moving toward distributed computer and data centers. There is a need to secure computer network transactions between these centers because critical information such as design specifications, product strategies, and future development plans may be sent over the network. Another motivation for security is the significant dependence on network applications such as electronic mail as a means to communicate.

5.1.3 Security Terminology and Abbreviations

The definitions of computer and network security terminology are provided in this section. The information in Table 5.1 is based on the ISO 7498-2 security architecture.

5.1.4 Security Threats

Security threats to a system may be classified as accidental or intentional and may be active or passive. *Accidental threats* are those that exist with no premeditated intent. An example of realized accidental threat may be system malfunction. *Intentional threats* may range from casual examination of computer or network data to sophisticated attacks using special system knowledge.

Passive threats are those that, if realized, would not result in any modification to any information contained in the system(s) and where neither the operation nor the state of the system change. Alteration of information or changes to the state or the operation of the system is defined as an *active threat* to a system. An example would be modification of the routing tables of a system by an unauthorized user.

5.1.5 Types of Attacks

Systems that exist on a network may be subject to specific types of attacks. In a *masquerade* one entity pretends to be a different entity. Typically, masquerade is used with other forms of active attack such as replay and modification of messages.

A *replay* occurs when a message, or part of a message, is repeated to produce an unauthorized effect. *Modification of a message* occurs when the content of a data transmission is altered without detection and results in an unauthorized effect, for example, if the message "Allow 'Pradeep Pate' to read confidential file 'paper.mss' " is changed to "Allow 'Jake Choudhary' to read confidential file 'paper.mss' ."

Denial of service occurs when an entity fails to perform its proper function or acts in a way that prevents other entities from performing their proper functions. The attack may involve suppressing traffic or generating extra traffic. The attack may also disrupt the operation of a network, especially if the network

Table 5.1
Security Terminology

Terminology	Description
Access control	The prevention of unauthorized use of a resource
Access control list	A list of entities, together with their access rights, that are authorized to have access to a resource
Accountability	Property that ensures that entity actions may be traced uniquely to the entity
Active threat	Threat of a deliberate unauthorized change in the state of the system
Authentication information	Information used to ensure validity of a claimed entity
Authentication exchange	Mechanism used to ensure identity of an entity by means of information exchange
Authorization	Granting of rights, including those based on access rights
Availability	Property of being accessible and usable upon demand by an authorized entity
Channel	Information transfer path
Ciphertext	Data produced through encipherment; the semantic content of the resulting data is not available
Cleartext	Intelligible data, the semantic content of which is available
Confidentiality	Property that information is not made available or disclosed to unauthorized individuals, entities, or processes
Credentials	Data transferred to establish the claimed identity of an entity
Cryptoanalysis	The analysis of a cryptographic system or its inputs and outputs to derive confidential variables or sensitive data, including cleartext
Cryptography	This determines the methods used in encipherment and decipherment; attack on a cryptographic principle, means, or method is cryptanalysis
Data Integrity	Property that data has not been altered or destroyed in an unauthorized manner
Decipherment	The reversal of a corresponding reversible encipherment
Decryption	*See decipherment*
Denial of service	Prevention of authorized access to resources or the delaying of time-critical operations
Digital signature	Data appended to, or a crytographic transformation of, a data unit that allows the recipient of the data unit to prove its source and integrity and protect against forgery (e.g., by the recipient)
Encipherment	The cryptographic transformation of data to produce ciphertext
Encryption	*See encipherment*

Table 5.1 (continued)

Terminology	Description
End-to-end encipherment	Encipherment of data within or at the source and system, with the corresponding decipherment occurring only with or at the destination end system
Identity-based security policy	A security policy on the identities or attributes of users, a group of users, or entities acting on behalf of the users and the resources or objects to which they have access
Key	A sequence of symbols that controls the operation of encipherment and decipherment
Key management	The generation, storage, distribution, deletion, archiving, and application of keys in accordance with a security policy
Link-by-link encipherment	The individual application of encipherment to data on each link of a communications system; therefore, data will be in cleartext form in relay entities
Manipulation detection	A mechanism used to detect whether a data unit has been modified (accidentally or intentionally)
Masquerade	The pretense by an entity to be a different entity
Notarization	The registration of data with a trusted third party that allows the later assurance of accuracy of its characteristics such as content, origin, time, and delivery
Passive threat	The threat of unauthorized disclosure of information without changing the state of the system
Password	Confidential authorization information, usually composed of a string of characters
Peer-entity authentication	The corroboration that a peer entity in an association is the one claimed
Physical security	The measures used to provide physical protection of resources against deliberate and accidental threats
Privacy	The right of individuals to control or influence what information related to them may be collected and stored and by whom and to whom that information may be disclosed
Repudiation	Denial by one of the entities involved in a communication of having participated in all or part of the communication
Routing control	The application of rules during the process of routing so as to chose or avoid specific networks, links, or relays

Table 5.1 (continued)

Terminology	Description
Rule-based security policy	A security policy based on global rules imposed on all user's the rules usually rely on a comparison of the sensitivity of the resources being accessed and the possession of corresponding attributes of users, a group of users, or entities acting on behalf of users
Security audit	An independent review or examination of system records or activities to test for adequacy of system controls, to ensure compliance with established policy and operations procedures, to detect breaches in security, and to recommend any indicated changes in control, policy, and procedures
Security audit trail	Data collected and potentially used to facilitate a security audit
Security label	The marking bound to a resource (may be a data unit) that names or designates the security attributes of that resource
Security policy	The set of criteria for the provision of security services
Security service	A service, provided by a layer of communicating open systems, that ensures adequate security of the systems or of data transfers
Selective field protection	The protection of specific fields within a message that is to be transmitted
Sensitivity	The characteristic of a resource that implies its value or importance and may include its vulnerability
Signature	*See digital signature*
Threat	A potential violation of security
Traffic analysis	The inference of information from observation of traffic flows (presence, absence, amount, direction, and frequency)
Traffic flow confidentiality	A confidentiality service to protect against traffic analysis
Trusted functionality	That which is perceived to be correct with respect to some criteria, such as established by a security policy

has relay entities that make routing decisions based on status reports received from other relay entities.

Insider attacks occur when legitimate users of a system behave in unintended or unauthorized ways. Most known computer crimes involved insider attacks that compromised the security of a system.

The techniques that may be used for *outsider attacks* include wiretapping, intercepting emissions, masquerading as authorized users of the system, and bypassing authentication or access control mechanisms. A *trapdoor* is added to a system when an entity of that system is altered to allow an attacker to produce an unauthorized effect on command or at a predetermined event or a sequence of events. An example would be modification of a password validation so that, in addition to its normal effect, it also validates an attacker's password.

When introduced to the system, a *Trojan horse* has an unauthorized function in addition to its authorized function. For example, a relay that also copies messages to an unauthorized channel is a Trojan horse.

5.1.6 Security Services

The security services that follow are included in the ISO 7498-2 security architecture. The services may be placed at appropriate layers. Security services that may be provided optionally within the OSI/RM include the following.

- *Authentication*: These services provide for the authentication of a communicating peer entity and the source of data (data origin). Peer entity authentication provides corroboration to the $(N + 1)$ entity that the peer entity is the claimed $(N + 1)$ entity. Data origin authentication provides corroboration to an $(N + 1)$ entity that the source of data is the claimed peer $(N + 1)$ entity.
- *Access Control*: This service provides protection against the unauthorized use of OSI or non-OSI resources accessible via OSI protocols.
- *Data Confidentiality*: This service provides for the protection of data from unauthorized disclosure. Data confidentiality services include connection confidentiality, connectionless confidentiality, selective field confidentiality, and traffic flow confidentiality.
- *Data Integrity*: This service provides protection against active threats. Data integrity services include connection integrity with recovery, connection integrity without recovery, selective field connection integrity, and selective field connectionless integrity.
- *Nonrepudiation*: *Repudiation* is defined as the denial by one of the entities involved in a communication of having participated in all or part of the communication. Nonrepudiation services may take one or both of two forms: nonrepudiation with proof of origin or nonrepudiation with proof of delivery.

5.1.7 Security Mechanisms

Security mechanisms implement security services. Security mechanisms are of two types: specific security mechanisms and pervasive security mechanisms.

Specific Mechanisms

Specific security mechanisms may be incorporated into an appropriate layer to provide some of the security services described earlier. Specific security mechanisms include the following.

- *Encipherment* may be used to provide confidentiality of either data or traffic flow information.
- *Digital signature mechanisms* may be used to define two procedures: signing a data unit and verifying a signed data unit.
- *Access control mechanisms* may be involved at the origin or any intermediate point to determine if the sender is authorized to communicate with the recipient or to use the resources. Mechanisms may be based on authentication information such as passwords, security labels, duration of access, time of access, or route of attempted access.
- *Data integrity mechanisms* include time stamping, sequence numbering, or cryptographic chaining, which may be used to provide integrity of a single data unit or field and the integrity of a stream of data units or fields.
- *Authentication* information such as passwords, use of characteristics or possessions of the entity, digital signature or notarization is another technique that may be applied.
- *Traffic padding* may be used to provide various levels of protection against traffic analysis.
- *In routing control*, routes may be chosen either dynamically or by prearrangement to use only physically secure subnetworks, relays, or links.

Each instance of communication may use a digital signature, encipherment, and integrity mechanisms as appropriate to the service being provided by the notary. Properties such as data origin, time, and destination can be assured by the provision of a *notarization* mechanism.

Pervasive Security Mechanisms

These mechanisms are not specific to any particular security service and are in general directly related to the level of security required.
 Trusted functionality may be used to extend the scope of or establish the effectiveness of other security mechanisms. *Security labels* may be used to indicate sensitivity level. Labels are additional data associated with the data transferred or may be implied by the use of a specific key to encipher data. *An audit trail* permits detection and investigation of breaches of security. The logging or recording of information is considered to be a security mechanism. *Security recovery* deals with requests from mechanisms–for example, event

handling and management functions, and takes recovery action as the result of applying a set of rules.

5.1.8 Security Management

OSI security management oversees the security services and mechanisms. Distribution of cryptographic keys, the setting of administratively imposed security selection parameters, and the reporting of security events are examples of the management and operation of services and mechanisms. Many security policies can be imposed by the administration of distributed open systems, and the OSI security management standards provide the support for such policies.

5.2 UNIX AND SECURITY

We examined information on the OSI/RM security architecture, the types of attacks or threats that an environment may experience, and the mechanisms defined within the architecture that can provide the basis for a security policy within your organization. In this section we examine, very specifically, mechanisms that can be used on UNIX systems to make the system more secure. Further, we take a look at some key protocols that UNIX systems support, protocols such as NFS and TFTP, and what we can do on a UNIX system to enable the secure use of these protocols.

How can a system administrator or manager use security-related utilities, files, and functions to define a model for a secure environment? Careful planning and awareness of the types of threats that a system may experience are key to defining a security policy that leads to a secure environment.

5.2.1 Super-User Sessions

What defines an account to be a *super-user account*? Any login name that has a UID of zero is a *super-user account*. Typically, on most UNIX systems the login name for a super-user account is **root**. The super-user account is the most privileged account on the system: it can read or write any file irrespective of the permissions defined, execute any file with an execute permission bit on, change any permission or ownership attribute, create device special files, and do other operations restricted to UID zero [2].

5.2.2 Passwords

Critical information associated with each user account is maintained in the **/etc/passwd** file. This is obviously the most important system file from the perspective of security. *No two users should have the same UID.* The file permission for **/etc/passwd** should be set to 644. The file must be owned by **root**. The password associated with the **root** account should be changed frequently. When manually editing the password file to add a new account it is important to indicate that the new user's password has aged. This directs *login* to force the user to choose a new password the first time the user logs in. In general, the *password aging* (discussed in the next section) interval must be set so that users change their password periodically.

Because the file **/etc/passwd** contains user account information including encrypted passwords, it is possible for a user to obtain a copy of **/etc/passwd** and decrypt the password entry for commonly used passwords. Passwords based on the following are relatively easy to decrypt: your user name, a word in a dictionary, individual names or pet names, addresses and places, any of the previously mentioned spelled backwards, and passwords less than six characters in length.

Passwords are the heart of security on any multiuser system.
Use the following rules when you create your password.

- Do not use your first, middle, last, nickname, or login name in any form.
- Do not use names of relatives and friends.
- Avoid using words in English and foreign language dictionaries, spelling lists, or other lists of words.
- Do not use words or numbers that are personal information, such as social security numbers, telephone numbers, and birthdate.
- Do not select a password where you repeat the same alphabet or digit.
- Use one with seven or more characters.
- Use one that mixes uppercase and lowercase letters.
- Use a password that includes nonalphabetic characters, such as punctuation symbols.
- Use a password that can be easily memorized, and do not write it down.
- Use a password that can be typed in quickly, making it harder for someone to steal.

Password Aging

Password aging is a mechanism that forces users to change their password. If you require a high level of security, then users should change their password every four to six weeks. The password changing mechanism also prevents a user from changing their password before a specified interval. The command format for password aging is

passwd -n minimum -x maximum -w warning username

where **-n minimum** defines the minimum number of days between password changes, **-x maximum** defines the maximum number of days that the password is valid, and **-w warning** sets the number of days before the password expires that the end user is warned, for example,

passwd -n 2 -x 45 -w 5 natasha

To disable password aging, set the maximum number of days to **-1**.

passwd -x -1 pabrai

5.2.3 System Accounts

Privileged accounts on the system are referred to as *system accounts*. Each system account performs a special function and has its summarizes system accounts typically found on UNIX hosts—do verify that a password is defined for each account (see Table 5.2).

5.2.4 Controlling Account Access

The **passwd** command may be used to control access to a given account. To prevent a user from changing their password, enter

passwd -n 8 -x 6 username

The **-n** option specifies the minimum time. The **-x** option specifies the maximum time. Since the minimum time is greater than the maximum time, the user will not be allowed to change his/her password. To get information about passwords, execute the command

Table 5.2
Important System Accounts

System Account	GID	Description
root	0	The most privileged account on a UNIX system
daemon	1	Controls background processing
bin	2	Owns most systems commands
sys	3	Owns many system files
adm	4	Owns some administration files
lp	8	Owns object and spooled data files for the printer
sysadmin	13	Owns administration tools such as *admintool*

 # passwd -s username
pabrai PS 10/15/93 4 45 5

If password aging is not enabled, then only the first two fields are displayed. The first field describes the login name (pabrai); the second provides information on the password status (PS):

- NP   indicates no password;
- LK   login is locked;
- PS   anything else.

The third field describes the date the password was last changed (10/15/93). The fourth field specifies the minimum number of days after the last time the password was changed before it can be changed again (4). The fifth field indicates the maximum number of days after the last password change that the user is forced to change the password (45). The last field describes the number of warning days before the password must be changed (5). To display the password status for all users, enter

 # passwd -s -a

To force a user to change their password, enter

 # passwd -f username

When the user next logs in, he/she will be forced to change their password. To get a display of logins with no passwords, enter

 # logins -p

To get information about login **nathan**, enter

 # logins -x -l nathan
nathan   740   other   1
         /export/home/nathan
         /bin/ksh
         PS 110293 -1 -1 -1

5.2.5 Logging Unsuccessful Logins

To log unsuccessful attempts to access your computer, you can create a file called **/var/adm/loginlog**. If the **/var/adm/loginlog** file exists and if five consecutive unsuccessful login attempts occur, then all those attempts are logged in the **loginlog** file. If the person attempts less than five times unsuccessfully, then none of the attempts is logged. Also, if the **/var/adm/loginlog** file does not exist, then no log is kept of unsuccessful attempts.

5.2.6 Search Path

When specifying your search path (PATH variable) refer to the "." last, if possible. An intruder may place a Trojan horse in place of a system command in a user area. If the current working directory is specified last in the search path, the Trojan horse will not be executed (assuming an application with the same name as the Trojan Horse exists in one of the system directories specified in your search path).

The syntax for setting the PATH variable is

    PATH=pathname:pathname:pathname. . . .   (in Bourne Shell)
    set path = (pathname pathname pathname)   (in C Shell)

For example, a typical definition for the search path in the **.profile** file may be

(In the **.profile** file for the Bourne Shell or the Korn Shell)
    PATH=/bin:/sys/bin:/usr/bin:usr/ucb:$HOME/bin:.
    export PATH

(In the **.cshrc** file for the C Shell)
    set path = (/bin:/sys/bin:/usr/bin:/usr/ucb:$HOME/bin:.)

If you need to frequently run applications from another area, then it is best to define an ALIAS in the **.cshrc** file that points to the program or application. For example, to display to the terminal the contents of the file *analysis* from **/home/kalidas/util**, in the **cshrc** file enter

alias analysis more /home/kalidas/util/analysis

Note that null entries in the path list point to the current working directory. It is a good practice to create a **$HOME/bin** directory in your area to hold private executables and scripts. The directory **$HOME/bin** may then be appended to the path list definition. Finally, open or temporary directories should not be included in the path list.

Create a file, **/tmp/test**, using the command

% touch /tmp/test

Edit the following program and save it as **who.c**:

#include <stdio.h>
main()
    {
        system ("/user/bin/who");
        system ("rm /tmp/test 2> /dev/null");
    }

Compile the program with the **cc** command

% cc -o who who.c

Edit the **.cshrc** file to change the path as follows:

set path = (. /bin /usr/bin /usr/ucb /etc /usr/etc)

Execute the following command and check the status of the file **/tmp/test**:

% **who**

5.2.7 Restricting Root Access

You should restrict access to the **root** account only to the console; thus, a user can only log in as **root** if he or she is at the console of the machine. If you need to log in to the **root** account remotely, first log in with your own username and then use the **su** command to become a super-user. To restrict **root** login to the console, uncomment the following line in the **/etc/default/login** file:

CONSOLE=/dev/console

The operating system records each time the **su** command is used; records are maintained in the log file, **/var/adm/sulog**. At any time, you can review the **/var/adm/sulog** file to determine which user is logged in as **root** on your system. The default conditions for the su command is specified in the file **/etc/default/su**.

If you would like to maintain a log for each time the su command is used to switch to another user, uncomment the following line in the **/etc/default/su** file:

SULOG=/var/adm/sulog

If you would like to see a display on the console each time an attempt is made to use the **su** command to log in as root, uncomment the following line in the **/etc/default/su** file:

CONSOLE=/dev/console

5.2.8 utmp and wtmp Files

The **utmp** and **wtmp** files contain user and accounting information for various commands–these commands include: **who**, **write**, and **login**. On a Sun system you can find these files in the **/var/adm** directory. The **utmp** and **wtmp** files provide specific information on:

- The username;
- The terminal line number;
- The device name;
- The process ID.

The **utmp** file records each time a user logs in, while the **wtmp** file records each time a user logs in or logs out. On some systems, you can determine the Internet address of the remote system from which the user established a connection.

5.2.9 syslog Facility

syslog is a general purpose facility that reads and forwards system messages to the appropriate log files and/or users, depending on the priority of the mesage and the system facility from which it originates. The configuration file, **/etc/syslog.conf**, is used to control where messages are forwarded. Upon startup, the *syslogd* daemon creates the file **/etc/syslog.pid**. This file contains the syslogd PID. On Sun Solaris systems, the *syslogd* daemon resides in the **/usr/sbin** directory. Some options that can be used with the *syslogd* daemon are **-d** to turn on debugging and **-f config file** to specify an alternate configuration file.

When *syslogd* starts, it reads the **/etc/syslogd.conf** file to determine events that need to be logged and where to log these events. Next, *syslogd* listens for log messages from three sources:

- **/dev/klog**: A special device that is used to read messages generated by the kernel;
- **/dev/log**: A UNIX domain socket that is used to read messages generated by processes running on the local system;
- **514/udp**: An Internet domain socket used to read messages generated over the network from other systems.

5.2.10 The last Command

The **last** command displays login and logout information about users and terminals. This command gets its information from the **/var/adm/wtmpx** file. The command format is

/usr/bin/last [-n number] [-f filename]

For example, the following use of the **last** command lists all **root** and other user sessions on the console terminal:

 # last root console

5.2.11 Directory and File Permissions

Table 5.3 summarizes file and directory permissions.

5.2.12 The umask Command

The **umask** command sets or displays your default permission; several programs set the default permission to 666 for ordinary files and 777 for directory and executable files. The file creation mask removes permissions from the default permissions, thus determining actual permissions assigned to a new file. The resulting permissions are the original permissions "ANDed" with the one's complement of the **umask** mask. For a high level of security, you may want to use a **umask** value of 077–this **umask** value denies access to group and others.

5.2.13 The chmod Command

The **chmod** command may be used to change the permission of any file owned by you. This command allows you to define file permissions in one of two ways: symbolic and absolute.

The *symbolic mode* allows you to use letters to modify file permissions. Table 5.4 summarizes **chmod** symbols.

For example,

    % chmod a+rwx   data.txt

The *absolute mode* is commonly used to set file permissions; in this mode you use octal values to define file permissions: these octal values are explained in Table 5.5.

Table 5.3
File and Directory Permissions

Symbol	Description
r	Read. Defined for files and directories. Files: Can open and read file contents. Directories: Can list files.
w	Write. Defined for files and directories. Files: Can modify (add, delete, change) file content. Directories: Can add or remove files/links in directories.
x	Execute. Defined for files and directories. Files: Can execute the file or run the file with the **exec** comand. Directories: Can **cd** to directory or subdirectories
-	Access Denied. Only defined for files. Files: Permission is not given to access files.

Table 5.4
Symbols Used With the **chmod** Command

Symbol	Description
u	User or owner
g	Group
o	Others
a	All
+	Add
-	Remove

Table 5.5
Absolute Mode Values Used with the **chmod** Command

Octal Value	Description (Permissions)
7	Read+write+execute
6	Read+write
5	Read+execute
4	Read
3	Write+execute
2	Write
1	Execute
0	Access denied

For example,

% **chmod 744 data.txt**

5.2.14 UIDs and GIDs

Discretionary access control may be applied on files, groups of files and directories. File permission and other information are stored as a 16-bit word within an *inode*. 9 bits are used to provide information on the actual file permissions. The file permissions may be **r**, **w**, **x** or - (access denied). 3 additional bits provide information relevant to file operation if the file is an executing program. All objects such as files and directories have attributes indicating their UID and GID. UIDs are defined in the **/etc/passwd** file. GIDs are defined in the **/etc/group** file. Each process is assigned four numbers to indicate who the process belongs to: real and effective UID and GID. Typically, the effective UID and GID is the same as the real UID and GID.

5.2.15 setuid, setgid, and the Sticky Bit

If the *set user identification (setuid)* permission bit is set on an executable file, then a process that runs this file is granted access based on the owner of the file instead of the user who created the process. Thus, a user can now access files and directories that would normally only be available to the owner. The setuid bit is the twelfth permission bit.

If the *set group identification (setgid)* permission bit is set, then the process's effective GID is changed to the owner of the group. Access is then granted based on permissions defined for the group. The setgid bit is the eleventh permission bit.

A program is typically given setuid/setgid attributes so as to allow its users the same access as the program's owner has to certain objects. setuid programs must be kept in write protected directories to prevent their replacement by unauthorized users. setuid programs created by the **root** account and setuid programs of any pseudouser accounts should be monitored frequently–since an intruder who has broken into the **root** account once may install and hide a setuid program that would enable super-user privileges even if the original security hole is fixed. To find all setuid/setgid files on your system enter

find / -perm -004000 -o -perm -002000 -type f -print

A program that has the *sticky bit* set will not be removed from swap space after the program has terminated. This is typically used by applications that are executed frequently. If a directory has the sticky bit set, then a file can only be deleted by

- The owner of the file;
- The owner of the directory;
- Root;
- The sticky bit is the tenth permission bit.

Table 5.6 provides information on setuid, setgid, and sticky bit permission symbols.

5.3 TCP/IP AND SECURITY

Securing access to a system on the network is as important as securing the system itself. We examine how to deny incoming and outgoing system access and look closely at securing application protocols such as NFS and TFTP.

5.3.1 telnet Versus rlogin

telnet and **rlogin** are commands used to login to another node on a TCP/IP network. Like most TCP/IP application layer protocols, **telnet** and **rlogin** are

Table 5.6
setuid, setgid, and Sticky Bit Permission Symbols

Symbol	Description
s	setuid or setgid bit is set
S	setuid bit is set but user execution bit is not set
t	Sticky bit is set, others execution bit is set
T	Sticky bit is set, others execution bit is not set

client/server applications. *telnet* is the name of the client application, while *telnetd* is the server application. After a connection is established with the remote system, the **telnet** application prompts the user for their username and password.

Each character entered by the user for their username and password is sent unencrypted over the network to the remote system. Using any network analyzer, you can set filters to capture usernames and passwords that are sent over the network. As far as **rlogin** is concerned, *rlogin* is the name of the client application while *rlogind* is the name of the server. The **rlogin** application does not require the user to enter their username or password–instead authentication is based on information in the files **/etc/hosts.equiv** and **~/.rhosts**.

As long as the user is trusted, wherein information on the user is contained in **hosts.equiv** or **.rhosts** file, the user is allowed access to the remote system without a password. If information on the user is not available in those two files, then **rlogin** prompts the user for the password. The **rsh** and **rcp** commands also base authentication on information specified in the **.rhosts** or **hosts.equiv** files. The **/etc/hosts.equiv** file specifies nodes on the network that are trusted and not trusted.

Any hostname listed in this file is a trusted system on the network. The user who connects from a remote system is authorized to login to the same username on the local system without a password; specifically, the user can execute the **rlogin**, **rsh**, and **rcp** commands. The file is scanned by the process from the beginning; as soon as a match is found, search stops. Consider the following **/etc/hosts.equiv** file.

```
nathan.netguru.com
natasha.netguru.com
tina.netguru.com
-@sales
+@engineers
```

This file specifies that any user on nodes **nathan**, **natasha**, and **tina** may log in to the same username on the local system without a password–**nathan**,

natasha, and **tina** are trusted nodes. The line **-@sales** indicates that hosts in the sales netgroup are not trusted and therefore not authorized to connect to the local system without a password. The line **+@engineers** specifies that all hosts listed in the engineers netgroup are trusted systems.

After searching the **/etc/hosts.equiv** file, the *rlogind* or *rshd* applications next scan the **.rhosts** file in the user's home directory. The **.rhosts** file may be used by a user to define systems from which the same username may connect without a password. A user can also authorize other users on a remote system to connect without a password. Consider a user named **weber**'s **.rhosts** file that includes the line

    koenen.netguru.com   pabrai

This implies that **pabrai** on node **koenen.netguru.com** could log in to **weber**'s account on the local system without a password.

5.3.2 Incoming FTP Connections

You can create a file, **/etc/ftpusers**, to specify a list of users who are not authorized to establish incoming **ftp** connections to your system. You should include pseudouser accounts in this file, accounts such as **root**, **bin**, and **daemon**. Also note that **ftp** access to a system will be denied unless the user's shell, specified in the **/etc/passwd** file, is listed in the file, **/etc/shells**, or the user's shell is one of the following:

- **/bin/sh** or **/usr/bin/sh**;
- **/bin/ksh** or **/usr/bin/ksh**;
- **/bin/csh** or **/usr/bin/csh**.

5.3.3 sendmail, SMTP, and Security

The SMTP is the protocol used by the *sendmail* application on UNIX systems to send mail messages to users on a TCP/IP network. In the past there have been many security break-ins that have occurred because of security holes in the *sendmail* program. For example, earlier versions of the *sendmail* program allowed a remote user to send mail directly to any file on the system, including **/etc/passwd**. *sendmail* can be compiled in "debug mode," which has been used by hackers in the past to have unrestricted access to the system. Note that the *sendmail* application runs as super-user, which makes its security holes all the more significant.

To verify that the *sendmail* program on your system does not still support security holes that have been used in the past, test that *sendmail* does not support the commands **debug**, **wiz**, or **kill**.

```
# telnet localhost smtp
Trying 127.0.0.1 ...
Connected to localhost.
Escape character is '^]'.
220 ganesh. Sendmail 5.0/SMI-SVR4 ready at Wed, 20 Oct 93 09:42:51
CST
debug
500 Command unrecognized
wiz
500 Command unrecognized
kill
500 Command unrecognized
```

5.3.4 Denying Incoming Network Access

The *inetd* daemon uses the **bind()** system call to attach itself to network ports and the **select()** system call to provide notification when a connection is made on any port. The **inetd.conf** file determines what application should run on the system when an incoming connection is detected. If an intruder gains access to this file, then he/she may modify an entry to start a shell or some other program upon *inetd* receiving a connection. If you would like to deny individuals from establishing a **telnet** connection with your system, then comment the **telnet** line in the **inetd.conf** file–the same is true for disabling incoming access for any network application specified in the **inetd.conf** file.

The ***inetd.conf*** *file contents must be examined on a regular basis.*

5.3.5 Denying Outgoing Network Access

If you would like to deny outgoing access for network applications such as **telnet** and **ftp** you could remove the client **telnet** and **ftp** applications from your system. Client network applications on a Sun Solaris system are in the **/bin** directory. Note that even if you remove the application from the system, it is still possible for a user to get a copy of the application from an outside source and install it in their directory–however, it at least makes the process of establishing outgoing connections for specific network applications more difficult.

5.3.6 NFS Security

NFS authenticates requests for files by authenticating the client system as opposed to the user. If the user on the client system has access to the **root** account, then he/she can impose as the owner of a file and access it. It is possible for a user to inject packets on the network imposing as a user or for the user to passively eavesdrop on NFS transactions–these transactions may be replayed later.

By default, if no restrictions are placed on the NFS server, then those resources can be mounted by any node on the network and it is possible to access those resources with read+write privileges. When configuring the system as a NFS server, consider using the following options:

- ro;
- rw=client[:client];
- root.

ro indicates that all clients have read only access to the NFS resource. **rw=client[:client]** gives read+write access to only the clients specified. The **root** option specifies that superuser on the NFS client has **root** privileges on the NFS directory or file system exported. The **ro** and **rw** options may be used to restrict access to a limited number of client nodes that have access to NFS resources. The following is an example of the file **/etc/exports**.

```
/usr        -access=natasha
/home       -access=natasha
#
/export/root/nathan -root=natasha, access=natasha
/export/swap/nathan -root=natasha, access=natasha
/export/exec/sun4c
```

If no **access=***client* is specified for a file system, then any host on the network can use NFS to mount the exported file system.

5.3.7 The Trivial File Transfer Protocol

The *trivial file transfer protocol* (TFTP) may be used to download the X server image and fonts to X terminals or to allow diskless workstations to boot over the network. Typically, implementations of TFTP have been known to have security holes. The Department of Energy's (DOE) *Computer Incident Advisory Capability* (CIAC) had reported, some time ago, that there were security holes related to *tftpd* and *rwalld* that leave certain systems vulnerable to intrusion. The holes, when used in a very specific scenario, permit an intruder to attack UNIX systems and assume super-user privileges.

The TFTP hole allows any user without first logging in to read any readable file and write any writeable file on a remote system using the Internet network. The hole existed in SunOS 3.x systems but has been fixed on most UNIX systems. The following test verifies that the version of TFTP installed on the system has been patched to prevent some security holes.

```
% tftp
tftp> connect hostname
tftp> get/etc/passwd stolen.passwd
Error code:1 File not found
tftp> quit
%
```

Note that there is no user login or validation within the TFTP protocol; therefore, the *tfpd* daemon must run in secure mode. On a UNIX system you need to run the *tfpd* daemon with the **-s** option. When accessed *tfpd* changes its root directory to *homedir* (typically,**/tftpboot**), which is specified in the **/etc/inetd.conf** file.

5.3.8 NIS+ Security

The motivation for NIS+ security is to protect information in the namespace and to prevent unauthorized access to the namespace.

For example, a system should not be able to change or destroy objects in the namespace. Every component in the namespace specifies the type of operation that it will accept and from whom (authorization); further, every request is authenticated.

5.3.8.1 Terminology

Principals

A NIS+ principal is a client or a client workstation whose credentials have been stored in the namespace. A user can log in to a NIS+ client and request access to the namespace based on his or her credentials. The user may also log in as super-user and request access to the namespace based on the credentials of the workstation.

Credentials

A credential is authentication information about an NIS+ principal that the client software sends with each request to an NIS+ server. The credential identifies the principal who sent the request. This information is used by the server to determine the principal's access rights for the objects it is trying to access.

Cred Table

This table stores LOCAL credentials and the information used to encrypt and decrypt DES credentials. The **org_dir** directory of every NIS+ domain includes a Cred table.

Access Rights

Access rights specify the type of operation that NIS+ principals–authenticated and unauthenticated–can perform on an NIS+ object. NIS+ supports four types of access rights:

- Read;
- Modify;
- Destroy;
- Create.

Authorization Categories

Each NIS+ object uses four authorization categories:

- Owner;
- Group;
- World;
- Nobody.

Access rights are granted by each object to each authorization category.

NIS+ Server Security Levels

NIS+ defines three security levels: 0, 1, and 2 (see Table 5.7).

NIS+ Client/Server Communication

A client always includes the credentials of the NIS+ principal making the request. The NIS+ server checks the credentials to determine whether the request is authenticated or unauthenticated. A client request is said to be authenticated if the server is able to identify the NIS+ principal who sent it; this identification is then used to determine the authorization category for the principal:

- Owner;
- Group;
- World.

A client request is unauthenticated if no credentials were sent or if wrong credentials were sent.

Table 5.7
NIS+ Security Levels

Server Security Level	Description
0	Lowest security level. Unauthenticated requests are placed in the Nobody category.
1	Accepts LOCAL or DES credentials. If credentials are not supplied, then these requests are considered unauthenticated and placed in the Nobody category.
2	Accepts only DES credentials. Requests that supply LOCAL credentials are considered unauthenticated and placed in the Nobody category.

Unauthorized requests are placed in the Nobody category. Depending upon the rights defined for the Nobody category, the request may be granted even though the sender may not be identified.

5.4 SECURITY-RELATED PRODUCTS AND APPLICATIONS

There are a number of security products and applications that can help make your computing environment more secure. We examine how to install, configure, and use some of these products and applications. We stepped through a number of security threats and problems to which UNIX systems on a TCP/IP network may be vulnerable. Products and applications of the type, discussed in this section, help secure computing resources.

5.4.1 ASET

The *Automated Security Enhancement Tool* (ASET) is a security package, enabling automated control and monitoring of system security. ASET runs at one of three security levels:

- Low;
- Medium;
- High.

At each level, the file control functions increase. ASET consists of seven tasks, each of which performs specific checks and adjustments to system files. Each task generates a report noting any detected security weaknesses and any changes the task has made to the system files. With ASET, as with any security product, tasks are disk-intensive and can impact system performance; hence, ASET should be scheduled to run when system activity is lowest.

ASET Tasks

Tasks are run at one of the three security levels, and each task generates a report. *Set System File Permissions (tune)*: **tune.rpt** set the permissions on system files to the designated security level: *low*, permissions are set to standard release values appropriate for an open information-sharing environment; *medium*, permissions are tightened producing adequate security for most environments; *high*, permissions are tightened to a very restrictive access. It is run when the system is installed and again to alter previously established levels. Therefore, this task is run only occasionally.

System Files Checklist (cklist): **cklist.rpt** examines system files and compares each one with a description of that file listed in a master file. The following criteria are checked for each file: owner and group, permission bits, size and checksum, number of links, and last modification time. ASET creates a snapshot of these files the first time it runs and when it runs at a new security level. ASET uses the snapshot as a master, comparing the file attributes at each execution with those of the master.

User/Group Checks (usrgrp): **usrgrp.rpt** check the consistency and integrity of user accounts and groups using the passwd and group files (see Figure 5.1). Both the local and NIS (or NIS+) password files are checked. The following violations are reported:

- Duplicate names or IDs;
- Incorrectly formatted entries;
- Accounts without passwords, invalid login directories;
- Nobody account;
- Plus sign (+) in **/etc/passwd** file on NIS (or NIS+) server.

System Configuration Files Check (sysconf): **sysconf.rpt** performs checks and modifications on the files: **/etc/default/login**, **/etc/hosts.equiv**, **/etc/**

A sample of **usrgrp.rpt** follows:

```
*** Begin User and Group Checking ***
: Password file, line 11, no passwd
:sync::1:1::/:/bin/sync
..end user check; starting group check ...
Checking /etc/group...
Checking /etc/passwd ...
Warning
*** End User and Group Checking ***
```

Figure 5.1 Sample ASET **usrgrp.rpt** file.

inetd.conf, /etc/aliases, /var/adm/utmp, /var/adm/utmpx, /.rhosts, /etc/vfstab, /etc/dfs/dfstab, /etc/ftpusers.

Environment Check (env): **env.rpt** checks the PATH and UMASK environment variables for **root** and other users in the **/.profile**, **/.login**, and **/.cshrc** files.

eeprom Check (eeprom): **eeprom.rpt** can be set to *none, command,* or *full*. ASET only reports recommendations in the *eeprom.rpt* file and does not change this setting.

Firewall (firewall): **firewall.rpt** ensures that the system can be safely used as a network relay. It disables the forwarding of IP packets and hides routing information from the external network. Runs at all security levels, but takes action only at the highest level.

ASET Reports

All report files generated are found in **/usr/aset/reports**. Subdirectory names indicate the date and time when the reports were generated. Each subdirectory contains all reports generated from one execution of ASET. The directory latest is a symbolic link pointing to the subdirectory containing the latest reports.

Task Report Files

Each report file is named after the task that generates it. Beginning and ending banner lines occur in each report; thus, a task that terminates prematurely can be identified. If a task does terminate prematurely, the report file will most likely contain a message indicating the reason for termination.

Report files should be examined closely for a period of time. When the report content stabilizes, use the **diff** utility to compare reports.

Execution Log

The execution log confirms that ASET executed and specifies any execution error messages. Figure 5.2 displays an example of messages seen on the screen when ASET is invoked.

Using ASET Interactively

/usr/aset/aset

To set the security level enter

/usr/aset/aset -l *level*

ASET running at security level low

Machine=shiva: Current time = 0112_11:00

aset: Using /usr/aset as working directory

Executing task list...

    env
    sysconfig
    usrgrp
    tune
    cklist
    eeprom

All tasks executing. Some background tasks may still be running.

Run /usr/aset/util/taskstat to check their status:
    % /usr/aset/util/taskstat aset_dir
Where aset_dir is ASET's operating directory, currently=/usr/aset

When the tasks complete, the reports can be found in:
    /usr/aset/reports/latest/*.rpt

You can view them by:
    more/usr/aset/reports/latest/*.rpt

Figure 5.2 ASET execution log.

To name the working directory enter

/usr/aset/aset -d *pathname*

The environment variable, ASETDIR, specifies the ASET working directory. ASETSECLEVEL specifies the security level (low, medium, high).

setenv ASETDIR /usr/testaset/asetdir
setenv ASETSECLEVEL med
aset

5.4.2 Computer Oracle Password System (COPS)

Computer Oracle and Password System (COPS) is a UNIX security audit program that performs various checks to determine if the UNIX system is vulnerable to security threats. COPS informs you of security problems–it does not alter the configuration of a machine to correct a risk. COPS was originally written by Dan Farmer.

You can get a copy of COPS from the following *ftp anonymous* site:

ftp anonymous Site Name: **ftp.cert.org**
Directory: **/pub/tools/cops/cops.tar.Z**

After you transfer the file to your system, enter the following command to *uncompress* and *untar* the package via

zcat cops.tar.Z | tar xvf -

Next, to create the COPS executable, enter

make

You can then execute the following command to execute the COPS suite of programs to create a report that summarizes the current state of the system:

cops -a sun4 -s /usr/secure

The audit report generated by COPS is itemized and categorized by risk level. There are several command arguments that can be used to perform subsets of an audit, or to change the output device, and other configuration options. In general, COPS examines the following system elements:

- Review boot strap files.
- Check file such as: **/etc/passwd**, **/etc/yppasswd**, **/etc/shadow**.
- User authorization file errors such as incorrect number of data-fields on a line, duplicate uids, nonnumeric uids, nonnumeric group ids, empty passwords, invalid shell commands, empty account fields, and poor or guessable passwords are checked.
- The **/etc/group** file is checked for syntax errors and vulnerabilities—syntax errors, nonalphanumeric group names, nonnumeric group ids, and duplicate group names are examined.
- The **/etc/fstab** file is checked for vulnerabilities of world or group writability.
- All SUID programs are found and compared against a valid listing of SUID programs; those SUID programs that don't show up in the valid list are announced during a COPS audit. COPS will also announce those programs that are found to not have the SUID bit set but are listed in the SUID database.
- Initialization files associated with the **root** account are checked for vulnerabilities. The contents of initialization files associated with the **root** account are checked for **umask** value, PATH variable, and shell environment settings.

- COPS will look for a **/etc/ftpusers** file and ensure that the **root** account is in it.
- The **/etc/hosts.equiv** file is checked for a single line containing a + character.
- COPS will monitor a database of files and announce changes in the sizes of files specified in it's database.

COPS is configured using several configuration databases. There is one main database that COPS uses to locate all other configuration databases. The default main database is called **/cops/lib/cops.dba**.

COPS, executed without parameters, will display all its output (security problems discovered) to *stdout*. The **-i** option may be specified to ignore messages, problems discovered, when it was last run. COPS has other, optional, command line parameters. The **-d** command line option can be used to specify other database configuration files. Table 5.8 summarizes parameters accepted by the **cops** command.

Table 5.9 is a summary of variables recognized by COPS in its main configuration database, **/cops/lib/cops.dba**.

Figure 5.3 describes a sample **cops.dba** file.

```
SECURE=/cops/bin
WRITEABLEDIRDBA=/cops/lib/dirchk.dba
PASSWORD=/etc/passwd
YPPASSWORD=/var/etc/passwd
ETCGROUP=/etc/group
WRITEABLEFILEDBA=/cops/lib/filechk.dba
SUIDDBA=/cops/lib/stopsample.dba
RHIDDENFILESDBA=/cops/lib/hiddenrfiles.dba
BOOTINITFILESDBA=/cops/lib/initbootfiles.dba
CRONTABSDIRDBA=/cops/lib/dircrontabs.dba
NOPASSWORDDBA=/cops/lib/validnopassword.dba
ROOTUIDDBA=cops/lib/uidroot.dba
ERRORLOG=/cops/lib/cops.error-NODENAME
WORDSDBA=/cops/lib/passwords.dba
SIZESDBA=/cops/lib/sizes.dba
MEMORYFILE=/cops/lib/mem-NODENAME]
SHADOWPASSWORD=/etc/passwd
C2=FALSE
YP=FALSE
```

Figure 5.3 Sample **cops.dba** file

COPS Messages

The COPS system will categorize all audit messages. A message will always be displayed with a category assignment number. The following is a list of messages

Table 5.8
Options Accepted by the **cops** Command

Option	Description
-i	Will instruct COPS to announce all security risks regardless if you have been told about them in a previous run.
-n	Will instruct COPS to not record output status in memory, thus leaving the status from the previous execution intact. This is used primarily for debug purposes.
-i and **-n**	Running COPS with the **-i** and **-n** options completely disables the memory feature of screening redundant information from the output status.
-s	Will instruct COPS to execute silently. Normally COPS outputs the time of the last run, the **-s** option will disable this. This is provided for use of COPS in crontab to avoid mail messages to root unless there is a security message.
-v	Instructs COPS to announce the check that is being performed during runtime.
-o filename	Instructs COPS to output to *filename* instead of the screen.
-d filename	Instructs COPS to read *filename* for configuration settings. The default COPS database is **cops.dba**.
-h	Prints helpful information about the COPS parameters.

and ID numbers that COPS will report and a brief description of what needs to be done to correct the problem.

111: Duplicate UIDs found in password file, *password_file*. Account(s): *account_name, account_name, . . .*

This is a problem, especially if the accounts have different permissions or privileges. When a user's account is deleted, one or more accounts may remain active. To correct, delete, or change one of the user's account.

112: Password file, *password_file*, line *line_num*, is blank.

To correct, delete all blank lines.

113: Password file, *password_file*, line *line_num*, does not have 7 fields Line: *password_line*

Dangerous, if a program checks for a field value using the *password_file*, the result is undetermined. To correct, ensure all fields of all lines in the **password_file** have legal values.

Table 5.9
Variables Specified in the **cops.dba** File

Variable Name	Description
WRITEABLEDIRDBA	The name of the database that contains a list of directories in which to check security vulnerabilities.
WRITLEABLEFILEDBA	The name of the database that contains a list of files on which to check security vulnerabilities.
XWRITLEABLEFILEDBA	The name of the database that contains a list of files to exclude from output if found to be writable in WRITLEABLEFILEDBA. This allows for easier configuration of the COPS program with the use of wildcards in the WRITLEABLEFILEDBA file. This variable is OPTIONAL.
PASSWORD	The name of the database that the user accounts are defined in (usually: **/etc/passwd**).
YPPASSWORD	The name of the NIS password file. This is ignored if the YP variable is set FALSE.
SHADOWPASSWORD	The name of the shadow password file, if password shadowing is enabled. If shadow password is not enabled, set this variable to FALSE.
ETCGROUP	The name of the group database. (usually: **/etc/group**).
SUIDDBA	The name of the database that contains a list of valid set UID filenames.
RHIDDENFILESDBA	The name of the database that contains a list of files that execute by root at login.
BOOTINITFILESDBA	The name of the database that contains a list of files that execute at boot time.
CRONTABSDIRDBA	The name of the database that contains a list of directories where cron table files are located.
NOPASSWORDDBA	The name of the database that contains a list of user accounts that are valid not to have a password for login.
ROOTUIDDBA	The name of the database that contains a list of user accounts that are valid to have a 0 UID.
C2	Set TRUE or FALSE. Set TRUE if C2 security is installed.
YP	Set TRUE or FALSE. Set TRUE if YP is installed, and the local machine is the master YP server.
ERRORLOG	The name of the file that will contain errors that occur while executing COPS.
WORDSDBA	The name of the database that contains a list of words to use in guessing passwords. If this variable is not set, extra password guessing is skipped.
MEMORYFILE	The name of the file to which memory is to be saved.
SIZESDBA	The name of the database that contains a list of system configuration files that the sizes should be monitored.
SECURE	Set to the directory where the COPS software and libraries are installed.

114: Password file, *password_file*, line *line_num*, Account name is Null Line: *password_line*

If an account has no name, unknown problems may surface. To correct, add an account name or delete the entry from the password file.

116: Password file, *password_file*, line *line_num*, non-numeric USER id Line: *password_line*

A user has an invalid user ID. Dangerous if it translates to an invalid number. To correct, change the field to a legal, unique numeric value.

117: Password file, *password_file*, line *line_num*, non-numeric GROUP id Line: *password_line*

A user has an invalid group ID. Dangerous if it translates to an invalid number. To correct, change the field to a legal, numeric value.

118: Password file, *password_file*, line *line_num*, invalid login directory Line: *password_line*

A user has a nonexistent or invalid login directory listed in the **passwd** file. Sometimes these are maintenance accounts, but it is discouraged. Examine the account to see if it should really exist. To correct, either delete the account or put in a valid login directory.

119: Password file, *password_file*, account has no password, Account: *account_name*

If an account has no password, anyone can log into the account. To correct, either have the user change her/his password or change it yourself or remove the account. If this account is authorized not to have a password, then add the account name to the database file specified with the variable, **NOPASSWOR-DDBA**.

120: Password file, *password_file*, has UID of ZERO: *account_name*

Ideally, no one but **root** should have a UID of 0. Anyone with a UID of 0 is considered a super-user. To correct, change the UID from 0 to some other valid number. If the account needs **root** privileges, include the account name specified with variable, **VALIDROOTDBA**.

121: Password file, *password_file*, line *line_num*, invalid character in account name. Line: *password_line*

To correct, delete or change the login to a valid login.

130: Group file, *group_file*, line *line_num*, is blank

To correct, remove all blank lines.

131: Group file, *group_file*, line *line_num*, does not have 4 fields Line:*group_line*

One or more of the groups will result in invalid results, depending on which field(s) is missing. To correct, ensure group has four valid fields.

132: Group file, *group_file*, line *line_num*, non-alphanumeric user id Line:*group_line*

To correct, change the invalid ID to a valid ID.

133: Group file, *group_file*, line *line_num*, has group password Line:*group_line*

To correct, change the password to an asterisk ("*").

135: Group file, *group_file*, line *line_num*, non-numeric group id Line:*group_line*

GIDs must be numeric. Testing a nonnumeric ID can give unpredictable results. To correct, change the ID to a valid GID.

136: Duplicate Group(s) found in *group_file* Account(s): *group_name, group_name, . . .*

This means that there are two or more groups with the same name in the **group_file**. This is a system accounting problem, unpredictable conditions may arise. To correct, remove all but one instance of each group in the group file.

137: Group *group_id* has duplicate user(s)

A group has the same user listed more than once. If all instances of the user are not deleted, they probably will remain with their old privileges. To correct, remove all but one instance of a user in each group of the **/etc/group** file.

150: NFS file system *line_data* exported with no restrictions

Anyone can mount the file system. May or may not be a problem, but look over it closely. To correct, specify a valid list of hosts and users that may mount it.

152: File *file_name* is World writable

This means that a file is world writable. To correct, change privileges on the file to remove write access for the world.

153: File *file_name* is Group readable

This means that a file is group readable. To correct, verify that this is okay or change privileges on the file to remove group readability.

160: Directory *directory_name* is World writable

This means that a directory is world writable. To correct, change privileges on the directory to remove write access for the world.

170: File *file_name* in cron file *cron_file* is World writable

This could be a problem if the cron file is owned by **root**. To correct, change file permissions to remove write access to the world.

175: File *file_name* is World writable and it is in the boot file, *boot_file*

These files are executed with **root** privileges at boot time. To correct, either delete the reference to **file_name** inside the file or change the permissions of the file to remove write access for the world.

181: Warning, Root's umask set to *xyz* in file: *file_name*

If **root**'s umask is set poorly, files that are created by root have permissions that allow world and/or group access. To correct, specify a value such as 077 with the **umask** command.

183: "." is in roots path!

To correct, remove the "." from the path in the initialization file.

201: Warning! User *user_id* home directory *home_dir* is mode *xyz*!

To correct, change directory permissions to remove access to the world.

202: Warning! User *user_id*: *init_file* is mode *xyz*!

If a user's file is world writable, anyone can modify it. It is possible for Trojan horse programs to be installed. To correct, change *init_file* permissions to remove access to the world.

5.4.3 TCP Wrapper

TCP Wrapper is a public domain security software that *prevents unauthorised network connections* for applications such as **ftp**, **telnet**, **finger**, **rlogin**, **rsh**, and **talk**. The software is available from the following *ftp anonymous* site:

ftp anonymous Site Name: **ftp.win.tue.nl**
Directory: **/pub/security/tcp_wrappers.7.tar.Z**

TCP Wrapper logs unsucessful attempts for network connections for applications such as **ftp**, **telnet**, **finger**, **rlogin**, **rsh**, and **talk**. TCP Wrapper does not replace any binaries on the system. The TCP Wrapper daemon monitors connections for applications such as:

- **ftp**;
- **telnet**;
- **finger**;
- **rlogin**;
- **rsh**;
- **talk**.

These network services are specified in the **inetd.conf** configuration file, which is referred to by the *inetd* process. Inside of *inetd* starting a network service daemon, such as *telnet* when an incoming *telnet* connection is received, it starts *tcpd*–a TCP Wrapper daemon. The *tcpd* daemon works with files such as **/etc/hosts.deny** and **/etc/hosts.allow** to determine which hosts are authorized to establish a connection with your system. TCP Wrapper logs unauthorized attempts in the file specified in **syslog.conf**. TCP Wrapper works with the following system files:

- The **/etc/inetd.conf** file is modified to specify the *tcpd* daemon.
- The **/etc/syslog.conf** file is modified to include the log file name.
- The **/etc/hosts.deny** file is created to specify hosts and services that are to be denied access.
- The **/etc/hosts.allow** file is created to specify hosts and services that are to be allowed access.

5.4.3.1 Configuration of TCP Wrapper

As indicated, TCP Wrapper can be downloaded from **ftp.win.tue.nl**. It is available as a compressed, tar file under **/pub/security/tcp_wrappers.7.tar.Z**. The white paper from W.Z.Venema, the author of this software, is also available in the same directory (as both *ps* and *text* files).

Step 1

Execute the following command to *uncompress* and *untar* the file.

zcat tcp_wrappers.7.tar.Z | tar xvf -

Step 2

Execute the following command to compile the package and make sure the second parameter is the operating system, for example, **aix** for IBM RS6000. This particular installation was done on a SPARC Tadpole running SunOS:

make sun

When **make** succeeds, *tcpd*, the tcp wrapper daemon, is generated. *tcpd* can monitor network services such as **telnet**, **finger**, **ftp**, **rlogin**, and **talk**. These network services can be wrapped in the **/etc/inetd.conf** file with *tcpd* either denying or allowing certain hosts in a given system. The following is an example entry for wrapping a network service:

finger stream tcp nowait nobody /opt/security/tcpd in.fingerd

After editing this file, you need to refresh the *inetd* daemon by executing the following command:

kill -HUP PID   (PID is *inetd*'s PID)

Now, you can deny access to the *tcpd* wrapped network services by entering the host name in the **/etc/hosts.deny** file.

5.4.4 Other Security-Related Applications

Table 5.10 summarizes information on important security-related software and applications that can help make your computing environment more secure.

5.5 KERBEROS

A major security problem in today's network is that once a user attempts to log onto a node on the network, the password information is sent unencrypted. Frequently executed applications, such as **telnet** and **ftp**, do not encrypt the password when it is sent from the client host to the server node for authentication.

Kerberos is the *authentication system* developed as a part of Project Athena at MIT. Kerberos requires a password for each network service transaction requested. Each user and every network service has a password, and the only entity that knows all passwords is the *Kerberos Authentication Server* (KAS). The password, when it is sent on the network, is always in an encrypted form. The authentication server itself must be physically secure. The following is a summary of terminology associated with the Kerberos system.

Kerberos	User and service authentication system.
TGS	The *ticket granting server* is responsible for assigning tickets to clients (users and services) on the network.

Table 5.10
Security-Related Software

Application	Description	ftp anonymous Site	Directory
TIS Firewall Kit	Provides the foundation needed for Internet firewalls	ftp.tis.com	/pub/firewalls/toolkit
tcpdump	Monitor traffic on a network	ftp.ee.lbl.gov	tcpdump2.2.1.tar.Z
traceroute	Determine the path between the source and destination systems	ftp.ee.lbl.gov	traceroute.tar.Z
SNMP	SNMP software that supports MIB-II objects	lancaster.andrew.cmu.edu	pub/snmp-dist
tripwire	Useful for determining the state of a system	ftp.cs.purdue.edu	/pub/spaf/COAST/Tripwire
crack	Password cracking program.	ftp.cert.org	/pub/tools/crack
CERT	CERT advisories on security threats and problems	ftp.cert.org	pub/cert_advisories

Ticket — Used by a user to provide credentials. In the Kerberos environment it is used to get a session key. A ticket contains the name of the server, client, Internet address of the client system, time stamp, session length, and a random session key.

Authenticator — System responsible for tickets assigned.

The objectives of Kerberos include:

- Unencrypted passwords should not be sent over the network.
- Unencrypted passwords should not be stored on the workstation.
- Define the length of time that a session is authenticated; if the session continues beyond that defined time, then the user has to authenticate himself or herself at that point.

Figure 5.4 describes the steps involved in Kerberos authentication [3].

In a Kerberos environment, the user enters his or her user name in response to the **login**: prompt. Before the password prompt is displayed, a message is sent across the network to the Kerberos authentication server. The message includes the *username* and the name of one particular Kerberos server, known as the Kerberos *ticket-granting server* (TGS) [3].

message = {username, TGS-name}

The message that is sent is not encrypted. The KAS looks up the user name and the TGS server in the Kerberos database and obtains a one-way encryption key for each. KAS next forms a response that it sends to the login program on the workstation. The response contains a *ticket* that grants the user access to the requested TGS. Tickets are always encrypted and consist of

ticket = {username, TGS-name, WS-IP-addr, TGS-session-key}

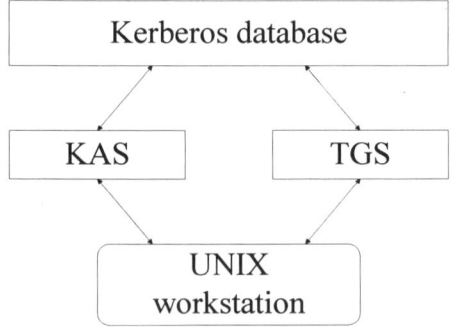

Figure 5.4 Kerberos authentication process.

The TGS-session key is a random number generated by KAS. The ticket also contains a time stamp and an expiration date. The lifetime of a ticket is typically eight hours, after which the user must be identified again to Kerberos, providing both the user namer and password. KAS encrypts the ticket using the encryption key of the TGS server. This produces what is called a *sealed ticket*. A message is then formed, consisting of the sealed ticket and the TGS-session key as follows:

message = {TGS-session-key, sealed ticket}

The message is encrypted using the user's password stored in the Kergeros database. The *login* program receives the encrypted message and then prompts for the password. The cleartext password entered is processed through the standard UNIX one-way encryption algorithm and the result, known as the *user's encryption key*, is used to decrypt the message (TGS-session key and sealed ticket) that was received. The cleartext password is then erased from memory. The workstation software saves a copy of the sealed ticket and the TGS-session key [3].

Next if a network service is requested, such as accessing a file from a file server or printing a file on a print server, the system requesting the service has to obtain a ticket for that particular service. The system requesting the service is known as the *end server*, and to obtain the ticket the workstation software contacts the Kerberos TGS [3].

5.6 WHAT DO WE NEED TO DO?

Note that very few computer break-ins are publicized—victims may not report computer crimes discovered for fear that their customers may lose faith in their operations. Experts agree that the most common computer crime is an internal threat as opposed to external—employees using system resources for personal gain. Information security professionals need to clearly articulate risks and exposures.

Further, it is imperative that a customized security policy be defined for the organization.

Security professionals also need to keep up with *rapidly changing technologies*, as they relate to security, in the areas of operating systems, networks, and applications. Security needs to be a key element in the integration of each new release of an operating system or an application.

Our advice to system and network administrators is to be paranoid about security, while senior management needs to recognize that security is a cost of doing business.

5.7 SUMMARY

We first examined the OSI/RM security architecture and defined terminology used in the areas of computer and network security. We then analyzed potential security problems on the UNIX system and steps that one can take to make the operating system more secure in a TCP/IP network. It is possible to significantly enhance the security of your UNIX system by following a few steps, which were outlined in this section and specifically related to disabling the direct **root** login, securing the use of protocols such as NFS and TFTP and verifying that all system-related accounts have passwords or an * in the password filed.

Increasingly, UNIX systems support the Kerberos authentication specification. Therefore, password information on the network will always be in an encrypted form. Kerberos will require resources such as a physically secure system to function as a Kerberos authentication server and resources to install and configure Kerberos for your environment.

REFERENCES

[1] International Standards Organization (ISO), *Information Processing Systems-OSI Reference Model-Part 2. Security Architecture*, Publication No. 7498 Part 2, 1989.
[2] Pabrai et al., *Understanding and Using Computer Networks*, second edition, Fermi National Accelerator Laboratory, September 1991.
[3] Stevens, W. R., *UNIX Network Programming*, Englewood Cliffs, NJ: Prentice-Hall, 1990.

SELECT BIBLIOGRAPHY

DeMax Software, *SecureMax/UX 2.0*, San Mateo, CA, 1992.

APPENDIX 5A: ABOUT ANONYMOUS FTP ACCOUNTS

Let us analyze how to configure and set up a secure account for distribution of software and other relevant information both internally, within your enterprise network, and possibly to nodes on the Internet. A useful feature of FTP is *anonymous* login. This special login allows users who do not have an account on your machine to have restricted access in order to transfer files from a specific directory. Anonymous FTP is useful if you wish to distribute software to the public at large without giving each person who wants the software an account on your machine.

Because the anonymous FTP feature allows anyone to access your system (albeit in a very limited way), it should not be made available on every host on the network. Instead you should choose one machine (preferably a server or stand-alone host) on which to allow this service. This makes monitoring for security violations much easier.

If you allow people to transfer files on your machine (using the world-writable **pub** directory, described later in this section), you should check often the contents of the directories into which they are allowed to write. Any suspicious files you find should be deleted.

5A.1 Anonymous FTP Account Configuration on Solaris 2.3 System

In order to securely set up anonymous FTP, you should follow specific instructions.

1. Create an account called *ftp*. Disable the account by placing an asterisk (*LK*) in the password field in the **/etc/shadow** file. Give the account a special home directory, such **as /usr/ftp or /usr/spool/ftp**. This directory should be in a file system with plenty of free disk space. Do not specify a valid shell name in the password entry of **ftp** user.
2. Make the home directory owned by **ftp** and unwritable by anyone:

   ```
   #    chown     ftp     ~ftp
   #    chmod     555     ~ftp
   ```

3a. Make the directory **~ftp/bin**, owned by the super-user and unwritable by anyone. Place a copy of the **ls** program in this directory. Link **~ftp/bin** to **~ftp/usr/bin**.

   ```
   #    mkdir      ~ftp/bin
   #    chown root         ~ftp/bin
   #    chmod 555          ~ftp/bin
   #    cp -p      /bin/ls         ~ftp/bin
   #    chmod 111          ~ftp/bin/ls
   #    mkdir ~ftp/usr
   #    ln -s      ~ftp/bin        ~ftp/usr/bin
   ```

3b. The following instructions apply to Solaris 2.x only; other vendors' systems will vary. Consult the documentation on *ftpd* for specific information on your system.

   ```
   #    mkdir ~ftp/dev
   ```

   Execute the following command to determine the major and minor numbers of the devices:

   ```
   #    ls -lL /dev/zero /dev/tcp /dev/udp /dev/ticotsord
   ```

   The major and minor numbers are the two numbers preceding the date in the output of **ls** *-lL.*

Execute the following command to create the devices:

```
# mknod ~ftp/dev/zero       c "major number" "minor number"
# mknod ~ftp/dev/tcp        c "major number" "minor number"
# mknod ~ftp/dev/udp        c "major number" "minor number"
# mknod ~ftp/dev/ticotsord  c "major number" "minor number"
```

Copy the libraries from the **/usr/lib** directory:

```
# mkdir       ~ftp/usr/lib
# chmod 555   ~ftp/usr/lib
# cp -p   /usr/lib/libc.so.*        ~ftp/usr/lib
# cp -p   /usr/lib/ld.so.*          ~ftp/usr/lib
# cp -p   /usr/lib/libdl.so.*       ~ftp/usr/lib
# cp -p   /usr/lib/libnsl.so.*      ~ftp/usr/lib
# cp -p   /usr/lib/libsocket.so.*   ~ftp/usr/lib
# cp -p   /usr/lib/libintl.so.*     ~ftp/usr/lib
# cp -p   /usr/lib/libw.so.*        ~ftp/usr/lib
```

You only need to copy the latest library version.

```
# chmod   444   ~ftp/usr/lib/*
```

4. Make the directory **~ftp/etc**, owned by the super-user and unwritable by anyone. Place copies of the password and group files in this directory, with all the password fields changed to asterisks (*LK*).

    For added security, you should delete all but the *ftp* account from the password file and all local groups from the group file. The only account that must be present is *ftp* (and some newer versions of *ftp* don't even require that). This prevents attackers from gaining a list of account names on your system by transferring your file.

```
# mkdir          ~ftp/etc
# chown root     ~ftp/etc
# chmod 555      ~ftp/etc
# cp -p /etc/passwd /etc/group /etc/shadow    ~ftp/etc
```

Edit **passwd**, **group** files and delete nonessential lines.

```
# chmod 444      ~ftp/etc/passwd   ~ftp/etc/group
# chmod 400      ~ftp/etc/shadow
```

5. Make the directory **~ftp/pub**, owned by *ftp* and world-writable. Users may then place files that are to be accessible via anonymous FTP in this directory:

```
# mkdir         ~ftp/pub
# chown ftp     ~ftp/pub
# chmod 777     ~ftp/pub
```

Note that by making this directory world-writable you are allowing people you do not know to place files on your system. This can be dangerous, since in addition to depositing their own files, these unknown users can replace your distribution files with modified versions containing Trojan horses or other problems.

An alternative method is to make the **pub** directory unwritable by the *ftp* account, which is used by anonymous users:

chmod 577   ~ftp/pub

Then create a second directory, *incoming*, which is writable. In this way, files can still be left by anonymous users, but the material in the **pub** directory can be "trusted" since they cannot modify it.

5A.2 Anonymous FTP Configuration on a SunOS 4.1.3 System

In order to securely set up anonymous FTP, you should follow specific instructions.

1. Create an account called *ftp*. Disable the account by placing an asterisk (*) in the password field in the **/etc/passwd** file. Give the account a special home directory, such as **/usr/ftp** or **/usr/spool/ftp**. This directory should be in a file system with plenty of free disk space. Do not specify a valid shell name in the password entry of **ftp** user.
2. Make the home directory owned by **ftp** and unwritable by anyone by entering:

   #   chown   ftp   ~ftp
   #   chmod   555   ~ftp

3a. Make the directory **~ftp/bin**, owned by the super-user and unwritable by anyone. Place a copy of the **ls** program in this directory. Link **~ftp/bin** to **~ftp/usr/bin**.

   #   mkdir   ~ftp/bin
   #   chown root   ~ftp/bin
   #   chmod 555   ~ftp/bin
   #   cp -p   /bin/ls   ~ftp/bin
   #   chmod 111   ~ftp/bin/ls
   #   mkdir ~ftp/usr
   #   chmod 555 ~ftp/usr
   #   ln -s   ~ftp/bin   ~ftp/usr/bin

3b. The following instructions apply to SunOS 4.1.3 only; other vendors' systems will vary. Consult the documentation on *ftpd* for specific information on your system.

mkdir ~ftp/dev

Execute the following command to create devices required for anonymous ftp:

mknod ~ftp/dev/zero c 3 12

Copy the libraries from the **/usr/lib** directory via

#	mkdir		~ftp/usr/lib
#	chmod 755		~ftp/usr/lib
#	cp -p	/usr/lib/ld.so	~ftp/usr/lib
#	cp -p	/usr/lib/libc.so.*	~ftp/usr/lib
#	cp -p	/usr/lib/libdl.so.*	~ftp/usr/lib

You only need to copy the latest library version.

chmod 444 ~ftp/usr/lib/*

4. Make the directory **~ftp/etc**, owned by the super-user and unwritable by anyone. Place copies of the password and group files in this directory, with all the password fields changed to asterisks (*).

   For added security, you should delete all but the *ftp* account from the password file and all local groups from the group file. The only account that must be present is *ftp* (and some newer versions of *ftp* don't even require that). This prevents attackers from gaining a list of account names on your system by transferring your file.

#	mkdir	~ftp/etc
#	chown root	~ftp/etc
#	chmod 555	~ftp/etc
#	cp -p /etc/passwd /etc/group	~ftp/etc

Edit **passwd, group** files and delete nonessential lines.

chmod 444   ~ftp/etc/passwd   ~ftp/etc/group

5. Make the directory **~ftp/pub**, owned by *ftp* and world-writable. Users may then place files that are to be accessible via anonymous FTP in this directory:

#	mkdir	~ftp/pub
#	chown ftp	~ftp/pub
#	chmod 777	~ftp/pub

Note that by making this directory world-writable you are allowing people you do not know to place files on your system. This can be dangerous, since in addition to depositing their own files, these unknown users can replace your distribution files with modified versions containing Trojan horses or other problems.

An alternative method is to make the **pub** directory unwritable by the *ftp* account, which is used by anonymous users:

chmod 577   **~ftp/pub**

Then create a second directory, *incoming*, which is writable. In this way, files can still be left by anonymous users, but the material in the **pub** directory can be "trusted" since they cannot modify it.

Client/Server Applications   6

There are many mechanisms available on UNIX systems to develop distributed applications. Communication between processes on the same system is referred to as *interprocess communication* (IPC). IPC mechanisms supported by UNIX systems include:

- Pipes;
- FIFOs;
- Messages;
- Semaphores;
- Shared memory.

Client/server applications refer to communication between two distinct entities. Typically, these entities reside on separate systems. For example, when you use the **telnet** command to connect to a remote system, you are actually invoking the **telnet** client application on the system on which the command was executed. The **telnet** client application through the *inetd* process establishes a connection with the **telnet** server application. Common mechanisms used to develop client/server applications include:

- Berkeley sockets;
- Transport layer interface (TLI);
- Remote procedure calls (RPCs).

As UNIX systems proliferate the commercial marketplace, there is an even greater need for distributed applications that take advantage of resources and information now available on the network. A distributed application may involve designing a client process that runs on the local system and uses the services provided by a server process that may be running on a remote system. The main advantage of a distributed software model is that, even in a heterogeneous environment, each part of the program can be developed independently of the others, thus taking advantage of special-purpose hardware and software.

TCP/IP-based distributed applications may be developed on the basis of Berkeley sockets or AT&T's System V *Transport Layer Interface* (TLI). Both

Berkeley sockets and AT&T System V TLI are *application program interfaces* (API) to underlying network protocols such as TCP, UDP, or IP.

Distributed applications, in general, are constructed to make use of the services available from network protocols such as TCP, UDP, or IP. These services may be grouped into two categories: *conection-oriented services* (TCP) and *connectionless services* (UDP). Connection-oriented services provide reliable, sequenced data delivery, whereas connectionless services are unreliable but considerably faster. Thus, performance and data integrity are issues that may determine how your application is developed.

For a connection to be established between two systems, five elements must be defined:

- Internet address of the local system;
- Internet address of the remote system;
- Local port number;
- Remote port number;
- Protocol.

These elements form what is referred to as an *association*. As long as any element in the quintuple is different, UNIX guarantees a unique connection.

6.1 INTERPROCESS COMMUNICATION MECHANISMS (IPCs)

A number of mechanisms are available on UNIX systems for a process to communicate with another process on the same system. These techniques are referred to as *interprocess communication* (IPC) mechanisms. As mentioned earlier, some IPC mechanisms are:

- Pipes;
- FIFOs or named pipes;
- Messages;
- Semaphores;
- Shared memory.

When a user executes a command such as

% **ps -ax | more**

output from the command "**ps -ax**" becomes input to the command "**more**". *Pipes* provide a one-way flow of data. Pipes are typically used to communicate between two different processes, as opposed to communication within a single process. *First In First Out* (FIFOs) or *named pipes* exist as special files, and any process with permission can open it for reading or writing. FIFOs, unlike pipes, have names associated with them, thus allowing unrelated processes access to a single FIFO. Figure 6.1 illustrates how pipes are created and used.

The processes communicating over a pipe must be related; typically, they are parent and child or two siblings. A disadvantage of using a pipe is that it may be too slow: data has to be transferred from the writing process to the kernel and back again to the reader; although no I/O is performed–the operation can take too long for some critical applications. Note that once a FIFO has been created, it must be opened for reading or writing. The **mknod**() system call is used to create special files on the UNIX system; these include named pipes or FIFOs, device files, and directories. The **open**() system call is used to read from or write to a FIFO.

Pipes and FIFOs use the streams model where there are no record boundaries, and data are not examined during read and write operations. Sometimes a process may want to impose structure on data being transferred. A *message* is typically a small amount of data (~ 500 bytes) that is sent to a message queue; any process with appropriate permissions can receive messages (first, last, any) from a queue.

```
/* Program Description: To demonstrate how pipes are created and used. */
#include <stdio.h>
main()
{
int pipefd[2], n;    /* pipefd[0] is used for reading, pipefd[1] is used for writing */
char buff[100];

if (pipe(pipefd) > 0 {
printf("pipe error\n");
exit(1);
}
printf("read fd = %d, write fd = %d\n", pipefd[0], pipefd[1] );
if (write(pipefd[1], "Welcome to UNIX Internetworking\n", 33) ! = 33) {
printf("write error");
exit(2);
}
if (n = read(pipefd[0], buff, sizeof(buff)) < = 0){
printf("read error");
exit(3);
}
printf("buff = %s\n", buff);
write(stdout, buff, n);         /* Note fd = 1 = stdout */
exit(0);
}
```

Figure 6.1 Using pipes on UNIX systems.

System V allows a process to pass messages to any other active process in the system. In the System V implementation of message queues, all messages are stored in the kernel and have an associated "message queue identifier." This identifier identifies a particular queue of messages. Processes can read or write messages to arbitary queues, each queue identified uniqely via it's "message queue identifier." Unlike other IPC mechanisms like pipes or FIFOs where it makes no sense to have a writer process unless a reader process exists as well; it is possible for a writer process to write a message to a queue, exit, and have a reader process retrieve the message at some later time.

Every message on a queue should be a structure that has, at the very least, two fields: (1) a long integer (used to multiplex messages in a single queue) and (2) a buffer to hold the message text (the text can contain binary or ASCII data).

A new message is created, or an existing message queue is accessed via the **msgget**(2) system call. Once a message queue is opened, a writer inserts data in the queue using a **msgsnd**(2) system call. Alternatively, a reader reads data from the queue using a **msgrcv**(2) sysem call. The program in Figures 6.2 to 6.4 demonstrates the use of message queues. There are two distinct entities: a server and a client. The server runs first and creates a message queue. It also populates the message queue with some text. The client can be run later; upon invocation, it opens the message queue, reads the data left for it by the server, deletes the message queue, and exits.

The header file described in Figure 6.2 should be included in both the server and client programs.

The server code is described in Figure 6.3. The client code is described in Figure 6.4. Compile the server and client programs as follows:

$ **cc -o msgserver msgserver.c**
$ **cc -o msgclient msgclient.c**

Run the server first:

$ **msgserver**

Issue the command **ipcs**(1). This command, with the **-q** option specified, displays all message queues owned by the user issuing the command

$ **ipcs -q**

IPC status from /dev/kmem as of Mon Mar 6 12:57:57 1995
T ID KEY MODE OWNER GROUP
Message Queues
q   400 0x000004d2 -rw-rw-rw- vkg usr

As can be observed, a message queue has been created. Its "message queue identifier" is 0x000004d2, or 1234L as specified in **msg.h**. Since this queue

```c
#ifndef _MSG_H
#define _MSG_H
#include <stdio.h>
#include <string.h>
#include <sys/types.h>
#include <sys/ipc.h>
#include <sys/msg.h>
#include <memory.h>
#include <sys/errno.h>

extern int errno;

#define Q_KEY 1234L            /* Our "message queue identifier" */
#define Q_PERMISSION 0666      /* Public queue: all can read/write */

/*
 * This is our message structure. As discussed above, it should contain
 * at the very least, the included two fields.
 */
#define MSG_BUF 512
typedef struct _Message {
long mtype;                    /* Message type */
char message[MSG_BUF];         /* The actual message */
} Message;

#endif
```

Figure 6.2 Header file for client/server message program.

was created as a public queue (mode 0666), any process can read from and write to this message queue as long as it knows about the "message queue identifier."

Now, if we run the client, it will connect to the message queue and retreive the message left for it by the server:

$ client
Message type = 1
Message   = Hello World!!
$

Since the client deletes the message queue before exiting, the server has to be rerun in order to create this queue again.

Four system calls are supported by UNIX for messages:

```
#include "msg.h"

int main(int argc, char *argv[])
{
int writeId;
Message msg;
/*
 * Step 1: Create the queue
 */
writeId = msgget(Q_KEY, Q_PERMISSION | IPC_CREAT);
if (writeId == -1) {
   fprintf(stderr, "%s: error creating message queue\n", *argv);
   perror("System error");
   return 1;
}
/*
 * Step 2: Prepare the message to be put in the queue
 */
memset((void *) &msg, 0, sizeof(msg));
msg.mtype = 1L;
strcpy(msg.message, "Hello World!!");

/*
 * Step 3: Now put the message in the queue
 */
if (msgsnd(writeId, (const void *)&msg, MSG_BUF, 0) != 0) {
   fprintf(stderr, "%s: error writing to message queue\n", *argv);
   perror("System error");
   return 1;
}

return 0;
}
```

Figure 6.3 Message server program.

- **msgget();**
- **msgctl();**
- **msgsnd();**
- **msgrcv().**

The call **msgget()** returns a message descriptor that defines a message queue. The call **msgctl()** includes options to set and return parameters associated with a message descriptor and also remove descriptors. The **msgsnd()** system call is used to send a message, and the **msgrcv()** call receives a message [4].

```
#include "msg.h"

int main(int argc, char *argv[])

{
   int readId, bytesRead;
   Message msg;

/*
* Step 1: Open an existing message queue
*/
readId = msgget(Q_KEY, 0);
if (readId == -1) {
   fprintf(stderr, "%s: error opening message queue\n", *argv);
   perror("Syetem error");
   return 1;
}

/*
* Step 2: Get ready to read in the message
*/
memset((void *) &msg, 0, sizeof(msg));
bytesRead = msgrcv(readId, (void *)&msg, MSG_BUF, 0L, 0);
if (bytesRead != MSG_BUF) {
   fprintf(stderr, "%s: number of bytes read (%d)", *argv, bytesRead);
   fprintf(stderr, " do not equal number written (%d)\n", MSG_BUF);
   return 1;
}
printf("Message type = %ld\n", msg.mtype);
printf("Message   = %s\n", msg.message);

/*
* Step 3: Delete the message queue
*/
if (msgctl(readId, IPC_RMID, (struct msgqid_ds *)0) < 0) {
   fprintf(stderr, "%s: cannot delete message queue\n", *argv);
   perror("System error");
   return 1;
}
return 0;
}
```

Figure 6.4 Message client program.

Semaphores are not used to exchange data between processes, instead they are used to synchronize two or more processes. They prevent two processes from simultaneously having access to a shared resource. A semaphore has only two values: 0 and 1. It is stored in the kernel. Calls associated with semaphores are:

- **semget()**;
- **semctl()**;
- **semop()**.

The **semget()** system call is used to create and to gain access to a set of semaphores. The **semctl()** call is used to perform various control operations on the set of semaphores, and the **semop()** system call manipulates the values of semaphores [4].

Note that both pipes and FIFOs transfer data between processes. However, the fastest way of moving data between two processes is not moving the data at all–both can share some memory. When data is written to a *shared memory* segment, it is immediately available to the other process. The system calls for access to shared memory are:

- **shmget()**;
- **shmat()**;
- **shmdt()**;
- **shmctl()**.

The **shmget()** call creates a new region of shared memory or returns an existing one. The **shmat()** system call attaches a shared memory region to the virtual address space of a process. The call **shmdt()** is used to detach a shared memory region from the virtual address space of a process, and the **shmctl()** system call accesses various parameters associated with the shared memory [4].

Semaphores are typically used in conjunction with shared memory to provide access control.

6.2 DISTRIBUTED APPLICATIONS

Distributed applications may be developed using mechanisms such as:

- Berkeley sockets;
- Transport layer interface (TLI);
- Remote procedure calls (RPCs).

By far, the most popular mechanism has been the Berkeley socket interface.

6.2.1 Berkeley Sockets

The basis for network applications in 4.3 BSD is an abstraction referred to as a *socket*. A socket is an endpoint of communication. Application programs request the operating system to create a socket when they need to access the network. The system in turns returns an integer that the applicaton uses to reference the socket. Note that sockets are similar to file descriptors and are actually maintained in the system process tables. Version 4.3 BSD, for example, refers to both socket and file descriptors as descriptors and differentiates between them only when necessary.

The main difference between *socket descriptors* and *file descriptors* is that the operating system binds a file descriptor to a specific file or device when the application calls open, but it can create sockets without binding them to a specific address. The application can choose to supply the destination address each time it uses the socket or it can choose to bind the destination address to the socket and thus avoid specifying the destination repeatedly. The former would be the case when UDP is the transport protocol and the latter would be an example of using TCP [1]. There are a number of different types of sockets [2]:

SOCK-STREAM	This is a stream socket used for connection-oriented, reliable services provided by the TCP protocol at the transport layer.
SOCK-DGRAM	This is a datagram socket used for connectionless services provided by the UDP protocol at the transport layer.
SOCK-RAW	This is a raw socket used to directly interface with the IP protocol at the network layer.

6.2.2 Transport Layer Interface (TLI)

Just as 4.3 BSD systems provide sockets and support for protocols such as Internet, XNS, and UNIX domain, the transport layer interface provides an interface to transport layer protocols. TLI is a set of user-callable C functions that hides the streams interface to the networking system. Streams provide a full-duplex connection between a user process and a device driver. TLI consists of two components: the transport endpoint and the transport provider.

The two processes that are communicating are referred to as *transport endpoints* by TLI. This is analogous to sockets in BSD systems, where a socket may also be viewed as a *half association*. The *transport provider* is the set of routines on the host computer that provides communication support for a user process. A system could have a transport provider for TCP/IP and another transport provider for Xerox network standard protocols. TLI itself provides the interface between the user process and the transport provider; it is not a transport provider. An example of this is that TLI does not define any restrictions on the structure of the transport address–that is left to the transport provider. TLI defines a generic structure that passes data between the TLI functions and user code.

System V Release 3.x computers do not supply a transport provider as a part of the operating system. System V Release 4 provides a TCP/IP transport provider.

6.2.3 Remote Procedure Calls (RPCs)

Sun Microsystems's Open Network Computing (ONC) architecture consists of two key components: *remote procedure calls* (RPCs) and *external data representation* (XDR). RPCs enable applications to use network services in a manner similar to calling a local function.

In the RPC model, the program that makes the remote procedure call to request an operation is called the *client*, whereas the *server* is a program that performs operations when requested and sends the return value back to the client. Thus, the RPC model extends the procedure call mechanism from a single host to multiple hosts on the network. The client calls a local procedure, referred to as the *client stub*. The function of the client stub is to package the arguments to the remote procedure and then build one or more network messages. The packaging of the client's arguments is known as *parameter marshalling* [3]. The stub modules are generated by the RPC compiler; stubs use RPC runtime library calls to communicate with the server.

The server stub calls the server routine and passes the parameters in a standard way. The server routine does not know it is being activated remotely because its immediate caller is a local procedure. When the server procedure is completed, it returns to the server stub, returning whatever its return values are. The return value is then sent over the network to the client system.

Thus, the stub routines make remote procedure calls look like local calls, enabling RPC clients and servers to use RPC facilities transparently. The stub routines are responsible for *marshalling* (data is copied to a RPC packet to be sent over the network) and *unmarshalling* (data is copied from the RPC packet) data.

External data representation is a machine-independent standard for the description and encoding of data. XDR is extremely useful for transferring data between different machine architectures. RPC transfers arbitrary data between machines of different architectures by converting them to an XDR format and then sending it over the network.

6.2.4 TCP and UDP Ports

Port numbers are addresses by which processes can be identified. This enables communication between processes on the TCP(UDP)/IP networks. *TCP and UDP protocol headers contain both the source and destination port numbers.* The port number is a 16-bit integer value, and it indentifies a communication channel to a specific user process. *TCP port numbers are independent of UDP port numbers.* As an analogy, in the telephone system, ports are the sockets into which modular telephones can be plugged, and port numbers are the telephone numbers of these sockets. To establish a connection to some other processes (remote or local) you need to dial their (port) numbers.

6.2.4.1 Types of Ports

A port number is an unsigned 16-bit integer, and its value ranges from 0 to 65535. *Port numbers are not equivalent to each other.* They are classified into different groups with different capabilities. Table 6.1 presents port categories, their range, and a brief description of each category [5]. Two parameters are required to communicate (identify) with a process: the Internet address of the host it is running on and a unique port number assigned to it by the system.

Port 0

In cases where there is no need to have a specific port assigned to a socket, a process can let the system automatically assign an unused port. This can be done by specifying a port number of 0 before calling the **bind()** system call. The port number assigned by the system is in the range of 1024 to 5000.

Auto-assignment of a regular port is done with the help of the **getsockname()** system call. This system call returns the name associated with a socket. Also returned are the local address and local process elements of an *association*. To let the system automatically assign a port, the application must specify a

Table 6.1
Port Numbers

Description	Port Range
System assigning port	0
Reserved port	1–1023
Well-known ports	1–1023
Auto assigned by **rresvport()**	512–1023
Nonreserved ports	1024–65535

port number of 0 before calling **bind()**. Following the call to **bind()**, a call to **getsockname()** is necessary. Figure 6.5 describes how to use the **bind()** system call.

After completing this section of code, the value of the variable *sin.sin_port* will no longer be 0, but some number in the range of 1024 to 5000.

```
int s, length;
struct sockaddr_in sin;
.
. sin.sin_port = htons(0);

/* instead of explicitly assigning a port number to sin.sin_port
 * give it a value of S
 */

if (bind(s, sin, sizeof (sin), 0) < 0) {
   perror("server: bind");
   exit(1);
}
if (sin.sin_port == 0) {
   length = sizeof(sin);
   if (getsockname(s, (struct sockaddr*)&sin, &length) < 0){
      perror ("getting socket name\n");
      exit(1);
   }
}
```

Figure 6.5 Using the **bind()** system call.

Reserved Ports: 1 to 1023

A port in the range 1 to 1023 is reserved; a process is not allowed to bind to (identify itself with) a reserved port unless its effective user ID is 0 (having super user or **root** privilege).

The job of the **rresvport()** system call is to have the machine automatically assign a reserved port. This function creates an Internet stream socket and binds a reserved port to the socket. The socket descriptor is returned as the value of the function, unless an error occurs, in which case 1 is returned. Note that the argument to this function is the address of an integer (a value-result argument), not an integer value. Figure 6.6 describes how the **rresvport()** system call is used.

The integer pointed to by *resvport* is the first port number to which the function attempts to bind. The caller typically initializes the starting port number to IPPORT_ RESERVED-1. The value of the constant IPPORT_RESERVED is defined to be 1024 in <**netinet/in.h**>. If the **bind()** system call fails with an *errno* of EADDRINUSE, then the function decrements the port number and tries again. If it finally reaches port 512 and finds it is already in use, it sends *errno* to EAGAIN and returns -1. If this function returns successfully, it not only returns the socket as the value of the function, but the port number is also returned in the location pointed to by *resvport*.

When requesting a reserved port, the preceding call is used in place of the **socket()** call and the **bind()** call.

```
int s, resvport = IPPORT_RESERVED-1;

struct sockaddr_in sin;

.

.

s = rresvport(&resvport);

if (s < 0) {

   perror ("server: socket");

   exit(1);

}

sin.sin_port = htons(resvport);
```

Figure 6.6 Using the **rresvport()** system call.

Well-Known Ports: 1 to 1023

Well-known ports, also referred to as *well-known addresses*, is a technique used by protocols such as TCP and UDP to identify well-known services that a host can provide. For example, the remote terminal protocol server named **telnet** is a well-known service with a port number of 23. Thus, every TCP/IP implementation that supports **telnet** assigns it the well-known port of 23 (decimal). All well-known port numbers are in the range 1 to 255. To list the services available on a UNIX system, simply examine the **/etc/services** file. To list the services available on a VAX/VMS system running MultiNet, use the MultiNet server configuration utility.

Nonreserved Ports

Port numbers in the range of 1024 to 65535 are considered nonprivileged and can be used by any process.

Ephemeral Ports

Ephemeral (transitional or short-lived) port numbers are unique port numbers typically assigned to client processes. The server determines the ephemeral port number from the TCP or UDP header and thus knows which process to communicate with at the remote system. Ephemeral port numbers are always greater than 1023.

6.2.4.2 portmapper Network Service

Sun Microsystems developed a network service, called the *portmapper*, that provides a standard way for client applications to determine the port number of any remote server application. The *portmapper* is started at boot-time and is assigned reserved port number 111 (i.e., TCP port number 111 and UDP port number 111). Server applications, on startup, request an available port from the system and then register their services and their corresponding port numbers with the *portmapper*.

The *portmapper* service is identical to the telephone system's 411 service. People get their phone numbers and request the phone company to publish their numbers. This way anybody can call you if they know the address (host Internet address, in the analogy) and your name with the help of the 411 operators. In general, the steps associated with the *portmapper* process are as follows.

Step 1

Server registers with *portmapper*. Here the server process is registering its port number with the *portmapper* process. Note that the *portmapper* process is running on the same system as the server process.

Step 2

Client requests server's port from *portmapper*. Here the client process is communicating with the *portmapper* pprcess on the server system.

Step 3

Client gets server's port from *portmapper*. The *portmapper* process responds with the port number of the server process.

Step 4

Client calls server. The client process now communicates directly with the server process.

Figure 6.7 illustrates how the *portmapper* network service works. The numbered steps in Figure 6.7 indicate the following.

- The server process registers with the *portmapper* to create a portmap entry. The following code segment is what a server executes to register its service and port number:

    /* Register this service with portmapper */

    if (!pmap_set(prognum, version, IPPROTO_TCP, port)
           fprint(stderr, "error in registering the service \n");

    else
           fprint(stdout, "Registering The service");

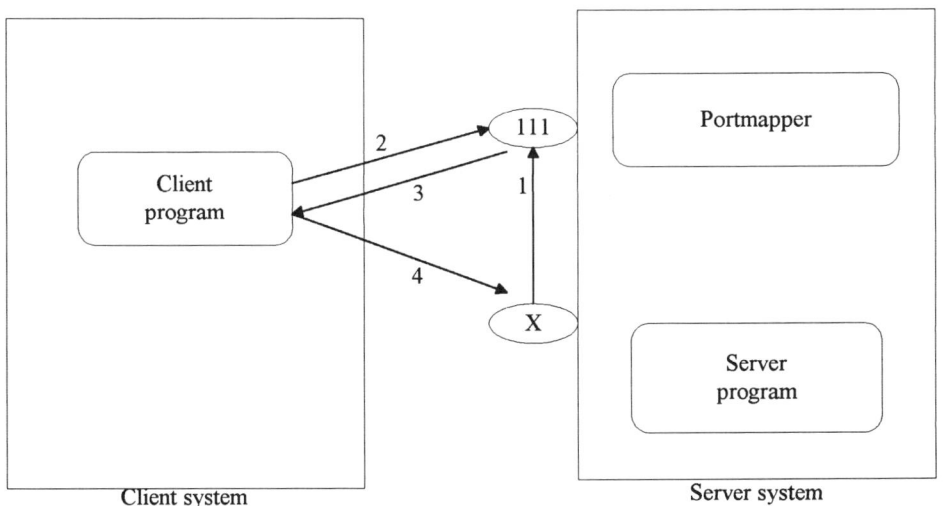

Figure 6.7 Portmapper network service.

- The function *pmap_set()* contacts the *portmapper* for registration. The arguments are **prognum**, an unsigned integer in the range of 0x40000000-0x5fffffff to identify the program; **version**, an unsigned integer to identify the version of the service (usually 1 if only one version is available); an integer constant identifying the **protocol** in use: IPPROTO_TCP for TCP services and IPPROTO_UDP for UDP services; and finally **port** (unsigned short), which is the port number to be registered.

The client process at any time can query the *portmapper* to determine the port number associated with a specific server application.

port = pmap_getport(&mapper_addr, program, version, IPPROTO_TCP);

The *portmapper* returns the appropriate port number associated with the specific server. The client process communicates directly with the server application.

The SunRPC library provides an interface to all *portmapper* procedures. A complete description of the portmap protocol and its use is specified in the **portmap man** pages. At the UNIX command prompt, enter:

% man 3 portmap

The *portmapper* is supported on a number of UNIX systems including AIX, ULTRIX, and IRIX.

6.3 BERKELEY SOCKET SYSTEM CALLS

First we define the two types of servers: concurrent and iterative. We then examine Berkeley socket system calls that are available on a UNIX system to develop client/server applications. Finally, calls associated with the *portmapper* are described.

6.3.1 Iterative and Concurrent Servers

Iterative servers are those processes that handle a client's request itself; typically the requests can be processed in a predetermined short amount of time. However, it is possible that the amount of time required to service the request depends on the request itself; therefore, the server does not know ahead of time how much time it will take to process the request. In this case, the server process invokes another process to handle each client request and then the server process goes to sleep waiting for the next client request. Such server processes are referred to as *concurrent servers*. The following steps apply to server processes:

1. Open a communication channel and inform the local host that it is ready to accept client requests on a specific address.

2. Wait for the client request to arrive at the specified address.
3. An iterative server processes the request itself and sends the client a response. A concurrent server forks a new process to handle the client request.
4. The server then goes back to Step 2.

The following steps apply to client processes:

1. Open a communication channel and connect to a specific address on the server system.
2. Send service request message to the server and process responses.
3. Close the communication channel when done.

6.3.2 System Calls

We now study some elementary socket calls and calls executed to transfer data between processes on client/server systems [2].

socket System Call

A process starts the network I/O by specifying the type of communication protocol with the help of the **socket()** system call.

#include <sys/types.h>
#include <sys/socket.h>

int socket(int domain, int type, int protocol)

The *domain* argument specifies the family of the protocol desired, in the case of TCP/IP applications it takes on the values of AF_INET. The *protocol* argument is typically set to 0 for most user applications.

The **socket()** system call is analogous to the **open()** system call for files and returns a socket descriptor. Table 6.2 summarizes the **socket()** system call combinations of arguments [3].

bind System Call

The **bind()** system call assigns a name (local or remote address) to an unnamed socket descriptor, specifying a local port number for the application. It links the socket to the local port specified in the address structure.

#include <sys/types.h>
#include <sys/socket.h>

Table 6.2
socket() System Call Arguments

Family	Type	Protocol	Actual Protocol
AF_INET	SOCK_DGRAM	IPPROTO_UDP	UDP
AF_INET	SOCK_STREAM	IPPROTO_TCP	TCP
AF_INET	SOCK_RAW	IPPROTO_ICMP	ICMP
AF_INET	SOCK_RAW	IPPROTO_RAW	(raw)

int bind(int socket-fd, struct sockaddr *an-address, int length-of-address)

The term *socket-fd* is the socket descriptor and *an-address* is a pointer to the address structure to be bound to the socket. The *length-of-address* is the size of the structure in bytes. Client applications are not required to be bound to a specific address or local port number–the opeating system takes care of it (ephermeral ports).

connect System Call

This system call is used by the client process to establish a connection with the server.

#include <sys/types.h>
#include <sys/socket.h>
int connect (int socket-fd, struct sockaddr *server-address, int length-of-address)

The first argument, *socket-fd*, is obtained from the **socket** system call, the second argument is a pointer to a socket address, and the last argument is the size of the structure. Typically, in connection-oriented applications the client program executes the **connect()** system call, which results in a connection between the local and remote systems.

listen System Call

This system call is used only by a connection-oriented server. It indicates the server's willingness to accept connections [3].

int listen (int socket-fd, int backlog)

The backlog argument specifies how many requests are to be queued by the system. The maximum value currently allowed is 5.

accept System Call

This system call is used by connection-oriented servers. The **accept()** system call takes the first network connection request from the queue and fills the address structure of the incoming client.

#include <sys/types.h>
#include <sys/socket.h>

int accept (int socket-fd, struct sockaddr *from, int address-length)

The **accept()** system call returns a socket with the same properties as the socket descriptor specified in the first argument, *socket-fd*. The *from* and *address-length* arguments return the address of the client process.

If the **accept()** system call is successful it creates a new socket that will be used for exchanging data with the client. The call **accept()** returns the new socket descriptor to the calling program. The original server socket continues to listen for incoming connection request messages. Each accepted client request is handled by a new process (created with the **fork()** system call). At this point, both the parent and the child processes inherit a copy of the newly created socket. The original parent process closes its copy of the new socket and calls **accept()** again to process another connection.

close System Call

The **close()** system call accepts both file and socket descriptors and closes the connection.

read and write System Calls

The standard **read()** and **write()** system calls do not differentiate between a socket and a file descriptor and can be used to read from and write to the network.

int read (int descriptor, char *buff, int sizeof-buff)
int write (int descriptor, char *buff, int sizeof-buff)

Note that **write()** blocks until data is transferred to socket buffers.

send and recv System Calls

These system calls are similar to the standard **read()** and **write()** system calls with one extra argument for additional options. The additional options may be used to glance at the data or for *out-of-band* (urgent) data to be exchanged between the server and the client processes.

#include <sys/types.h>
#include <sys/socket.h>

int send(int descriptor, char *buff, int sizeof-buff, int flag)
int recv(int descriptor, char *buff, int sizeof-buff, int flag)

The flags argument could have a value of 0.

sendto and recvfrom System Calls

These system calls are used in connectionless applicatons. The **sendto()** and **recvfrom()** calls are similar to the **send()** and **recv()** calls, except that they have two additional arguments that relate to the destination address and the size of the address in bytes.

#include <sys/types.h>
#include <sys/socket.h>

int sendto(int descriptor, char *buff, int sizeof-buff,
    int flag, struct sockaddr *to, int address-length)
    int recvfrom(int descriptor, char *buff, int sizeof-buff,
    int flag struct sockaddr *from, int address-length)

The *to* argument in the **sendto()** system call contains the destination address of the message (datagram) sent to the network. The *from* argument in the **recvfrom()** system call contains the source address of the message received from the network.

6.3.3 Using the *portmapper* Service

There are several ways for a process to request a TCP or UDP port number. The process can request a specific port. This is typical for servers that need to assign a well-known port to a socket. The process can also let the operating system automatically assign a port. The **rresvport()** system call must be used if the operating system is to assign a reserved port (between 512 and 1023). To have the system assign a nonprivileged port you must specify a port number of 0 and call **getsockname()** before calling **bind()**.

Both TCP and UDP server/client processes may interact with the *portmapper* process. The functions supported by the *portmapper* service are:

- pmap_set();
- pmap_unset();
- pmap_getport().

pmap_get() portmapper Function

The *pmap_set()* function may be used by the server to register its service and port number with the *portmapper* process. Thus, in the client application, you need not hardcode the port number of the server. The client first communicates with the *portmappper* to determine the port number of the server process.

#include <rpc/rpc.h>
bool_t pmap_set (prognum, versnum, protocol, port)
    u_long prognum, versnum;
    int protocol;
    u_short port;

This leads to a mapping between the triplet (*prognum, version, protocol*) and a port on the local machines *portmapper* service. The value of protocol can be either IPPROTO_UDP or IPPROTO_TCP. This routine returns TRUE if it succeeds, FALSE otherwise.

pmap_unset() portmapper Function

The *pmap_unset()* function may be used by the server to deregister its service from the *portmapper*.

#include <rpc/rpc.h>
bool_t pmap_unset(prognum, versnum)
    u_long prognum, versnum;

This deregisters all mappings between the triplet (*prognum, versnum,* *) and ports on the local machines' *portmapper* service.

pmap_getport() portmapper Function

The *pmap_getport()* function is exectuted by the client to request the port number of the server from the *portmapper* process on the server system.

#include <rpc/rpc.h>
u_short pmap_getport(addr, prognum, versnum, protocol)

```
    struct sockaddr_in *addr;
    u_long prognum, versnum, protocol;
```

This returns the port number of a server process. The address is returned in *addr*, which should be preallocated. The value of protocol can be either IPPROTO_UDP or IPPROTO_TCP. A return value of 0 means that the mapping does not exist or that the RPC system failed to contact the remote *portmapper* service.

6.4 SUMMARY

First, we examined mechanisms that can be used to develop interprocess communication applications. We analyzed the advantages and disadvantages of mechanisms such as pipes, FIFOs, messages, semaphores, and shared memory. We then explored the various possibilities available to application developers to design client/server applications. These include Berkeley sockets, the transport layer interface, and remote procedure calls.

Next, we discussed the various types of port numbers. Port numbers identify the application protocols with which you are communicating. For example, port number 23 identifies the **telnet** application, and port number 69 is associated with **tftp**. One of the things that you need to decide when you are developing a TCP/IP client/server application is what port number you will use for your application. You should also consider registering the port number that you will be using with the *portmapper* process. If that is the case, the client application will first communicate with the *portmapper* process on the server system to find out the port number of the server and then connect to the server process.

Finally, we examined various systems calls available to develop client/server applications based on Berkeley sockets. We would also recommend that you consider using the *portmapper* service, because with the *portmapper* you do not have to hardcode the port number of the server process in the client application. An excellent reference for a more detailed discussion on Berkeley sockets is *UNIX Network Programming* by William Stevens [3].

REFERENCES

[1] Comer, D. E., *Internetworking with TCP/IP*, third edition, Englewood Cliffs, NJ: Prentice-Hall, 1995.
[2] Abar, F., U. Pabrai, and J. Weber, *Designing Distributed Applications*, Fermilab, Computing Division Document GG0013, September 1991.
[3] Stevens, W., *UNIX Network Programming*, Englewood Cliffs, NJ: Prentice-Hall, 1990.
[4] Bach, M., *The Design of the UNIX Operating System*, Englewood Cliffs, NJ: Prentice-Hall, 1986.
[5] Abar, F., U. Pabrai, and J. Weber, "Open Systems: Port Numbers and TCP/IP Socket-Based Networking Applications," *VAX Professional Technical Journal*, December 1991.

SELECT BIBLIOGRAPHY

SGI IRIS UNIX System V - *Programmers Guide.*

APPENDIX 6A: BERKELEY SOCKET CLIENT/SERVER APPLICATION

6A.1 Server Application

```
/*
 * This server application was developed on a VMS system running MultiNet.
 * The server application receives text from the client application and converts
 * it to uppercase.
 *
 * To compile and link this server:
 *   $ CC SERVER.C
 *   $ LINK SERVER,sys$input:/opt
 *   multinet_root:[multinet.library]rpc/lib
 *   multinet:multinet_socket_library/share
 *   sys$share:vaxcrtl/share
 *
 *   $ SERVER == "$ [current_directory]SERVER.EXE"
 *
 * To run this client, use the following syntax:
 *   $ SERVER
 */

#include <stdio.h>
#include <stdlib.h>
#include <sys/types.h>
#include <sys/socket.h>
#include <netinet/in.h>
#include <netdb.h>
#include <arpa/inet.h>
#include <rpc/rpc.h>

int writen();
int readline();
void session ();
char *my_strchr();
```

```
#define MAXQUE 5
#define MAXLINE 512

u_long prognum=0x40000001;
u_long version=1;
u_short port;

main(argc,argv)

int argc;
char *argv[];

{
int     sockfd,newsockfd;
int     length;
int     clilen;
struct      sockaddr_in serv_addr, cli_addr;

if ( (sockfd = socket(AF_INET, SOCK_STREAM, 0)) < 0){ /* Create an Internet
                                                         family, */
    fprintf(stderr,"error in creating stream socket \n");   /* connection-
                                                              oriented socket */
exit(1);
}

bzero((char *) &serv_addr, sizeof(serv_addr));
serv_addr.sin_family = AF_INET;
serv_addr.sin_addr.s_addr = htons(INADDR_ANY);
serv_addr.sin_port = htons(0);

if ( bind(sockfd, (struct sockaddr *) &serv_addr, sizeof(serv_addr), 0) < 0 ){
    fprintf(stderr,"error in binding \n");
    exit(1);
}

length=sizeof(serv_addr);
if (getsockname(sockfd,(struct sockaddr *)&serv_addr,&length) < 0 )
    fprintf(stderr," error in getting socket name \n");

port=ntohs(serv_addr.sin_port);

/* Register this service to portmapper */
```

```
if (!pmap_set(prognum,version,IPPROTO_TCP,port))
    fprintf(stderr," error in registering the service \n");
else
    fprintf(stdout," Registering The service %s under \n program number: %d
\n version number: %d    \n with assign port number: %d \n",argv[0], pro-
gnum, version, port);

listen(sockfd,MAXQUE);

clilen = sizeof(cli_addr);
newsockfd = accept(sockfd, (struct sockaddr *) &cli_addr, &clilen);

/* blocking */

if ( newsockfd > 0 )
   session(newsockfd);

close(newsockfd);
/* If the server is finished you must unregister the service. */

if (!pmap_unset(prognum,version))
fprintf(stderr," error in unregistering the service \n");
else
fprintf(stderr," service is unregisterged \n");
}

void session (sockfd)
int sockfd;
{
int n, fd;
int i, length;
char line[MAXLINE];
char *ptr;
FILE *inputfile;

line[MAXLINE-1]='\0';
if ( (inputfile = fopen("test.data", "r")) == (FILE *) NULL ) {
    fprintf(stderr, "Cannot open input file\n");
    return;
}

n=readline(inputfile,line,MAXLINE);

printf("reading line from local file: \n %s \n",line);
```

```
/* upper case it */

length=strlen(line);

for(i=0;i<=(length-1);i++)
line[i]=(char)toupper((int)line[i]);

if ((n=writen(sockfd,line,length))!= length)
fprintf(stderr,"session: writen error to socket \n");
return;
}
int writen(fd, ptr, nbytes)

register int fd;
register char *ptr;
register int nbytes;

{

int nleft, nwritten;

nleft = nbytes;

while (nleft > 0 ) {
nwritten = write(fd,ptr,nleft);
if ( nwritten <= 0 )
return(nwritten);

nleft -= nwritten;
ptr += nwritten;

}
return(nbytes-nleft);
}

int readline (fd, ptr, maxlen)

register int fd;
register char *ptr;
register int maxlen;
{

int n,rc;
char c;
```

```
for (n=1; n<maxlen; n++) {
if ( (rc=read(fd,&c,1)) == 1) {
*ptr++ = c;
if ( c == '\n' )
    break;
} else if (rc == 0 ) {
if ( n == 1 )
    return(0);          /* EOF, no data read */
else
    break;              /* EOF, some data was read */
} else
return(-1);             /* Error */

}

*ptr = 0;
return(n);
}


char *my_strchr(pstring, chr)
char *pstring;
int chr;

{
while (*pstring != '\0') {
if(*pstring == chr)
return(pstring);
++pstring;
}
return(0);
}
```

6A.2 Client Application

```
#include <stdio.h>
#include <stdlib.h>
#include <sys/types.h>
#include <sys/socket.h>
#include <netinet/in.h>
#include <arpa/inet.h>
#include <netdb.h>
#include <rpc/rpc.h>
```

```c
int writen();
int readline();
void session ();

#define MAXQUE 5
#define MAXLINE 512
#define PMAP_PORT 111

u_long prognum=0x40000001;
u_long version=1;
u_short port;

void main(argc, argv)
int argc;
char *argv[];
{

int sockfd;
struct sockaddr_in mapper_addr,serv_addr;
struct hostent *hostptr;
struct in_addr *thsptr;

if ( (hostptr = gethostbyname("ganesh")) == '\0'){
fprintf(stderr," gethostbyname: error for mapper host ganesh \n");
exit(1);
}

bzero((char *) &mapper_addr, sizeof(mapper_addr));
mapper_addr.sin_family = AF_INET;
thsptr = (struct in_addr *) hostptr->h_addr_list[0];
mapper_addr.sin_addr.s_addr = inet_addr(inet_ntoa(*thsptr));
mapper_addr.sin_port = htons(PMAP_PORT);
port=pmap_getport(&mapper_addr, prognum, version, IPPROTO_TCP);

if ( port > 0 )
fprintf(stdout," requesting The service %s under \n program number: %d \n version number: %d \n\n The assign port number returned: %d \n",argv[0],
prognum,
version,port);
else{
printf("error in getting the remote port \n");
exit(1);
}
```

```
if ( (sockfd = socket(AF_INET, SOCK_STREAM, 0)) < 0){
fprintf(stderr,"error in creating stream socket \n");
exit(1);
}

if ( (hostptr = gethostbyname("ganesh")) == '\0'){
fprintf(stderr," gethostbyname: error for server host lakshmi \n");
exit(1);
}

bzero((char *) &serv_addr, sizeof(serv_addr));
serv_addr.sin_family = AF_INET;
thsptr = (struct in_addr *) hostptr->h_addr_list[0];
serv_addr.sin_addr.s_addr = inet_addr(inet_ntoa(*thsptr));
serv_addr.sin_port = htons(port);

if( connect(sockfd, (struct sockaddr *) &serv_addr, sizeof(serv_addr)) < 0) {
fprintf(stderr,"error in connecting to server \n");
exit(1);
}

session(sockfd,argv[1]);
close(sockfd);
exit(0);
}

void session (sockfd,mess)
int sockfd;
char *mess;

{
int n;
char line[MAXLINE];

n=strlen(mess);
/*
if (writen(sockfd,mess,n) != n)
   fprintf(stderr,"session: writen error to socket \n");

if (writen(sockfd,"\n",strlen("\n")) != strlen("\n"))
   fprintf(stderr,"session: writen error to socket \n");
*/
printf("reading the server response \n");
```

```
n= readline(sockfd, line, MAXLINE-1);
line[n]='\0';
printf("%s",line);

if ( n < 0)
   fprintf(stderr,"session: readline error \n");
}

int writen(fd, ptr, nbytes)

register int fd;
register char *ptr;
register int nbytes;

{
int nleft, nwritten;

nleft = nbytes;

while ( nleft > 0 ) {
nwritten = write(fd,ptr,nleft);
if ( nwritten <= 0 )
return(nwritten);

nleft -= nwritten;
ptr += nwritten;

}
return(nbytes-nleft);
}

int readline (fd, ptr, maxlen)

register int fd;
register char *ptr;
register int maxlen;
{

int n,rc;
char c;

for (n=1; n<maxlen; n++) {
if ( (rc=read(fd,&c,1)) == 1 {
```

```
    *ptr++ = c;
    if ( c == '\n' )
        break;
} else if (rc == 0 ) {
    if ( n == 1 )
        return(0);        /* EOF, no data read */
    else
        break;            /* EOF, some data was read */
} else
    return(-1);           /* Error */

}

*ptr = 0;
return(n);
}
```

APPENDIX 6B: UDP BROADCAST CLIENT/SERVER APPLICATION

6B.1 Server Application

```
/*
 * Server Program to test UDP broadcast messages.
 */

#include <sys/types.h>
#include <sys/time.h>
#include <sys/socket.h>
#include <netinet/in.h>
#include <netdb.h>

main()
{
struct    hostent *h_name;
int       sockfd;
char      buf[10];
struct    sockaddr_in mine, your, rcvaddr;
int       addlen;

h_name = gethostbyname("broadcast");
```

```
mine.sin_family = AF_INET;
mine.sin_port = htons(4000);
mine.sin_addr.s_addr = INADDR_ANY;

if ((sockfd = socket(AF_INET, SOCK_DGRAM, 0)) < 0)
    {
    printf("Socket error\n");
    exit(1);
    }

if (bind(sockfd, (struct sockaddr *)&mine, sizeof(mine)) < 0)
    {
    close(sockfd);
    printf("Bind Error\n");
    exit(1);
    }

recvfrom(sockfd, buf, sizeof(buf), 0, &rcvaddr, &addlen);
printf("%s\n", buf);
}
```

6B.2 Client Application

```
/*
*Client program to test broadcasting on a TCP/IP Network.
*
*/

#include <sys/types.h>
#include <sys/time.h>
#include <sys/socket.h>
#include <netinet/in.h>
#include <netdb.h>

main()
{
struct    hostent *h_name;
int    sockfd;
char    buf[10];
struct    sockaddr_in mine, your;

h_name = gethostbyname("broadcast");
```

```
mine.sin_family = AF_INET;
mine.sin_port = htons(0);
mine.sin_addr.s_addr = INADDR_ANY;
your.sin_family = AF_INET;
your.sin_port = htons(4000);

your.sin_addr.s_addr = *(u_long *) h_name->h_addr;
if ((sockfd = socket(AF_INET, SOCK_DGRAM, 0)) < 0)
    {
    printf("Socket error\n");
    exit(1);
    }
if (bind(sockfd, (struct sockaddr *)&mine, sizeof(mine)) < 0)
    {
    close(sockfd);
    printf("Bind Error\n");
    exit(1);
    }

strcpy(buf,"ok");

if (sendto(sockfd, buf, strlen(buf), 0, &your, sizeof(your)) != strlen(buf))
    {
    close(sockfd);
    exit(0);
    }
}
```

/* End Main */

Internetworking 7

So far we examined how to connect UNIX systems to a TCP/IP network. We also stepped through the process of configuring NFS, NIS, and DNS servers based on UNIX. In this chapter, we focus on how to interconnect UNIX hosts with Novell NetWare (IPX/SPX), Macintosh (AppleTalk), and Windows NT systems. Further, we emphasize how the X Window system may be used to integrate UNIX and PC environments.

7.1 NOVELL'S NETWARE ARCHITECTURE

In a Novell environment, a workstation or PC used by the end user is referred to as a *client system*. On the network are *server systems*–there may be one or several. The software for the end-user system and servers are referred to as *Novell Netware*. The portion of NetWare installed on the client system is known as a NetWare shell, which enables remote resources to appear as though they were locally attached. The other component of NetWare is operation system software installed on a PC-based system, which acts as a server and typically is configured with disk drives, communication devices, and printers.

Client systems request services; the servers provide services. The network architecture describes how client and server systems communicate. Figure 7.1 provides information on the Novell NetWare architecture and protocol stack.

7.1.1 Novell NetWare Protocols

At the lowest layers, physical and data link, Novell supports protocols such as Ethernet, token ring, and ARCNET. Novell's network layer protocol, *Internetwork packet exchange* (IPX), is primarily responsible for connecting different networks. At the transport layer, Novell supports two protocols: *sequenced packet exchange* (SPX) and *packet exchange protocol* (PXP). Other protocols such as *error*, *echo*, and *service advertisement protocol* (SAP) are used for advertisement of services such as printing and for error detection.

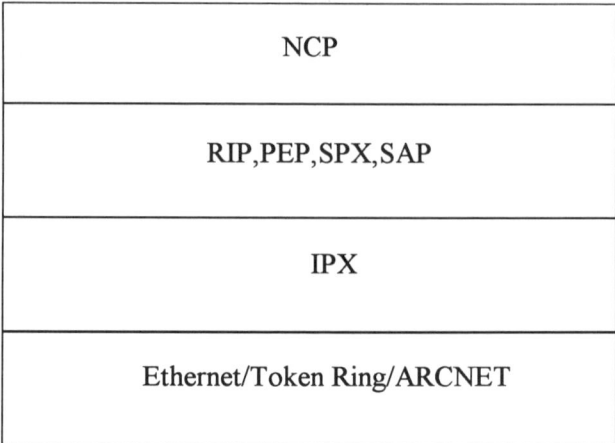

Figure 7.1 Novell NetWare architecture.

7.1.1.1 IPX

Novell's *Internetwork packet exchange* (IPX) protocol is a derivative of Xerox's *Internetwork datagram protocol* (IDP). IPX, like IDP, works at the network layer and is primarily responsible for the forwarding of packets. IPX provides its services to programs at a higher layer through the use of a *socket*. A socket may be viewed as an address of a higher layer protocol that is using the services of IPX. For an IPX client to communicate with its peer, it needs to know three things:

- Network number of the remote host;
- Local address on that remote network;
- Socket number of the program with which it is communicating.

IPX is an example of a connectionless protocol; it makes a best effort to deliver data but does not guarantee that data will be delivered to the destination system. Figure 7.2 describes the format of an IPX header.

The following is a description of fields in the IPX header:

- *Checksum* (1 byte): Checksum is always set to all ones (binary).
- *Length* (2 bytes): Packet length of the IPX header is 30 bytes. If a router is not involved in communication between the source and the destination, the maximum length of an IPX datagram is 576 bytes. If a router is present, then the maximum length is 512 bytes.
- *Transport Control* (1 byte): Transport control is a 1-byte field that specifies the number of routers a packet has passed through. It is initially set to 0.

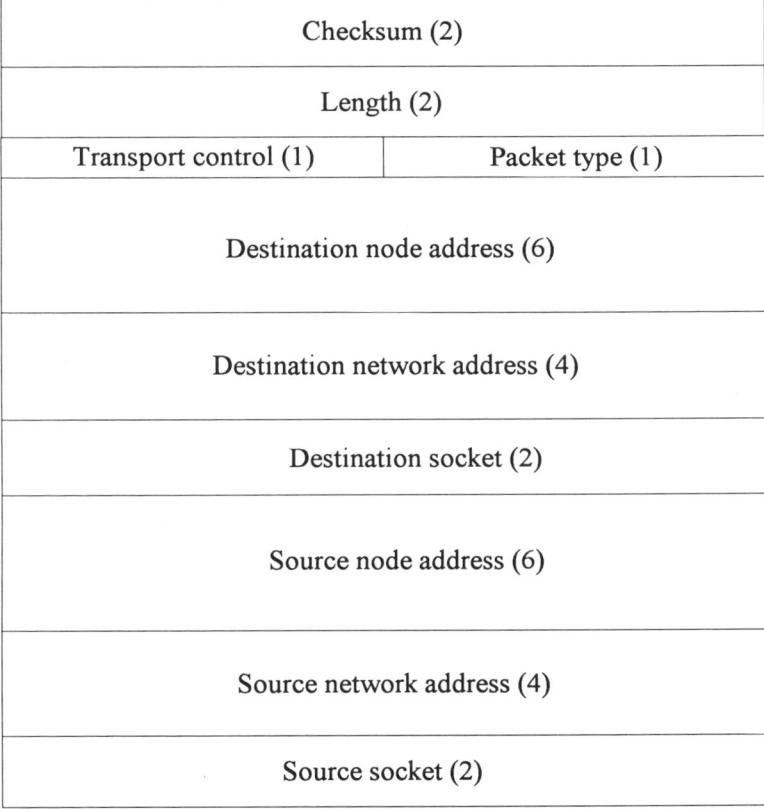

Figure 7.2 IPX header format.

- *Packet Type* (1 byte): Packet type indicates which higher layer protocol is to process the packet after IPX (similar to the protocol type field in an IP header). Examples of higher layer protocols are RIP (01$), Echo (02$), Error (03$), PXP (04$), SPX (05$), NCP (11$).
- *Destination Node and Network Address* (10 bytes): Destination node and network number specify the address of the destination network (4 bytes) and the host on that network (6 bytes).
- *Destination Socket* (2 bytes): Destination socket is a 2-byte field that specifies the address of the destination application receiving data.
- *Source Node and Network Address* (10 bytes): Source node and network number specify the address of the source network (4 bytes) and the host on that network (6 bytes).
- *Source Socket* (2 bytes): Source socket is a 2-byte field that indicates which application on the source generated the data.

7.1.1.2 SPX

The *sequenced packet exchange* (SPX) protocol is a transport layer protocol that uses the services of the internetwork packet exchange. SPX guarantees the delivery of data between the server and client. It takes care of problems such as duplicate data and lost data. Like TCP, SPX uses the concept of a *sliding window protocol*; several packets may be sent before an acknowledgment is received. Then a single acknowledgment may be sent for all packets received.

Client programs execute a series of SPX listen commands after opening an SPX connections. Space is reserved in memory for incoming packets. When SPX receives a packet for a given connection, it moves the packet into the indicated buffer space and notifies the client program. The SPX header is 42 bytes in length. Figure 7.3 describes an SPX header. The first 30 bytes are the same for the internetwork packet exchange and SPX, the only difference is that the packet type field is set to 05$ for SPX packets. The remaining 12 bytes provide information on fields such as:

- Data stream type specifies which application layer protocol is to process the data.

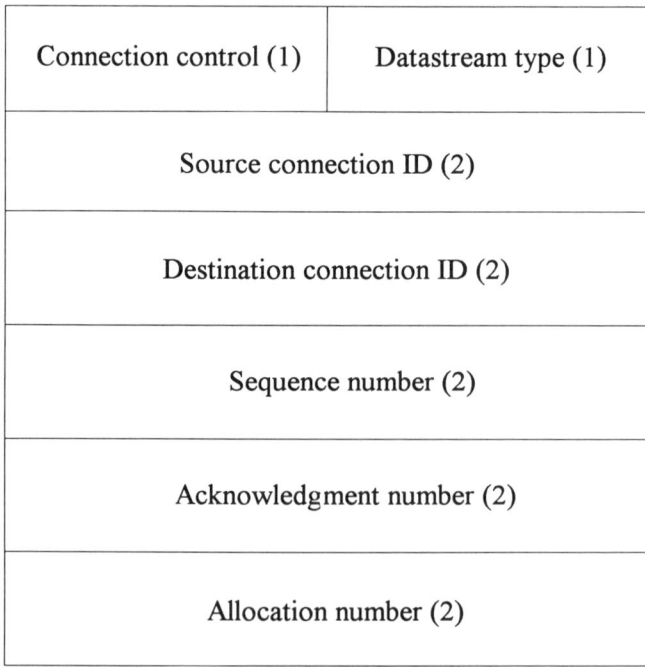

Figure 7.3 SPX header.

- Source and destination connection ID is used by the application to identify individual sessions.
- Sequence and acknowledgment numbers to guarantee that the destination received data sent by the source system.
- Allocation number provides information on buffers available on the source node (typically between 512 and 4096 bytes).

All SPX connections involve a two-step handshaking process, and after that a virtual session is said to be established.

7.1.1.3 NCP

The *NetWare core protocol* (NCP) provides operating system services such as printer, file, and queue management; bindery; and support for basic communication services. NCP is a key user of the network protocol, IPX. NCP uses a protocol similar to XNS's PEP as a transport layer protocol. This transport layer protocol is considered to be a part of NCP. NCP allows a user access to remote data, print files, and some other functions. Figure 7.4 describes how a Novell client system communicates with a Novell server using NCP. The client system generates an NCP request message. The response generated by the Novell server is referred to as an NCP reply.

Novell client systems communicate their requests to Novell servers using NCP. Some or all of the NCP services are provided by programs that reside both on servers and workstations. The server system runs the NetWare operating system; the client side or the workstation runs NetWare software in conjuction with the workstation operating system, DOS or OS/2. This software, the NetWare shell, extends the services of the operating system onto the network. The NetWare shell intercepts calls from application programs and the operating system and packages them as NCP requests for sending over the network.

The NCP header is encapsulated within an Ethernet, IPX, SPX frame. Figure 7.5 describes how NCP relates to IPX and SPX.

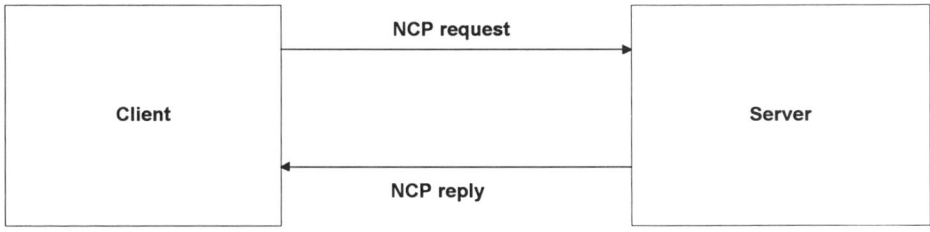

Figure 7.4 NCP request and reply messages exchanged between Novell Systems.

| Ethernet header | IPX header | SPX header | NCP header | Data |

Figure 7.5 An NCP packet on the network.

The NetWare server maintains several connections with workstations. It maintains security using the *bindery*. The bindery is a server database used to keep track of users, groups, workgroups, and other objects. Each entry in the bindery is referred to as a bindery object. Properties are attributes of the bindery object, an example of which is a user password [5]. The NetWare server maintains integrity among multiple users of data by using lock manager, which prevents users from making incompatible requests simultaneously.

Each NCP client request is followed by a server reply–hence, NCP is often referred to as a "ping-pong" protocol. The NCP request header is slightly different from an NCP reply header. The NCP request header consists of five fields. Figure 7.6 describes the format of an NCP request header.

The NCP request header is 6 bytes in length and is sent from the client system to the server. Following the NCP request header (in the same message) there is additional NCP data that identifies the client's request. The following is a brief description of fields in the NCP request header:

- *Request Type* (2 bytes): Identifies the type of NCP request. It may be set to:

1111	Create a service connection
2222	Service request
5555	Destroy service connection
7777	Burst mode transfer

- *Sequence Number* (1 byte): Is used to verify the sequence of the communication between the client and server systems. The last sequence number plus 1 is inserted by client systems in this field.
- *Connection Number Low* (1 byte): When a connection is established with the server, it assigns a service connection number to the client. The service connection number is placed in this field.
- *Task Number* (1 byte): Identifies which client task is making the request. The server automatically deallocates resources when a task ends.

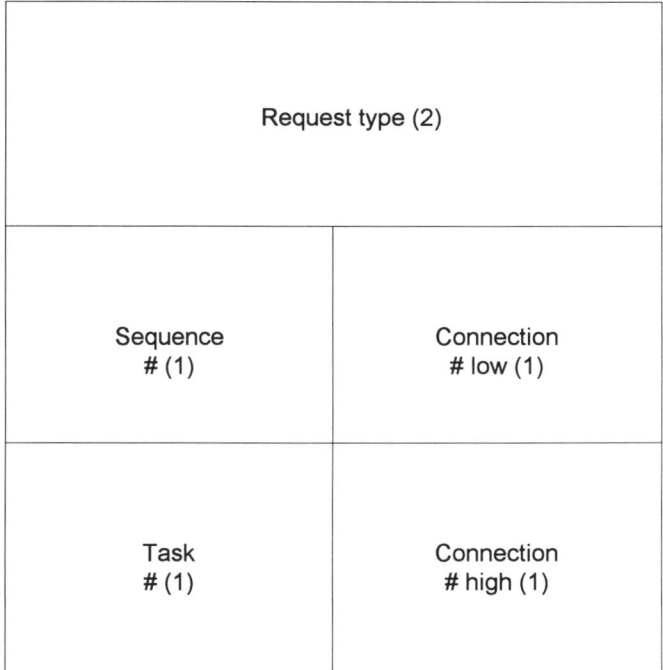

Figure 7.6 An NCP request header.

- *Connection Number High* (1 byte): This field is not currently used and is set to 0.

  The format of an NCP reply header is described in Figure 7.7. The following is a brief description of fields in the NCP reply header:

- *Reply Type* (2 bytes): Specifies the type of reply being sent. It may be set to:

  3333   Service reply
  7777   Burst mode connection
  9999   Request being processed

- *Completion Code* (1 byte): Specifies if the client's request was successful. 0 implies that the request was successful while a nonzero number indicates that some error occurred in processing the client's request.
- *Connection Status Flags* (1 byte): This field must be checked in all incoming NCP replies from a server. For example, if the DOWN command is entered at the command prompt, then the fourth bit in this byte is set to 1.

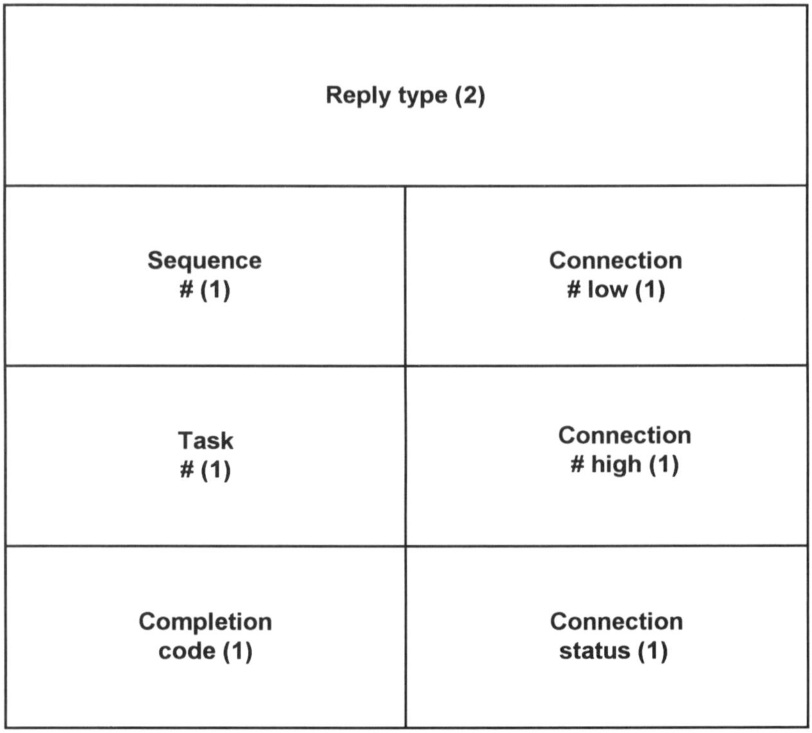

Reply type (2)	
Sequence # (1)	Connection # low (1)
Task # (1)	Connection # high (1)
Completion code (1)	Connection status (1)

Figure 7.7 An NCP reply header.

7.1.1.4 Service Advertisement Protocol (SAP)

The *service advertisement protocol* (SAP) is used to determine the address of the remote program. SAP specifies what services are available on a server system. These messages are broadcast every sixty seconds. The server system then sends messages known as *SAP responses*.

7.1.2 Case Study: Novell System Configuration

We step through the process of installing and configuring Novell NetWare 3.12 server and client systems.

Novell v3.12 File Server Configuration

Step 1

Insert the *Install diskette* in drive A: and reboot your computer, or change to drive A: and type

A: INSTALL <Enter>

Step 2

Select **Install new Netware v3.12** from the "Select an Installation Option" menu.

Step 3

Determine your DOS disk partition requirements.

> Select Create a new DOS partition. If your hard disk contains a previous DOS partition, continuing with the next step will erase that partition and destroy all data. Be sure you have backup copies of those files before continuing.
> Select Create a DOS partition.
> Enter the size (in megabytes) of the new partition. We chose 15 MB as the DOS partition size (recommended is 5 MB).
> Press any key to restart INSTALL. You must reboot your server so that DOS recognizes the new partition. Pressing any key automatically reboots the server. Make sure that the *Install diskette* is in drive A:.

Step 4

Format the newly created DOS partition. When the Install program starts again, it prompts you for formatting.

> Press <Enter> to continue.
> INSTALL now loads FORMAT.COM.
> Warning All existing data on nonremovable disk c: will be destroyed!— Continue (Y/N)?
> Type "Y" to continue.
> Press any key to continue.

Step 5

Name the file server.

SHIVA   (*we called the file server SHIVA*)

Step 6

Assign an IPX internal network number.

2E541330   (we accepted the number prompted by the installation process)

Step 7

Press <Enter> to copy the server boot files to the hard disk from *System_1 Diskette* to the default directory C:\SERVER.312. Files copied include SERVER.EXE, INSTALL.NLM, Disk drivers, and LAN drivers. During the copy process, insert the *NetWare diskettes* for which you are prompted into the source drive and press <ENTER>.

Step 8

You will next be prompted for the following information:

Country Code: 001 (United States)
Code Page: 437 (United States English)
Keyboard mapping: None
Accept these defaults by pressing <F10>
Select the format you desire and press <ENTER>
DOS filename format (recommended)
NetWare filename format

Step 9

Select the DOS filename format for which you are asked if you want to specify a startup set of commands.

Step 10

Select "NO".

Step 11

Press <F10> to save the start-up commands.

Step 12

Do you want AUTOEXEC.BAT to load SERVER.EXE? Choose "YES".

Step 13

The system console will appear prompting supported I/O port values for ISA device driver as 1F0, 170.

Choose 1F0
Supported interrupt no. values are E, B, F, C
Choose E

Step 14

At this step you will get the File Server prompt.

SHIVA:

Step 15

Load the Disk Driver Loadable Module at **SHIVA**: prompt.

SHIVA: load AHA1540 <ENTER>

The system will prompt for port=330. We accept this value.

Step 16

Create Netware Disk Partition Tables.
    Load INSTALL by typing

    SHIVA: load install

    From the Installation Options menu, select Disk Options.
    From the Available Disk Options menu, select Partition Tables.
    From the Partition Options menu, select Create Netware Partition.

    Partition type: netware 386 partition
    Partition size: 987 MB
    Hot fix information:
    Data area: 967.2 MB
    Redirection area: 512 blocks, 2%

Step 17

From the Installation Options menu, choose Volume Options.

    Press <Ins> on the "Volumes" screen.

    To create volume **sys** enter in the following:

Volume name: **sys**
Blocks: **26000**
Mem: **101 Meg**
Create volume **sys1** following Steps 17a and 17b

The size of the **sys1** volume is 865 MB

Step 18

Mount both volumes, **sys** and **sys1**:

From the Installation Options menu, choose Volume Options.
Select the **sys** volume, highlight the status option, and toggle it to mounted.

Follow the same steps for mounting the **sys1** volume.

Step 19

Copy SYSTEM and PUBLIC files.

> From the Installation Options menu, choose System Options.
> Select Copy System and Public Files from the Available System Options menu. Insert the diskettes as directed, the whole process may take between 2 and 3 hours.

Step 20

Next, take the server down:

SHIVA: **DOWN**
SHIVA: **EXIT**

C:\SERVER.312> **cd **

Step 21

Then we copied LAN driver files from 3-Com EtherlinkIII diskette to C:

c:\> copy a:\netware\4&312sw\3c*.* c:

Step 22

Reboot the server; you will get the SHIVA prompt.

SHIVA:
SHIVA: **LOAD INSTALL**

Select system options and edit the AUTOEXEC.NCF file to include the following information:

file server name SHIVA
ipx internal net 2E541330

mount all
load c:\3c5x9 port=300 int=10 Frame=Ethernet_II Name=IPNET
load c:\3c5x9 port=300 int=10 Frame=Ethernet_802.3 Name=IPXNET
load tcpip rip=no trap=192.136.118.54
load snmp Monitor=control=private
load snmplog
bind ip to IPNET ADDR=192.136.118.250 netmask ff.ff.ff.00
bind ipx to IPXNET net=F009
load clib
load mathlib
load tli
load ipxs
load spxs
load aiocomx

The AUTOEXEC.NCF file is responsible for loading TCP/IP without RIP. SNMP traps are sent to the indicated IP address. The SNMP NLM is loaded with monitor and control community names as *private*. The file server IP address and IPX numbers are allocated as shown above. Libraries such as CLIB and MATHLIB are loaded so that the NLMs that need these libraries can access them.

The STARTUP.NCF file included the following entry:

load AHA1540 port=330 int=B dma=5

Step 23

Down the file server.

SHIVA: **DOWN**
SHIVA: **EXIT**

Step 24

Enter the following command:

c:\server.312> SERVER

The server is up with TCP/IP enabled. You should be able to PING the server from another machine on the network. If another machine is configured as a Novell client, you should be able to login to the server.

Step 25

From a Novell client login as *supervisor*, invoke the **syscon** utility and select the option Edit System Login Script. Enter the following lines:

pccompatible
MAP ROOT F:= SHIVA/SYS1:USERS\\%LOGIN_NAME
MAP ROOT INS S1:= SHIVA/SYS1:USERS\\%LOGIN_NAME\\WIN31
MAP ROOT INS S2:= SHIVA/SYS1:APPS
MAP ROOT INS S3:= SHIVA/SYS:PUBLIC

The pccompatible line indicates to the system that it should ignore the version of DOS that is running. The INS lines specify that the system should search the paths indicated before C:\ search paths. S1, S2, and S3 will correspond to logical **z**, **y**, and **x** drives, respectively.

Step 26

Create an account with supervisor privileges. The account name we specified was *lakshmi*. You need to create this account because the supervisor account name exceeds the DOS 8 character file name convention. If we use the supervisor account, we may have problems of being unable to map the F: drive for user, *supervisor*.

Novell Client System Configuration

We stepped through the following to configure a PC as a Novell client system.

Install the **3c509** (Ethernet) board in the PC expansion slot.
Insert the 3 COM Etherlink III diskette drive A: and enter:

A:\> INSTALL

Press **y** for agreeing to license. Press the Enter key to continue.
Select NETWARE DOS ODI CLIENT.
You will be prompted for a password, just press <Enter>.
After a number of messages, you will see a message stating that the configuration is complete.
Press <ESC> to cancel. Reboot the machine.

7.1.3 Open Data Link Interface (ODI)

Novell's *open data-link interface* (ODI) adds functionality to NetWare by supporting multiple protocols and multiple LAN adapters in a single system. ODI creates a "logical network board" to allow multiple frame formats over a single network board and cable. Some benefits associated with ODI include [6]:

- It can run multiple protocols such as IPX/SPX, TCP/IP, and AppleTalk without adding extra network boards.

- It can communicate with a variety of workstations, file servers, and mainframe computers via different protocol stacks without rebooting your PC.
- Protocols written to ODI specification can communicate through any LAN adapter written to ODI specification.
- It can use the NET.CFG file to configure the LAN driver for any possible hardware configuration.

You can convert a standalone PC into a DOS ODI network system by adding one or more network boards, cabling, and DOS ODI software. Three sets of files allow Novell ODI-based systems to communicate with each other and other hosts on the network.

- LSL.COM: The *link support layer* (LSL) file enables the workstation to communicate using several protocols.
- LAN Drivers: Driver files such as NE2000.COM and NE2.COM communicate directly with LAN boards.
- Protocol stacks: Files such as IPXODI.COM and TCPIP.EXE manage communication between systems on the network.

7.1.4 Internetworking Products

We now examine different ways of internetworking Novell nodes with other systems on the network.

7.1.4.1 UNIXWare

Univel was a company formed by Novell, Inc., and UNIX System Laboratories, Inc., to integrate Novell's NetWare network operating system with UNIX. In 1992, Univel introduced an integrated NetWare and UNIX package that runs on 32-bit Intel microprocessors (Intel 386 and 486 processors) for network servers and clients.

The integrated package provided UNIX clients access to information from both UNIX and NetWare servers. The offerings from Univel were based on UNIX System V Release 4.2. Products available are marketed as UNIXware—UNIXWare version 2.0 is available in the market today. The two key products from Univel are *UNIXware Application Server* and *UNIXWare Personal Edition*. UNIXWare includes built-in support for IPX/SPX.

The UNIXWare Application Server is targeted for users who want to use UNIX as a server for database, transaction processing, and other aplications. The UNIXware Application Server supports multiple concurrent login sessions for TCP/IP or IPX/SPX. The UNIXWare Personal Edition lets UNIX clients communicate with NetWare servers using IPX/SPX and NCP.

7.1.4.2 LAN WorkPlace for DOS

LAN WorkPlace for DOS brings the TCP/IP protocol stack not only to the Novell client system but to PCs in general. LAN WorkPlace for DOS supports Microsoft Windows and uses Novell's ODI to provide PC clients access to both NetWare servers and UNIX hosts on the same network. The NetWare server routes the TCP/IP packets from the client PC to the UNIX machine. The LAN WorkPlace for DOS software includes [7]:

- TCP/IP transport system software;
- HostAccess utilities;
- NetBIOS software.

The TCP/IP transports system software, TCP/IP protocol software, and utilities for monitoring and administering an Ethernet network. The HostAccess utilities enable Pcs to communicate with remote hosts and nodes on the local network. Using these utilities you can [7]:

- Transfer files to and from remote hosts.
- Use your DOS workstation as a terminal and log onto a remote host. Print files on a printer attached to a remote host.
- Execute commands on a remote host.

The NetBIOS application program interface lets you run, without modification, all PC network applications designed for the standard NetBIOS interface.

Also included in LAN WorkPlace for DOS are a number of TCP/IP network information utilities, a large number of which are Windows based. This release supports Berkeley UNIX print queue management via utilities such as LPR, LPT, and LPQ. Further included with the package is XPC, which combines the **telnet** application with the client functionality of X windows; thus, a PC can function as a X Windows client.

Let us now examine the steps you need to follow to install and configure LAN WorkPlace on a PC.

Step 1

Insert the first LAN WorkPlace disk in your A drive.

Step 2

Type **A:INSTALL**. Press the <Enter> key.

Step 3

Press the <ESC> key to continue.

Step 4

The following menu will be displayed:
Select the components you wish to install:

(Required)   ODI Workstation services
(Required)   LAN WorkPlace v4.2 TCP/IP Transport
(Required)   LAN WorkPlace v4.2 DOS application

YES   LAN WorkPlace v4.2 Windows Application

Press <ESC> to accept and choose "YES" to save changes.

Step 5

Choose the **C** drive as the destination drive.

Step 6

Select **C:\net** as the target directory.

Step 7

Now, answer the following questions.

Does your workstation boot from a file server? **NO**
Do you want INSTALL to update your system files? **YES**

Step 8

Choose the network board that you have installed in your computer from the menu. If the network board that is installed on your system is not listed, then select any board from the list—later after the installation is complete you can modify the following files:

\net\bin\lanwp.bat
\net\nwclient\net.cfg

Step 9

Answer the following questions, based on the configuration of your network:

- Are TCP/IP parameters provided automatically by a BOOTP server?
- Enter the IP address of the workstation.
- Does your network have subnets?
- Does your network use an IP router?
- Does your network have a DNS server?

Step 10

Finally the message "Installation successfully completed" signals that the installation is complete. Reboot the PC.

7.1.4.3 NetWare NFS and NFS Gateway

NetWare NFS is a NetWare 3.11 network loadable module. It lets NetWare servers act as NFS file servers for UNIX systems. It provides features such as bidirectional printing (between UNIX and NetWare networks) and remote screen monitoring of a NetWare server from a UNIX workstation [8]. Features associated with NetWare NFS software include:

- The new NetWare server backup and restore utility, **sbackup**, is fully integrated with NetWare NFS and supports NFS specific file attributes.
- The NetWare utility **nfsadmin** allows NFS configuration files and parameters to be administered from the NetWare console.
- The utility **ftpserv** allows file transfer between the NetWare server and any host supporting a client implementation of the FTP protocol.

7.1.4.4 NetWare SunLink

The SunLink NetWare product runs on the Solaris operating system. With this product you can use a Sun SPARCstation as a file server for Novell client systems. This product works with other Sun products such as SunLink X.25, SunLink DECnet, SunLink SNA, and SunLink OSI. Further, NetWare clients could be on a DOS-, OS/2-, or Microsoft Windows–based system. SunLink NetWare supports IPX routing, Ethernet, token ring, and other NetWare administration products. Vendors such as Oracle and Ingres have indicated that their products will work with SunLink NetWare in the near future.

Another product that Sun introduced some time ago was *PC/NFS*, which provides DOS/Windows systems with support for the TCP/IP family of protocols. The PC/NFS product allows PCs to be integrated into UNIX networks.

7.2 UNIX–MACINTOSH INTEGRATION

Let us now understand the AppleTalk architecture and how to integrate Macintosh systems on a LocalTalk or AppleTalk environment with UNIX hosts on a TCP/IP network.

7.2.1 The AppleTalk Environment

The AppleTalk network environment consists of the Protocol architecture and its components. The protocol architecture consists of network protocols that include application, delivery, and connection protocols, which determine how the various components provide services. The components include all of the network's functional parts: hardware devices such as computers, printers, servers, cables and connectors and software such as the network control software and network services. AppleTalk networking capabilities are built into the Macintosh computer.

7.2.2 AppleTalk and the OSI/RM

Table 7.1 describes the relationship between AppleTalk protocols and the OSI/RM.

7.2.3 AppleTalk Addressing

The AppleTalk network system uses a combination of node and network numbers to identify devices on the network. Thus, a LaserWriter printer or a Macintosh are nodes on the network. An AppleTalk node is dynamically assigned a node address by AppleTalk software when it is powered on. This is also referred to as *dynamic node assignment*. It is therefore possible that a node may not have the same address each time it is turned on.

Table 7.1
AppleTalk Protocols

Layers	Protocols
Application	AppleShare file server
	AppleShare print server
AppleShare PC	
Presentation	AppleTalk filing protocol (AFP)
Postscript	
Session	AppleTalk session protocol (ASP)
	Printer access protocol (PAP)
	AppleTalk data stream protocol (ADSP)
	Zone information protocol (ZIP)
Transport	AppleTalk transaction protocol (ATP)
	AppleTalk echo protocol (AEP)
	Name binding protocol (NBP)
	Routing table maintenance protocol (RTMP)
Network	Datagram delivery protocol (DDP)
Data link and physical	EtherTalk link access protocol (ELAP)
	TakenTalk link access protocol (TLAP)
	LocalTalk

AppleTalk Phase 2 provides extended addressing that allows up to 16 million nodes to be on the same network. *AppleTalk Phase 1* networks were limited to 254 nodes. Note that the LocalTalk network continues to support a maximum of 254 nodes, which is primarily for smaller organizations that may not require extended addressing. Also, under Phase 2, up to 256 zone names can be defined for a single network. A zone in an AppleTalk network provides a way of conceptually grouping devices to make it easier for users to locate and gain access to network services. AppleTalk zones are defined by the placement of routers on the network.

7.2.4 AppleTalk Protocols

The *name binding protocol* (NBP) and the *AppleTalk filing protocol* (AFP) are important protocols in the AppleTalk environment.

Name Binding Protocol

Users on an AppleTalk network can specify names as opposed to node and network numbers. The translation between names and network and node numbers is a function of the name binding protocol (NBP). When a device is connected to the network, NBP assigns a name to the device. Users can also specify a name for the device that would then be used by NBP.

AppleTalk Filing Protocol

Communication between a user's system and a file server is made possible by the AppleTalk filing protocol (AFP). AFP server software runs on a variety of platforms: Macintosh systems, MS-DOS hosts, and VAX/VMS nodes. With AFP, files and applications are reached and used as if they were located on the user's system [9].

7.2.5 AppleTalk Network Types

AppleTalk protocols can operate on a number of different network types. These include *LocalTalk, EtherTalk, and TokenTalk*, each of which supports a variety of media and topologies.

LocalTalk

A LocalTalk network is characterized by the following:

- Transmission speed of 230.4 Kbps;
- A bus or star topology;

- Optional shielded twisted-pair, unshield twisted-pair, or infrared light media;
- Cable systems that can connect up to 32 devices on a single network.

LocalTalk networks can be connected to each other through a backbone network such as Ethernet.

TokenTalk

A TokenTalk network transmits AppleTalk protocols over IEEE 802.5 token-ring networks. Token-ring networks operate at either 4 Mbps or at 16 Mbps and use either shielded twisted-pair or unshield twisted-pair cables. A single network can support up to 260 devices. To connect a Macintosh to a token-ring network you need to install TokenTalk software and a token-ring interface card. TokenTalk conforms to the IEEE 802.5 standard for token-ring networks.

7.2.6 Internetworking Services

Network services are typically provided by server systems. AppleTalk networks are characterized by many types of servers: file servers, print servers, e-mail servers, and modem servers.

File Services

The AppleTalk filing protocol is used to communicate between the user's computer and the file server. AppleTalk file services can be centralized or distributed. In a *centralized file service*, a single system provides access to user files and a system on the network that has the file-sharing software installed. Thus, each user's computer is like a file server, and resources can be shared among systems.

A *distributed file service* is useful when a small number of users need to share files. Centralized file service is appropriate when a large number of users need to share files and other data. It also simplifies the process of backup and security.

The AppleShare file server is a central location in which the AppleTalk users can store and share information and applications. AppleShare consists of server and administrative software that runs on a Macintosh computer and computer-specific workstation software for other hardware [9]. AppleShare provides file security through password verification and access privileges to specific volumes and folders.

A built-in feature of System 7 is Macintosh file sharing, which enables users to share information on their Macintosh computers with other people on the network. A number of companies have implemented the AFP file service protocol. These include Novell NetWare for DOS systems; VAXShare, AlisaShare, and PacerShare for VMS systems; and AT&T's StarGROUP LAN Manager Server, PacerShare, and IPT's ushare for UNIX systems. Thus a Digital VAX computer can be used as an AFP file server and print server. The same is true for DOS, OS/2, and Windows 3.x systems. For example, the VAX file system appears on the Macintosh as a series of hierarchical file system volumes, with VMS directories being represented as folders and VAX files represented as documents.

Print Services

The very first AppleTalk networks were LocalTalk networks that connected Macintosh computers to a shared LaserWriter printer. Printing can be set up in two ways: by using a *shared printer* or by using a *print server*. Shared printing is good for environments that have a small network and people who may print at different times. It is possible to use background printing with shared printing. However, if the computer is turned off or its connection to the network is broken, the print job will not be completed. The PrintMonitor application program included with Macintosh software is an example of a *background printer*.

Another way to set up network printing is to use a print server, also referred to as a *spooler*. The server allows several users to send documents to the same printer, regardless of whether or not that printer is busy. Users send their files to be printed and immediately gain control of their computer for other tasks. When the server receives a print job it stores the file on its hard disk and sends it to the printer when it is available for printing. A print server is ideal for large networks. It enables the network administrator to manage a resource centrally and frees the user's computer for other tasks.

E-mail Services

E-mail can be used across AppleTalk zones and network types such as LocalTalk, Ethernet, and token ring. Typically, e-mail services use a mail system that acts as a server that can store and forward mail messages. Some commonly used e-mail products for AppleTalk networks are:

- Microsoft Mail;
- cc:Mail;
- QuickMail;
- InBox from Sitka.

7.2.7 Internetworking Software

MacTCP and MacX are used to communicate with nodes on a TCP/IP-based network.

MacTCP

MacTCP is a software product that provides TCP/IP transmission services as a basis for developing applications. MacTCP supports the following protocols: IP, TCP, UDP, ARP, RARP, ICMP, BOOTP, RIP, and the domain name server. It also facilitates IP subnetting. MacTCP is coresident with AppleTalk Protocols; thus, TCP/IP and AppleTalk applications can operate concurrently. MacTCP runs over both Ethernet and LocalTalk networks.

Wollongong's Pathway Access product and InterCon's TCP/Connect II support TCP/IP application layer protocols such as **telnet** and **ftp**. For *NFS client* functionality, so that the Macintosh system can mount UNIX disks, you can use Wollongong's Pathway client NFS or Intercon's NFS/Share.

Products such as VersaTilities from Synergy Software, MacSLIP from Terisoft, and NCSA/BYU from Brigham Young University provide support for SLIP. Thus, Macintosh nodes can connect to a TCP/IP network with a modem instead of Etherrnet.

MacX

MacX is an X Window display server for the Macintosh operating system. It provides support for the following protocols: TCP/IP, AppleTalk data stream protocol, and DECnet.

Applications that have been written to support the X Window protocol are typically referred to as *X clients*. These applications can be displayed on the Macintosh because the Macintosh functions as an X server. Some features associated with MacX are [10] that it provides for concurrent execution of X Window and Macintosh applications under the MulitiFinder operating system software and can work in two different modes: rooted and rootless. In the rootless mode of operation, the root window as defined by the X Window system is made invisible—you can see the Macintosh desktop in the background. In the rooted mode of operation, X Windows appear inside a Macintosh window—this represents the visible portion of the X screen. Both modes may be used concurrently, on a per client basis.

To use MacX on TCP/IP networks, you must first install and configure MacTCP on your Macintosh. MacX runs on Mac A/UX and MacOS (Finder) systems.

SNMP Support

Products such as AppleTalk Connection and TCP/IP Connection for Macintosh enable you to manage Macintosh computers with the *simple network management protocol* (SNMP). The AppleTalk and TCP/IP connection products support the following agents:

- Network agent, which collects data on the data link layer;
- TCP/IP agent, which collects data on the TCP/IP protocol;
- AppleTalk agent, which collects data on AppleTalk protocols;
- Mac agent, which collects data on Macintosh hardware and software.

7.3 X WINDOW SYSTEM

X is increasingly being accepted as the common thread for user interfaces across heterogeneous computer systems.

X is the graphical user interface (GUI) that users interact with on UNIX systems. The X Window System is supported on Windows and Macintosh environments.

Therefore, whether a person is working with a Digital DECstation running ULTRIX or an IBM RS/6000 running AIX, the end-user interface is fairly consistent because both operating systems support the X standard and their graphics user interface is based on X. Further, we examine the various components of the X standard and how the X protocol relates to the network architecture supported by UNIX systems, TCP/IP. Finally, the role of serial line protocols such as SLIP and PPP, and X is examined.

7.3.1 MIT's Project Athena and X

The Massachusetts Insitute of Technology's *Project Athena* was funded by MIT, IBM, and Digital. Athena was the goddess of wisdom, who suddenly sprang from the head of Zeus. The technologies developed from this joint venture have become industry standards. These include the X Window System graphical user interface. *Today, it is difficult to find a computer system that does not support the X standard.*

However, MIT's project was no sudden achievement: It took eight years, about $50 million from IBM and DEC, and about $20 million from MIT itself. But the gains from this investment are very impressive; several resulting technologies have been submitted to and accepted by the Open Software Foundation (OSF).

The motivation for developing the X Window System standard was to have a common way for applications on computer systems to communicate with the display device. The emphasis was to keep X independent of operating system technology (such as MVS, VMS, VM, or UNIX) and system hardware (SPARC-, PA-, RISC-, POWER-based systems). Some other technologies developed at MIT's Project Athena include:

- Kerberos;
- Moira;
- Hesiod;
- Zephyr.

Kerberos is a user authentication specification and software. Because users are always moving from one machine to another, it is critical to authenticate the user over the network as opposed to the user's system. Kerberos enables a user to enter a password that is encrypted during transmission. Kerberos then transparently grants *tickets* that give the user access to network services such as file and print servers. *Moira* is a system database. This relational database contains information about files, users, and services. It enables Athena administrators to install and update software from a central location.

Hesiod is a mapping system. Hesiod works with Kerberos and Moira and describes associations between logged-in users and their system preferences and files. *Zephyr* is a real-time messaging service. In addition to electronic mail that Athena provides, Zephyr lets users or services send messages of immediate concern exclusively to individuals who are logged in on the network.

Today, the X Window system has an organization of its own: the X Window Consortium. The consortium is composed of many vendors who support the X standard on a variety of platforms. Project Athena ended in June 1991. All hardware and software associated with the project was transferred to MIT's in-house computer services department.

Some other joint projects have had a significant impact on distributed computing. The development of the *Andrew File System* (AFS) by Carnegie-Mellon University was funded by IBM. AFS is a part of OSF's DCE subsystem. Carnegie-Mellon University also developed the *Mach multiprocessor operating system*. This is being used on the NeXT workstation and has been incorporated in the OSF/1 operating system.

7.3.2 The X Standard

X, also referred to as the X Window system, is a network transparent window system.

The X Window System consists of the following major components:

- X server;
- Xlib;

- Toolkit intrinsics;
- X clients;
- X protocol.

X is based on an asynchronous network protocol, called *X protocol*. To mask protocol encoding and transport interactions the X Window system includes an interface library. *Xlib* is the C language interface library provided by MIT. Xlib includes about 400 functions, which may be used for drawing objects such as circles, polygons, and lines; creating and moving windows; displaying text; and defining colors. The X protocol and the X library do not specify menus, scroll bars, dialog boxes, or how an application should respond to user input.

Toolkits, such as the X toolkit, provide menus, scroll bars, and dialog boxes. Toolkits include routines that make it easier to draw an object such as a scroll bar. Toolkits hide the details associated with Xlib, and the main motivation for toolkits is to make the process of developing X applications easier.

Graphics libraries, such as the GKS library, transform abstract object descriptors into graphics requests. Toolkits, graphics libraries, and user interface management systems are implemented on top of Xlib. Two major user interface toolkits and window managers are MOTIF and OpenLook. MOTIF is a part of the OSF specifications, whereas OpenLook was developed at Sun Microsystems. Windowing systems such as DECwindows available from Digital and AIXwindows from IBM are based on X and MOTIF, and the OpenWindow system included with Sun SPARCstations is based on the OpenLook standard.

7.3.3 X Terminology

Terms commonly used in an X environment are:

- Icons;
- Cursor;
- Screen;
- Window manager;
- X server;
- X client;
- xterm.

Icons are small symbols that represent a window. A cursor is what tracks the pointer position. A display may consist of more than one *screen*—for example, two monitors may be connected to the same UNIX system to form a single display. The *window manager* enables you to indicate the size and position of icons and windows on your display; it is an example of an X client application. The *X server* is responsible for processing input received from the keyboard, mouse, and X client applications. An *X client* is an application displayed on the X server system. *xterm* is an example of an X client application—it emulates terminals such as Digital's VT100. The *xterm* application opens a window that enables you to log in to a system on the network.

7.3.4 X Servers and Clients

The software that manages the display, keyboard, and mouse and understands the X protocol in X is referred to as the *server*. This is different from the concept of a file server or a CPU server, which are systems with extensive disk or CPU resources that are made available to other hosts on the network. The X server makes available its *display* for X client applications. The main functions of the X server are to:

- Multiplex keyboard and mouse input back onto the network to the X client;
- Perform two-dimensional graphics on the display;
- Demultiplex requests from each X client.

The X server software could be downloaded from the host or stored in internal ROM. The X client is an application displayed on the X server's screen. Examples of X client applications are *xcalc*, *xclock*, and *xterm*. X clients communicate with the server by executing Xlib calls. Xlib calls in turn are translated into X protocol requests and passed to the local or remote X server. Inputs form the keyboard and mouse are captured by the X server and passed to the appropriate X clients in the form of X protocol events.

The *window manager* is an X client responsible for the layout and management of windows on the screen. The window manager may be local to the X display device or served remotely.

7.3.5 X Protocol

The X protocol is designed to communicate all the information necessary to operate a window system over a single asynchronous, bidirectional stream of 8-bit bytes. In terms of the OSI/RM, the X protocol is implemented above the transport layer. In order to communicate X messages between the server and client processes, the lower layers must:

- Be bidirectional;
- Deliver bytes in sequence;
- Deliver unduplicated bytes.

Note that if the X client and the X server processes are on the same system (i.e., they are communicating over the network), then the connection is typically based on local interprocess communication mechanisms [12].

So how is the X protocol implemented? The protocol has been implemented over a number of languages and operating systems. X clients implement the protocol by using a programming library that interfaces to a single underlying network protocol, typically TCP/IP or DECnet. The C language programming library provided by MIT, called *Xlib*, uses *sockets* to communicate. Sockets, as described earlier, are an application program interface to communication protocols such as TCP/IP. The interfaces defined in MIT's implementation of Xlib are standard; however, the code is not. Therefore, vendors may modify or optimize the library code for their systems as long as it matches the specification of Xlib provided with the MIT distribution of X software [12]. For example, AT&T's implementation of Xlib uses *System V streams*. Streams, like sockets, are another application programming interface to communication protocols such as TCP/IP.

X servers typically understand underlying protocols such as TCP/IP and DECnet. Hence, the server can accept connections from TCP/IP or DECnet clients.

Protocol Packet Types

All X protocol packets have a length in multiples of 4 bytes. This simplifies the implementation of the protocol on architectures that require alignment of values on 16- or 32-bit boundaries [12]. There are four types of X protocol packets:

- Requests;
- Replies;
- Events;
- Errors.

An X request is generated by the client and sent to the server. A protocol request can carry a variety of information, such as specification for drawing a line or an inquiry about the current size of a window. An X reply is sent from the server to the client in response to certain requests. Not all requests are answered by replies—only the ones that ask for information. Requests that specify drawing, for example, do not generate replies, but requests that inquire about the current size of the window do.

An X event is sent from the server to the client and contains information about a device action or about a side effect of a previous request. All events are stored in a 32-byte-long structure to simplify queueing and handling. The X server is capable of sending many types of events to the client, only some of which are needed by most clients. X provides a mechanism whereby the client can express interest in certain events but not others. Not only does this prevent wasting of network resources on unneeded events, it also speeds and simplifies clients by avoiding the testing and destruction of unnecessary events.

An error is like an event but is handled differently by clients. Unlike events, which are queued by the client library to be read later, errors are sent immediately upon arrival to an error-handling routine by the client-side programming library. Every error packet includes an 8-bit error code. Error packets are basically treated just like events, including the routine in the client library that receives them. At this point they are sent to the error-handling routine instead of being queued.

In the TCP/IP Environment

TCP/IP and DECnet are the two network protocols commonly supported in the X environment. RARP, BOOTP, NFS, FTP, and TFTP are some other network protocols commonly used in the X environment. The X display device determines the protocols supported by the system. In the case of X terminals these protocols are installed in internal ROMs. It is possible for the X terminal to determine its network address dynamically from a host on the network. With TCP/IP, either RARP or BOOTP may be used for this purpose.

In the DECnet world, the *maintenance operations protocol* (MOP) would provide the same functionality. BOOTP is a bootstrap protocol based on UDP that allows a diskless workstation or an X terminal to determine its Internet address, the Internet address of the server, and the path name of the file to be loaded into memory. RARP is a similar protocol, but it allows a system to determine only its network address.

Increasingly, UNIX systems are being shipped with protocols such as RARP, BOOTP, and/or DHCP. Once the address information and file path are determined, TFTP is the protocol typically used to download the X server software.

Fonts

X terminals can get fonts from their internal ROM or from a host. The two protocols most commonly used to get fonts from the host to the X display device are TFTP and NFS.

With TFTP, the path name of the font directory must be entered in the ROM setup for an X terminal. The X terminal then uses TFTP to transfer font files as required. If the X terminal has the NFS client code in ROM, it has access to fonts by mounting the host's font directory [13].

7.3.6 XDMCP

The *X display manager control protocol* (XDMCP) provides a uniform mechanism for an autonomous display to request login service from a remote host [14]. The word *autonomous* indicates that the display consists of hardware and processes that are independent of any particular host where login service is desired. X terminals are a good example of autonomous display devices.

The result of XDMCP negotiations is the X protocol communication between the client and server. XDMCP uses datagrams to communicate. The display device is responsible for sequencing and retransmission.

The *xdm* process on most systems supports the XDMCP protocol. In terms of functionality, *xdm* provides the same function as the *getty* and *login* processes do for extablishing a login session to a UNIX system. After you log onto a host using *xdm*, the display manager initiates an X session and starts X applications as specified in X intialization files, such as **.xsession**.

7.3.7 X and Serial Line Protocols

Almost all X display devices have an RS-232 interface to support serial line communication. Most systems connected via serial lines run at 9600 bps or less. The protocols typically used over serial lines include the *serial line Internet protocol* (SLIP), Xremote, GraphOn, and *point-to-point protocol* (PPP). Xremote and GraphOn are proprietary protocols provided by NCD and GraphOn, respectively.

SLIP was introduced by Rick Adams on a UNIX system in 1984. SLIP was later distributed as a part of 4.3BSD. SLIP is defined in RFC 1055. RFC 1144 describes the CSLIP (compressd SLIP) specification.

The following subsection is based mostly on [15], which provides an excellent comparison of serial line protocols SLIP and PPP. SLIP defines a method of encapsulating IP packets for transmission over a serial line and then sends a special character, Hex 0xC0, to indicate the end of the IP packet. This is similar to the technique used by Kermit, where each packet starts with Hex 0x01. Once two systems are connected by SLIP, users can initiate TCP/IP-based applications such as **telnet**, **ftp**, or X Window sessions. SLIP is supported on a number of UNIX systems and X terminals.

The two significant improvements to SLIP have been dial-up capability and header compression. Dial-up SLIP has become important because most X terminals support it. It is a convenient way to use an X terminal from home with a modem. The code for dial-up SLIP differs from the original SLIP in that the code negotiates modem control on the serial port. TCP/IP packets typically contain about 40 bytes of header information; if the data bytes are few, this results in a significant overhead. Van Jacobson under a DOE contract modified the SLIP protocol to improve TCP/IP throughput over serial lines. The technique used was to cache TCP/IP header information so that it does not have to be sent with each packet.

However, SLIP continues to have a few deficiencies: lack of error correction, inability to support more than one protocol, no compression, and no method of dynamically assigning network addresses. For this reason the Internet community developed a new protocol that could address SLIP's deficiencies and meet future needs. PPP is the result of that effort. PPP uses the ISO standard *high-level data link control* (HDLC) protocol for framing packets. HDLC begins and ends each transmission with a Hex 0x7e character. It provides support for a 16-bit *cyclic redundancy check* (CRC) for error correction. HDLC operates over synchronous as well as asynchronous serial links.

PPP implements an ISO extension to HDLC by using the first 16 bits of the data packet to specify the type of protocol packet being transmitted. Thus, multiple protocol types can use the serial connection. Upon initiating a PPP connection, PPP sends a *line control protocol* (LCP) frame. This frame contains information that lets the two connected hosts nogotiate the type of connection they want. All PPP implementations by default are able to handle a 1,500-byte frame size. After the connection is negotiated with LCP, the host will transmit a network control protocol packet to further negotiate options associated with the type of network protocol desired. If the host wants to transmit IP packets then *Internet protocol control protocol* (IPCP) packets are exchanged to negotiate parameters specific to IP transmission, such as the dynamic assignment of addresses and header compression.

After the connection negotiations are complete, actual protocol packets can then be transmitted and, in the case of the IP protocol, **ftp**, **telnet**, and X sessions may be initiated. LCP frames can be used to terminate or renegotiate the connection. Only a few X terminal vendors currently support PPP.

An interesting use of PPP has been in dial-up IP routers. These are units that contain modems and reside on the Ethernet network. They are capable of negotiating dial-up PPP and SLIP connections with remote X terminals and workstations and routing IP packets to appropriate networks. With PPP, a remote workstation does not need a static, previously defined network address as with SLIP. Upon dial-up, PPP can request a suitable network address for a remote workstation.

Physical interfaces such as RS-232, RS-422, or V.35 can be used for PPP-based communication. RFCs 1171 and 1172 provide further details on PPP.

7.3.8 X Commands and Applications

Let us now look at commands and applications commonly used in an X environment. Ascertain that the **path** variable includes **/usr/bin/X11** (this is typically specified in your **.login** or **.profile** files).

7.3.8.1 xinit

The **xinit** command is executed to start the X server. Typically, it also creates an **xterm** window in the upper left corner of the display, which is referred to as the *login xterm* window. The background window is called the *root window*.

    % xinit

7.3.8.2 xterm

You can use the **xterm** command to start a terminal window:

    % xterm&

7.3.8.3 xhost

The **xhost** command may be executed to add or delete hosts that are authorized to connect to the X server. By default, only locally run programs can use the X server. Systems specified in the **/etc/X*.hosts** file can also connect to the X server (*is the display number of the server). The command format is

    xhost [options]

For example:

    % xhost + hostname

enables the specified *hostname* to connect to the local X server. In

    % xhost - hostname

the *hostname* specified is not authorized to connect to the local X server. By

    % xhost +

access is granted to all nodes on the network. However, for

    % xhost -

only nodes specified in the **/etc/X*.hosts** file have access to the X server. Note that the host names followed by two colons (::) indicates a DECnet node name.

7.3.8.4 xclock

The **xclock** application displays the time in digital or analog format. The default is an analog clock with a black foreground on a white background. For example,

    % xclock -analog -hd navyblue &

The **hd** option specifies the color of the hands of the analog clock. Some other options include:

- **analog**   Draws a 12-hour clock face;
- **digital**   Displays date and time in digital format;
- **bg color**   Specifies that the background color; white is the default;
- **bd color**   Specifies the border color; the default is black;
- **fg color**   Foreground color;
- **fn font**   Font required.

7.3.9 PCs, UNIX, and the X Window System

To better understand how to integrate the X Window System environment on a PC with DOS/Windows installed, let us step through and examine how to configure NCD's PC XWare product. The configuration steps described are based on a Toshiba laptop system with DOS v6.22 and Windows 3.1.

NCD's PC Xware product brings the entire X Window System environment to a PC. The following steps detail how to install and configure NCD's PC XWare product.

> In the Windows 3.1 environment, choose the FILE Menu and select RUN. Now enter: **A:\SETUP** (after inserting the **Setup Disk** of PC Xware in the A drive).
>
> Select Standard Install.
>
> Choose NCD TCPIP. Select the location for the install directory as **C:\PCXWARE** and **C:\PCXNET**. Follow the instructions displayed on the screen and insert diskettes as requested. The serial number and the key are provided on the diskettes.
>
> Next, you are prompted for information on the LAN card. We selected OTHER. We inserted the Xircom driver diskette in the A: drive. On the command line, enter:
>
> **A:\CENDIS.EXE.** The system will display the contents of the PROTOCOL.INI file. Modify the entries:
>
> > [CENDIS]
> > DRIVERNAME=XIRCOM$
>
> The system will then ask for the host name of the PC, it's IP address, and other network parameters.
>
> You are then asked if you want to change some parameters. Enter, "NO". Reboot the machine.

The system will perform a network test and ask you to enter the IP address of another system on the network. Now, try to send X displays from other nodes on the network to the PC where you installed NCD's PC XWare software.

7.4 WINDOWS NT

Windows NT is Microsoft's response to UNIX. Windows NT is not just for Intel systems—it also runs on MIPS and ALPHA processors. NT is a multithreaded, multitasking operating system. NT supports DOS, Windows, and OS/2 applications—it also supports 16-bit Windows and POSIX-based applications.

Window NT operates in two modes: user mode and privileged or kernel mode. Application programs run in user mode. The NT Executive, which is the heart of Windows NT, performs such tasks as managing input and output, virtual memory, and all processes. The Executive controls communication between NT and the hardware. The Executive operates in kernel mode.

Windows NT supports a variety of protected subsystems within user mode. The Security subsystem is an example of a protected subsystem, which supports a UNIX-like secure login and C2 security. Win32 API is another example of a protected subsystem.

The server version of NT, referred to as Windows NT Advanced Server, supports LANManager, centralized administration, and fault tolerance (disk mirroring and stripping). The server can also be set up as an AppleTalk server. The Windows NT Advanced Server system can support up to 4 GB of RAM. The Advanced Server uses 64-bit addressing to access the disk drive—thus, it can support up to 408 TB of disk storage.

Another feature built into the Advanced Server is that it allows users to transparently access all network resources with a single network logon. The operating system includes graphical tools to centrally manage groups of NT servers and desktops. There is a separate protected virtual address space for each application to guard against application or software failure—the operating system elements are protected from each other and from applications. The Advanced Server protects against hard disk failure by supporting disk mirroring and striping with parity—RAID 5. As far as fault tolerance is concerned, the Advanced Server protects against:

- Application failure;
- Hard disk failure;
- Power failure.

The server system can support DOS, Windows, Windows for Workgroups, NT, OS/2, and Macintosh client systems. The NT operating system supports the following network protocols:

- NetBEUI;
- IPX/SPX;
- AppleTalk;
- TCP/IP.

The network programming interfaces supported include:

- Windows sockets;
- RPC;
- NetBIOS.

7.4.1 NT and TCP/IP

As fas as TCP/IP support is concerned, protocols such as UDP, TCP, IP, ARP, and ICMP are integrated in the NT operating system. Other application layer protocols supported include:

- FINGER;
- TELNET;
- FTP;
- RCP;
- REXEC;
- RSH.

Utilities that are a part of the NT system include:

- ARP;
- HOSTNAME;
- IPCONFIG;
- NETSTAT;
- PING;
- ROUTE;
- PPP.

The operating system supports an SNMP agent for network management transactions. A key protocol supported by NT is DHCP. As explained earlier, DHCP is an important protocol used for assigning IP addresses for TCP/IP client/server systems.

To configure TCP/IP on an NT system, you need to determine several factors. Is DHCP going to be used? If yes, is there a DHCP server system on the network? What is the DHCP server system's IP address? If DHCP is not used, you need to determine the following:

- What is the IP address for each network adapter?
- What is the subnet mask for each network adapter?
- What is the IP address of default gateway?
- If system is using DNS, what are the IP addresses of DNS servers on the network?

- If system is using WINS, what are the IP addresses of WINS servers on the network?
- Is this system a DHCP server? This is only possible on Windows NT Advanced Server systems.
- Is this system a WINS server? This is only possible on Windows NT Advanced Server systems.
- Is this system a WINS proxy agent?

To configure SNMP on an NT system, you need to know:

- Community name (public and private);
- Trap destination;
- IP address(es) of NMS.

TCP/IP configuration on an NT system requires you to be a member of the *administrators* group. Once logged in, you need to start the Network option in the Control Panel. Then, choose the Add Software button in the Network Settings dialog box. You will now see the Network Software Installation dialog box. Select TCP/IP Protocol and Related Components from the Network Software list. Choose the Continue button.

In the Windows NT TCP/IP Configurations Options dialog box, specify values for such options as:

- Adapter;
- IP address;
- Subnet mask;
- Default gateway.

Also, if you have a WINS server and would like to use it, select Query WINS for Windows Name Resolution. You then need to enter the IP address of the primary and secondary WINS servers. For DNS support, choose the DNS button in the TCP/IP Configuration dialog box to specify DNS related options. At this point, you will see the DNS Configuration dialog box. Specify:

Host Name: shiva
TCP Domain Name: ngt.com
Name Resolution Search Order: (*here you will have the following choices*)
    DNS Only
    DNS First, Then Hosts File
    Hosts File First, Then DNS
    Hosts File Only
(*Select one of the above four choices*)

Next, specify if you would like to Enable WINS Resolution. This implies that the system will first consult WINS servers on the network to resolve host names and then use whatever other option is selected (such as Hosts File only). Then you need to specify the DNS Search Order, which is the dotted decimal IP address of DNS servers on the network. Up to three DNS server addresses can be specified. In the Domain Suffix Search Order box, enter the domain suffixes to add to the domain suffix search list. Use the Add button to add the suffix to the list. There can be up to six domain suffixes. This list specifies DNS domain suffixes to be appended to host names during name resolution.

NT and DHCP

In the Windows NT environment, on the Advanced Server system, an administrator can configure DHCP parameters by working with the DHCP Administrator Tool. The DHCP Administrator Tool may be used for address allocation, leases, and other options.

WINS

The Windows Internet Name Service (WINS) is server software that runs on an NT Advanced Server–its primary function is to maintain a database that maps host names to IP addresses. WINS centralizes the management of host names and IP addresses. On NT systems, options available to resolve names include:

- WINS;
- DNS;
- LMHOSTS.

The *domain name system* (DNS) is commonly used on UNIX-TCP/IP networks for resolving host names. Windows NT also supports broadcast name resolution–this is a mechanism wherein systems broadcast their name on the network. The protocol used is the b-node protocol defined in RFCs 1001 and 1002.

On NT systems, the local text file that maps IP addresses to host names may be the HOSTS or LMHOSTS file. These files are located in the **\WINNT\-SYSTEM32\DRIVERS\ETC** directory. If DNS resolution fails, then the HOSTS file is consulted. The LMHOSTS file is read when WINS or broadcast name resolution fails. With WINS there is minimal need to work with the LMHOSTS file. On a given network, there may be one or more WINS servers. The WINS database is replicated among all WINS servers on the enterprise network.

WINS supports the concept of proxies. A proxy WINS server is a WINS-enabled system that listens to name query broadcasts on the network. The proxy system responds to those names that are not on the local subnet. The proxy system communicates with the WINS server to resolve names. Names resolved by the proxy system are cached for some time.

Like other client/server applications, WINS consists of two components: (1) WINS server, which is responsible for handling name queries and registrations; and (2) WINS clients, which send queries for name resolution.

As a part of NT configuration, you can enable WINS on the system. If WINS is not enabled, then the system can register its name by broadcasting name registration packets on the local subnetwork. To find a system, the non-WINS host broadcasts name query request packets on the local subnetwork. If the name is not resolved, then the local LMHOSTS file is consulted. If WINS is enabled, the system sends its query directly to the WINS server. In the event that no response is received, the system broadcasts its name registration and query requests on the subnetwork.

7.4.2 NT Installation and Configuration

Let us examine the steps involved in installing and configuring NT 3.5 server and client systems. The configuration steps detail how TCP/IP support is provided, so that NT systems can communicate with UNIX hosts on the network.

NT 3.5 Server Configuration

This is based on installing NT 3.5 software on a Toshiba Laptop system. The following is a summary of software and other system elements used for the installation.

- MS-DOS 6.22 diskettes;
- Windows 3.1 diskettes;
- Windows NT 3.5 Server CD;
- Diskette for MS-DOS 5-0 with CD-ROM driver (diskette includes driver for Trantor cable - this is a SCSI/parallel port cable);
- NT/Novell Network Driver diskette (drivers were obtained from the Xircom bulletin board - network driver is for Xircom's PCMCIA Ethernet Combo card);
- CD-ROM drive.

Step 1

Install MS-DOS 6.22.

Step 2

Install Windows 3.1.

Step 3

Boot the PC from the DOS 5.0 diskette with the CD-ROM driver. Load the NT 3.5 server CD in the CD-ROM.

Step 4

cd to the **D:** drive (where the CD-ROM drive is located) by entering

C:\> **cd D:\ I386**
D: \I386> **winnt/b**

This procedure will copy all NT 3.5 files from CD-ROM to the hard disk of the PC. This step takes about an hour.

Step 5

The system will prompt for setup, now run Express setup. Choose the installation path as **c:\windows**.

Step 6

The system will prompt for Domain Controller (Primary or Backup) or Server. Choose Server.

Step 7

When asked for the computer name, set as **ngtlap6**. Language selected is American/English. When prompted for Printer Installation, select Cancel.

Step 8

Now the system asks for the LAN (Network Interface) card. Choose "continue" to select the adapter manually.

Choose **continue**.
Select **Other**.

You need to enter the LAN driver diskette in the **a:** drive. Next, you will be prompted for the path of the driver. Enter, **a:\ndis_nt**. The system will then prompt for the card's I/O address:

Memory Address
IRQ Level
Transceiver Type (should be **10 bt**) then press **continue**.

Step 9

Select the Protocol Stacks to be loaded:

- NW Link IPX/SPX;
- TCP/IP;
- NETBEUI Transport.

Step 10

Now the system asks for TCP/IP Configuration Parameters.

IP Address	192.136.118.206
Subnet Mask	255.255.255.0
Default gateway	192.136.118.1
Primary wins Server	192.136.118.206
Secondary wins Server	
DHCP Server	192.136.118.206

Step 11

Now, you will be asked to define a password for the administrator account. Create another account **ngtusr** (enter the password as **ngtusr**).

Step 12

Select Central Zone (US or Canada) as the the Time Zone.

Step 13

The system then detects the video card. Test the display pattern by pressing the Test button. Next, press <Enter>. The system will then ask: Did you test? Say "YES", save the settings, and enter **OK** for the bit map.

Step 14

You are then asked for: creating a Emergency Repair Disk. Put in a new diskette—the system will make a repair diskette.

Step 15

Reboot the PC at this point. Login as **Administrator**, go to the Control Panel, and then to Services. Start the service called "Server".

Step 16

From the Accessories menu, you can now **telnet** to any node on the network.

NT 3.5 Workstation Configuration

This is based on installing NT 3.5 workstation software on a Toshiba Laptop system.

- MS-DOS 6.22 diskettes;
- Windows 3.1 diskettes;
- Windows NT 3.5 Workstation CD;
- Diskette for MS-DOS 5.0 with CD-ROM driver (diskette includes driver for Trantor cable—this is a SCSI/parallel port cable);
- NT/Novell Network Driver diskette (drivers were obtained from the Xircom bulletin board—network driver is for Xircom's PCMCIA Ethernet Combo card);
- CD-ROM drive.

Step 1

Install MS-DOS 6.22.

Step 2

Install Windows 3.1.

Step 3

Boot the PC from the DOS 5.0 diskette with the CD-ROM driver. Load the NT 3.5 workstation CD in the CD-ROM.

Step 4

cd to the **D:** drive (where the CD-ROM drive is located)

C:\> **cd D:\ I386**
D: \I386> **winnt/b**

This procedure will copy all NT 3.5 files from CD-ROM to the hard disk of the PC. This step takes about an hour.

Step 5

The system will prompt for setup, now run Express setup. Choose the installation path as **c:\windows**.

Step 6

The system will prompt for Domain Controller (Primary or Backup) or Server. Choose Server.

Step 7

When asked for the computer name, set as **ngtlap6**. Language selected is American/English. When prompted for Printer Installation, select Cancel.

Step 8

Now the system asks for the LAN (Network Interface) card. Choose "continue" to select the adapter manually.

Choose **continue**.
Select **Other**.

You need to enter the LAN driver diskette in the **a:** drive. Next, you will be prompted for the path of the driver. Enter, **a:\ndis_nt**. The system will then prompt for the card's I/O address.

Memory Address
IRQ Level
Transceiver Type (should be **10 bt**) then press **continue**.

Step 9

Select the Protocol Stacks to be loaded:

- NW Link IPX/SPX;
- TCP/IP;
- NETBEUI Transport.

Step 10

Now the system asks for TCP/IP Configuration Parameters.

IP Address	192.136.118.205
Subnet Mask	255.255.255.0
Default gateway	192.136.118.1
Primary wins Server	192.136.118.206
Secondary wins Server	
DHCP Server	192.136.118.206

(The client system is not DHCP enabled in our installation.)

Step 11

Now, you will be asked to define a password for the administrator account. Create another account **ngtusr** (enter the password **ngtusr**).

Step 12

Select Central Zone (US or Canada) as the the Time Zone.

Step 13

The system then detects the video card. Test the display pattern by pressing the Test button. Next, press <Enter>. The system will then ask: Did you test? Say "YES", save the settings, and enter **OK** for the bit map.

Step 14

You are then asked for: creating • Insert a new diskette in drive A–label it as Emergency Repair Disk when done.

Step 15

Reboot the PC at this point. Login as **Administrator**, go to the Control Panel, select Services. Start the service called "workstation". If you login as **ngtusr** and an **ngtusr** account exists on the Novell file server, then you can log on to that account.

7.5 SUMMARY

We examined how to internetwork UNIX systems with:

- Novell-based PCs;
- Macintosh systems;
- Windows NT PCs.

We looked closely at Novell's NetWare, the architecture, and its key protocols in order to better understand how to internetwork IPX/SPX nodes with UNIX systems. Next, we analyzed the AppleTalk architecture and some key protocols associated with it. You can install products such as Pathway Access from Wollongong or InterCon's TCP/Connect II to bring the TCP/IP protocol stack to your Macintosh system. You can use the NFS protocol to export disks from UNIX systems and mount them on Macintosh computers; products such as Pathway NFS Client and InterCon's NFS/Share support the NFS client specifications on a Macintosh system.

We then stepped through the various components of the X Window system. X is increasingly found in a variety of computing environments. X is supported on almost all flavors of UNIX, and you can install X server software on both PCs and Macintoshes. Vendors such as Hummingbird, Quarter Deck, and NCD have products that support the X specification on PCs. Intercon's Planet X product supports the X Window system on Macintoshes.

Finally, we examined how to internetwork NT systems with UNIX nodes on the network. Wherever possible, several examples of installing, configuring and using internetworking software was provided–the main motivation for configuration information was to give you a feel for what it takes for PCs, Novell, X, Macintosh, and NT systems to communicate with UNIX hosts on the network.

SELECT BIBLIOGRAPHY

Apple Computer, Inc., *A Guide to Apple Networking and Communications Products*, 1990.
Apple Computer, Inc., *Planning and Managing AppleTalk Networks*, Reading, MA: Addison-Wesley Publishing Company, 1991.
Comer, D. E., *Internetworking with TCP/IP*, Vol. 1, second edition., Englewood Cliffs, NJ: Prentice-Hall, 1991.
Ki Research, *Guide to Using DAP*, kiNET, 1992.
Levitt, J., "Two Protocols Worth Observing," *UNIX Today*, January 7, 1991, pp. 33–36.
Levitt, J., "X Terminals: The Ratings Are In," *UNIX Today*, April 1, 1991, pp. 44–48.
Malamud, C., *Analyzing Sun Networks*, New York: Van Nostrand Reinhold, 1992.
Mikes, S., and B. Keller, "What's New in X11 Release 5," *The XJ.*, January–February 1992.
Novell, *LAN WorkPlace for DOS User's Guide*, Novell Part # 100-000881-001, December 1990.
Novell, *NetWare NFS Supervisor's Guide*, Novell Part # 100-000955-001, February 1991.
Novell, *NetWare ODI Shell for DOS*, Novell Part # 100-000871-001, October 1990.
Nye, A., *X Protocol References Manual: Volume Zero*, second edition, Sebastopol, CA: O'Reilly & Associates, 1990, pp. 3–36.

Packard, K., "X Display Manager Control Protocol," *MIT X Consortium Standard, Version 1.0* Cambridge, MA: MIT X Consortium, 1989, pp. 1–2.

Rose, M. T., *The Simple Book*, Englewood Cliffs, NJ: Prentice-Hall, 1991.

Shah, H., "vt100/vt200 Emulation," Fermilab Tech. Notes TIBM001, TSUN011, TSUN017, TSG1004, TDG001, 1992.

Siyan, K., *NetWare: The Professional Reference*, Carmel, IN: New Riders Publishing, 1992.

Managing UNIX Networks   8

The objective of this chapter is to understand how to troubleshoot problems on a UNIX-TCP/IP network. On any TCP/IP network, you are likely to find some or all of the following communication devices:

- Repeaters;
- Bridges;
- Routers;
- Brouters;
- Gateways and protocol converters;
- Hubs;
- CSU/DSU.

To effectively troubleshoot problems, it is important to understand the role these devices play in moving information between systems on the network. Next, we analyze how routing protocols work and the role played by SNMP-based network management systems such as SunNet Manager in effectively identifying problems on the network. In many instances these potential problemsmay be identified before they even occur. Finally, if there are specific problems on the network, you can work with TCP/IP's troubleshooting protocol, ICMP, to determine the cause.

8.1 COMMUNICATION DEVICES

Let us review important communication devices such as bridges and routers. These devices are very typical on a UNIX-TCP/IP network.

8.1.1 Repeaters

Repeaters are low-level devices that operate at the physical layer of the OSI/RM. They amplify electrical signals. Repeaters are needed to provide current to drive long cables. Repeaters copy bits as they arrive.

8.1.2 Bridges

Bridges operate at the data link layer. A bridge can be used to connect two networks with different data link layers or two networks with the same data link layers. For example, a bridge may be used to connect an Ethernet network to a token-ring network or a bridge may be used to connect two Ethernet networks. A bridge accepts an entire frame and passes it to the data link layer, where the checksum is verified. Then the frame is sent to a different layer for forwarding on a different subnet. Because they are data link layer devices, they do not deal with headers at network layer and above. A bridge understands addressing used at the data link layer. Therefore, a bridge understands Ethernet, token ring, or FDDI addresses, depending on which networks it is interconnecting.

8.1.3 Routers

Routers are conceptually similar to bridges, except that they operate at the network layer. A router is needed to forward or route packets from one network to another. Networks connected by a router can differ much more than those connected by a bridge. Routers understand the format of addresses used at the network layer in the OSI/RM; therefore, as far as UNIX hosts on a TCP/IP network are concerned, routers understand Internet addresses. Routers on a TCP/IP network make routing decisions on the basis of Internet addresses. Routers also talk to each other using routing protocols. Examples of routing protocols used on a TCP/IP network are:

- Routing information protocol (RIP);
- Open shortest path first (OSPF);
- Exterior gateway protocol (EGP);
- Border gateway protocol (BGP).

Routers exchange routing tables, and thus they have a sense of the entire network.

8.1.4 Brouters

A *brouter* is a device that operates at both the data link and network layers of the OSI/RM. A brouter includes the functionality of both a bridge and a router. Brouters are typically deployed in multirotocol environments. For example, if your network supports Digital's DECnet and the Internet architectures, then you could use a brouter to bridge DECnet packets and route TCP/IP datagrams.

8.1.5 Gateways and Protocol Converters

A *gateway* can operate at any layer. The job of a gateway or a protocol converter is much more complex than that of a router. Typically, a gateway must convert from one protocol stack to another. For example, a gateway may connect an AppleTalk network to nodes on a DECnet network.

8.1.6 Hubs

Hubs are devices that operate at the physical layer. A hub may be viewed as a *network concentration point*–a single device that interconnects different systems. It is an example of systems connected in a star topology.

The new generation of hubs, referred to as *smart hubs* or *intelligent hubs*, support bridging and some basic routing functions besides support for protocols such as SNMP. Hubs are increasingly becoming critical in designing and configuring LANs, extended LANs, and virtual LANs. Intelligent hubs are evolving to integrate switching capabilities.

To handle the increased traffic on today's networks there are basically two options: (1) reduce the number of users per system per segment, and (2) increase the bandwidth available to the end user per system (migrate from Ethernet to FDDI or 100 Mbps Ethernet).

One way to increase the bandwidth available is by moving to a higher speed standard such as FDDI–this requires changing adapters, re-wiring the building and maybe changing system software–another option available is *switching*.

8.1.7 CSU/DSU

Data communication equipment (DCE) is a modem or a type of a communication device. *Data terminal equipment* (DTE) is typically a terminal but could be a computer, bridge, or a router. The DCE is between a DTE and the circuit that provides connectivity to the remote site. The DCE terminates a circuit and provides clocking for the circuit. If you work with analog lines, then the DCE is a modem; if you work with digital lines, then the DCE is a *channel service unit/data service unit (CSU/DSU)*.

The CSU is a high-speed device that terminates digital circuits–it provides additional functions such as:

- Filtering;
- Line equalization;
- Line conditioning;
- Signal regeneration;
- Circuit testing.

CSUs typically provide a T1 circuit interface. The DSU is a lower speed device that terminates digital circuits. Fixed-rate DSUs operate at 19.2 Kbps and less or at 56 Kbps; it is possible to get DSUs with a secondary channel for network management. The functionality of both the CSU and the DSU can be found in a single device referred to as a *digital data set* (DDS). CSU/DSU interfaces include 56 Kbps, T1, V.35, and the high-speed serial interface (HSSI) for DS-3 connectivity. CSUs and DSUs operate at the physical layer.

8.2 Routing

Let us now step through concepts associated with routing. First, we examine terminology such as:

- Interior routing protocols;
- Exterior routing protocols;
- Autonomous systems;
- Core.

Next, emphasis is placed on routing protocols used on networks with UNIX systems: protocols such as RIP, OSPF, and EGP. Further, information is provided on how to configure a UNIX system for *static* or *dynamic routing*.

First, what does the term routing mean? *Routing may be defined as the process of selecting a path over which to send packets.* The routing software may take into account factors such as:

- Network load;
- Datagram length;
- Type of service specified in the IP header.

If two UNIX systems need to communicate and they are on the same network, then their packets do not go through a router. The sending entity encapsulates the datagram in a Ethernet frame, binds the destination Internet address to an Ethernet address, and transmits the resulting frame directly to the destination. This process is also referred to as *direct routing*. The address resolution protocol is an example of a direct routing protocol.

The sender knows that the destination system is on the same physical network as itself if the network portion of both their adresses is the same. If two UNIX systems need to communicate and they are not on the same physical network, then they have to send the IP datagram to a router for delivery. Whenever a router is involved in the process of communication, it is referred to as *indirect routing*. Indirect routing involves two key elements: (1) the router needs to know where to sent the datagram, and (2) the host needs to know which router to use for given destination.

Routing does not lead to changes in the original datagram. The source and destination Internet addresses remain the same. The source address always specifies the address of the original source system, and the destination address is that of the target or final host. After a router determines the address of the system to which the datagram is to be sent next, it does not store this addresss in the IP datagram; no field is defined to hold the address of the *next hop* system. Instead, after executing the routing algorithm, IP passes the datagram and the next hop address to the network interface software responsible for the physical network over which the datagram must be sent.

The network interface software binds the next hop address to a physical address. Therefore, a new frame is formed using that physical address. The rest of the datagram is encapsulated in the new frame. The frame is then transmitted. After using the next hop address to find a physical address, the network interface software discards the next hop address.

When an IP datagram arrives at a UNIX host, for example, the network interface software delivers it to the IP software for further processing. If the datagram's destination address matches the host's Internet address, the IP software accepts the datagram and passes it to the appropriate higher level protocol software (e.g.,TCP or UDP) for further processing. If the address does not match, then the host is required to discard the datagram.

When an IP datagram arrives at a gateway, it is delivered to the IP software. It is possible that the datagram may have reached its final destination. If it has, then the IP software passes the datagram to the higher layers. If the addresses are different, the router processes the packet using the standard routing algorithm and information in the local routing table.

There are two types of routing protocols: interior routing protocols and exterior routing protocols. *Interior routing protocols* are those you use within (interior to) your organizational network. Examples of interior routing protocols are *routing information protocol* (RIP) and *open shortest path first* (OSPF). As the term implies, exterior routing protocols are those routing protocols that are used outside of your organization's network. The *exterior gateway protocol* (EGP) is an example of such a protocol.

Some terms associated with routing are autonomous system, exterior gateways, and interior gateways. An *autonomous system* is one that is managed by a single organizational entity, which includes all networks and gateways managed by that entity. If gateways belong to different autonomous system and they exchange routing information, they are referred to as *exterior gateways*.

8.2.1 RIP

The routing information protocol is commonly found on Berkeley-based systems. RIP uses UDP at the transport layer and the associated port number 520. All routing update messages originate at this port. RIP packets are limited to a maximum datagram size of 512 bytes. Most routers on the Internet are configured to handle 576 byte packets. Therfore, RIP packets are not fragmented.

RIP is based on the concept of timers. Every 30 seconds a node, such as a router, sends a complete RIP response to its neighbors. All RIP requests are sent as broadcast packets. If a router has sent an update for a particular route for 180 seconds, then that route is marked as invalid.

Note that RIP is based on the *vector distance algorithm*; distance is also defined as *hops*. RIP limits the total distance of a node to 15 hops. A node that is 16 hop counts away is considered unreachable. Internet standards describing ICMP formats and usage include:

- RFC 792: The ICMP Standard;
- RFC 896: Implementing Congestion Control;
- RFC 950: Subnet Mask Messages;
- RFC 1016: Use of Source Quench Messages.

On UNIX systems, the command **/etc/route** is used to manually manipulate system's routing tables. This command is typically executed at boot time by the **/etc/rc.local** script. In a relatively small network, *static routing* is an efficient solution and is not difficult to administer. An example of defining a *static route* on your system may be

/usr/etc/route add target-node router-node 1

where *target-node* is the node that you need to access and *router-node* is the router through which you need to go in order to access that node. The number **1** indicates how many hop counts away the target node is.

Support for *dynamic routing* on UNIX systems is provided with the routing daemon */etc/routed*. It is responsible for communicating with directly connected hosts and networks. The routing tables are maintained by *routed*, and when it receives a request packet it formulates a reply based on information in its internal tables. The response that it generates contains a list of known routes, each marked with a hop count. Figure 8.1 describes the format of a RIP protocol packet.

In the RIP header, the *command field* is used to specify the following operations, by command number:

1. Request for partial or full routing information.
2. Response containing network-distance pairs.
3. Turn on trace mode (obsolete).
4. Turn off trace mode (obsolete).
5. Reserved for Sun Microsystems internal use.

The *family of network* field has a value of 4 for IP addresses. There are 14 bytes reserved for the address field; because we are concerned only with

Command	Version	Must be zero
Family of network 1		Must be zero
IP address of network 1		
Must be zero		
Must be zero		
Distance to network 1		
Family of network 2		Must be zero
IP address of network 2		
Must be zero		
Must be zero		
Distance to network 2		
... ...		

Figure 8.1 RIP header format.

IP, the first 4 bytes are used to specify the IP address. The *distance to network* field indicates how many hop counts away that network is located.

8.2.2 OSPF

A disadvantage of a routing protocol such as RIP is that routes are selected on the basis of the closest path (fewest hops) between the source system and the destination system. No emphasis is placed on factors such as bandwidth available, multiple connections, and security. The *open shortest path first* (OSPF) is a new interior gateway routing protocol proposed by the *Internet Engineering Task Force* (IETF) that overcomes many of the shortcomings of a protocol such as RIP. Some features associated with OSPF are:

- Various types of service routing;
- Load balancing;
- Network areas;
- Authenticated exchanges;
- Host- and network-specific route support.

It is possible to install multiple routes to a given destintion; each route may by defined on the basis of a service such as high bit rate and security. If there are multiple routes to a given destination and all routes have the same cost associated with them, then OSPF distributes traffic evenly over all routes. OSPF provides the ability to partition a network into areas, which provides for growth and organization. Each area's internal topology is hidden from other areas.

All exchanges between routers using the OSPF protocol are authenticated. OSPF allows the use of various authentication schemes. This is important because only a trusted system should propagate routing information. OSPF allows the definition of host- or network-specific routes. There are different types of OSPF messages.

- Hello;
- Database description;
- Link status request;
- Link status update;
- Link status acknowledgment.

Each OSPF messages starts wih a fixed 24-byte header. RFC 1131 describes OSPF. Figure 8.2 describes the format of OSPF header.

As indicated previously, there are five different types of OSPF messages, and this is indicated in the *type field*. The *source gateway IP address* is the Internet address of the gateway sending the OSPF message, and the *authentication type field* specifies information on security: *authentication type* 0 indicates no authentication: 1 is a simple password.

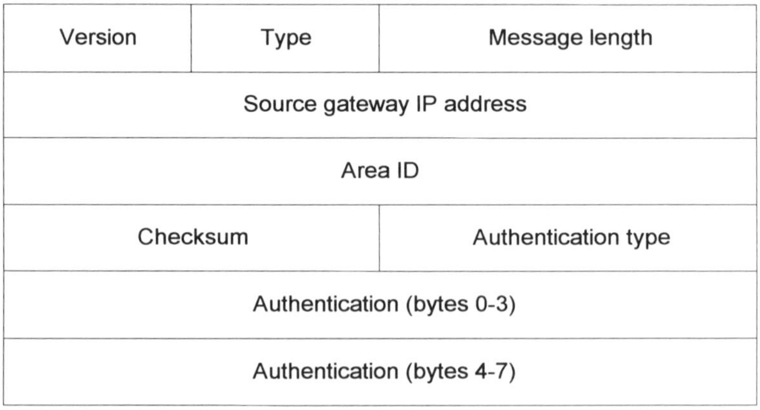

Version	Type	Message length
Source gateway IP address		
Area ID		
Checksum		Authentication type
Authentication (bytes 0-3)		
Authentication (bytes 4-7)		

Figure 8.2 OSPF header format.

8.2.3 EGP

The exterior gateway protocol (EGP) is used to communicate reachability information between exterior gateway systems. It is especially important because this routing protocol is used to provide information to the *Internet core* system. There are different types of EGP messages, which can be summarized in four groups.

- Neighbor acquisition;
- Hello exchange;
- Routing update;
- Error message.

The *neighbor acquisition* message is used by gateway to request that another system exchange routing information. This process is referred to as *acquiring an EGP peer*. *Hello exchanges* are used to test if the neighbor is responding to requests, and finally the *routing update* messages are used to exchange reachability information. Figure 8.3 describes the format of the EGP header.

The *autonomous system number* indicates the autonomous system number of the router sending the message.

8.2.4 What About OSI's IS-IS?

The *intermediate system-to-intermediate system* (IS-IS) is the OSI routing protocol to exchange routing tables among nodes on an OSI network. OSPF is to a large extent based on IS-IS. Most routing vendors have announced support for the IS-IS routing protocol. Digital's *integrated* IS-IS protocol supports both OSI and TCP/IP routing; thus routers in TCP/IP and OSI networks can share routing

Version	Type	Code	Status
Checksum		Autonomous system #	
Sequence number			

Figure 8.3 EGP header format.

data. Integrated IS-IS is considered by many as the way to introduce OSI into TCP/IP networks. Vendors such as CISCO Systems, Proteon, Retix, Vitalink, Well Fleet, and 3 Com plan to support Integrated IS-IS.

8.3 NETWORK AND SYSTEM MANAGEMENT

We now examine the elements of network management. As we move to integrate UNIX systems in our computing environment we are faced with the challenge of managing devices all over our network. We first look at the model of network management and then study elements of the system that also need to be managed effectively.

8.3.1 Model for Network Management

As we move toward distributed computing and client/server architectures there is an even greater need for central access to information about resources on the network. Although the immediate gain is that it allows us to troubleshoot problems on the network centrally, it also provides the ability to configure and manage these devices from a single point of reference.

A network management strategy is key to bring about consistency in the configuration and management of heterogeneous systems and to provide for growth and organization of the network.

This requires the systems on the network to talk a common language, enabling them to exchange information about packets, protocols, and network data. A network management protocol facilitates nodes on the network to share information that may be necessary for troubleshooting network-related problems. The model for network and system management consists of three elements:

- Managed nodes;
- Network management stations;
- Network management protocol.

An effective network management strategy includes:

- Fault management;
- Security management;
- Configuration management;
- Accounting management;
- Performance management.

Managed Nodes

All managed nodes are on the network: these include host systems such as workstations or PCs and media devices such as bridges, hubs, routers, or multiplexors. One can see that managed nodes are very diverse, but the thing that binds them together is that they are nodes on the network. Managed nodes must support protocols that enable key systems on the network to communicate with them.

Network Management Stations (NMS)

A *network management station* (NMS) is a system that supports a network management protocol and the applications necessary for it to process and access information from entities (managed nodes) on the network.

Network Management Protocol

Each managed node stores information about its interactions with the network, for example, the number of packets it generated or the number of collisions. A network management protocol provides the framework for reading and writing information, information that may be resident on managed nodes thereby providing the ability for the network management station to communicate with the managed nodes. A network management protocol also provides for a traversal operation and a trap operation. A traversal operation allows a management station to determine which variables a managed node supports. With traversal operations, a management station can gain access to or modify information maintained by managed nodes. A trap operation allows a managed node to report an extraordinary event to a management station. If a problem or fault is detected, then a trap message is sent to the NMS entity.

8.3.2 ASN.1

Abstract syntax notation 1 (ASN.1) is a specification language adopted for the OSI/RM, giving standards developers a common method for defining protocols and related standards. The objective is to define data without regard to operating systems or machine architectures. ASN.1 is a language that defines the formats of packets exchanged by the network management protocol. It is also the basis for defining objects that are to be managed.

ASN.1 defines a hardware architecture-independent language for data structures. The *basic encoding rules* (BER) provide the mechanism for transmitting those data structures, unambiguously, over the network. BER is a transfer syntax notation.

The *management information base* (MIB) uses the ASN.1 tree architecture to organize all information. Each piece of information in the tree is referred to as a *labeled node*. A labeled node specifies an *object identifier* and a *short text description*. The *object identifier*, also referred to as OID, is a series of integers separated by periods that names the node and specifies the exact traversal of the ASN.1 tree. An example of an object identifier is: **1.3.6.1.2.1.1.2.0**. The short text description describes the labeled node.

8.3.3 SNMP

The *simple network management protocol* (SNMP) originated in the Internet community as a means of managing TCP/IP and Ethernet networks. The protocol was introduced as a standard by the Internet Architecture Board in 1988. SNMP is based on the *simple gateway management protocol* (SGMP), which was developed to manage routers on the global Internet. Since 1989 SNMP's appeal has broadened considerably beyond the Internet, and today organizations are increasingly basing their network management strategy on the SNMP specifications. SNMP can also be used to manage non-SNMP devices with *proxy agents*. The SNMP proxy agent acts as a protocol converter, translating SNMP manager commands into the network management protocol supported by the device. The advantages associated with SNMP are:

- Its simplicity makes it easier for vendors to implement the standard.
- Its memory and CPU cycle requirements are lower than those of the *common management information protocol* (CMIP), OSI's network management protocol.
- The protocol has been tested and used on the Internet for some time.
- Products are available from hundreds of vendors.

SNMP, like CMIP, is based on a query-response mechanism; authority to query is not delegated on the network but rather centralized at the NMS. It is likely that, in the near future, network management protocols will provide support for delegating certain functions to other nodes on the network. The SNMP architecture consists of the following components:

- Manager (NMS);
- Agent (managed nodes);
- MIB (database of information);
- SMI (management of database);
- Protocols (commands).

Today, SNMP is supported on many different systems, including bridges, PCs, workstations, routers, brouters, terminal servers, gateways and protocol converters, hub repeaters, and concentrators such as multiport Ethernet, token-ring, and FDDI devices.

Manager

The term *manager* refers to the NMS entity: it may request a terminal server to report its Internet address and subnet mask, for example. A manager reacts to trap messages.

Agents

Agents are entities based on managed nodes. Agents respond to requests from the NMS and send specific information about a device.

MIB-I

The *management information base* (MIB) defines those objects to be implemented by managed nodes on the Internet. The first Internet standard MIB was designed to include the minimal number of objects that would be useful for managing nodes. This standard is also referred to as MIB-I and includes the objects in Table 8.1, which are divided into eight groups [16]. MIB-I thus defines a total of 114 objects. The successor to MIB-I was MIB-II; the main motivation was to create new objects for network management.

MIB-II

MIB-II is compatible with MIB-I and SMI and includes support for a total of 171 objects [16]. The new groups include transmission and SNMP. The

Table 8.1
MIB-I Objects

Group	Number of Objects	Description
System	3	Managed node itself
Interfaces	22	Interfaces on a device
At	3	IP address translation
IP	33	IP address related
ICMP	26	ICMP protocol related
TCP	17	TCP related
UDP	4	UDP protocol related
EGP	6	EGP protocol related

transmission objects support interfaces such as token ring and loopback. The SNMP *objects* enable the NMS to manipulate the SNMP portion of the entities that it manages. The groups defined in MIB-II are:

- System;
- Interfaces;
- Address translation;
- IP;
- ICMP;
- TCP;
- UDP;
- EGP;
- CMOT;
- Transmission;
- SNMP.

The *system group*, OID 1.3.6.1.2.1.1, includes information about the system on which the entity resides. Objects in this group are useful for fault management and configuration management. All MIB-II objects discussed below are based on the information in RFC 1213. Table 8.2 summarizes objects defined in the system group in MIB-II.

The *interfaces group*, OID 1.3.6.1.2.1.2, contains information about each interface on a network device. This group provides useful information for:

- Fault management;
- Configuration management;
- Performance management;
- Accounting management.

Table 8.3 summarizes objects defined in the Interfaces group in MIB-II.

The *address translation group*, OID 1.3.6.1.2.1.3, is no longer a separate group. The address translation group objects have been incorporated into other protocol groups. The *IP group*, OID 1.3.6.1.2.1.4, provides information about IP in the following areas:

- Errors and types of IP packets seen;
- IP addresses in the entity;
- IP routing table entries;
- Mapping IP addresses to other addresses.

The IP group includes objects that support fault, configuration, performance, and accounting management. Table 8.4 gives a summary of these objects.

Table 8.2
MIB-II System Group

Object	Access Control	Management Application	Description
sysDescr (1) Display String (SIZE (0..255))	Read only	Configuration	A textual description of the entity. This value should include the full name and version identification of the system's hardware type, software operating-system, and networking software. It is mandatory that this only contain printable ASCII characters.
sysObjectID (2) OBJECT IDENTIFIER	Read only	Fault	The vendor's authoritative identification of the network management subsystem contained in the entity. This value is allocated within the SMI enterprises subtree (1.3.6.1.4.1) and provides an easy and unambiguous means for determining "what kind of box" is being managed. For example, if vendor "Flintstones, Inc." was assigned the subtree 1.3.6.1.4.1.4242, it could assign the identifier 1.3.6.1.4.1.4242.1.1 to its "Fred Router".
sysUpTime (3) TimeTicks	Read only	Fault	The time (in hundredths of a second) since the network management portion of the system was last re-initialized.
sysContact (4) Display String (SIZE (0..255))	Read write	Configuration	The textual identification of the contact person for this managed node, together with information on how to contact this person.
sysName (5) Display String (SIZE (0..255))	Read write	Configuration	An administratively assigned name for this managed node. By convention, this is the node's fully qualified domain name.

Table 8.2 (continued)

Object	Access Control	Management Application	Description
sysLocation (6) Display String (SIZE (0..255))	Read write	Configuration	The physical location of this node (e.g., "telephone closet, 3rd floor").
sysServices (7) INTEGER (0..127)	Read only	Fault	A value that indicates the set of services primarily offered by this entity.

The *ICMP group*, OID 1.3.6.1.2.1.5, contains objects that provide more information about ICMP on the entity. Note that the entity is responsible for processing every ICMP packet that is received–this obviously impacts the overall performance of the entity. See Table 8.5 for a summary of MIB-II ICMP objects.

The *TCP group*, OID 1.3.6.1.2.1.6, provides information about TCP on the entity. A table of values is provided for each TCP connection–the table changes with the establishment and termination of each session. See Table 8.6 for an analysis of MIB-II TCP objects.

The *UDP group*, OID 1.3.6.1.2.1.7, provides information about UDP on the entity. UDP group objects specify information on current UDP applications accepting datagrams on the entity. This group does not provide information about current connections since UDP is not a connection-oriented protocol. Table 8.7 describes UDP objects.

The EGP protocol provides information on reachability to other IP networks. Objects in the *EGP group*, OID 1.3.6.1.2.1.8, provides information about EGP on the entity. The objects describe fault, configuration, performance, and accounting management information. Table 8.8 summarizes objects in the EGP group.

The *CMOT group*, OID 1.3.6.1.2.1.9, only exists for historical reasons. There are no objects defined in this group. The *Transmission group*, OID 1.3.6.1.2.1.10, provides information about specific media used at the physical and data link layers of the OSI/RM. At present, Token Ring and FDDI objects are in the process of being defined. The *SNMP group*, OID 1.3.6.1.2.1.11, provides information about SNMP packets entering and leaving the entity. The SNMP group objects describe all five areas of network management: fault, performance, accounting, security, and configuration. Table 8.9 summarizes the objects in the SNMP group.

Table 8.3
MIB-II Interfaces Group

Object	Access Control	Management Application	Description
ifEntry (1) SEQUENCE	Not applicable	Not applicable	An interface entry containing objects at the subnetwork layer and below for a particular interface.
ifTable (2) SEQUENCE OF IfEntry	Not applicable	Not applicable	A list of interface entries. The number of entries is given by the value of ifNumber.
ifNumber (2.1) INTEGER	Read only	Configuration	The number of network interfaces (regardless of their current state) present on this system.
ifIndex (2.1.1) INTEGER	Read only	Not applicable	A unique value for each interface. Its value ranges between 1 and the value of ifNumber. The value for each interface must remain constant at least from one re-initialization of the entity's network management system to the next re-initialization.
ifDescr (2.1.2) Display String (SIZE 0..255))	Read only	Configuration	A textual string containing information about the interface. This string should include the name of the manufacturer, the product name, and the version of the hardware interface.
ifType (2.1.3) INTEGER	Read only	Configuration	The type of interface, distinguished according to the physical/link protocol(s) immediately "below" the network layer in the protocol stack.
ifMtu (2.1.4) INTEGER	Read only	Configuration	The size of the largest datagram that can be sent/received on the interface, specified in octets. For interfaces that are used for transmitting network datagrams, this is the size of the largest network datagram that can be sent on the interface.

Table 8.3 (continued)

Object	Access Control	Management Application	Description
ifSpeed (2.1.5) Gauge	Read only	Configuration	An estimate of the interface's current bandwidth in bits per second. For interfaces that do not vary in bandwidth or for those where no accurate estimation can be made, this object should contain the nominal bandwidth.
ifPhysAddress (2.1.6)	Read only	Fault Configuration	The interface's address at the protocol layer immediately "below" the network layer in the protocol stack. For interfaces that do not have such an address (e.g., a serial line), this object should contain an octet string of zero length.
ifAdminStatus (2.1.7) INTEGER	Read write	Fault Configuration	The desired state of the interface.
ifOperStatus (2.1.8) INTEGER	Read only	Fault	The current operational state of the interface.
ifLastChange (2.1.9) TimeTicks	Read only	Fault	The value of sysUpTime at the time the interface entered its current operational state. If the current state was entered prior to the last re-initialization of the local network management subsystem, then this object contains a zero value.
ifInOctets (2.1.10) Counter	Read only	Performance Accounting	The total number of octets received on the interface, including framing characters.
ifInUcastPkts (2.1.11) Counter	Read only	Performance Accounting	The number of subnetwork-unicast packets delivered to a higher layer protocol.
ifInNUcastPkts (2.1.12) Counter	Read only	Performance Accounting	The number of nonunicast (i.e., subnetwork-broadcast or subnetwork-multicast) packets delivered to a higher layer protocol.

Table 8.3 (continued)

Object	Access Control	Management Application	Description
ifInDiscards (2.1.13) Counter	Read only	Performance	The number of inbound packets that were chosen to be discarded to prevent their being deliverable to a higher layer protocol. One possible reason for discarding such a packet could be to free up buffer space.
ifInErrors (2.1.14) Counter	Read only	Performance	The number of inbound packets that contained errors preventing them from being deliverable to a higher layer protocol.
ifInUnknownProtos (2.1.15) Counter	Read only	Performance	The number of packets received via the interface that were discarded because of an unknown or unsupported protocol.
ifOutOctets (2.1.16) Counter	Read only	Performance Accounting	The total number of octets transmitted out of the interface, including framing characters.
ifOutUcastPkts (2.1.17) Counter	Read only	Performance Accounting	The total number of packets that higher level protocols requested be transmitted to a subnetwork-unicast address, including those that were discarded or not sent.
ifOutNUcastPkts (2.1.18) Counter	Read only	Performance Accounting	The total number of packets that higher level protocols requested be transmitted to a nonunicast (i.e., a subnetwork-broadcast or subnetwork-multicast) address, including those that were discarded or not sent.
ifOutDiscards (2.1.19) Counter	Read only	Performance	The number of outbound packets that were chosen to be discarded even though no errors had been detected to prevent their being transmitted. One possible reason for discarding such a packet could be to free up buffer space.

Table 8.3 (continued)

Object	Access Control	Management Application	Description
ifOutErrors (2.1.20) Counter	Read only	Performance	The number of outbound packets that could not be transmitted because of errors.
ifOutQLen (2.1.21) Gauge	Read only	Performance	The length of the output packet queue (in packets).
ifSpecific (2.1.22) OBJECT IDENTIFIER	Read only	Configuration	A reference to MIB definitions specific to the particular media being used to realize the interface. For example, if the interface is realized by an ethernet, then the value of this object refers to a document defining objects specific to Ethernet. If this information is not present, its value should be set to the OBJECT IDENTIFIER { 0 0 }, which is a syntactically valid object identifier, and any conformant implementation of ASN.1 and BER must be able to generate and recognize this value.

SMI

The *Structure of Management Information* (SMI) defines how objects contained in the MIB are to be managed. It provides a method for identifying objects and includes data types that describe what these objects are. So, although SMI does not actually define any objects, it specifies how objects should be defined. The objects are defined in the MIBs.

Commands: How SNMP Works

All SNMP tasks are accomplished by five types of commands or verbs, referred to as *protocol data units* (PDUs).

- GetRequest;
- GetNextRequest;

Table 8.4
MIB-II IP Objects

Object	Access Control	Management Application	Description
ipForwarding (1) INTEGER	Read write	Configuration	The indication of whether this entity is acting as an IP gateway in respect to the forwarding of datagrams received by, but not addressed to, this entity. IP gateways forward datagrams. IP hosts do not (except those source-routed via the host).
ipDefaultTTL (2) INTEGER	Read write	Performance	The default value inserted into the time-to-live (TTL) field of the IP header of datagrams originated at this entity, whenever a TTL value is not supplied by the transport layer protocol.
ipInReceives (3) Counter	Read only	Performance	The total number of input datagrams received from interfaces, including those received in error.
ipInHdrErrors (4) Counter	Read only	Performance	The number of input datagrams discarded due to errors in their IP headers, including bad checksums, version number mismatch, other format errors, time-to-live exceeded, and errors discovered in processing their IP options.
ipInAddrErrors (5) Counter	Read only	Performance	The number of input datagrams discarded because the IP address in their IP header's destination field was not a valid address to be received at this entity. This count includes invalid addresses (e.g., 0.0.0.0) and addresses of unsupported classes (e.g., Class E). For entities that are not IP gateways and therefore do not forward datagrams, this counter includes datagrams discarded because the destination address was not a local address.

360   UNIX Internetworking

Table 8.4 (continued)

Object	Access Control	Management Application	Description
ipForwDatagrams (6) *Counter*	Read only	Performance	The number of input datagrams for which this entity was not their final IP destination, as a result of which an attempt was made to find a route to forward them to that final destination. In entities that do not act as IP gateways, this counter will include only those packets that were source-routed via this entity, and the source-route option processing was successful.
ipInUnknownProtos (7) *Counter*	Read only	Performance	The number of locally addressed datagrams received successfully but discarded because of an unknown or unsupported protocol.
ipInDiscards (8) *Counter*	Read only	Performance	The number of input IP datagrams for which no problems were encountered to prevent their continued processing but which were discarded (e.g., for lack of buffer space). Note that this counter does not include any datagrams discarded while awaiting reassembly.
ipInDelivers (9) *Counter*	Read only	Performance Accounting	The total number of input datagrams successfully delivered to IP user-protocols (including ICMP).
ipOutRequests (10) *Counter*	Read only	Performance Accounting	The total number of IP datagrams that local IP user-protocols (including ICMP) supplied to IP in requests for transmission. Note that this counter does not include any datagrams counted in ipForwDatagrams.

Table 8.4 (continued)

Object	Access Control	Management Application	Description
ipOutDiscards (11) Counter	Read only	Performance	The number of output IP datagrams for which no problem was encountered to prevent their transmission to their destination but which were discarded (e.g., for lack of buffer space). Note that this counter would include datagrams counted in ipForwDatagrms if any such packets met this (discretionary) discard criterion.
ipOutNoRoutes (12) Counter	Read only	Performance	The number of IP datagrams discarded because no route could be found to transmit them to their destination. Note that this counter includes any packets counted in ipForwDatagrams that meet this "no-route" criterion. Note that this includes any datagrams that a host cannot route because all of its default gateways are down.
ipReasmTimeout (13) INTEGER	Read only	Performance	The maximum number of seconds that received fragments are held while they are awaiting reassembly at this entity.
ipReasmReqds (14) Counter	Read only	Performance	The number of IP fragments received that needed to be reassembled at this entity.
ipReasmOks (15) Counter	Read only	Performance	The number of IP datagrams successfully reassembled.
ipReasmFails (16) Counter	Read only	Performance	The number of failures detected by the IP reassembly algorithm (for whatever reason such as timed out and errors). Note that this is not necessarily a count of discarded IP fragments since some algorithms (notably the algorithm in RFC 815) can lose track of the number of fragments by combining them as they are received.

Table 8.4 (continued)

Object	Access Control	Management Application	Description
ipFragOKs (17) Counter	Read only	Performance	The number of IP datagrams that have been successfully fragmented at this entity.
ipFragFails (18) Counter	Read only	Performance	The number of IP datagrams that have been discarded because they needed to be fragmented at this entity but could not be, e.g., because their Don't Fragment flag was set.
ipFragCreates (19) Counter	Read only	Performance	The number of IP datagram fragments that have been generated as a result of fragmentation at this entity.
ipAddrTable (20) SEQUENCE OF	Not applicable	Configuration	The table of addressing information relevant to this entity's IP address.
ipRouteTable (21) SEQUENCE OF	Not applicable	Fault Configuration	This entity's IP Routing table.
ipNetTo MediaTable (22) SEQUENCE OF	Not applicable	Fault	The IP Address Translation table used for mapping from IP addresses to physical addresses.
ipRoutingDiscards (23) Counter	Read only	Performance	The number of routing entries that were chosen to be discarded even though they are valid. One possible reason for discarding such an entry could be to free up buffer space for other routing entries.

- SetRequest;
- GetResponse;
- Traps.

An agent will inspect the value of MIB variables after receiving either a *GetRequest* or *GetNextRequest* command from a manager. The *SetRequest* command may be sent by a manager to alter certain MIB variables. An SNMP agent responds to GETRequest and GetNextRequest PDUs with a GetResponse PDU. The GetResponse PDU includes the original request followed by the

Table 8.5
MIB-II ICMP Objects

Object	Access Control	Management Application	Description
icmpInMsgs (1) Counter	Read only	Performance	The total number of ICMP messages that the entity received. Note that this counter includes all those counted by icmpInErrors.
icmpInErrors (2) Counter	Read only	Performance	The number of ICMP messages that the entity received but determined as having ICMP-specific errors (e.g., bad ICMP checksums and bad length).
icmpInDestUnreachs (3) Counter	Read only	Performance	The number of ICMP Destination Unreachable messages received.
icmpInTimeExcds (4) Counter	Read only	Performance	The number of ICMP Time Exceeded messages received.
icmpInParmProbs (5) Counter	Read only	Performance	The number of ICMP Parameter Problem messages received.
icmpInSrcQuenchs (6) Counter	Read only	Performance	The number of ICMP Source Quench messages received.
icmpInRedirects (7) Counter	Read only	Performance	The number of ICMP Redirect messages received.
icmpInEchos (8) Counter	Read only	Performance	The number of ICMP Echo (request) messages received.
icmpInEchoReps (9) Counter	Read only	Performance	The number of ICMP Echo Reply messages received.
icmpInTimestamps (10) Counter	Read only	Performance	The number of ICMP Timestamp (request) messages received.
icmpInTimestampReps (11) Counter	Read only	Performance	The number of ICMP Timestamp Reply messages received.
icmpInAddrMasks (12) Counter	Read only	Performance	The number of ICMP Address Mask Request messages received.
icmpInAddrMaskReps (13) Counter	Read only	Performance	The number of ICMP Address Mask Reply messages received.

Table 8.5 (continued)

Object	Access Control	Management Application	Description
icmpOutMsgs (14) Counter	Read only	Performance	The total number of ICMP messages that this entity attempted to send. Not that this counter includes all those counted by icmpOutErrors.
icmpOutErrors (15) Counter	Read only	Performance	The number of ICMP messages that this entity did not send due to problems discovered within ICMP such as a lack of buffers. This value should not include errors discovered outside the ICMP layer such as the inability of IP to route the resultant datagram. In some implementations there may be no types of error that contribute to this counter's value.
icmpOutDestUnreachs (16) Counter	Read only	Performance	The number of ICMP Destination Unreachable messages sent.
icmpOutTimeExcds (17) Counter	Read only	Performance	The number of ICMP Time Exceeded messages sent.
icmpOutParmProbs (18) Counter	Read only	Performance	The number of ICMP Parameter Problem messages sent.
icmpOutSrcQuenchs (19) Counter	Read only	Performance	The number of ICMP Source Quench messages sent.
icmpOutRedirects (20) Counter	Read only	Performance	The number of ICMP Redirect messages sent. For a host, this object will always be zero, since hosts do not send redirects.
icmpOutEchos (21) Counter	Read only	Performance	The number of ICMP Echo (request) messages sent.
icmpOutEchoReps (22) Counter	Read only	Performance	The number of ICMP Echo Reply messages sent.
icmpOutTimestamps (23) Counter	Read only	Performance	The number of ICMP Timestamp (request) messages sent.
icmpOutTimestampReps (24) Counter	Read only	Performance	The number of ICMP Timestamp Reply messages sent.

Table 8.5 (continued)

Object	Access Control	Management Application	Description
icmpOutAddrMasks (25) *Counter*	Read only	Performance	The number of ICMP Address Mask Request messages sent.
icmpOutAddrMaskReps (26) *Counter*	Read only	Performance	The number of ICMP Address Mask Reply messages sent.

requested information. And finally, a trap is a special, unsolicited command type that agents send to a manager after sensing a prespecified condition.

SNMP currently uses Ethernet and UDP to transport data. Each SNMP message is represented completely within a single UDP datagram. The SNMP message consists of:

- Version identifier;
- SNMP community name;
- PDU.

The SNMP version identifier is the RDC version. An SNMP community name consists of an agent and its associated applications. A SNMP PDU is one of the five command types. The SNMP protocol entity receives most messages at UDP port 161. Traps are received on UDP port 162. RFC 1157 describes the SNMP standard. RFC 1158 describes MIB-II. RFC 1155 describes SMI. Later RFCs describe enhancements to SNMP specifications.

8.3.4 SNMPv2

SNMPv2 is a new version of the SNMP protocol, currently defined as a standard by the Internet community. SNMPv2 supports SNMP specifications and also introduces security enhancements and greater control over the network. Proxy agents would be used in SNMPv2 to translate between SNMP and SNMPv2 commands. SNMPv2 specifically supports:

- Bulk file transfer;
- Several security mechanisms;
- An event-driven polling mechanism;

Table 8.6
MIB-II TCP Objects

Object	Access Control	Management Application	Description
tcpRtoAlgorithm (1) INTEGER	Read only	Configuration	The algorithm used to determine the timeout value used for retransmitting unacknowledged octets.
tcpRtoMin (2) INTEGER	Read only	Configuration	The minimum value permitted by a TCP implementation for the retransmission timeout, measured in milliseconds.
tcpRtoMax (3) INTEGER	Read only	Configuration	The maximum value permitted by a TCP implementation for the retransmission timeout, measured in milliseconds.
tcpMaxConn (4) INTEGER	Read only	Configuration	The limit on the total number of TCP connections the entity can support. In entities where the maximum number of connections is dynamic, this object should contain the value -1.
tcpActiveOpens (5) Counter	Read only	Accounting	The number of times TCP connections have made a direct transition to the SYN-SENT state from the CLOSED state.
tcpPassiveOpens (6) Counter	Read only	Accounting	The number of times TCP connections have made a direct transition to the SYN-RCVD state from the LISTEN state.
tcpAttemptFails (7) Counter	Read only	Performance	The number of times TCP connections have made a direct transition to the CLOSED state, from either the SYN-SENT state or the SYN-RCVD state, plus the number of times TCP connections have made a direct transition to the LISTEN state from the SYN-RCVD state.

Table 8.6 (continued)

Object	Access Control	Management Application	Description
tcpEstabResets (8) *Counter*	Read only	Performance	The number of times TCP connections have made a direct transition to the CLOSED state from either the ESTABLISHED state or the CLOSE-WAIT state.
tcpCurrEstab (9) *Gauge*	Read only	Configuration	The number of TCP connections for which the current state is either ESTABLISHED or CLOSE-WAIT.
tcpInSegs (10) *Counter*	Read only	Performance Accounting	The total number of segments received, including those received in error. This count includes segments received on currently established connections.
tcpOutSegs (11) *Counter*	Read only	Performance Accounting	The total number of segments sent, including those on current connections but excluding those containing only retransmitted octets.
tcpRetransSegs (12) *Counter*	Read only	Performance	The total number of segments retransmitted–that is, the number of TCP segments transmitted containing one or more previously transmitted octets.
tcpConn Table (13) SEQUENCE OF	Read only	Accounting	A table containing TCP connection-specific information.
tcpConnEntry	Read only	Accounting	Information about a particular current TCP connection. An object of this type is transient in that it ceases to exist when (or soon after) the connection makes the transition to the CLOSED state.
tcpConnState	Read only	Accounting	The state of this TCP connection.

Table 8.6 (continued)

Object	Access Control	Management Application	Description
tcpconnLocalAddress IP Address	Read only	Accounting	The local IP address for this TCP connection. In the case of a connection in the listen state that is willing to accept connections for any IP interface associated with the mode, the value 0.0.0.0 is used.
tcpConnLocalPort	Read only	Accounting	The local port number for this TCP connection.
tcpConnRemAddress IP Address	Read only	Accounting	The remote IP address for this TCP connection.
tcpConnRemPort	Read only	Accounting	The remote port number for this TCP connection.
tcpInErrs (14) Counter	Read only	Performance	The total number of segments received in error (e.g., bad TCP checksums).
tcpOutRsts (15) Counter	Read only	Performance	The number of TCP segments sent containing the RST flag.

- Management of not just networks but also applications on end-user systems;
- SNMPv2 will support Novell, AppleTalk, and OSI network layer protocols. SNMP messages have always been limited to 460 bytes. SNMPv2 includes support for a new message format, referred to as *GetBulk*, which enables a system to retrieve larger sized messages. Another improvement over SNMP has been in the area of error messages, which are more imformative.

8.3.5 System Management

Today, system administrators not only install and maintain systems but are often called upon to understand and improve the performance of systems, such as UNIX workstations. You can use a number of UNIX commands and utilities to understand how system resources are being utilized. Just like a network may experience problems such as high load or a high error rate, the problems that a system may experience include:

Table 8.7
MIB-II UDP Objects

Object	Access Control	Management Application	Description
udpInDatagrams (1) Counter	Read only	Performance Accounting	The total number of UDP datagrams delivered to UDP users.
udpNoPorts (2) Counter	Read only	Performance	The total number of received UDP datagrams for which there was no application at the destination port.
udpInErrors (3) Counter	Read only	Performance	The number of received UDP datagrams that could not be delivered for reasons other than the lack of an application at the destination port.
udpOutDatagrams (4) Counter	Read only	Performance Accounting	The total number of UDP datagrams sent from this entity.
udpTable (5) SEQUENCE OF UdpEntry	Not applicable	Accounting	A table containing UDP listener information.
udpEntry (5.1) SEQUENCE	Not applicable	Not applicable	Information about a particular current UDP listener.
udpLocalAddress (5.1.1) IPAddress	Read only	Not applicable	The local IP address for this UDP listener. In the case of a UDP listener which is willing to accept datagrams for any IP interface associated with the node, the value 0.0.0.0 is used.
udpLocalPort (5.1.2) INTEGER	Read only	Accounting	The local port number for this UDP listener.

- CPU bottleneck;
- Memory bottleneck;
- I/O bottleneck.

For example, some symptoms of your system being CPU bound include:

- Processes waiting for CPU;
- CPU is not idle;
- Significant time spent in user or system code.

Table 8.8
MIB-II EGP Group Objects

Object	Access Control	Management Application	Description
egpInMsgs (1) Counter	Read only	Performance	The number of EGP messages received without error.
egpInErrors (2) Counter	Read only	Performance	The number of EGP messages received that proved to be in error.
egpOutMsgs (3) Counter	Read only	Performance	The total number of locally generated EGP messages.
egpOutErrors (4) Counter	Read only	Performance	The number of locally generated EGP messages not sent due to resource limitations within an EGP entity.
egpNeighTable (5) SEQUENCE OF	Not applicable	Not applicable	The EGP neighbor table.
egpNeighEntry SEQUENCE	Not applicable	Not applicable	Information about this entity's relationship with a particular EGP neighbor.
egpAs (6) INTEGER	Read only	Configuration	The autonomous system number of this EGP entity.
egpNeighState (6.1) INTEGER	Read only	Configuration	The EGP state of the local system with respect to this entry's EGP neighbor. Each EGP state is represented by a value that is one greater than the numerical value associated with said state in RFC 904.
egpNeighAddr (6.2) IPAddress	Read only	Configuration	The IP address of this entry's EGP neighbor.
egpNeighAs (6.3) INTEGER	Read only	Configuration	The autonomous system of this EGP peer. Zero should be specified if the autonomous system number of the neighbor is not yet known.
egpNeighInMsgs (6.4) Counter	Read only	Performance	The number of EGP messages received without error from this EGP peer.
egpNeighInErrs (6.5) Counter	Read only	Performance	The number of EGP messages received from this EGP peer that proved to be in error (e.g., bad EGP checksum).
egpNeighOutMsgs (6.6) Counter	Read only	Performance	The number of locally generated EGP messages to this EGP peer.

Table 8.8 (continued)

Object	Access Control	Management Application	Description
egpNeighOutErrs (6.7) Counter	Read only	Performance	The number of locally generated EGP messages not sent to this EGP peer due to resource limitations within an EGP entity.
egpNeighInErrMsgs (6.8) Counter	Read only	Performance	The number of EGP-defined error messages received from this EGP peer.
egpNeighOutErrMsgs(6.9) Counter	Read only	Performance	The number of EGP-defined error messages sent to this EGP peer.
egpNeighStateUps (6.10) Counter	Read only	Fault	The number of EGP state transitions to the UP state with this EGP peer.
egpNeighStateDowns (6.11) Counter	Read only	Fault	The number of EGP state transitions from the UP state to any other state with this EGP peer.
egpNeighInterval Hello (6.12) INTEGER	Read only	Configuration	The interval between EGP Hello command retransmissions (in hundredths of a second). This represents the t1 timer as defined in RFC 904.
egpNeighIntervalPoll (6.13) INTEGER	Read only	Configuration	The interval between EGP poll command retransmissions (in hundredths of a second).
egpNeighMode (6.14) INTEGER	Read only	Configuration	The polling mode of this EGP entity, either passive or active.
egpNeighEvent Trigger (6.15) INTEGER	Read only	Configuration	A control variable used to trigger operator-initiated Start and Stop events. When read, this variable always returns the most recent value to which egpNeighEventTrigger was set. If it has not been set since the last initialization of the network management subsystem on the node, it returns a value of "stop."

Table 8.9
MIB-II SNMP Objects

Object	Access Control	Management Application	Description
snmpInPkts (1) *Counter*	Read only	Performance Accounting	Total number of SNMP messages delivered to the SNMP entity from the transport service.
snmpOutPkts (2) *Counter*	Read only	Performance Accounting	Total number of SNMP messages that were passed from the SNMP protocol entity to the transport service.
snmpInBadVersions (3) *Counter*	Read only	Performance Accounting	The total number of SNMP messages that were delivered to the SNMP protocol entity and were for an unsupported SNMP version.
snmpInBad CommunityNames (4) *Counter*	Read only	Security	The total number of SNMP messages delivered to the SNMP protocol entity that used a SNMP community name not known to said entity.
snmpInBad CommunityUses (5) *Counter*	Read only	Security	The total number of SNMP messages delivered to the SNMP protocol entity that represented an SNMP operation that was not allowed by the SNMP community named in the message.
snmpInASNParseErrs (6) *Counter*	Read only	Fault	The total number of ASN.1 or BER errors encountered by the SNMP protocol entity when decoding received SNMP messages.
snmpInTooBigs (8) *Counter*	Read only	Fault	The total number of SNMP PDUs that were delivered to the SNMP protocol entity and for which the value of the error-status field is "tooBig".
snmpInNoSuchNames (9) *Counter*	Read only	Fault	The total number of SNMP PDUs that were delivered to the SNMP protocol entity and for which the value of the error-status field is "noSuchName".

Table 8.9 (continued)

Object	Access Control	Management Application	Description
snmpInBadValues (10) Counter	Read only	Fault	The total number of SNMP PDUs that were delivered to the SNMP protocol entity and for which the value of the error-status field is "badValue".
snmpInRead Onlys (11) Counter	Read only	Fault	The total number of valid SNMP PDUs that were delivered to the SNMP protocol entity and for which the value of the error-status field is "readOnly". It should be noted that it is a protocol error to generate an SNMP PDU that contains the value "readOnly" in the error-status field, as such this object is provided as a means of detecting incorrect implementations of the SNMP.
snmpInGenErrs (12) Counter	Read only	Fault	The total number of SNMP PDUs that were delivered to the SNMP protocol entity and for which the value of the error-status field is "genErr".
snmpInTotalReqVars (13) Counter	Read only	Performance	The total number of MIB objects that have been retrieved successfully by the SNMP protocol entity as the result of receiving valid SNMP Get-Request and Get-Next PDUs.
snmpInTotalSetVars (14) Counter	Read only	Performance	The total number of MIB objects that have been altered successfully by the SNMP protocol entity as the result of receiving valid SNMP Set-Request PDUs.
snmpInGetRequests (15) Counter	Read only	Performance	The total number of SNMP Get-Request lPDUs that have been accepted and processed by the SNMP protocol entity.

Table 8.9 (continued)

Object	Access Control	Management Application	Description
snmpInGetNexts (16) Counter	Read only	Performance	The total number of SNMP Get-Next PDUs that have been accepted and processed by the SNMP protocol entity.
snmpInSetRequests (17) Counter	Read only	Performance	The total number of SNMP Set-Request PDUs that have been accepted and processed by the SNMP protocol entity.
snmpInGetResponses (18) Counter	Read only	Performance	The total number of SNMP Get-Response PDUs that have been accepted and processed by the SNMP protocol entity.
snmpInTraps (19) Counter	Read only	Performance Accounting	The total number of SNMP Trap PDUs that have been accepted and processed by the SNMP protocol entity.
snmpOutTooBigs (20) Counter	Read only	Fault	The total number of SNMP PDUs that were generated by the SNMP protocol entity and for which the value of the error-status field is "tooBig".
snmpOutNoSuch Names (21) Counter	Read only	Fault	The total number of SNMP PDUs that were generated by the SNMP protocol entity and for which the value of the error-status is "noSuchName".
snmpOutBadValues (22) Counter	Read only	Fault	The total number of SNMP PDUs that were generated by the SNMP protocol entity and for which the value of the error-status field is "badValue".
snmpOutGenErrs (24) Counter	Read only	Fault	The total number of SNMP PDUs that were generated by the SNMP protocol entity and for which the value of the error-status field is "genErr".
snmpOutGetRequests (25) Counter	Read only	Performance	The total number of SNMP Get-Request PDUs that have been generated by the SNMP protocol entity.

Table 8.9 (continued)

Object	Access Control	Management Application	Description
snmpOutGetNexts (26) Counter	Read only	Performance	The total number of SNMP Get-Next PDUs that have been generated by the SNMP protocol entity.
snmpOutSetRequests (27) Counter	Read only	Performance	The total number of SNMP Set-Request PDUs that have been generated by the SNMP protocol entity.
snmpOutGet Responses (28) Counter	Read only	Performance	The total number of SNMP Get-Response PDUs that have been generated by the SNMP protocol entity.
snmpOutTraps (29) Counter	Read only	Performance Accounting	The total number of SNMP Trap PDUs that have been generated by the SNMP protocol entity.
snmpEnableAuthen Traps (30) Counter	Read write	Security	Indicates whether the SNMP agent process is permitted to generate authentication-failure traps. The value of this object overrides any configuration information; as such, it provides a means whereby all authentication-failure traps may be disabled.

On a UNIX system you can execute the **uptime** command to get information on the system load. Other related commands are **vmstat, nice,** and **iostat.** The way to use these commands is to execute them when you believe your system is performing well. Then when you are experiencing problems on the system you can execute the **uptime** or other commands and compare the output to determine what the problem may be. For the **uptime** command, if the load average numbers are significantly higher (compared to when the system performance was acceptable) when the system is performing poorly, then it indicates that the system, among other things, may be CPU bound.

8.3.6 NMS Product: SunNet Manager, Installation and Usage

We examine the SunNet Manager product as a way to manage systems on the network. SunNet Manager, HP OpenView, and IBM's NetView/6000 are some dominant network management products available in the industry today. Sun-Net Manager, developed by Sun Microsystems, is a product whose primary purpose is to manage distributed systems on a large network. The product uses a "manager/agent" model of network management. The management process running on the management station communicates with a number of agent processes running on all the managed nodes on the network. Each agent process monitors a specific resource and reports back to the manager:

- Either on demand;
- After a specified interval;
- When a specific event occurs.

Problems with which SunNet Manager can deal include:

- Notifying a system administrator when a system goes down;
- Notifying if a user file system exceeds a certain usage level;
- Notifying if a file server's CPU usage is very high.

The agent processes provide information about resources on the network. Typically, there is one agent for each resource being monitored. The agent processes are implemented using Sun's RPC calls. Some agents supported by SunNet Manager include:

- *diskinfo*;
- *etherif*;
- *hostif*;
- *rpcnfs*;
- *lpstat*;
- *SNMP*.

Each of the agents typically monitors several attributes. For example, the *diskinfo agent* can monitor such things as the capacity of the file system or the number of inodes that are used and free. Users can create agents for new types of devices and new attributes for existing devices. In SunNet Manager, agent processes always have an na prefix; for example, *na.etherif*.

SunNet Manager: Installation and Configuration

The entire process of installing and configuring SunNet Manager v2.0 on a SunOS 4.1.3 (BSD) system is described in this section. SunNet Manager v2.2 and higher releases run on Solaris 2.x systems.

All responses required and commands entered at the command prompt (#) are in **bold italics**.

Enter the following commands to start the installation process:

#	***mkdir /cdrom***
#	***mount -r -t hsfs /cdrom***
#	***cd /cdrom***
#	***./cdmanager***

You will then see the following display:

2.0_SNM : Begin Installation of SunNet_Manager

* NOTICE *
Many non-Sun vendors provide management applications that run on the SNM platform. If you are using such as application, check with the vendor for compatibility with SNM 2.0 *before* you install the SNM 2.0 software.

The SunNet Manager run-time database format has changed since the 1.X releases. Before upgrading to SunNet Manager 2.0 from a 1.X release please be sure to save all existing run-time databases in ASCII format. After completing the installation of SunNet Manager 2.0, you may reload your saved ASCII files.

Please refer to the SunNet Manager User's Guide for more information.

Do you wish to continue with the installation? [n] ***y***
OK.
SunNet Manager 2.0 requires at least SunOS 4.1.1, with the "Networking Tools and Programs" option installed.

The sun4 package requires about 9000 KB.

This package is usually installed into the directory /usr/snm. In most cases, it should be installed into /export/exec/ARCH/snm (ARCH is your current machine architecture), which is a link to /usr/snm. You may specify a different directory.

When performing a server installation, if the software you are installing does not match the server's architecture, the server's system files will not be modified to run SunNet Manager 2.0.

Installation requires five to fifteen minutes.

Supported architecture is: sun4.

Do you want to install into /export/exec [y]   ***y***

It is recommended that you do not change the elements.schema file. You may add your own element schema by creating a personalized file with a .schema extension in one of the directories specified in the "Schema Locations" field in the SunNet Manager console property sheet.

Don't worry if you don't know what this means.

Would you like to install the Sun SNMP agent? [y]   **y**

The Sun SNMP agent's default community strings are:

read: public
write: private

You should at least change the write community string.

New read community string? [public]   **public**
New write community string? [private]   **private**

To run the Sun SNMP agent at each reboot, the following lines need to be added to the end of /etc/rc.local:

if [-f /etc/snmpd.conf -a -x /usr/etc/snmpd]; then
   /usr/etc/snmpd -c /etc/snmpd.conf && echo 'Starting snmpd."
fi

Would you like me to do this for you? [y]   **y**

By default, SunNet Manager database and log files are placed under the directory /var/adm/snm that will be created during this installation. A minimum of 10 Mb to 15 Mb of free space in the default database location is recomended. If you would like to put the databases in an alternate directory by default, a link will be created from /var/adm/snm to the new location. The current usage for /var/adm/snm is:

Filesystem kbytes used avail capacity Mounted on
/dev/sd0a 165606 49942 115664 30% /

Would you like the databases to be written to a new default directory?

[n]   **n**Creating /var/adm/snm directory ... done.

Some of the SunNet Manager daemons create log files that can grow over 1 Mb each in size, depending on the number of nodes you are managing. The default directory for these log files is /var/adm/snm. Here is the current usage for /var/adm/snm:

Filesystem kbytes used avail capacity Mounted on
/dev/sd0a 165606 49943 115663 30% /

Would you like the log files to be written somewhere else (like /usr/snm/logs)? [n]   **n**

I'm about to install SunNet Manager 2.0 into /export/exec for sun4, OK? [y]   **y**

x sun4/snm/agents/na.activity, 32768 bytes, 64 tape blocks
x sun4/snm/agents/na.diskinfo, 24576 bytes, 48 tape blocks
x sun4/snm/agents/na.etherif, 32768 bytes, 64 tape blocks
x sun4/snm/agents/na.event, 106496 bytes, 208 tape blocks
x sun4/snm/agents/na.hostif, 32768 bytes, 64 tape blocks
x sun4/snm/agents/na.hostmem, 32768 bytes, 64 tape blocks
x sun4/snm/agents/na.hostperf, 114688 bytes, 224 tape blocks
x sun4/snm/agents/na.iostat, 32768 bytes, 64 tape blocks
x sun4/snm/agents/na.ippath, 32768 bytes, 64 tape blocks
x sun4/snm/agents/na.iproutes, 32768 bytes, 64 tape blocks
x sun4/snm/agents/na.layers, 32768 bytes, 64 tape blocks
x sun4/snm/agents/na.logger, 40960 bytes, 80 tape blocks
x sun4/snm/agents/na.lpstat, 32768 bytes, 64 tape blocks
.
.
.
x sun4/snm/struct/elements.schema, 11919 bytes, 24 tape blocks
x sun4/snm/struct/example.db, 12434 bytes, 25 tape blocks
x sun4/snm/snm.conf, 2917 bytes, 6 tape blocks

Copying snmpd to /usr/etc ... done.
Copying snmpd.conf to /etc ... done.
Starting SNMP daemon ... Starting snmpd.
done.

Backing up your old /etc/rc.local ... done.

It looks like there may be an exit statement in /etc/rc.local.
You should remove it.

Creating a new /etc/snm.conf ... done.

Creating /var/adm/snm/snmp.hosts file ... done.
Creating /var/adm/snm/snmp.traps file ... done.

Building oid.dbase...
Parsing /export/exec/sun4/snm/agents/enterprises.oid
Parsing /export/exec/sun4/snm/agents/snmp.oid

Parsing /export/exec/sun4/snm/agents/sun-snmp.oid
Writing /var/adm/snm/oid.dbase
done.

Linking libnetmgt to /usr/lib ... done.
Linking libnetmgt_db to /usr/lib ... done.
Running ranlib on new libraries ...done.

Adding agent definitions to /etc/rpc ... done.
Your old /etc/rpc has been saved as /etc/rpc.377

Adding SNMP definitions to /etc/services ... done.
Your old /etc/services has been saved as /etc/services.377

Adding agents to /etc/inetd.conf ... done.
Your old /etc/inetd.conf has been saved as /etc/inetd.conf.377

Asking inetd to re-read its config file... done.

Generating /var/tmp/ngtcs4.db file ... done.

An example database file called /var/tmp/ngtcs4.db has been created.

Before using SunNet Manager, you should set the environment variable SNMHOME to the directory /usr/snm. You may also want to add /usr/snm/bin to your PATH environment variable.

You may then use "snm" to start the SunNet Manager Console, or use "snm /var/tmp/ngtcs4.db" to start SunNet Manager with the example database. Please refer to the SunNet Manager User's Guide for information on how to set the location of SunNet Manager Databases with the SNMDBDIR environment variable.

Finished Installation on ngtcs4.

A log of the installation is in /usr/tmp/unbundled/2.0_SNM.log. You should check this log for any errors that may have occurred during the installation process.

SunNet Manager 2.0 Installation Completed on Fri Oct 28 13:37:34 CDT 1994

At this point the installation of SunNet Manager version 2.0 is complete.

SunNet Manager: Usage

Step 1

Check if the SNMHOME environment variable is set. If not, set the environment variable **SNMHOME** to the directory where SunNet Manager is installed.

setenv SNMHOME /usr/snm

Step 2

snm is the command to start the GUI of SunNet Manager. To start SunNet Manager with a new run-time session, use the **-i** option. Enter:

/usr/snm/bin/snm -i

Step 3

Next, use the Discovery Tool to build your initial run-time databases.

- Pull down the Tools menu.
- Select Discover.
- Enter the **root** password in the pop-up window.

At this point, you will see glyphs of the network.

8.4 ICMP: TCP/IP's TROUBLESHOOTING PROTOCOL

The Internet control messages protocol (ICMP) is often referred to as *TCP/IP's troubleshooting protocol*. Often, when a UNIX system is unable to communicate with other nodes on the network an ICMP message will be generated. By analyzing the ICMP message, a network engineer can determine the location of the problem on the network and the type of problem a system or application may be experiencing.

Thus, for anyone responsible for supporting UNIX systems on a TCP/IP network, an understanding of ICMP messages is a must.

Users on a UNIX system may experience problems using applications such as NFS, **telnet**, and **ftp**. In the section on "Network Application Problems" we step through the types of problems a user may experience accessing resources on the network and how the network engineer can determine what the problem may be and how to correct it. ICMP is a required part of the TCP/IP protocol stack. ICMP uses the services of IP at the network layer in the Internet architecture. It allows hosts and gateways on the Internet to report errors. ICMP provides a single mechanism for all Internet control and information messages. Note that not every error results in an ICMP error message. ICMP messages are always sent back to the source node. Further, ICMP messages are encapsulated within IP datagrams. The datagram includes the IP header, the ICMP header, and ICMP data. The protocol field in the IP header is set to 1 if an ICMP message I encapsulated. Figure 8.4 describes the first three fields of any ICMP message. There are many types of ICMP messages.

The three fields of any ICMP message are:

- *Message Type* (1 byte): Uniquely identifies the ICMP type.
- *Code* (1 byte): Provides a more specific description of the type.
- *Checksum* (2 bytes): Applied to the message.

The remaining fields and message formats are determined by the type of ICMP message. Table 8.10 summarizes the types of ICMP messages.

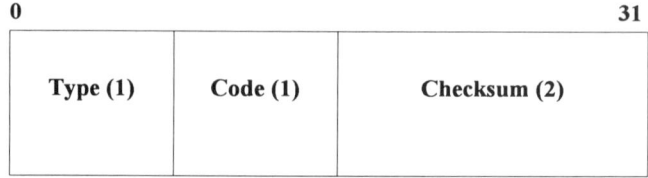

Figure 8.4 Three fields in an ICMP message.

Table 8.10
Types of ICMP Messages

ICMP Type Field	ICMP Message
0	Echo reply
3	Destination unreachable
4	Source quench
5	Redirect
8	Echo request
11	Time exceeded
12	Parameter problem
13	Timestamp request
14	Timestamp reply
15	Information request (obsolete)
16	Information reply (obsolete)
17	Address mask request
18	Address mask reply

The ICMP standard is described in RFC 792. It defines a total of 15 message formats (2 are now obsolete). Other ICMP related documents are:

- RFC 896: Implementing Congestion Control;
- RFC 1016: Use of Source Quench Messages;
- RFC 950: Subnet Mask Messages;

8.4.1 ICMP Destination Unreachable Message

The ICMP Destination Unreachable message is used when a router or a host is unable to deliver a datagram. The network may be unreachable for a number of reasons: protocol or port number may not be available on the target host or the destination node may be down. Figure 8.5 describes the format of an ICMP destination unreachable message.

The following is a brief description of each field in the destination unreachable message.

- *Type* (1 byte): The Type field is set to 3.
- *Code* (1 byte): The Code field describes, in more detail, the reason why information cannot be delivered. Table 8.11 summarizes the different codes defined for an ICMP destination unreachable message.
- *Checksum* (2 bytes): The Checksum field contains the checksum applied to the entire message.
- *Unused* (4 bytes): 32-bits unused.

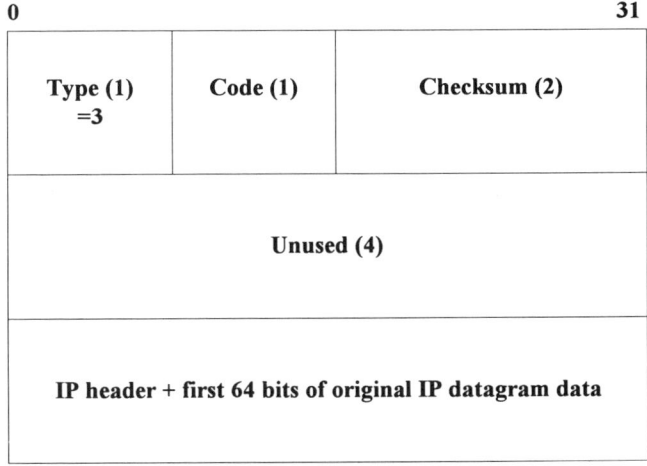

Figure 8.5 ICMP destination unreachable message format.

Table 8.11
Destination Unreachable Code Field Description

Destination Unreachable Code	Description
0	Network unreachable
1	Host unreachable
2	Protocol unreachable
3	Port unreachable
4	Fragmentation required but "Don't Fragment" bit is set
5	Source route failed
6	Destination network unknown
7	Destination host unknown
8	Source host is isolated
9	Communication with destination network is not allowed (administratively)
10	Communication with destination host is not allowed (administratively)
11	Network is unreachable for the type of service specified
12	Host is unreachable for the type of service specified

- *Internet Header Plus Data*: The first 8 bytes beyond the IP header are included to help the host diagnose the failure in the transmission process.

8.4.2 ICMP Time Exceeded Message

An ICMP Time Exceeded message may be generated when a datagram gets lost or has been on the network for an excessive amount of time. If the time-to-live field in the IP header expires or if congestion prevents all fragments of a datagram from being reassembled within the destination host's required time, then an ICMP time exceeded message is generated. Figure 8.6 shows the format of the ICMP time exceeded message.

The following is a brief description of the ICMP time exceeded message:

- *Type* (1 byte): This field is set to 11.
- *Code* (1 byte): There are two codes defined:
- Code 0 : Time-to-Live field in the IP header is 0.
- Code 1 : Fragment reassembly Time Exceeded.
- *Checksum* (2 bytes): This field contains the checksum applied to the entire message.
- *Unused* (4 bytes): 32-bits unused and filled with zeros.

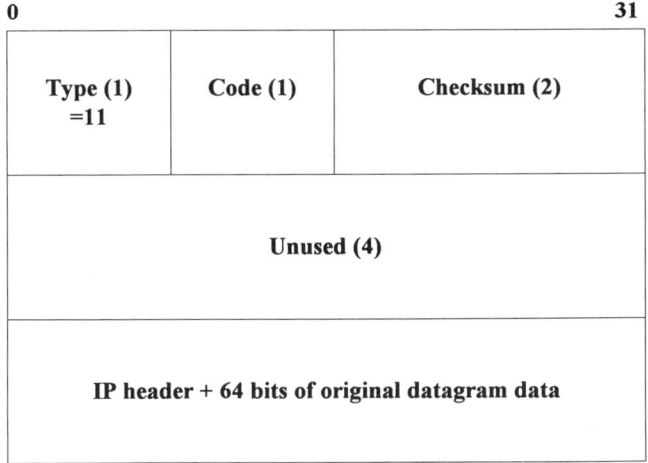

Figure 8.6 ICMP time exceeded message format.

- *Internet Header Plus Data*: This field contains a portion of the offending datagram.

8.4.3 ICMP Parameter Problem Message

If a system is unable to process a message because it encountered some problem with a field in the header, then an ICMP parameter problem message is generated. Invalid option fields are the most usual sources of problems in the header. Figure 8.7 provides an example of an ICMP parameter problem message.

The following is a brief description of fields in the ICMP parameter problem message:

- *Type* (1 byte): This field is set to 12.
- *Code* (1 byte): There are two codes defined for an ICMP parameter problem message.
- Code 0 : The value in the pointer field identifies the octet where an error occurred.
- Code 1 : A required option is missing.
- *Checksum* (2 bytes): This field contains the checksum applied to the entire message.
- *Pointer* (1 byte): This field contains a pointer that identifies the octet with the error.
- *Unused* (3 bytes): 24-bits unused and filled with zeros.
- *Internet Header Plus Data*: This field contains a portion of the data.

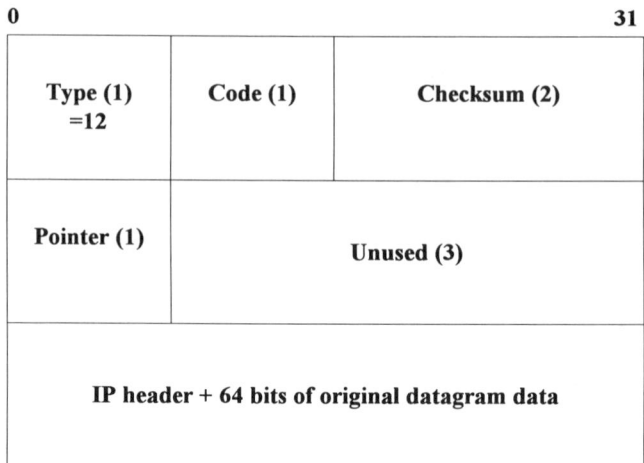

Figure 8.7 ICMP parameter problem message format.

8.4.4 ICMP Source Quench Message

An ICMP source quench message is generated by routers as a way to control the amount of congestion it experiences. Source quench messages report that a network device is discarding datagrams due to lack of resources; a router may be congested and is requesting nodes to slow the rate at which data is generated. Source quench messages are delivered to the upper layer application, however, it is up to the implementor to determine exactly how the congested system should execute a source quench. Figure 8.8 shows the ICMP source quench message format.

The following is a brief description of fields in the source quench message.

- *Type* (1 byte): This field is set to 4.
- *Code* (1 byte): This field is set to 0.
- *Checksum* (1 byte): This field contains the checksum applied to the entire message.
- *Unused* (4 bytes): 32-bits unused and filled with zeros.
- *Internet Header Plus Data*: This field contains a portion of the datagram that triggered the request.

8.4.5 ICMP Redirect Message

An ICMP redirect message is generated if a host system does not choose the correct destination address for a datagram it transmits. Hosts do not always choose the correct destination address for a particular datagram. This occurs

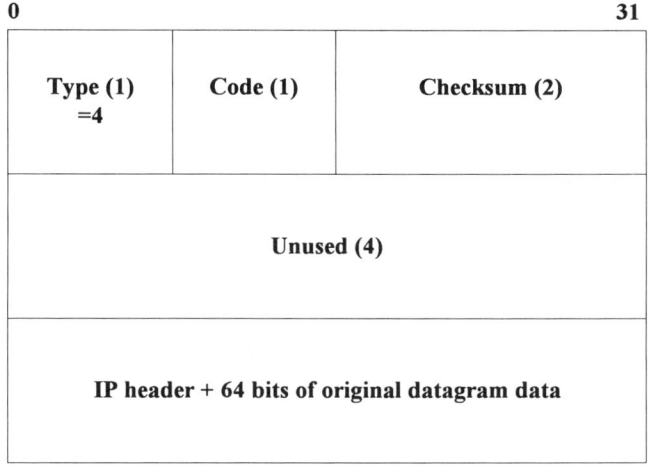

Figure 8.8 ICMP source quench message format.

when the host is initialized and its routing tables are incomplete. When a routing mistake occurs, the router receiving the datagram improperly will return a redirect message to the host identifying a better route. Figure 8.9 is an example of an ICMP redirect message.

The following is a brief description of fields in the ICMP redirect message.

- *Type* (1 byte): This field is set to 5.

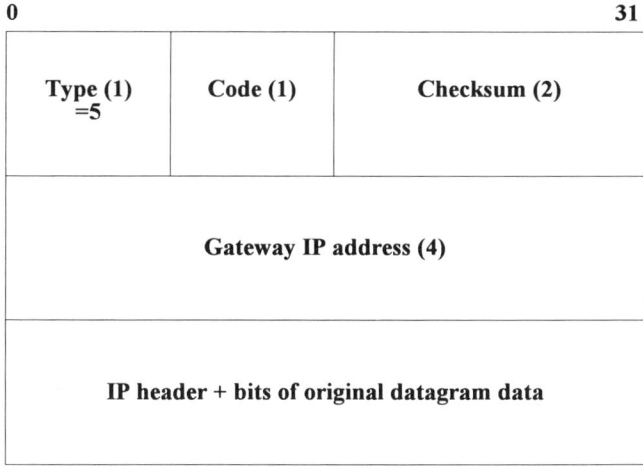

Figure 8.9 ICMP redirect message format.

- *Code* (2 bytes): Four codes are defined specifying the redirection of datagrams:
- Code 0 for the network;
- Code 1 for the host;
- Code 2 for the type of service and network;
- Code 3 for the type of service and host.
- *Checksum* (2 bytes): This field contains the checksum applied to the entire message.
- *Gateway Internet Address* (4 bytes): The redirect message contains the correct router address to reach the desired destination.
- *Internet Header Plus Data*: This field contains a portion of the datagram to aid in the diagnostic process.

8.4.6 ICMP Echo Request Message

The ICMP echo request message is the most frequently used ICMP message. The **ping** utility generates an ICMP echo request and echo reply messages. This message is primarily used to test the communication path between nodes on the network. Figure 8.10 is an example of an ICMP echo request message.

The following is a brief description of fields in the ICMP echo request message.

- *Type* (1 byte): This field is set to 8.
- *Code* (1 byte): This field is set to 0.

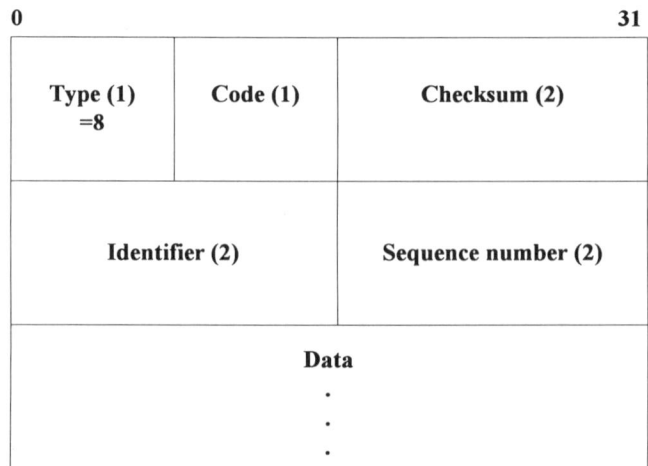

Figure 8.10 ICMP echo request message format.

- *Checksum* (2 bytes): This field contains the checksum applied to the entire message.
- *Sequence Number* (2 bytes): This field is used when sending a sequence of echo messages (to test whether the network is dropping messages and to estimate average throughput and round trip time). The value is incremented for each message.
- *Identifier* (2 bytes): This field is used to match a reply with its original request. It is held fixed when sending a sequence of echo messages.
- *Data*: The sender selects the amount of data in this field.

8.4.7 ICMP Echo Reply Message

The ICMP echo reply message is the reponse to the ICMP echo request message. When the destination receives the echo request message, it reverses the source and destination addresses, recomputes the checksum, and returns an echo reply message. Figure 8.11 is an example of the format of an ICMP echo reply message.

The following is a brief description of fields in the ICMP echo reply message.

- *Type* (1 byte): This field is set to 0.
- *Code* (1 byte): This field is set to 0.
- *Checksum* (2 bytes): This field contains the checksum applied to the entire message.
- *Identifier* (2 bytes): This field is used to match a reply with its original request.

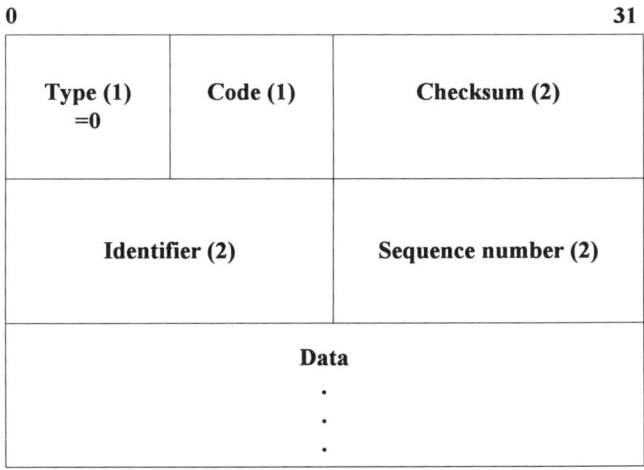

Figure 8.11 ICMP echo reply message format.

- *Sequence Number* (2 bytes): This field is used when sending a sequence of echo reply messages (in response to a sequence of echo messages).
- *Data*: The responder must send back the same data it receives.

8.4.8 ICMP Timestamp Request Message

Used with the timestamp reply message to measure the round-trip transit time between two machines and to synchronize their clocks. Figure 8.12 is an example of an ICMP timestamp request message.

The following is a brief description of fields in the timestamp request message.

- *Type* (4 bytes): This field is set to 13.
- *Code* (4 bytes): This field is set to 0.
- *Checksum* (4 bytes): This field contains the checksum applied to the entire message.

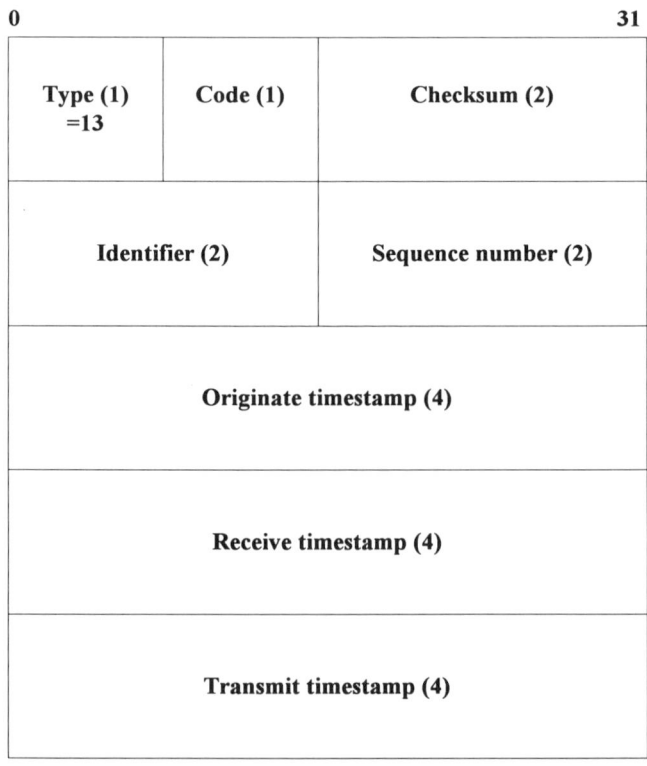

Figure 8.12 ICMP timestamp request message format.

- *Identifier Number* (2 bytes) and *Sequence Number* (2 bytes): These fields are used to match a reply with its original request.
- *Originate Timestamp* (4 bytes): The time the sender last touched the message.
- *Receive Timestamp* (4 bytes): The time the echoer first touched it.
- *Transmit Timestamp* (4 bytes): The time the echoer last touched it.

The timestamp-related fields are measured in milliseconds since midnight, Universal Time (UT–formerly Greenwich Mean Time).

When the requester receives the reply it can estimate the remote processing and round-trip transit times.

- *Remote processing time* = Received timestamp minus *Transmit timestamp*
- *Round-trip transit time* = Timestamp reply message arrival time minus Originate timestamp

These two calculations are used to synchronize the two clocks. Note that these are only estimates because network delay is a highly dynamic and variable measurement. The *network time protocol* (NTP) is far more capable and has been defined for Internet time synchronization.

8.4.9 ICMP Timestamp Reply Message

The timestamp reply is used with the timestamp request message. The recipient of the timestamp request message fills in the receive timestamp when it receives the request. The recipient also fills in the transmit timestamp when it sends the timestamp reply message. Figure 8.13 is an example of an ICMP timestamp reply message.

The following is a brief description of fields in the timestamp reply message.

- *Type* (1 byte): This field is set to 14.
- *Code* (1 byte): This field is set to 0.
- *Checksum* (2 bytes): This field contains the checksum applied to the entire message.
- *Identifier Number* (2 bytes) and *Sequence Number* (2 bytes): These fields are used to match a reply with its original request.
- *Originate Timestamp* (4 bytes): The time the sender last touched the message.
- *Receive Timestamp* (4 bytes): The time the echoer first touched it.
- *Transmit Timestamp* (4 bytes): The time the echoer last touched it.

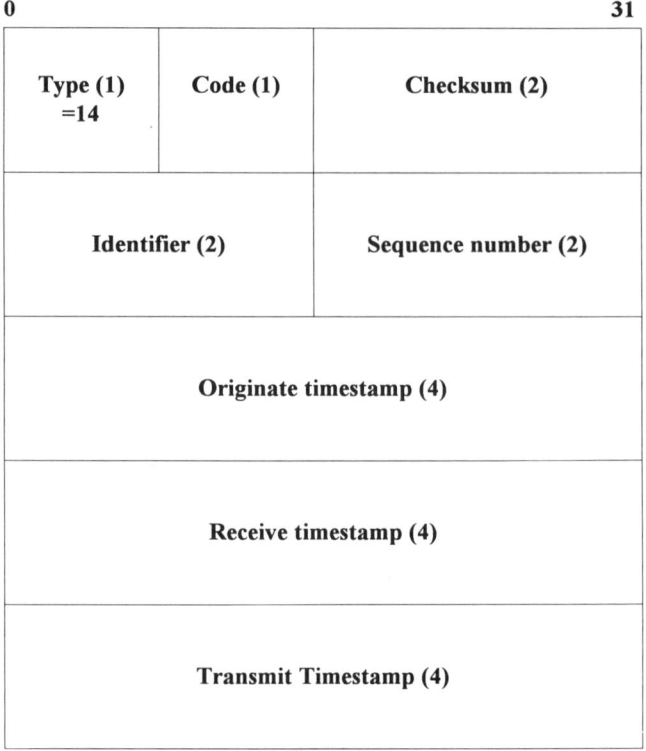

Figure 8.13 ICMP timestamp reply message format.

8.4.10 ICMP Address Mask Request Message

The address mask request is used to determine the subnet mask of the local IP network. The requesting host (already knows its own internet address) broadcasts an address mask request message to the destination address [255.255.255.255]. The address mask field of the ICMP message would be filled with all zeros. The requesting host waits to receive an address mask reply message from a neighboring router who knows the appropriate mask. Figure 8.14 is an example of an ICMP address mask request meaasge.

The following is a brief description of fields in the address mask request message.

- *Type* (1 byte): This field is set to 17.
- *Code* (1 byte): This field is set to zero.
- *Checksum* (1 byte): This field contains the checksum applied to the entire message.

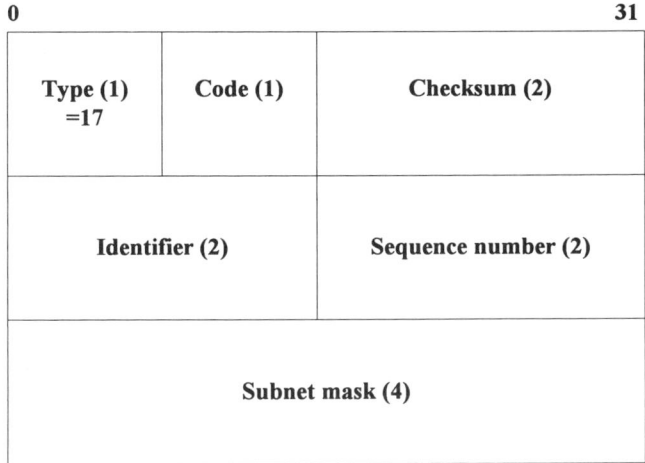

Figure 8.14 ICMP address mask request message format.

- *Identifier Number* (2 bytes) and *Sequence Number* (2 bytes): Generally, these fields can be ignored.
- *Subnet Mask* (4 bytes): This field is not used for a request.

8.4.11 ICMP Address Mask Reply Message

The address mask reply is generated in response to an address mask request message. An authorized address mask server sends the response. A response for a Class B network (without subnetting) would be [255.255.0.0], while a response from a Class B network with an 8-bit subnet field would be [255.255.255.0]. Figure 8.15 is as example of an ICMP address mask reply message.

The following is a brief description of an ICMP address mask reply message.

- *Type* (1 byte): This field is set to 18.
- *Code* (1 byte): This field is set to zero.
- *Checksum* (1 byte): This field contains the checksum applied to the entire message.
- *Identifier Number* (2 bytes) and *Sequence Number* (2 bytes): Generally, these fields can be ignored.
- *Subnet Mask* (4 bytes): This field differentiates between various subnetworks. The reply will put *1s* into the network and subnet fields of a 32-bit address mask field.

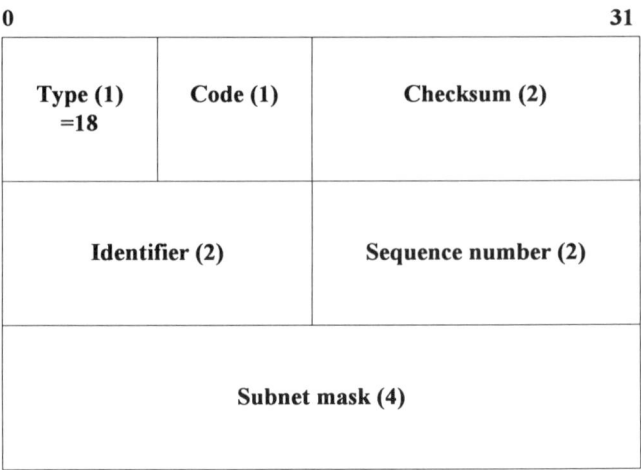

Figure 8.15 ICMP address mask reply message format.

8.4.12 ICMP Information Request and Reply

The ICMP information request and reply messages are now considered obsolete. These ICMP messages were used to find the address of the local IP network. The ICMP type field was set to 15 for information request messages and 16 for information reply messages.

8.5 NETWORK APPLICATION (TELNET, FTP) PROBLEMS

If users have a problem using **telnet**, **ftp**, or any other application layer protocol you should check the following areas to determine the cause.

- Is the client side of the application running on the local system?
- Can you **ping** the remote system? If the remote system is on the other side of a router, can you ping the interfaces on the router?
- Is the *inetd* process running on the remote system? If the *inetd* daemon is not running, then applications such as **telnet**, **ftp**, **tftp**, **rlogin** and others cannot be accessed.
- Is the service listed in the **/etc/services** file on the remote system?
- Is there any other application using the same port number as the user's application?
- Is the protocol specified in the **/etc/protocols** file?
- Is the **inetd.conf** file set up correctly?
- Does the server application get initialized by *inetd*?

8.6 NETWORK FILE SYSTEM (NFS) PROBLEMS

Let us examine specific problems that users may experience with NFS and what the administrator can do to troubleshoot NFS errors.

8.6.1 File System Errors

If you try to NFS mount a directory from the server and get the following error message:

mount -F nfs shiva:/export/home /export/home
nfs mount: shiva:/export/home: access denied

the directory may not have been exported to the client system. To find out if the directory or file system is exported to your system, enter the following command on the NFS client system:

dfshares -F nfs shiva

On the NFS server system, check if the **/etc/dfs/dfstab** file contains an entry for the NFS client system. Here is a sample **dfstab** file.

```
#
#
share [-F fstype] [ -o options] [-d "<text>"] <pathname> [resource]
# .e.g.,
# share -F nfs -o rw=engineering -d "home dirs" /export/home2
share -F nfs -o anon=0 /opt share -F nfs -o anon=0 /export/home
```

8.6.2 Read Only Errors

If you try to create a file by writing to a NFS mounted directory and get the following message:

cat /etc/passwd > mypasswd
ksh: mypasswd: cannot create

then the directory may be exported **read only** to your system. To find out if the directory was exported **read only**, enter the following command on the NFS client system:

dfshares -F nfs shiva

where, **shiva** is the name of the NFS server system.

8.6.3 *mountd* Daemon Problems

If you try to NFS mount a directory and get the following error message:

mount -F nfs shiva:/export/home /export/home
nfs mount: shiva:: RPC: Program not registered

the *mountd* daemon may not be running on the server. To find out if the *mountd* daemon is running on the system, type the following command on the NFS server:

ps -ef | grep mountd

8.6.4 *nfsd* Daemons Problems

If you try to NFS mount a directory from the server and get the following error message:

mount -F nfs shiva:/export/home /export/home
nfs mount: shiva: NFS service not responding

or, if you try to access files on an NFS mounted directory and get the following message:

cd /export/home
ls

NFS server shiva not responding still trying, then check if the *nfsd* daemon is running on the server system. To find out if the *nfsd* is running on the server system, enter the following command on the NFS server:

ps -ef | grep nfsd

8.7 SUMMARY

We examined the fundamentals of:

- Communication devices;
- Routing;
- Network and system management.

Those concepts are important to troubleshoot network and application problems. The section on ICMP is critical in understanding how the TCP/IP

network is performing and to identify the types of problems that the network is experiencing.

SELECT BIBLIOGRAPHY

Feit, Sidnie, *TCP/IP Architecture, Protocols, and Implementation*, New York: McGraw-Hill, Inc., 1993.

Appendix A: RFC 1340

RFC 1340 is an RFC that contains important network information. We have particularly found the following sections to be useful in managing UNIX systems on the network:

The VERSION NUMBERS section refers to the version number field in the IP header. The PROTOCOL NUMBERS section identifies higher layer protocols that can be encapsulated in an IP datagram. This section relates to the 8-bit protocol field in the IP header.

WELL-KNOWN PORT NUMBERS are port numbers controlled and assigned by the IANA. These port numbers are in the range 0 to 1023. These are privileged ports on UNIX systems.

REGISTERED PORT NUMBERS are not controlled by te IANA. These ports may be used by end users—no special privileges are required. Registered ports are in the range 1024 to 65535.

The INTERNET MULTICAST ADDRESSES section refers to host extensions to IP multicasting, as described in RFC 1112. The IP addresses specified in this section are required of a host implementation of IP to support multicasting. Note that on an Ethernet network, the 23 lower order bits of the IP multicast address are placed in the lower order 23 bits of the Ethernet multicast address.

The IANA ETHERNET ADDRESS BLOCK summarizes Ethernet address blocks owned by the IANA. These addresses may be used for multicasting or for other purposes.

IP TOS PARAMETERS specify valid bit values in the 8-bit TOS field in the IP header. The TOS values defined are:

- Low delay;
- High throughput;
- High reliability;
- Low cost.

In the IP TIME-TO-LIVE PARAMETER section is a recommendation for the default value of the 8-bit TTL field in the IP header (default recommended is 64).

DOMAIN SYSTEM PARAMETERS summarize resource record types defined for DNS.

BOOTP PARAMETERS describe vendor extensions to the BOOTP header.

NETWORK MANAGEMENT PARAMETERS provide useful information on object identifiers in the management subtree of Internet.

The ETHERNET NUMBERS OF INTEREST specify Ethernet type field values.

ETHERNET VENDOR ADDRESS COMPONENTS are summaries of the first 24 bits of the Ethernet address assigned to vendors.

The ADDRESS RESOLUTION PROTOCOL PARAMETERS section describes values for the hardware type field in the ARP header.

TELNET OPTIONS describe options that may be negotiated between a **telnet** server and a **telnet** client.

Appendix B: Glossary

The information in this glossary is based on *Understanding and Using Computer Networks*, second edition, Fermi National Accelerator Laboratory, 1992; *Data and Computer Communications*, William Stallings, 1988; and the *Glossary of Telecommunication Terms*, FED-STD-1037A, National Communications Systems, 1986.

AAL	ATM adaption layer.
Access point	Networkwide reference to a device and directory at a server node running DFS.
Administrative domain	A collection of systems and subnetworks operated by a single organization or administrative authority. It may be subdivided into a number of routing domains.
AppleTalk	A set of protocols used in the Macintosh networking environment.
Area	The group of systems that constitute a single Level 1 routing subdomain in a DECnet network. It is a contiguous grouping of addresses for purposes of routing in DECnet Phase IV and in OSI networks.
ARP	The address resolution protocol is used to map network access layer addresses (such as Ethernet) to an Internet address.
ARPANET	Services provided included file transfer, e-mail, and remote login. Services are supported by protocols such as FTP, SMTP, and TELNET. ARPANET was an advanced research and development tool for DARPA and an operational network supporting many DARPA-sponsored researchers in universities, national laboratories, and industry. ARPANET has also served as a test for the development of protocols, such as TCP/IP. In 1983, the ARPANET was divided into a research network (ARPANET) and a military network (MILNET).

Asynchronous	Signals that are sourced from independent clocks. These signals generally have no relation to each other and have different frequencies and phase relationships.
Asynchronous transfer mode (ATM)	A form of LAN data transmission based on fixed-length packets, called cells, that can carry data, voice, and video at high speeds.
Asynchronous transmission	Transmission in which each information character is individually synchronized.
AAL 1	Supports connection-oriented services that require constant bit rates and have specific timing and delay requirements (e.g., DS-3 circuit emulation service).
AAL 2	Supports connection-oriented services with variable bit rates such as some video schemes.
AAL 3/4	These layers are intended for both connectionless and connection-oriented variable rate services. Originally two distinct layers, they have merged into a single AAL called AAL 3/4.
AAL 5	Supports connection-oriented variable bit rate data services such as the typical "bursty" data traffic found in today's LANs. Also known as the simple and efficient adaptation layer (SEAL).
ATM	See asynchronous transfer mode.
ATM endpoint	The point in an ATM network where an ATM connection is either terminated or initiated. This includes ATM-attached workstations, ATM-attached servers, ATM-to-Legacy LAN bridges, or routers.
ATM layer	The layer of the ATM protocol that relays cells from one connection to another. The ATM layer operates differently in endpoints and switches.
Attenuation	A decrease in magnitude of current, voltage, or power of a signal in transmission between points.
Balanced transmission	Signals having equal amplitude and opposite polarity, carried on a line consisting of two parallel metallic conductors separated a dielectric.
Bandwidth	The difference between the limiting frequencies of a continuous frequency spectrum.

Baseband	Transmission of signals without modulation of carrier signal. In a baseband local network, digital signal (1's and 0's) are inserted directly onto the cable as voltage pulses. The entire spectrum of the cable is consumed by the signal. This scheme does not allow frequency division multiplexing.
Big-endian	A format for storage or transmission of binary data in which the most significant byte (bit) comes first. The Internet's standard network byte order is big-endian.
BITNET	A store and forward network supporting basic research and educational facilities. Consists of about 175 sites in the United States and about 260 sites in Europe (supported via EARN). Services include file transfer, e-mail, and remote job entry.
BOOTP	A TCP/IP application layer protocol that supports the functionality of RARP and provides additional features such as file names. Uses the services of UDP and IP.
Bridge	A bridge can be used to connect to networks with the same or different data link layers but typically the same network layer. Bridges operate at layer 2, the data link layer.
Broadband	The use of coaxial cable for providing data transfer by means of analog (radio frequency) signals. Digital signals are passed through a modem and transmitted over one of the frequency bands of the cable.
Broadcast	The simultaneous transmission of data to a number of stations.
CATV	Community antenna television. CATV cable is used for broadband local networks.
Cell	The fixed-length transmission unit used by ATM. Each cell is 53 bytes long with a 5-byte header containing its connection identifier and a 48-byte payload. See CLP, HEC, PTI, VCI, VPI.
Cell loss priority (CLP)	A one-bit descriptor found in ATM cell headers, indicating the relative importance of a cell. If set to 0, the cell should not be discarded. If set to 1, the cell may be discarded if necessary. The cell is set by the AAL.

Circuit	Virtual communication path between nodes. Circuits operate over physical lines and are the medium on which all I/O occurs. They refer to a logical stream of data between two users of the network.
Circuit switching	A method of communicating in which a dedicated communication path is established between two devices through one or more intermediate switching nodes. Unlike packet switching, digital data are sent as a continuous stream of bits. Bandwidth is guaranteed, and delay is essentially limited to propagation time. The telephone system uses circuit switching.
Clearinghouse	In DNA, a collection of (copies of) directories stored on a particular node.
CLP	See cell loss priority.
Coaxial cable	An electromagnetic transmission medium consisting of a center conductor and an outer, concentric conductor.
Codec	Coder-decoder. Transforms analog data into digital bit stream (coder) and digital signals into analog data (decoder).
Collision	A condition in which two packets are being transmitted over a medium at the same time. Their interference makes both unintelligible.
Connection admission control (CAC)	The set of actions taken by the network during the connection setup phase in order to determine whether a connections requested QoS can be accepted or should be rejected. CAC is also used when routing a connection through an ATM network.
Connectionless data transfer	A protocol for exchanging data in an unplanned fashion and without prior coordination (e.g., datagram).
Connection-oriented	A type of communication in which a connection must be provided between a sender and a receiver before transmission can occur.
Connection-oriented data transfer	A protocol for exchanging data in which a logical connection is established between the endpoints (e.g., virtual circuits).
Contention	The condition when two or more stations attempt to use the same channel at the same time without scheduling or reservation scheme.

Controller	One of the main components of the Ethernet physical architecture. It controls the exchange of data between the coaxial cable and the attached station.
CRC	Cyclic redundancy check. A numeric value derived from the bits in a message. The transmitting station calculates a number and attaches it to a message. The receiving station performs the same calculation. If the result differs, then one or more bits are in error.
CSMA	A medium access control technique for multiple-access transmission media. A station wishing to transmit first senses the medium and transmits only if the medium is idle.
CSMA/CD	A refinement of CSMA in which a station ceases to transmit if it detects a collision.
CSNET	Purpose of the network is to facilitate research and advance development in computer science by providing a means for increased collaboration among those working in the field. CSNET has merge with BITNET.
Data circuit terminating equipment (DCE)	In a data station, the equipment that provides the signal conversion and coding between the DTE and the line (e.g., a modem).
Data exchange interface (DXI)	The local interface between a packet-based router and an ATM capable DSU. One of the ATM specifications.
Datagram	In packet switching, a self-contained packet, independent of other packets, that does not require acknowledgment and that carries information sufficient for routing from the originating DTE, without relying on earlier exchanges between the DTEs and the network.
DELNI	DIGITAL's local network interconnect product that provides eight separate network interfaces from a single transceiver tap.
DEMPR	DIGITAL's multiport repeater that provides eight Thinwire Ethernet drops from a single standard Ethernet connection.
DEQNA	DIGITAL's network adapter that connects MicroVAX- and Q-bus-based systems to Ethernet.
DESTA	DIGITAL's station adapter that acts as a thinwire Ethernet transceiver. A DESTA allows you to connect a workstation with a transceiver cable to Thinwire Ethernet.

DEUNA	Digital's network adapter that connects VAX- and UNIBUS-based systems to Ethernet.
Distributed computing environment (DCE)	An OSF specification for designing and developing distributed applications.
Distributed file service (DFS)	Allows remote files to appear as though they were locally mounted on a system. DFS uses DNS to locate files. Analogous to NFS.
Distributed management environment (DME)	An OSF specification to managing client/server systems on the network.
DIGITAL Network Architecture (DNA)	DNA defines standards for protocols, interfaces, and communications functions. These standards allow various operating systems, communication devices, and computer hardware to function in a network. DNA is the basis for the design of all DECnet products.
Distributed name service (DNS)	DNS is the domain name service for the internet providing node name translations. DEC DNS is a directory lookup service that provides a name translation, such as A DECnet node name to DECnet address, and is also used to locate DEC DFS files.
Domain	In the Internet, a part of the naming hierarchy. A domain name consists of a sequence of names (labels) separated by periods (dots).
Data terminal equipment (DTE)	Equipment consisting of digital end instruments that convert user information into data signal for transmission or reconvert the received data signal into user information (e.g., a terminal).
DXI	See data exchange interface.
executor node	The DECnet term for the node at which a NCP command actually executes. Usually the executor is the local node.
Full-duplex	Data transmission in both directions at the same time.
Gated	Gateway daemon. A program that runs under 4.3 BSD UNIX on a gateway (router) to allow the gateway to collect information from one autonomous system and to advertise routes to another autonomous system.

Appendix B: Glossary

Gateway	Is a network or higher layer device that stores and forwards packets. Networks connected by a gateway can differ much more than those connected by a bridge. Gateways are used to connect networks with incompatible addressing formats. Typically, gateways transfer 10,000 packets/s.
Generic flow control (GFC)	The first four bits of the ATM UNI cell header; used when passing through the User–Network Interface.
GFC	See generic flow control.
Half-duplex	Data transmission in either direction, one direction at a time.
Header error control (HEC)	The HEC field is an 8-bit cyclic redundancy code (CRC) computed on all fields in an ATM header; capable of detecting single-bit and certain multiple-bit errors. HEC is used by the physical layer for cell delineation.
HEC	See header error control.
High-performance parallel interface (HIPPI)	HIPPI is a high-speed serial line protocol developed at Los Alamos National Laboratory for real-time scientific visualization and is being considered by an ANSI task group (X3T9.3) as the industry standard for high-speed super computer networks. HIPPI allows transmission at peak rates of 800 Mbps to 1.6 GBps. HIPPI transfer 32 bits of data in parallel across distances of up to 25m.
ILMI	See interim local management interface.
Inetd	One of the most important network deamons on a UNIX system. Checks the specifications of the /etc/inetd.conf and /etc/services for incoming connection requests.
Interim local management interface (ILMI)	The standard specification used to manage an ATM network. The ILMI uses the SNMP protocol and an ATM UNI MIB to provide the administrator with status and configuration information.
IP address	An identifier for a node; expressed as four fields separated by decimal points (e.g., 136.19.9.5). The IP address is site-dependent and is assigned by an administrator.
Integrated services digital network (ISDN)	A planned worldwide telecommunication service that uses digital transmission and switching technology to support voice and digital data communication.

Isochronous	Signals that are dependent on some uniform timing or carry their own timing information embedded as part of the signal.
Internet	A collection of packet-switched and broadcast networks that are connected together via gateways.
Internet protocol (IP)	An internetworking protocol that provides connectionless service across multiple packet-switched networks. IP works at the network layer.
Internetworking	Communication between devices across multiple networks.
Kermit	A character-oriented computer file transfer protocol developed at Columbia University.
LAN	Any physical network technology that operates at high speed (usually tens of Mbps through several Gbps) over short distance (up to few thousand meters). Examples include Ethernet and token-ring networks.
LAN emulation	How an ATM network emulates enough of the MAC protocol of an existing LAN technology, such as Ethernet or token ring, to allow existing higher layer protocols and applications to be used unchanged over an ATM network.
Level 1 router	A router that performs routing within a single area in both the DECnet and OSI context. Messages for destinations in other areas are routed to the nearest Level 2 router.
Level 2 router	A router that acts as a Level 1 router within its own area but, in addition, routes messages between areas in both the DECnet and OSI contexts.
Line	The network management component that provides a distinct physical data path.
Link	Any connection on a network that links two separate devices such as an ATM switch and an endpoint/endstation.
Little-endian	A format for storage or transmission of binary data in which the least significant byte (bit) comes first.
Local loop	Transmission path, generally twisted-pair, between the individual subscriber and the nearest switching center of the public telecommunication network.

Logical link	A carrier of a single stream of full-duplex traffic between two user-level processes.
MAN	Any physical network technology that operates at high speeds (usually hundreds of Mbps through few Gbps) over distances sufficient for a metropolitan area.
Manchester encoding	A way of encoding to get zero-DC binary wave form. In this encoding scheme, half of the bit interval is transmitted with a positive signal and the other half is transmitted with a negative signal.
Message switching	A switching technique using a message store-and-forward system. No dedicated path is established. Rather, each message contains a destination address and is passed from source to destination through intermediate nodes. At each node, the entire message is received, stored briefly, and then passed on to the next node.
MFENET	Magnetic Fusion Energy NETwork. Formerly, a network used to link laboratories and computers performing similar research. Now, the collection of applications used by the original network.
Message handling system (MHS)	A system for handling messages following the model specified by CCITT. An MHS has three components: the OSI network, the message transfer service (MTS), and the user agent.
Microwave	Electromagnetic waves in the frequency range of about 2 GHz to 40 GHz.
Multiplexing	In data transmission, a function that permits two or more data sources to share a common transmission medium such that each source has its own channel.
Modem	Device that converts data signals to analog signals and back for transmission over the voice telephone network.
Multicast	Similar to a broadcast, except that the receipts of a multicast message represent only a subset in the same broadcast domain. Multicast messages are not the same as a point-to-multipoint connection and, instead, should be supported by multipoint-to multipoint connection and, instead, should be supported by multipoint-to multipoint connections.

Multipoint-to-multipoint	A connection based on a full mesh of point-to-multipoint VCCs or VPCs between all the associated endpoints. In a multipoint-to-multipoint connection, all the endpoints are roots and can send cells to all the other endpoints. See also point-to-multipoint and point-to-point.
Name resolution	The process of mapping a name into a corresponding address. The Internet domain name system resolves machine names into Internet addresses for those machines.
Name server	A system supporting name service.
Namespace	A tree of directories starting at root.
National Science Foundation Network (NSFNET)	Function is to provide e-mail an file transfer services as well as access to super computing centers and national research facilities. Consists of a T3 and T1 (1.5 Mbps) terrestrial transcontinental backbone that interconnects regional networks such as BARRNET, Merit, and SURANET.
NetBIOS	The standard interface to networks on IBM/PC compatibles.
Network control program	A DECnet-VAX utility that accepts terminal commands to configure, control, monitor, and test a DECnet network.
Network synchronization	The consistent timing within a network; provided by the selection of a single clock used throughout the network.
Network-to-node interface (NNI) (SS)	The interface between ATM switches or an ATM switch and an entire switching system. Also called network-to-network interface.
Network file system (NFS)	An application layer protocol used on TCP/IP networks to distribute file systems to nodes on the network.
Network information service (NIS)	A distributed database lookup service that maintains a set of data bases and propagates updated databases among systems on the IP network ensuring consistency.
NN	See network-to-node interface.
Null modem	A configuration (enabled by interconnecting leads) that allow two DTEs to signal each other.
NNI	See network-to-node interface.

Offered load	The actual load or traffic demand presented to a local network.
Operations and maintenance (OAM)	A number of preventative maintenance principals recommended by the ITU for B-ISDN networks. In an ATM network, OAM information is generally passed around in special cells.
Packet assembler/ dissembler (PAD)	A device used with an X.25 network to provide service to asynchronous terminals.
Packet switching	A method of transmitting messages through a communication network in which long messages are subdivided into short packets. The packets are then transmitted as in message switching. Usually, packet switching is more efficient and rapid than message switching.
Payload type identifier (PTI)	A 3-bit descriptor found in ATM cell headers, indicating what type of payload the cell contains. Payload types include user and management cells.
PDU	See protocol unit.
Permanent virtual circuit (PVC)	A logical (rather than physical) connection between endpoints established by an administrator that stays intact until manually torn down.
Physical layer	The layer below the ATM layer in the protocol reference model that passes cells from the media to the ATM layer and vice versa. Also refers to OSI Layer 1.
Piggybacking	A technique used to increase acknowledgment efficiency during packet transmission. A response number is included in the message header of a user data packet being sent by the receiving station.
Pipelining	A technique used to increase acknowledgment efficiency during packet transmission. Several packets are sent, and the acknowledgment signifies receipt of that packet and all lower numbered packets.
Point-to-multipoint	A connection with one root endpoint and several nonroot end nodes. End nodes can send data back to the root only, not to each other. See multipoint-to-multipoint, point-to-point.
Point-to-point	A connection with only two endpoints. See multipoint-to-multipoint and point-to-multipoint.
P-NNI	See private network-to-node interface.

Private network-to-node interface (P-NNI)	The interface between two ATM switches or between an ATM switch and an entire switching system (SS) in a private network. Also known as a private network-to-network interface.
Protocol converter	Is a device used to connect dissimilar networks at the transport layer and above. Its primary function is to convert from one protocol to another.
Protocol data unit (PDU)	A unit of data consisting of control information and user data exchanged between peer layers.
PTI	See payload type indentifier.
PVC	See permanent virtual circuit.
RARP	The reverse address resolution protocol is used by diskless UNIX systems and X terminals to determine their Internet address at boot time.
Repeater	Is a physical layer device that receives, re-times, and regenerates electrical signals. Its function is to copy individual bits between cable segments.
Round robin	A medium access protocol in which everybody takes a turn.
Routed	RIP daemon. A program that runs under 4.3 BSD UNIX to propagate routes among machines on a local network. Pronounced "route-d."
Routing domain	A collection of systems and subnetworks that operate according to the same routing procedures and that is wholly contained within a single administrative domain.
RS-232-C	A standard interface between terminals and communications equipment. Designed for speeds up to 19.2 Kbps over a maximum distance of 15m.
RS-449/RS-422-A/ 423-A	A newer standard issued by the EIA to replace RS-232-C. RS-422-A/423-A defines the electrical characteristics of the DTE-DCE interface. RS-422-A specifies balanced transmissions and achieves 100 Kbps at 1200m to 10 Mbps at 12m. RS-423-A specifies unbalanced transmission and achieves 2 Kbps at 1000m to 300 Kbps at 10m. RS-449 defines the mechanical, functional, and procedural characteristics of the new interface.
Simplex	Data transmission in one preassigned direction only.

...en ring	A medium access control technique for rings. A token circulates around the ring. A station may transmit by seizing the token, inserting a packet onto the ring, and then retransmitting the token.
...ology	The structure, consisting of paths and switches, that provide the communications interconnection among nodes of a network.
...fic policing	A mechanism used to detect and discard or modify cells/traffic that violate the traffic or quality of service (QoS) contract agreed to at connection setup. Although applicable to both public and private networks, traffic policing will most likely be used by public ATM service providers where tariffing may be based on guaranteed QoS.
...ic shaping	A mechanism used to achieve or modify traffic characteristics in order to match a desired quality of service (QoS) contract.
...sceiver	A device that provides a single physical connection between standard Ethernet and Ethernet communication equipment.
...smission ...ium	The physical path between transmitters and receivers in a communication system.
...ted pair	A transmission medium consisting of two parallel insulated wires arranged in a spiral pattern.
...NET	A proprietary data link protocol supporting very high speed (250–500 Mbps) access between systems.
...lanced ...smission	Signals are transmitted on a single conductor. Transmitter and receiver paths may share a common ground. Also refers to twisted pairs with one conductor grounded as in RS423.
...: parameter ...rol (UPC)	The set of actions used by the network to monitor and control traffic. Its purpose is to protect network resources from both malicious and unintentional misbehavior that may adversely affect the QoS of already established connections by detecting violations of negotiated quality of service parameters and taking policing actions.
	See user-to-network interface.
...ET	A UNIX news facility, based on the UUCP network, that provides a news bulletin board service.

Slot time	An upper bound on the time it take sion using the CSMA/CD algorithm ing quantum for retransmission.	
Systems network architecture (SNA)	A network architecture, designed l a coherent environment for loose] uted processing. Arbitrary topol LANs are supported.	
Socket	An API to communication protoco a socket; specifies the service desi stream delivery; binds the socke vice desired; and then sends or r	
Subnet address	An extension of the Internet add allows a site to use a single Intern ple physical networks. Beyond t addressing, routing continues a the destination address into an l a local portion.	
SVC	See switched virtual circuit.	
Switched virtual circuit (SVC)	A logical (not physical) conne points established by the ATM after receiving a connection req root, which it transmits using protocol.	
Synchronous	Signals that are sourced from t ence and have the same freque	
Synchronous transmission	Data transmission in which th of each signal representing a b time frame.	
T1 system	A digital communication syste 24 voice channel at 64 Kbps e	
Tap	An analog device that permits or removed from a twisted pa	
TELENET	A public packet-switched net ated by GTE that uses the CC	
TELNET	Terminal-remote host prot TCP/IP. It is the Internet stand terminal connection service (f gous to SET HOST functiona	
Terminator	A special connector used on Ethernet segment that provid tion resistance needed for th	

User-to-network interface (UNI)	Generally described as any connection that directly links a user's device to an ATM network, through an ATM switch. See NNI.
UUCP	File transfer and remote command execution are the main objectives. Most host machines run the UNIX operating system. In addition to mail, much traffic is generated in response to USENET news.
Value-added network	A privately owned packet-switched network whose services are sold to the public.
VCC	See virtual channel connection.
VCI	See virtual channel identifier.
Virtual channel connection (BCC)	A concatenation of virtual channel links between two endpoints where higher layer protocols are accessed. By definition, ATM cell sequence must be preserved over a BCC.
Virtual channel identifier (NCI)	An identifying value found in the header of each ATM cell.
Virtual circuit	A packet-switching service in which a connection (virtual circuit) is established between two stations at the start of transmission. All packets follow the same route. Thus, packets do not carry a complete address and always arrive in sequence.
Virtual local area network (VLAN)	A logical collection of member endpoints and network devices grouped together in a secure, autonomous domain where no broadcast and multicast traffic can enter or leave that domain. Membership in a VLAN is not restricted by physical location. VLANs in ATM networks may be built upon emulated LANs. See LAN emulation.
Virtual path connection (VPC)	A concatenation of virtual path links between two points in which the VCI values are either reassigned or terminated. Several VCCs may be bundled into one VPC.
Virtual path identifier (VPI)	An identifying value found in the header of each ATM cell.
VLAN	See virtual local area network.
VPC	See virtual path connection.
VPI	See virtual path identifier.

X.21	A network access standard for connecting stations to a circuit-switched network. Includes OSI layers 1–3 functionality.
X.25	The CCITT three-layered interface architecture for packet switching connecting a DTE to a DCE.
X.75	An internetworking protocol that provides virtual circuit service across multiple X.25 networks.
X.400	CCITT developed the X.400 family of standards for MHS. The standard defines the MHS model consisting of user agents and message transfer agents, discusses naming and addressing, defines interpersonal messaging and message transfer services.
X.500	CCITT standard for directories for OSI networks.
XMI	A 100-Mbps bus used to connect CPUs, BI buses and memory on VAX 6200 series of parallel processors.
Yellow Pages or Network Information Service	A distributed database lookup service that maintains a set of databases and propagates updated databases among systems on the IP network to ensure consistency.

Appendix C: Acronyms

AAL	ATM adaptation layer
ABR	Available bit rate
AFI	Authority and format identifier
ANSI	American National Standards Institute
ARP	Address resolution protocol
ARPANET	Advanced Research Projects Agency Network
ASCII	American standard code for information interchange
ASN	Abstract syntax notation
BBN	Bolt Beranek and Newman Communications Corporation
BECN	Backwards explicit congestion notification
BGP	Border gateway protocol
B-ICI	Broadband inter-carrier interface
B-ISDN	Broadband integrated services digital network
BITNET	Because It's Time Network
CAC	Connection admission control
CBR	Constant bit rate
CATV	Community antenna TV (cable television)
CCITT	International Consultative Committee on Telegraphy and Telephony
CERT	Computer emergency response team
CI	Computer interconnect
CIAC	Computer Incident Advisory Council
CISC	Complex instruction set computer
CLNP	Connectionless network protocol
CLNS	Connectionless-Mode Network Service
CLP	Cell loss priority
CO	Central office
CORBA	Common object request broker architecture
CONS	Connection-mode Network Service
CMIP	Common management information protocol
CMOT	CMIP on TCP/IP

COSE	Common open software environment	
CPC	Common part convergence sublayer	
CPE	Customer premise equipment	
CRC	Cyclic redundancy check	
CS	Convergence sublayer	
CSMA/CD	Carrier-sense multiple access with collision detection	
CSNET	Computer Science Network	
CSU	Channel service unit	
DAP	Data access protocol	
DARPA	Defense Advanced Research Projects Agency	
DCE	Data circuit-terminating equipment	
DCE	Distributed computing environment	
DDCMP	Digital data communications message protocol	
DEBNA	Digital Ethernet BI network adapter	
DELNI	Digital Ethernet local network interconnect	
DELUA	Digital Ethernet LAN UNIBUS adapter	
DEMPR	Digital Ethernet multiport repeater	
DEQNA	Digital Ethernet LAN Q-bus adapter	
DES	Data encryption standard	
DESPR	Digital Ethernet single-port repeater	
DESTA	Digital Ethernet station adapter	
DESVA	Digital Ethernet small VAX adapter	
DFS	Distributed file system	
DLCI	Data link connection indicator	
DME	Distributed management environment	
DNA	Digital network architecture	
DNS	Domain name service	
DQS	Distributed queuing service	
DS-1	Digital signal level 1	
DS-3	Digital signal level 3	
DSP	Domain specific part	
DSAP	Destination service access point	
DSU	Digital service unit	
DTE	Data terminal equipment	
DXI	Data exchange interface	
EARN	European Academic Research Network	
EBCDIC	Extended binary coded decimal interchange code	
EGP	Exterior gateway protocol	
EIA	Electronics Industries Association	
EMA	Enterprise management architecture	
EN	Enterprise Network Roundtable	

ESI	End station identifier	
FAL	File access listener	
FCS	Frame check sequence	
FDM	Frequency division multiplexing	
FDDI	Fiber distributed data interface	
FECN	Forwards explicit congestion notification	
FIPS	Federal information processing standard	
FTAM	File transfer, access, and management	
FTP	File transfer protocol	
Gbps	Gigabits per second	
GCRA	Generic cell rate algorithm	
GOSIP	Government open systems interconnect profile	
HDLC	High-level data link control	
HIPPI	High–performance parallel interface	
HSC	Hierarchical storage controller	
ICMP	Internet control message protocol	
IDI	Initial domain identifier	
IDP	Initial domain part	
IDRP	Inter-domain routing protocol	
IEEE	Institute of Electrical and Electronic Engineers	
IETF	Internet Engineering Task Force	
IGRP	Interior gateway routing protocol	
ILMI	Interim local management interface	
IMP	Interface message processor	
IP	Internet protocol	
IPX	Internet packet exchange	
ISDN	Integrated services digital network	
IS-IS	Intermediate system to intermediate system protocol	
ISSI	Inter-switching system interfaces	
ISO	International Standards Organization	
ITU	International Telecommunications Union (formerly CCITT)	
JANET	Joint Academic Network	
LAN	Local area network	
LAP-B	Link access protocol - balanced	
LAT	Local area transport protocol	
LAVc	Local area VAX cluster	
LBA	Leaky-bucket algorithm	
LEC	LAN emulation client	
LENNI	LAN emulation NNI	

LES	LAN Emulation Service
LIS	Logical IP subnetworks
LLC	Logical link control
LSP	Link state PDU
LUNI	LAN emulation UNI
MAC	Medium access control
MAN	Metropolitan area network
Mbps	Millions of (mega) bits per second
MFENET	Magnetic Fusion Energy Network
MHS	Message handling systems
MIB	Management information base
MICE	Management information, control, and exchange
MNP	Microcom networking protocol
MOTIS	Message-oriented text interchange systems
MPEG	Motion Picture Experts Group
MTU	Maximum transfer unit
NBMA	Nonbroadcast multiple access
NBS	National Bureau of Standards
NCS	Network computing system
NDIS	Network driver interface specification
NetBIOS	Network basic input output system
NCL	Network control language
NCP	Network control program
NeWS	Network extensible window system
NFS	Network file system
NHRP	Next hop resolution protocol
NIC	Network information center
NIS	Network Information Service
NNI	Network node interface
NLPID	Network layer protocol ID
NPDU	Network layer protocol data unit
NRZI	Nonreturn to zero inverted
NSAP	Network service access point
NSF	National Science Foundation
NSFNET	National Science Foundation Network
NSP	Network services protocol
OAM	Operations and maintenance
OC-n	Optical carrier-n
ODI	Open datalink interface
OSF	Open Software Foundation

OSI	Open systems interconnection
OSI/RM	Open systems interconnection/reference model
OSPF	Open shortest path first
PAD	Packet assembler disassembler
PBX	Private branch exchange
PCSA	Personal computing systems architecture
PDN	Public data network
PDU	Protocol data unit
PING	Packet Internet groper
PMD	Physical medium dependent
PMDF	Pascal memo distribution facility
P-NNI	Private network-to-node interface
POTS	Plain, ordinary telephone system
PSN	Packet switch node
PTI	Payload type identifier
PVC	Permanent virtual circuit
QoS	Quality of service
RARP	Reverse address resolution protocol
RBOC	Regional Bell operating company
RIP	Routing information protocol
RISC	Reduced instruction set computers
RMS	Record management services
ROLC	Routing over large clouds
RPC	Remote procedure call
SAA	System application architecture
SAAL	Signaling ATM adaptation layer
SAR	Segmentation and reassembly
SCA	System communication architecture
SDH	Synchronous digital hierarchy
SEAL	Simple and efficient adaptation layer
SMDS	Switched Multimegabit Data Service
SMTP	Simple mail transfer protocol
SNAP	Sub network access protocol
SNMP	Simple network management protocol
SONET	Synchronous optical network
SPARC	Scalable processor architecture
SRTS	Synchronous residual time stamp
SS	Switching system
SSCS	Service specific convergence sublayer
SSCO	Service specific connection-oriented protocol

SSAP	Source service access point
STM	Synchronous transfer mode
STS-n	Synchronous transport signal-n
SVC	Switched virtual circuit
TC	Transmission convergence
TCP	Transmission control protocol
TCP/IP	Transmission control protocol/Internet protocol
TDM	Time division multiplexing
TFTP	Trivial file transfer protocol
TLI	Transport layer interface
TOP	Technical and office protocols
UBR	Unspecified bit rate
UDP	User datagram protocol
UI	UNIX International
UNI	User-to-network interface
UNMA	Unified network management architecture (AT&T)
UPC	Usage parameter control
USL	UNIX System Laboratories
UUCP	UNIX to UNIX copy
VAN	Value-added network
VMTP	Versatile message transaction protocol
VBR	Variable bit rate
VC	Virtual channel
VCC	Virtual channel connection
VCFC	Virtual connection flow control
VCI	Virtual channel identifier
VLAN	Virtual local area network
VP	Virtual path
VPC	Virtual path connection
VPI	Virtual path identifier
VTAM	Virtual telecommunications access method
VTP	Virtual terminal protocol
WABI	Windows application binary interface
WAN	Wide area network
WOSA	Windows open services architecture
XDR	External data representation
XNS	Xerox network standard
YP	Yellow Pages (now called NIS)

Appendix D: InterNIC Internet Service Providers List

The following information was made available courtesy of InterNIC Information Services, General Atomics (GA), P.O. Box #85608, San Diego, CA 92186-9784.

Service Provider	Phone Number	Fax Number	e-mail Address
Alternet	(800) 4UUNET3		alternet-info@uunet.uu.net
ANS	(800) 456-8267	(703) 758-7717	info@ans.net
BARRNet	(415) 725-1790	(415) 725-3119	info@barrnet.net
CERFnet	(800) 876-2373 or (619) 455-3900	(619) 455-3990	sales@cerf.net
CICnet	(800) 947-4754 or (1313) 998-6703	(313) 998-6105	info@cic.net
CO Supernet	(303) 273-3472	(303) 273-3475	gcook@csn.org
CONCERT	(919) 248-1999	(919) 248-1405	info@concert.net
CSUnet	(310) 985-9661		nethelp@csu.net
Digintal Express Group, John Todd	(800) 969-9090	(301) 220-0477	sales@access.digex.net
EarthLink Network, Inc.	(213) 644-9500	(213) 644-9510	info@earthlink.net
Fxnet	(704) 338-4670	(704) 338-4679	info@fx.net
HoloNet	(510) 704-0160	(510) 704-8019	support@holonet.net
Global Enterprise Services, Inc	(800) 35-TIGER	(609) 897-7310	market@jvnc.net
IACNet	(513) 887-8877		info@iac.net
ICNet	(313) 998-0090		info@ic.net
Interaccess	(708) 498-4542		tom@interaccess.com

International Connections Manager	(703) 904-2230		rcollet@icml.icp.net
Internetworks	(503) 233-4774	(503) 233-4773	info@i.net
Interpath	(800) 849-6305 or (919) 890-6305	(919) 890-6319	info@interpath.net
Los Nettos	(310) 822-1511	(310) 823-6714	los-nettos-info@isi.edu
MCSNet	(312) 248-8649	(312) 248-8649	info@mcs.net
MichNet/Merit	(313) 764-9430	(313) 747-3185	info@merit.edu
MIDnet	(402) 472-7600	(402) 172-5640	nic@westie.mid.net
MRNet	(612) 342-2570	612) 342-2873	info@MR.Net
MSEN	(313) 998-4562	(313) 998-4563	info@msen.com
NEARNET	(617) 873-8730	(617) 873-5620	nearnet-join@near.net
NETCOM	(800) 501-8649 or (408) 554-8649	(408) 241-9145	info@netcom.com
netILLINOIS	(708) 866-1825	(708) 866-1857	p-roll@nwu.edu
NevadaNet	(702) 784-4827	(702) 784-1108	braddlee@nevada.edu
Northcoast Internet	(707) 443-8696		support@northcoast.com
NorthwestNet	(206) 562-3000	(206) 562-4822	info@nwnet.net
NYSERNet	(315) 453-2912	(315) 453-3052	info@nysernet.org
OARnet	(614) 292-8100	(614) 292-7168	alison@oar.net
PACCOM	(808) 956-3499		torben@hawaii.edu
PREPnet	(412) 268-7870	(412) 268-7875	twb+@andrew.cmu.edu
PSCNET	(412) 268-4960	(412) 268-5832	pscnet-admin@psc.edu
PSINet	(800) 82PSI82 or (703) 620-6651	(703) 620-2430 or (800) 79FAX79 (FAXBACK)	info@psi.com
Red River Net	(701) 232-2227		lien@rrnet.com
SeaNet	(206) 343-7828	(206) 628-0722	igor@seanet.com
Sesquinet	(713) 527-4988	(713) 527-6099	farrell@rice.edu
SprintLink	(800) 817-7755	(703) 904-2680	info@sprintlink.net
SURAnet	(301) 982-4600	(301) 982-4605	kdonalds@sura.net
Synergy Communications	(402) 346-4638	(402) 346-0208	jsaker@synergy.net
THEnet	(512) 471-2444	(512) 471-2449	f.sayre@utexas.edu
VERnet	(804) 924-0616	(804) 982-4715	net-info@ver.net
Westnet	(303) 491-7260	(303) 491-1958	pburns@yuma.acns.colostate.edu
WiscNet	(608) 262-8874	(608) 262-4679	tad@cs.wisc.edu
WVNET	(304) 293-5192	(304) 293-5540	cc011041@wvnvms.wvnet.edu

Appendix E: Internet Address Application

Appendix E is a copy of the form required to obtain an Internet address.

This form must be completed as part of the application process for obtaining an Internet Protocol (IP) Network Number. To obtain an Internet number, please provide the following information online, via electronic mail, to HOSTMASTER@INTERNIC.NET. If electronic mail is not available to you, please mail hard copy to:

Network Solutions
InterNIC Registration Services
505 Huntmar Park Drive
Herndon, VA 22070

–OR–

FAX to (703) 742-4811

Once Registration Services receives your completed application we will send you an acknowledgment, via electronic or postal mail.

Note: This application is solely for obtaining a legitimate IP network number assignment. If you're interested in officially registering a domain please complete the domain application found in templates/domain-template.txt. If FTP is not available to you, please contact HOSTMASTER@INTERNIC.NET or phone the NIC at (703) 742-4777 for further assistance.

ATTENTION:

European network requests should use the European template (templates/european-ip- template.txt). Please follow their instructions for submission.

Networks that will be connected/located within the geographic region maintained by the Asian-Pacific NIC should use the APNIC template (templates/apnic-001.txt). Please follow their instructions for submission.

*** NONCONNECTED NETWORKS ***

If the networks you are requesting address space for will NEVER TO BE CONNECTED TO THE INTERNET, YOU ARE REQUIRED TO REFER TO AND ADHERE TO THE GUIDELINES SET FORTH IN RFC 1597, UNDER SECTION 3 "PRIVATE ADDRESS SPACE". This RFC contains important information regarding the Policies/Procedures that are to be implemented when IP address space is requested for networks that will NEVER be connected to the Internet. A large portion of address space (one (1) class A, sixteen (16) class Bs and two-hundred fifty-six (256) class Cs) has been reserved for address allocation for non-connected networks. Please obtain the IP address space you require by utilizing the IP address range(s) that have been reserved by the IANA for use by all non-connected networks specified in this RFC. RFC 1597 may be obtained via anonymous FTP from DS.INTERNIC.NET (198.49.45.10).

YOUR APPLICATION MUST BE TYPED.

Step 1

If the network will be connected to the Internet, you must provide the name of the governmental sponsoring organization or commercial service provider, and the name, title, mailing address, phone number, net mailbox, and NIC Handle (if any) of the contact person (POC) at that organization who has authorized the network connection. This person will serve as the POC for administrative and policy questions about authorization to be a part of the Internet. Examples of such sponsoring organizations are: DISA DNS, The National Science Foundation (NSF), or similar government, educational or commercial network service providers.

NOTE: IF THE NETWORK WILL NEVER BE CONNECTED TO THE INTERNET, PLEASE UTILIZE THE ADDRESS SPACE RESERVED FOR NON-CONNECTED NETWORKS THAT IS SPECIFIED IN RFC 1597. IF YOU INTEND TO CONNECT THIS NETWORK TO THE INTERNET BUT HAVE NOT YET CHOSEN A SERVICE PROVIDER, LEAVE THIS SECTION BLANK, BUT INDICATE THE APPROXIMATE DATE OF YOUR INTERNET CONNECTION IN SECTION 9 OF THIS TEMPLATE. IF YOU INTEND TO CONNECT TO THE INTERNET AND HAVE ALREADY CHOSEN A PROVIDER, YOU ARE REQUIRED TO SUBMIT THIS REQUEST TO YOUR SERVICE PROVIDER FOR PROCESSING. SERVICE PROVIDERS ARE ALLOCATED BLOCKS OF ADDRESSES TO SUPPORT THE NETWORKING NEEDS OF THEIR CUSTOMERS. THIS PROCEDURE WILL ENSURE THAT THE NUMBER OF ENTRIES ADDED TO THE INTERNET ROUTING TABLES IS KEPT TO A MINIMUM, AND CIDR IS USED AS EFFICIENTLY AS POSSIBLE. THE ABOVE PROCEDURES PERTAIN EXCLUSIVELY TO REQUESTS FOR CLASS C ADDRESS(ES).

Sponsoring organization:
Contact name (lastname, firstname):
Contact title:
Mail Address:
Phone:
Net mailbox:
NIC handle (if known):

Step 2

Provide the name, title, mailing address, phone number, and organization of the technical Point-of-Contact (POC). The on-line mailbox and NIC Handle (if any) of the technical POC should also be included. This is the POC for resolving technical problems associated with the network and for updating information about the network. The technical POC may also be responsible for hosts attached to this network.

Technical POC name (Lastname, Firstname):
NIC handle (if known):
Technical POC title:
Mail address:
Phone:
Net mailbox:

Step 3

Supply the SHORT mnemonic name for the network (up to 12 characters). This is the name that will be used as an identifier in Internet name and address tables. The only special character that may be used in a network name is a dash (-). PLEASE DO NOT USE PERIODS OR UNDERSCORES. The syntax XXXX.com and XXXX.net are not valid network naming conventions and should only be used when applying for a domain.

Network name:

Step 4

Identify the geographic location of the network and the organization responsible for establishing the network.

Postal address for main/headquarters network site:
Name of organization:

Step 5

Question #5 is for MILITARY or DoD requests, ONLY. If you require that this connected network be announced to the NSFNET please answer questions 5a, 5b, and 5c. IF THIS NETWORK WILL BE CONNECTED TO THE INTERNET VIA MILNET, THIS APPLICATION MUST BE SUBMITTED TO HOSTMASTER-@NIC.DDN.MIL FOR REVIEW/PROCESSING.

Do you want MILNET to announce your network to the NSFNET? (Y/N):
Do you have an alternate connection, other than MILNET, to the NSFNET? (please state alternate connection if answer is yes):
If you've answered yes to 5b, please state if you would like the MILNET connection to act as a backup path to the NSFNET? (Y/N):

Step 6

Estimate the size of the network to include the number of hosts and subnets/segments that will be supported by the network. A "host" is defined as any device (PC, printer, etc.) that will be assigned an address from the host portion of the network number. A host may also be characterized as a node or device.

Host Information

_____

    Initially:
    Within one year:
    Within two years:
    Within five years:
Subnet/Segment Information

_____

    Initially:
    Within one year:
    Within two years:
    Within five years:

Step 7

Unless a strong and convincing reason is presented, the network (if it qualifies at all) will be assigned a single class C network number. If a class C network number is not acceptable for your purposes, you are required to submit substantial, detailed justification in support of your requirements.

THE NIC WOULD STRONGLY SUGGEST YOU CONSIDER SUBNETTING CLASS C ADDRESSES WHEN MULTIPLE SEGMENTS WILL BE USED TO SUPPORT A MINIMAL AMOUNT OF HOST ADDRESSES. MULTIPLE CLASS C NUMBERS SHOULD BE UTILIZED WHEN IT IS NECESSARY TO SUPPORT MORE THAN 256 HOSTS ON A SINGLE NETWORK. YOU MAY WISH TO CONFER WITH A NETWORK CONSULTANT AND ROUTER VENDOR FOR ADDITIONAL INFORMATION.

(Note: If there are plans for more than a few local networks, and more than 100 hosts, you are strongly urged to consider subnetting. [Reference RFC 950 and RFC 1466])

Reason:

Step 8

Networks are characterized as being either Research, Educational, Government-Non Defense, or Commercial, and the network address space is shared between these four areas. Which type is this network?

Type of network:

Step 9

What is the purpose of the network?

Purpose:

For further information contact InterNIC Registration Services:

Via electronic mail:	HOSTMASTER@INTERNIC.-NET
Via telephone:	(703) 742-4777
Via postal mail:	Network Solutions InterNIC Registration Service 505 Huntmar Park Drive Herndon, VA 22070

SELECT BIBLIOGRAPHY
(Available via anonymous FTP from DS.INTERNIC.NET or 198.49.45.10 or call 1-619-455-4600.)

Gerich, E., *Guidelines for Management of IP Address Space*, Ann Arbor, MI: Merit Network, Inc.; May 1993; RFC 1466. 10 p. (DS.INTERNIC.NET RFC1466.TXT). Rekhter, Y., Moskowitz. B., Karrenberg, D., and de Groot, G., *Address Allocation for Private Internets*, IBM Corp., Chrysler Corp., RIPE NCC; March 1994; RFC 1597 (DS.INTERNIC.NET RFC1597.TXT).

Braden, R. T., and J. B. Postel, *Requirements for Internet Gateways*, Marina del Rey, CA: University of Southern California, Information Sciences Inst., June 1987; RFC 1009 (DS.INTERNET.NET POLICY RFC1009.TXT).

Internet Engineering Task Force, R. T. Braden, *Requirements for Internet Hosts–Communication Layers*, Marina del Rey, CA: University of Southern California, Information Sciences Inst., October 1989, RFC 1122 (DS.INTERNIC.NET RFC1122.TXT).

Internet Engineering Task Force, R. T. Braden, *Requirements for Internet Hosts–Application and Support*, Marina del Rey, CA: University of Southern California, Information Sciences Inst., October 1989, RFC 1123 (DS.INTERNIC.NET RFC1123.TXT).

Internet Activities Board, Internet Official Protocol Standards, March 1994, RFC 1600 (DS.INTERNIC.NET POLICY RFC1600.TXT). [Note: the current version is available as "STD 1".]

Mogul, J., and J. B. Postel, *Internet Standard Subnetting Procedure*, Stanford, CA: Stanford University, August 1985, RFC 950 (DS.INTERNIC.NET POLICY RFC950.TXT).

Postel, J. B., *Internet Control Message Protocol*, Marina del Rey, CA: University of Southern California, Information Sciences Inst., September 1981, RFC 792 (DS.INTERNIC.NET POLICY RFC792.TXT).

Postel, J. B., *Transmission Control Protocol*, Marina del Rey, CA: University of Southern California, Information Sciences Inst., September 1981, RFC 793 (DS.INTERNIC.NET POLICY RFC793.TXT).

Postel, J. B., *Address Mappings*, Marina del Rey, CA: University of Southern California, Information Sciences Inst., September 1981, RFC 796 (DS.INTERNIC.NET POLICY RFC796.TXT). Obsoletes: IEN 115 (NACC 0968-79).

Postel, J. B., *User Datagram Protocol*, Marina del Rey, CA: University of Southern California, Information Sciences Inst., August 28, 1980, RFC 768 (DS.INTERNIC.NET POLICY RFC768.TXT).

Postel, J. B., *Internet Protocol*, Marina del Rey, CA: University of Southern California, Information Sciences Inst., September 1981, RFC 791 (DS.INTERNIC.NET POLICY RFC791.TXT).

Reynolds, J. K., and J. B. Postel, *Assigned Numbers*, Marina del Rey, CA: University of Southern California, Information Sciences Inst., July 1982, RFC 1340 (DS.INTERNIC.NET POLICY RFC1340.TXT). [Note: the current version is available as "STD 2".]

Appendix F: Domain Registration Application

Appendix F is a copy of the form required to register a domain.

To establish a domain, the following information must be sent to the InterNIC Registration Services (HOSTMASTER@INTERNIC.NET). Either this template, or the "short form" following this template, may be used.

The name of the top-level domain to join (EDU, GOV, COM, NET, ORG).

Top-level domain:

The name of the domain (up to 24 characters). This is the name that will be used in tables and lists associating the domain with the domain servers addresses. While domain names can be quite long, the use of shorter, more user-friendly names is recommended.

Complete domain name:

The name and address of the organization for which the domain is being established.

Organization name:
Organization address:

The date you expect the domain to be fully operational.

Date operational:

Note: The key people must have electronic mailboxes (even if in the domain being registered) and "handles" (unique InterNIC database identifiers). If you have access to "WHOIS", please check to see if the contacts are registered and if so, include only the handle and changes (if any) that need to be made in the entry. If you do not have access to "WHOIS", please provide all the information indicated and a handle will be assigned.

The handle of the administrative head of the organization in (3) or this person's name, postal address, phone number, organization, and network e-mailbox. This is the contact point for administrative and policy questions about the domain.

Administrative Contact
    Handle (if known):
    Name (Last, First):
    Organization:
    Postal Address:
    Phone Number:
    Net Mailbox:

The handle of the technical contact for the domain or this person's name, mailing address, phone number, organization, and network mailbox. This is the contact point for problems and updates regarding the domain or zone.

Technical and Zone Contact
    Handle (if known):
    Name (Last, First):
    Organization:
    Postal Address:
    Phone Number:
    Net Mailbox:

Note: Domains must provide at least two independent servers for translating names to addresses for hosts in the domain. The servers should be in physically separate locations and on different networks if possible. The servers should be active and responsive to DNS queries BEFORE this application is submitted. Incomplete information in Sections 7 and 8 or inactive servers will result in delay of the registration.

The primary server information.

Primary Server Hostname:
Primary Server Netaddress:
Primary Server Hardware:
Primary Server Software:

The secondary server information.

Secondary Server Hostname:
Secondary Server Netaddress:
Secondary Server Hardware:
Secondary Server Software:

Please briefly describe the organization for which this domain is being registered. If the domain is for an organization that already has a domain registered, please describe the purpose of this domain.

For further information contact InterNIC Registration Services:

Via electronic mail:	HOSTMASTER@INTERNIC.NET
Via telephone:	(703) 742-4777
Via facsimile:	(703) 742-4811
Via postal mail:	Network Solutions
	InterNIC Registration Services
	505 Huntmar Park Drive
	Herndon, VA 22070

The party requesting registration of this name certifies that, to her/his knowledge, the use of this name does not violate trademark or other statutes. Registering a domain name does not confer any legal rights to that name and any disputes between parties over the rights to use a particular name are to be settled between the contending parties using normal legal methods. (See RFC 1591)

Top-level domain......:
Complete Domain Name.:

Organization name....:
Organization address.:

Operational Date.....:

Administrative Contact:
    NIC Handle (if known):
    Name (Last, First)...:
    Organization.........:
    Postal Address.......:
    Phone Number.........:
    Net Mailbox..........:

Technical/Zone Contact:
    NIC Handle (if known):
    Name (Last, First)...:
    Organization.........:
    Postal Address.......:
    Phone Number.........:
    Net Mailbox..........:

    Prime Server Hostname...:
    Prime Server Netaddress.:
    Prime Server Hardware...:
    Prime Server Software...:

Second Server Hostname..:
Second Server Netaddress:
Second Server Hardware..:
Second Server Software..:

Domain/Org Purpose/Desc.:
Notes: In Sections 3b, 5d, & 6d use multiple lines for addresses. If contacts are registered, only 5a and 6a are needed. If servers are registered, only 7a, b and 8a, b are needed. If there is more than one secondary server, just copy Section 8. The party requesting registration of this name certifies that, to her/his knowledge, the use of this name does not violate trademark or other statues.

Registering a domain name does not confer any legal rights to that name and any disputes between parties over the rights to use a particular name are to be settled between the contending parties using normal legal methods. (See RFC 1591.)

SELECT BIBLIOGRAPHY

Albitz, P., and C. Liu, *DNS and Bind Help for UNIX System Administrators*, O'Reilly and Associates, Inc., October 1992.

Postel, J., *Domain Name System Structure and Delegation*, Marina del Rey, CA: University of Southern California, Information Sciences Inst. March 1994, RFC 1591 <rs.internic.net:policy/rfc1034.txt>.

Cooper, Postel, *The US Domain*, Marina del Rey, CA: University of Southern California, Information Sciences Inst., December 1992, RFC 1480 <rs.internic.net:policy/rfc1480.txt>.

Stahl, M. K., *Domain Administrators Guide*, Menlo Park, CA: SRI International, DDN Network Information Center, November 1987, RFC 1032 (.internic.net:policy/rfc1032.txt>.

Lottor, M., *Domain Administrators Operations Guide*, Menlo Park, CA: SRI International, DDN Network Information Center, November 1987, RFC 1033 <rs.internic.net:policy/rfc1033.txt>.

Mockapetris, P., *Domain Names–Concepts and Facilities*, Marina del Rey, CA: University of Southern California, Information Sciences Inst., November 1987, RFC 1034 <rs.internic.net:policy/rfc1034.txt>.

Mockapetris, P., *Domain Names–Implementation and Specification*, Marina del Rey, CA: University of Southern California, Information Sciences Inst., November 1987, RFC 1035 <rs.internic.net:policy/rfc1035.txt>.

Mockapetris, P., *DNS Encoding of Network Names and Other Types*, Marina del Rey, CA: University of Southern California, Information Sciences Inst., April 1989, RFC 1101 <rs.internic.net:policy/rfc1101.txt>.

Appendix G: IP Version 6

Appendix G describes how the new version of IP, referred to as IP version6 or IPv6, works.

The current version of IP is 4. The new version of IP is 6. It is in a draft phase with the final specifications not yet complete. You can get a copy of the draft document from **ftp.cnri.reston.va.us**. The Internet Engineering Task Force (IETF) selected IPv6 from several competing proposals, one of which was called TCP and UDP with Bigger Addresses (TUBA). The OSI/RM's addressing structure was used in the TUBA proposal.

The main objective of IPv6 is to enable the Internet to grow and support over a million interconnected networks. Further, compatibility with IPv4 is also important, since it provides the basis for the Internet and TCP/IP networks today.

Some important features of IPv6 are:

- Addressing structure has been increased from 32 bits (IPv4) to 128 bits (IPv6). This may be viewed as eight 16-bit double bytes (octets). The address is represented in hexadecimal (similar to Ethernet addresses). For example, 10A6:1534:242B:1234:3410:9817:24AB:1050.
- IPv4 features such as fragmentation are now handled as options in IPv6.
- Checksum field has been removed.
- Support is provided for IPv4-mapped IPv6 address. The IPv4 address space is directly represented in the IPv6 address space.

Figure G-1 describes the IPv6 header.
The following is a brief description of fields in IPv6:

- Version (4 bits): IP version number. Set to 6.
- Flow Label (28 bits): A way to uniquely identify a specific set of packets. It may be used for prioritizing packet processing.
- Payload Length (16 bits): Provides the same function as the datagram-length field in IPv4. The overall size of an IP datagram is still limited to 64 KB.

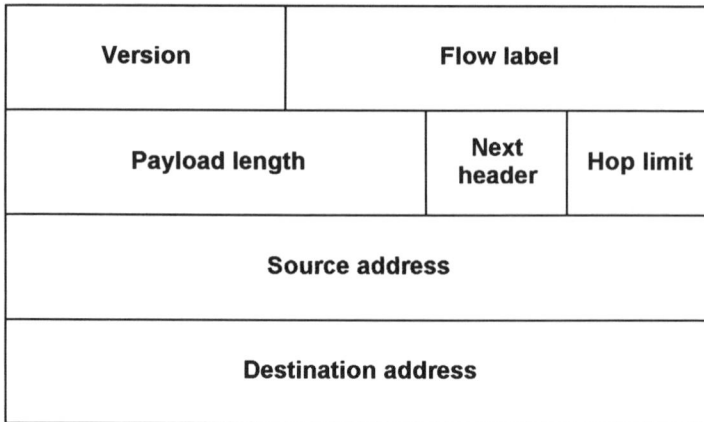

Figure G-1 IPv6 header format.

- Next Header (8 bits): Provides the same function as the protocol type field in IPv4—it identifies if the next higher layer protocol encapsulated is TCP, UDP, or ICMP.
- Hop Limit (16 bits): Provides the same function as the Time-to-Live (TTL) field in IPv4. The hop limit value is decremented each time the datagram is forwarded by a router—the timer decrement is no longer supported.
- Source Address (128 bits): Address of the system that generated this message.
- Destination Address (128 bits): Final (target) system address.

About the Author

Uday O. Pabrai, recognized nationally for his work in network computing, is the author of several texts including a forthcoming title on security to be published by McGraw-Hill. Mr. Pabrai has consulted extensively on various network, operating system, and related application technologies. Previously, Mr. Pabrai led the System Integration Group at Fermi National Accelerator Laboratory. Projects executed by Mr. Pabrai include benchmarking of RISC-based systems and the design and development of client/server applications which established connectivity between Solaris, AIX, ULTRIX, VMS, and mainframe systems.

As a key member of the Supercomputing Task Force, he designed procedures for global (LAN/WAN) access to open UNIX systems. While working as a network manager at Teradyne's Telecom Division, Mr. Pabrai worked with X and NFS to determine network load and configuration of client/server systems.

In addition to his industry work, Mr. Pabrai has presented for Net Guru Technologies, Inc., several classes including Hands-On Security for UNIX and TCP/IP Networks, Network Fundamentals, TCP/IP Internetworking, SNMP Network Management, Introduction to UNIX, and UNIX Internetworking throughout the United States. Mr. Pabrai has published numerous papers in various technical magazines, including the *IEEE Communications*, *DataPro*, *UNIX Review*, and the *VAX Professional*. Mr. Pabrai received his BS degree in Computer Engineering from Clemson University and his MS degree in Electrical Engineering from Illinois Institute of Technology. His thesis subject was "Network Security Design for UNIX Systems in a Distributed Environment."

Mr. Pabrai may be reached at Net Guru Technologies, Inc., at (708) 574–4878 or e-mail pabrai@eagle.ais.net.

Note: If you have an interest in any classes on TCP/IP, Internet connectivity, Windows NT, UNIX or networks, you may reach NGT at (708) 574–4878.

Index

3BSD, 4
100Base-X, 43–46
100VG-AnyLAN, 44–46

AAL. *See* ATM adaptation layer
Absolute mode, 227
Abstract syntax notation 1, 349–50
accept system call, 277
Access, to client/server
    using nischmod command, 189
    control of, 218–19
    demand priority, 45
    frame relay rates, 50–51
    restricted, 178–79
    rights to, 235
    unrestricted, 179
Account access, 222–23
Acknowledgment flag field, 74
Acknowledgment number field, 74
Acknowledgment message, 97
Active monitor, 46
Adapter card, 45
Additional packet mode bearer service, 47
    See also Frame relay
Address(es)
    AppleTalk, 311–12
    broadcast, 41
    determination of, 28
    DHCP, 97–98
    Ethernet, 111–12
    Internet, 32, 37–41
    loopback, 39, 108
    mapping, 107
    multicast, 41

    next hop, 343
    notation, 38
    routing and, 343
    subnet masks, 40–41
    UNIX, 124
    well-known, 271–72
    Windows NT, 329
Address extension bit, 49
address-length argument, 277
Address mask reply message, 393–94
Address mask request message, 392–93
Address resolution protocol, 32, 36
    and ATM, 62
    header, 65–67
    and Internet layer, 65–66
Address space, 23
ADN. *See* Advanced digital network
Advanced digital network, 50
Advanced Interactive Executive. *See* AIX
Advanced Research Projects Agency
    Network, 3
AES. *See* Application environment
    specification
AFP. *See* AppleTalk filing protocol
AFS. *See* Andrew File System
Agents, 351
AIX, 8–9
aliases file, 171
American National Standards Institute, 47
ANDing, 40
Andrew File System, 317
Anonymous FTP account, 253–57

ANSI. *See* American National Standards Institute
Any-to-any connectivity, 52
a option, 126, 136, 156
API. *See* Application program interface
AppleTalk, 31, 310–13
AppleTalk filing protocol, 312
Application environment specification, 6
Application layer, 37
    bootstrap protocol, 94–96
    dynamic host configuration protocol, 96–98
Application program interface, 260
ARP. *See* Address resolution protocol
arp command, 135–36
ARPANET. *See* Advanced Research Projects Agency Network
ASET. *See* Automated security enhancement tool
ASN.1. *See* Abstract syntax notation 1
Asset, 213
Assignments, 103
Association, 260, 269
Asynchronous transfer mode, 25, 52
    at desktop, 62–63
    cells, 59–60
    cell switch, 104
    characteristics of, 101–2
    and FDDI, 46
    and IP and ARP, 62
    layers, 55–57
    need for, 53–54
    network characteristics, 54–55
    planes, 58
    service classes, 58
    standards, 53
    vendors, 63
    virtual channels/paths, 61–62
ATM. *See* Asynchronous transfer mode
ATM adaptation layer, 53, 55, 57
ATMARP, 62
ATM Forum, 53
Attacks, security, 214, 217–18
Audit trail, 219
Authentication
    Kerberos system, 249–51
    network file system, 233
    network information service +, 180
    as security service, 218–19
Authorization
    categories for, 235
    network information service +, 180
Auto-configuration, 23

auto-direct file, 167
auto-master file, 166
Automated security enhancement tool, 236–39
Automatic IP address allocation, 98
automount command, 122, 168
Automounter, 165–68
Autonomous system, 322, 343, 347

Backbone switch, 104
Backlog argument, 277
Backward explicit congestion notification, 49
Bandwidth-on-demand, 54
Bank assignment, 103
Baseband transmission, 102
Basic encoding rules, 349
BECN. *See* Backward explicit congestion notification
BER. *See* Basic encoding rules
Berkeley Internet name domain service, 201
Berkeley sockets, 267
    client/server application, 281–89
    system calls, 274–80
Berkeley Software Distribution, 2–4
Berkeley Software Distribution UNIX, 3, 153–58
BGP. *See* Border gateway protocol
B-ICI. *See* B-ISDN Intercarrier Interface
Bind tool, 123
Bindery, 298
Binding the domain, 123
bind system call, 275–76
biod command, 122, 155
B-ISDN. *See* Broadband-integrated services digital network
B-ISDN Intercarrier Interface, 53
Boolean AND operation, 40
bootp command, 321
bootpd command, 112, 121–122
bootptab file, 112–13
Bootstrap protocol, 32, 94–96, 321
Border gateway protocol, 340
Bound state, 97
Bridges, 105, 340
Broadband-integrated services digital network, 53, 55–57
Broadband transmission, 102
Broadcast address, 32, 41
Brouters, 340
BSD. *See* Berkeley Software Distribution
Bus topology, 42

Caching only server, 204, 208–10
Caching server, 203

Index 441

Capture, token ring, 46
Carrier sense, multiple access/collision detect, 41–42, 45
CBS. See Committed burst size
CCITT, 47–48
CD-ROM, 28
Cell loss priority, 59
Cell relay, 52, 105
Cells, ATM, 59–61
   delineation, 56
   header generation, 56
   reordering, 55
   multiplexing, 56
   rate decoupling, 56
Centralized file service, 313
Channel identifier, 55
Channel service unit, 105, 341–42
Checksum field, 74, 92
Child directory, 181
Child process, 16
chmod command, 227–28
CIR. See Committed information rate
CISC. See Complex instruction set computer
CIX. See Commercial Internet Exchange
cklist.rpt, 237
Client configuration
   network file system, 164–65
   network information service, 170, 177
   network information service +, 195–97
   Novell environment, 293
   RPC model, 268
   X, 319
Client node, 2, 27
Client only configuration, DNS, 206–8
Client/server, 25, 27–28
   applications, 259–60
   Berkeley sockets, 267, 274–89
   interprocess communication, 260–66
   iterative/concurrent servers, 274–75
   network information service, 171
   portmapper service, 278–80
   remote procedure calls, 268
   system calls, 275–78
   system strategies, 27–28
   TCP and UDP ports, 269–74
   transport layer interface, 267–68
   UDP broadcast application, 289–91
Client stub, 268
CLNS. See Connectionless-mode network service
close system call, 277
CLP. See Cell loss priority

CMIP. See Common management information protocol
CMOT group, MIB-II, 354
Coherent operating system, 12
Collision detect, 42
Command field, 344
Command/response bit, 49
Commercial Internet Exchange, 144
Committed burst size, 50
Committed information rate, 50–51
Common management information protocol, 350
Common Open Software Environment, 9, 24
Communication devices
   bridges, 105, 340
   brouters, 340
   CSU/DSU, 341–42
   gateways/protocol converters, 341
   hubs, 341
   repeaters, 339
   routers, 340
Complex instruction set computer, 2, 25–26
Compressed serial line Internet protocol, 322
Computer Oracle Password System, 239–47
Concurrent servers, 274–75
Congestion control, 47, 51, 92
Connectionless services, 4, 68, 260, 294
Connection-oriented services, 53, 260
Connection set up, 91
Connection termination, 91
connect system call, 276
Context switching, 23
Control plane, 58
Convergence sublayer, 57
COPS. See Computer Oracle Password System
COSE. See Common Open Software Environment
C/R bit. See Command/response bit
CRC. See Cyclic redundancy check
Credentials, 235
CS. See Convergence sublayer
CSLIP. See Compressed serial line Internet protocol
CSMA/CD. See Carrier sense, multiple access/collision detect
CSU. See Channel service unit
Cursor, 318
Cyclic redundancy check, 323

DARPA. See Defense Advanced Research Projects Agency
Data communication equipment, 341
Data confidentiality, 218

Data exchange interface, 53
Data field, 71, 75
Data file, 172
Datagram ID number, 70
Datagram length field, 70
Datagrams
    defined, 68
    Internet protocol, 36, 72
Datagram server, 120
Data integrity, 218–19
Dataless workstation, 25, 27–28
Data link connection identifier, 48
Data packet priority, 46
Data service unit, 341–42
Data superhighway, 35
Data terminal equipment, 341
Data transmission modes, 101–2
DCE. *See* Data communication equipment; Distributed computing environment
DDS. *See* Digital data set
DE. *See* Discard-eligible
Dedicated access, 50
defaultdomain file, 182
Defense Advanced Research Projects Agency, 3–4
Demand priority, 45
Denial of service, 214
Departmental switch, 104
Destination address
    ARP, 66
    Ethernet, 42–43
    Internet, 70
Destination port field, 74, 92
Destination unreachable message, 383–84
dfmounts command, 163
dfstab file, 158, 160
DFS. *See* Distributed file system
dfshares command, 163
DHCP. *See* Dynamic host configuration protocol
Dial-up capability, 322–23
diff utility, 238
Digital data set, 342
Digital network architecture, 31
Digital service unit, 105
Digital signal hierarchy, 106
Digital signature mechanism, 219
Direct maps, 165–67
Directory permissions, 227
Direct routing, 342
dir file extension, 172
Dirty page clustering, 122

Discard-eligible, 49, 51
Discover message, 97
Disk drives, 29
Diskless workstation, 25, 28, 66, 94
Distance to network field, 345
Distributed applications, 24–25, 259–60, 266
    Berkeley sockets, 267
    remote procedure calls, 268
    TCP and UDP ports, 269–74
    transport layer interface, 267–68
Distributed computing environment, 6
Distributed file system, 7, 313
Distributed management environment, 6
Distributed system management interface tool, 8
DLCI. *See* Data link connection identifier
DME. *See* Distributed management environment
DNA. *See* Digital network architecture
DNS. *See* Domain name service
Domain, 170–71, 182, 202
Domain argument, 275
domainname command, 137
Domain name service, 201–2, 329
    caching only system, 208–10
    client only configuration, 206–8
    master server configuration, 204–6
    nslookup command, 210–11
    processes related to, 123
    server types, 202–4
    uses of, 151
Dotted decimal notation, 38
DSMIT. *See* Distributed system management interface tool
DSU. *See* Data service unit; Digital service unit
DTE. *See* Data terminal equipment
DXI. *See* Data exchange interface
Dynamic host configuration protocol, 96–98, 327–29
Dynamic IP address allocation, 98
Dynamic node assignment, 311
Dynamic routing, 344
Dynamic switching, 103–4

EA bit. *See* Address extension bit
EBS. *See* Excess burst size
Echo protocol, 293
Echo reply message, 389–90
Echo request message, 388–89
EGP. *See* Exterior gateway protocol
EIA. *See* Electronics Industries Association
Electronics Industries Association, 44
E-mail, 314

Encipherment, 219
Encryption, 187, 249–51
End of message, 102
Endpoint, 57, 267
End server, 251
End-to-end layer. *See* Transport layer
Enhanced security, 5–6
Enterprise Systems Architecture, 8
EOM. *See* End of message
Error protocol, NetWare, 293
Error(s)
    codes, 190
    file system, 395
    messages, 382
    packet switching, 105
    read only, 395–96
ES. *See* Enhanced security
ESA. *See* Enterprise Systems Architecture
Ethernet, 3
    at network access layer, 41–46
    Fast Ethernet, 43–45
    reliability of, 25
Ethernet 100VG-AnyLAN, 44–46
Ethernet frames, 36, 65–66
Ethernet local area network switch, 104
ethers file, 111–12, 171
Excess burst size, 50
Execution log, 238
Export function, 151
exportfs command, 156
Export rules, NFS server, 163–64
exports file, 154
Exterior gateway protocol, 340, 343, 347
    MIB-II group, 354, 370–71
External data representation, 9, 152, 268

Family of network field, 344
Fast Ethernet, 43–45
Fast packets, 52, 104–5
FCS. *See* Frame check sequence
FDDI. *See* Fiber distributed data interface
FECN. *See* Forward explicit
        congestion notification
Fiber distributed data interface, 25, 46
Fiber-optic networks, 53–54
FIFO. *See* First in first out
File descriptor, 267
File handle, 153, 163
File permission, 227
File services, AppleTalk, 313–14
File sharing, 313–14
File system, 15–16, 395
File transfer protocol, 139

anonymous account configuration, 253–57
    incoming connections, 231
FIN field, 74
finger command, 147
First in first out, 260
Flag fields, 70, 74
Fonts, 321
f option, 195
Fork system call, 16–17
Forward explicit congestion notification, 49
Forwarding server, 204
Four-wire connection, 44, 101
Fractional T1, 105
Fractional T3, 105
FRAD. *See* Frame relay access device
Fragmentation, Internet datagram, 72
Fragment offset, 70
Frame check sequence, 48
Frame relay
    access rates, 50–51
    at network access layer, 47–52
    congestion control, 51
    Ethernet, 42–43
    header, 44, 48–49
    IEEE, 43
    management, 51–52
    PVC and SVC, 49
    service providers, 51–52
    standards for, 47–48
Frame relay access device, 50
Frame Relay Forum, 47–48
from argument, 277–78
fstab file, 154
fstypes file, 160
FT1. *See* Fractional T1
FTP. *See* File transfer protocol
ftp anonymous account, 145, 203
ftp command, 139–41, 394
Full duplex operation, 101

Gateways, 341
Generic flow control, 59
getsock-name system call, 269
Getty process, 23
GFC. *See* Generic flow control
GID, 228
Global addressing, 51
Graphical user interface, 9, 316
Graphics libraries, 318
GraphOn, 322
group file
    GID definition in, 228
    NIS, 171

group file (cont.)
    specifications for, 20–21
Group of Four, 48
GUI. See Graphical user interface

Half association, 267
Half duplex operation, 101
Hardware length field, 66, 94
Hardware type field, 65, 94
HDLC. See High-level data link control
Header checksum field, 70
Header error control, 56, 60
Header length field, 69, 74
Header(s)
    ARP, 65–67
    ATM cell, 59–60
    bootstrap protocol, 94–96
    Ethernet, 42–44, 66, 68
    frame relay, 48–49
    IEEE specifications, 43
    Internet protocol, 69–71
    Internetwork packet exchange, 294–95
    NetWare core protocol, 298–300
    open shortest path first, 346
    RARP, 68–69
    routing information protocol, 344
    sequenced packet exchange, 296
    transmission control protocol, 73–75
    user datagram protocol, 92
HEC. See Header error control
Hello exchange message, 347
Hesiod, 317
High-level data link control, 48, 323
High-speed serial interface, 342
Hops, 344
Hops field, 94
host.deny file, 247
hostname command, 137
hostname files, 185
Host names
    Ethernet, 111–12
    mapping, 107
hosts.allow file, 247
hosts.deny file, 248
hosts.equiv file, 230–31
hosts file, 39
    changes to, NIS, 172–73
    used in mapping, 107–8
    NIS, 171
    UNIX, 155
    Windows NT, 329
Hosts map, 165, 167
Host-to-host layer. See Transport layer

HP-UX, 7
HSSI. See High-speed serial interface
Hubs, 341
HUP signal, 121
Hybrid workstation, 28

IAB. See Internet Architecture Board
ICMP. See Internet control messages protocol
Icons, 318
IDP. See Internetwork datagram protocol
IEEE. See Institute of Electrical and
        Electronic Engineers
IETF. See Internet Engineering Task Force
ifconfig command, 124–25
Import function, 151
Incremental drive, 29
Index file, 172
Index node. See Inode
Indirect maps, 165–66
Indirect routing, 342
inetd command, 108–9, 114, 120–21
inetd.conf file, 232, 247
Information node. See Inode
Information request and reply message, 394
Initialization, 21–23
    address determination, 28
    client, 196
    and bootptab file, 112
    master server, 174
    and memory management, 23
    root master server, 191
    slave server, 176
    See also Start-up
Initializing state, DHCP, 97
init process, 23
init.d/nfs files, 159–60
inittab file, 21
Inode, 16, 228
Insider attack, 217
Institute of Electrical and Electronic
        Engineers, 43
    LAN standards, 63–64
Integrated services digital network, 50
Interdata 8/32 system, 2
Interface, 32
Interfaces group, MIB-II, 352, 355–58
Interior routing protocol, 343
Intermediate system-to-intermediate
        system, 347–48
International Standards Organization, 33, 213
    See also Security, ISO
Internet architecture
    addresses, 37–41

compared to OSI/RM, 35
layers, 36–37
NII, 35–36
NSF/NREN, 33–35
Internet Architecture Board, 31, 33
Internet control messages
    protocol, 72, 344, 381–83
    address mask messages, 392–94
    destination unreachable message, 383–84
    echo messages, 388–90
    information request and reply, 394
    MIB-II group, 354, 363–65
    parameter problem message, 385–86
    redirect message, 386–88
    source quench message, 386
    time exceeded message, 384–85
    timestamp messages, 390–92
Internet Engineering Task Force, 53, 345
Internet layer, 36, 64–65
    address resolution protocol, 65–66
    reverse address resolution protocol, 66–68
Internet protocol, 31–32, 68–72
    addresses, 97–98
    and ATM, 62
    datagram, 36
    packet report, 71–72
    See also Transmission control protocol/
        Internet protocol
Internet protocol control protocol, 323
Internet protocol group, MIB-II, 352, 359–62
Internet resources, 144–47
Internetwork datagram protocol, 294
Internetworking. *See* Novell Netware; UNIX-
        Macintosh integration; Windows NT;
        X Window
Internetwork packet exchange, 31, 293–95
Interprocess communication, 259–66
i option, 126, 137
IP. *See* Internet protocol
IPC. *See* Interprocess communication
IPCP. *See* Internet protocol control protocol
ipcs command, 262
IPX. *See* Internetwork packet exchange
ISDN. *See* Integrated services digital network
IS-IS. *See* Intermediate system-to-
        intermediate system
ISO. *See* International Standards Organization
Iterative server, 274–75

KAS. *See* Kerberos authentication server
Kerberos Authentication Server, 249–51, 317
Kernel, 13–14, 21–23, 28
Kernel mode, 326

keylogin command, 196
keyserv daemon, 187, 196
k option, 163

Labeled node, 350
Labels. *See* Security labels
LAN. *See* Local area network
LAN WorkPlace, 308–10
LAPD. *See* Link access procedures on
        D-channel
last command, 226
Layers, 32
    application, 37, 94–98
    ATM, 55–57
    Internet, 36–37, 64–72
    network access, 36
    OSI/RM, 34
    transport, 37
    transmission control protocol, 72–91
    user datagram protocol, 92–93
    See also Network access layer
LCP. *See* Line control protocol
Line control protocol, 323
Link, 16
Link access procedures on D-channel, 48
LIS. *See* Logical IP subnetwork
listen system call, 276–77
LLC. *See* Logical link control
LMI. *See* Local management interface
Local area network, 3
    IEEE standards, 63–64
    reliability of, 25
Local management interface, 48
LocalTalk network, 312–13
Logical devices, 15, 50
Logical IP subnetwork, 62
Logical link control, 46
Login program, 23
Logins, unsuccessful, 223
Loopback address, 32, 39, 108
l option, 136, 139, 142
Loss rate, ATM network, 55

MAC. *See* Media access control
Mach operating system, 6, 317
MacTCP, 315
MacX, 315
Maintenance operations protocol, 321
makefile, 171, 178
MAN. *See* Metropolitan area network
Managed nodes, 349
Management information base, 350
Management information base-I, 351

Management information base-II, 351–52
    EGP group objects, 370–71
    ICMP objects, 363–65
    interfaces group table, 355–59
    IP objects table, 359–62
    SNMP objects, 372–75
    system group table, 353–55
    TCP objects table, 366–68
    UDP objects table, 369
Management plane, 58
Manager, 351
Manual IP address allocation, 98
Maps
    automounter, 165–66
    master, 165–66
    modification/propagation, 172–73
    network information service, 170–73
    Windows NT, 329
Marshalling, 268
Masks, 113–14
Masquerade, 214
Master maps, 165–66
Master server, 170, 173–75, 191–95, 199–201, 203–6
Matrix switching, 103
Maximum segment size, 74–75
Maximum transmission unit, 75
Media access control, 46, 63
Memory management, 23
Message-framed data, 101
Message length field, 92
Message queues, 262–65
Message(s), 37
    ARP, 65–66
    COPS, 241–42
    defined, 261
    discover, 97
    error, 382
    exterior gateway protocol, 347
    modification, 214
    offer, 97
    open shortest path first, 346
    SNMP, 365
    See also Internet control messages protocol
Metropolitan area network, 63
MIB. See Management information base
Microkernel, 6
MIPS, 25
MK. See Microkernel
mknod system call, 261
MLS. See Multilevel security
Module assignment, 103

MOP. See Maintenance operations protocol
m option, 126, 195
MOTIF, 6
mountall command, 162
mount command, 154, 156–57, 160, 162
mountd daemon, 155–56, 161, 163, 396
mnttab file, 160
MP. See Multiple processors; Multiprocessing plus
msgctl system call, 264
msgget system call, 262, 264
msgrcv system call, 262, 264
msgsnd system call, 262, 264
mtab file, 154, 156
MTU. See Maximum transmission unit
Multicast address, 32, 41
Multicasting, 51
Multilevel security, 5
Multiple access, 42
Multiple processors, 5
Multiplexer, 105
Multiprocessing plus, 5–6
Multithreaded server, 120

Name binding protocol, 312
named.boot file, 204, 208–9
named.ca file, 205–6, 208–9
named daemon, 123, 201
named.local file, 204–205
Named pipes, 260
Namespace, 181
National Information Infrastructure, 35–36
National Institute of Standards and Technology, 24
National Research and Educational Network, 33–35
National Science Foundation, 33–35
NBP. See Name binding protocol
NCP. See NetWare core protocol
Neighbor acquisition message, 347
netgroups file, 155–56
Netmask. See Subnet mask
netmasks file, 113–14, 171
netstat command, 125–35
NetWare core protocol, 297
NetWare NFS, 310
Network access denial, 232–233
Network access layer, 36
    ATM, 52–63
    Ethernet, 41–43
    Ethernet 100VG-AnyLAN, 44–46
    Fast Ethernet, 43–44
    FDDI, 46

Index

frame relay, 47–52
IEEE LAN standards, 63–64
token ring, 46
Network architectures, 31
   OSI/RM, 32–33
   TCP, 100
   See also Internet architecture; Transmission control protocol/Internet protocol
Network file system, 9, 25, 28, 92
   automounter, 165–68
   BSD UNIX and, 153–58
   client configuration, 164–65
   design and working, 151–52
   future direction, 168–69
   problem troubleshooting, 395–96
   procedures for, 153
   processes related to, 122
   security, 233
   server configuration, 163–64
   stateless protocol, 152–53
   SVR4 UNIX and, 158–63
Network information center, 203
Network information service, 9, 169
   client configuration, 177
   client/server model, 171
   files, 171
   maps, 171–73
   motivation for, 170
   password files, 177–79
   processes related to, 122–23
   server configuration, 173–75
   slave server configuration, 175–77
   terminology, 170
   usage, 179–80
   uses of, 151
Network information service +, 169, 180
   client configuration, 195–97
   commands, 188–90
   daemons, 185–87
   directories, 181
   files, 182–85
   replica configuration, 197–99
   security, 234–36
   server configuration, 191–95, 199–201
   terminology, 181–82
   uses of, 151
Network information systems center, 144
Network management
   abstract syntax notation, 349–50
   model for, 348–49
   SNMP, 350–65

SNMP v2, 365–68
SunNet Manager, 375–81
system management, 368–75
Network management protocol, 349
Network management station, 349, 375–81
Network mask, 113–14
Network-network interface, 54, 59
networks file, 171
Network time protocol, 391
Next hop address, 343
NeXTStep, 11
NFS. *See* Network file system
nfsd daemon, 122, 155, 161, 163, 396
NFS Gateway, 310
nfsstat command, 157–58
ngt.hosts file, 206
NIC. *See* Network information center
NIS. *See* Network information service
nisaddcred command, 188, 194–95
nisaddent command, 194
NISC. *See* Network information systems center
nis-cachemgr daemon, 186–87
nischgrp command, 192
nischmod command, 189, 192
nischttl command, 189–90
NIS_COLDSTART file, 184
niserror command, 190
nisgrpadm command, 193–94
nisinit command, 184–85, 196
nismkdir command, 197
nisping command, 190
NIS_SHARED_DIRCACHE, 184–85
nisshowcache command, 185, 190
NIST. *See* National Institute of Standards and Technology
nistest command, 190
NMS. *See* Network management station
NNI. *See* Network-network interface
NNSC. *See* NSFNET Network Service Center
Nodes
   client, 27
   configuration, 96
   dependency between, 25
   dynamic node assignment, 311
   labeled, 350
   managed, 349
   server, 27
Nonrepudiation, 218
n option, 126, 142
Notation. *See* Dotted decimal notation

Novell NetWare
    configuration case study, 300–306
    internetworking products, 307–10
    open data link interface, 306–7
    protocols, 293–300
NQS, 25
NREN. *See* National Research and Educational Network
NSF. *See* National Science Foundation
NSFNET network service center, 144
nslookup command, 136–37, 210–11
nsswitch.conf file, 182–84
NTP. *See* Network time protocol

Object identifier, 350
Objects, 181
ODI. *See* Open data-link interface
Offer message, 97
ONC. *See* Open Network Computing
Open data-link interface, 306–7
Open Network Computing, 9, 268
Open shortest path first, 340, 343, 345–46
Open Software Foundation, 6–8, 24
open system call, 261
Open system interconnect/reference model, 31
    AppleTalk protocols and, 311
    architecture, 32–33, 35
    layer functions, 34
Operating system versus kernel, 13–14
Operation field, 94
Option length field, 74
Options field, 70
Option type field, 74
OSF. *See* Open Software Foundation
OSI/RM. *See* Open system interconnect/reference model
OSPF. *See* Open shortest path first
Outsider attack, 217
Oversubscription, 51

Packet exchange protocol, 293
Packet(s)
    delivery reliability, 73
    fast, 104–5
    sequencing, 73
    service, 105
    switching, 102, 104–5
    X protocol, 320–21
Padding field, 71
pag file extension, 172
Paging, 23, 27
Parameter marshalling, 268
Parameter problem message, 385–86

Parent directory, 181
Parent process, 16
PA-RISC processor, 7
Partitioning, 15
passwd file, 18
    changes to, NIS, 172–73
    network information service, 171, 177–79
    UID definition in, 228
    UNIX security, 220–22
    yppasswd command, 180
Passwords, 220–21
    aging, 221–22
    encryption, 249–51
    See also passwd file
Payload type identifier, 59
PC/ix. *See* Personal computer interactive executive
PDN. *See* Public data network
PDP-11 system, 2
PDP-7 system, 2
PDU. *See* Protocol data unit
Peripheral devices, 28–29
Permanent virtual circuit, 49–50
Permission bits, 229–30
Permissions setting, 237
Personal computer interactive executive, 8
Personal computers, 325
Pervasive security mechanism, 219–20
Physical layer, 55–56, 103
Physical medium-dependent sublayer, 56
PID. *See* Process identifier
Pipes, 260–61
Planes, ATM, 58
PMD sublayer. *See* Physical medium-dependent sublayer
Point-to-point protocol, 322–23
Portable operating system interface for computer environments, 24
Port assignment, 103
portmap process, 123–24
portmapper network service, 272–74, 278–80
Ports
    ephemeral, 272
    nonreserved, 272
    reserved, 270–71
    TCP and UDP, 269–74
    well-known, 271–72
POSIX. *See* Portable operating system interface for computer environments
PowerPC RISC processor, 8
Power processor, 8
PPP. *See* Point-to-point protocol

Primary server, 203
Principals, 234
Print services, AppleTalk, 314
Privileged mode, 326
Processes, 14
Process identifier, 14
Process layer. *See* Application layer
Processor technology, 25–26
Programs, 14
Project 1003, 24
Project Athena, 316–17
Protocol argument, 275
Protocol converter, 341
Protocol data unit, 358
Protocol field, 66, 70
Protocol(s)
    ARP, 6, 66
    defined, 32
    Ethernet, 42–43
    types of, 32
protocols file, 108–9, 171
Proxy agents, 350, 365
ps -ax command, 260
PSH. *See* Push function field
PTI. *See* Payload type identifier
Public data network, 51
Push function field, 74
PVC. *See* Permanent virtual circuit
PXP. *See* Packet exchange protocol

QIC. *See* Quarter-inch cartridge
QoS. *See* Quality of service
Quality of service, 54, 57
Quarter-inch cartridge, 29

RARP. *See* Reverse address resolution protocol
rarpd process, 111, 121
rc.local script, 156
rcp command, 141
rc script file, 159
read and write system call, 277–78
Read only errors, 395
Real-time processing, 5
recvfrom system call, 278
recv system call, 278
Redirect message, 386–88
Reduced instruction set computer, 2, 26
Relay service, 105
Remote procedure call, 8–9, 120, 152, 268
Remote shell command, 141–42
Repeaters, 339
Replay, 214
Replica configuration, 197–99

Reply, ARP, 65
reports file, 238
Repudiation, 218
Request for comments, 145
Requesting state, 97
Request packet, 65
Reserved field, 74
Reset connection field, 74
Reverse address resolution protocol, 32, 36, 66, 68–69, 121
rev.ngt.com file, 206
RFC. *See* Request for comments
rhosts file, 230–31
Ring controller, 46
RIP. *See* Routing information protocol
RISC. *See* Reduced instruction set computer
rlogin command, 139, 229–31
rmt protocol, 29
ROLC. *See* Routing over large clouds
Root access, 225
Root account, 220–21, 229, 233
Root directory, 181
Root domain, 191–95
root file, 23
rootkey file, 184
Root server, 202–3
r option, 126, 192
routed daemon, 121, 344
Routing, 340, 342–43
    exterior gateway protocol, 347
    IS-IS, 347–48
    open shortest path first, 345–46
    security control, 219
    in T carrier services, 105
Routing information protocol, 121, 340, 343–45
Routing over large clouds, 62
Routing update message, 347
RPC. *See* Remote procedure call
rpcbind command, 123
rpcinfo command, 137–38
rpc.lockd daemon, 122
rpc.mountd daemon, 122
rpc.nisd daemon, 185–86
rpc.statd daemon, 122
rresvport system call, 270, 278
RS/6000, 8
rsh command, 141–42
RST. *See* Reset connection field

SAP. *See* Service advertisement protocol
SAR. *See* Segmentation and reassembly sublayer

Scalable technology, 55
SCO UNIX, 11
Screen, 318
Sealed ticket, 251
Search path, 224–25
Secondary server, 203
Security
    anonymous FTP account, 253–57
    Automated security enhancement
        tool, 236–39
    Computer Oracle Password System, 239–47
    credentials, 187–88
    ISO
        attack types, 214, 217–18
        definition of, 213
        management, 220
        mechanisms, 218–20
        motivation for, 213–14
        services, 218
        terminology, 215–17
        threats, 214
    Kerberos, 249–51
    SVR4, 5
    TCP/IP
        FTP connections, 231
        incoming network access, 232
        network file system, 233
        network information service +, 234–36
        outgoing network access, 232–33
        sendmail and SMTP, 232
        telnet versus rlogin, 229–31
        trivial file transfer protocol, 233–34
    TCP Wrapper, 247–48
    UNIX
        account access, 222–23
        chmod command, 227–28
        directory/file permissions, 227
        last command, 226
        passwords, 220–22
        root access, 225
        search path, 224–25
        setuid/setgid/sticky bit, 229
        super-user sessions, 220
        syslog facility, 226
        system accounts, 222
        UIDs and GIDs, 228
        umask command, 227
        unsuccessful logins, 223
        utmp/wtmp files, 225–26
Security labels, 219
Security recovery, 219
Segmentation and reassembly sublayer, 57
Selecting state, 97
Semaphores, 266
semctl system call, 266
semget system call, 266
semop system call, 266
sendmail, 232
send system call, 278
sendto system call, 278
Sequenced packet exchange, 31, 293, 296–97
Sequence number field, 74
Serial line Internet protocol, 322
Serial line protocols, 322–23
Server node, 2, 27
Servers
    AppleTalk Network, 313–14
    domain name service, 201–4
    end, 251
    iterative and concurrent, 274–75
    master, DNS, 203–6
    master, NIS, 170, 173–75
    master, NIS +, 191–95, 199–201
    network file system, 163–64
    Novell, 293
    RPC model, 268
    slave, DNS, 204
    slave, NIS, 170, 175–77
    Windows NT, 330–35
    X, 318–19
Service advertisement protocol, 293, 300
Service classes, ATM, 58
Service field, 70
services file, 109–11, 171
setgid. *See* Set group identification
Set group identification, 229–30
Set system file permissions, 237
setuid. *See* Set user identification
Set user identification, 229–30
SGMP. *See* Simple gateway
        management protocol
shadow file, 18–20
shareall command, 161
share command, 160–61
Shared memory, 266
sharetab file, 160–61
shmat system call, 266
shmctl system call, 266
shmdt system call, 266
shmget system call, 266
Short text description, 350
showmount command, 157
Signal degradation, 102
Signals, 15

Simple gateway management protocol, 350
Simple mail transfer protocol, 232
Simple network management protocol, 316
  advantages, 350
  architecture, 350–52
  objects, 352–65, 372–75
  version 2, 365–68
Simplex circuit operation, 101
Single-threaded server, 120
Slave server, 170, 175–77, 204
Sliding window protocol, 296
SLIP. *See* Serial line Internet protocol
SMDS. *See* Switched multimegabit service
SMI. *See* Structure of management information
SMIT. *See* System management interface tool
SMTP. *See* Simple mail transfer protocol
SNMP. *See* Simple network
           management protocol
Snoop command, 142–44
SOA record, 205
Socket descriptor, 267
Sockets, 267, 294, 320
socket system call, 275
Solaris, 9–11
SOM. *See* Start of message
SONET, 54, 55
s option, 126, 197
Source address, Ethernet, 42–43
Source hardware address, ARP, 66
Source IP address, ARP, 66
Source port field, 74, 92
Source quench message, 386
Source-to-destination layer.
           See Transport layer
SPARC processor, 10
Spec 1170, 24
Specific security mechanism, 219
Spooler, 314
SPX. *See* Sequenced packet exchange
start argument, 159
Start of message, 102
Start-up
  init.d/nfs.client, 159
  rc.boot, 154
  See also Initialization
Start-up drive, 29
Stateless protocol, 152
Static routing, 344
Static switching, 103
Sticky bit, 229–30
stop argument, 159
Streaming drives, 29

Stream-oriented service, 92
Streams, 320
Structure of management information, 358
Subnet address, 32
Subnet mask, 40–41
Subnetting, 113–14
SunLink, 310
SunNet Manager, 375–81
SunOS, 9–10
Super block, 16
Super-user sessions, 220
SVC. *See* Switched virtual circuit
SVID. *See* System V Interface Definition
SVR4. *See* System V Release 4
Swapping, 23, 28
Switched access, 50
Switched-media standard, 55
Switched multimegabit service, 102
Switched virtual circuit, 49, 58
Switching
  ATM network, 52
  dynamic, 103–4
  fast packet, 104–5
  and hubs, 104, 341
  static, 103
  virtual LAN, 102–3
  virtual path/virtual channel, 62
Symbolic mode, 227
Synchronization field, 74
Synchronous transmission, 46, 101–2
syslog.conf file, 247
syslog facility, 226
System accounts, 222
System calls, 13, 16–17
  Berkeley socket, 275–78
System files, 17
  group, 20–21
  inittab, 21
  passwd, 18
  shadow, 18–20
System files checklist, 237
System group, MIB-II, 352–54
System management interface tool, 8
System V interface definition, 6–7, 24
System V Release 4, 5–6, 158–63

Tables, 182
Tape drives, 29
T carrier services, 105
TCP. *See* Transmission control protocol
TCP/IP. *See* Transmission control protocol/
           Internet protocol
TCP Wrapper, 247–48

TC sublayer. *See* Transmission convergence sublayer
telnet command, 139, 229–31, 394
TFTP. *See* Trivial file transfer protocol
TGS. *See* Ticket granting server
Threads, 6
Threats, security, 213–14
Ticket granting server, 249–51
Tickets, 249–51
Time exceeded message, 384–85
Timestamp reply message, 391–92
Timestamp request message, 390–91
Time to live field, 70
Time-to-live value, 189–90
TLI. *See* Transport layer interface
to argument, 278
Token, 46
Token bus, 64
Token ring network, 3
   at network access layer, 46
   IEEE 802.5 standard, 64
   reliability of, 25
TokenTalk network, 313
Toolkits, 318
TOS. *See* Type of service
Traffic padding, 219
Traffic switched backplane, 104
Transmission control protocol, 32, 37, 72–91
   MIB-II group, 354, 366–68
   packet reports, 75–90
   ports, 269–74
Transmission control protocol/Internet protocol, 31
   architecture, 100
   and Windows NT, 327–30
   and X environment, 321
   See also Internet architecture; Security, TCP/IP
Transmission convergence sublayer, 56
Transmission objects, 352
Transmission types, 101
Transport endpoint, 267
Transport layer, 37
   transmission control protocol, 72–91
   user datagram protocol, 92–93
Transport layer interface, 259, 267–68
Transport provider, 267
Trapdoor, 218
Trivial file transfer protocol, 92, 233–34
Trojan horse, 218, 224
Troubleshooting protocol. *See* Internet control messages protocol

Trusted functionality, 219
tune.rpt command, 237
Two-wire connection, 44, 101
type field, 346
Type of service, 70

UDP. *See* User datagram protocol
UID, 220-221, 228, 242
ULTRIX, 7
umask command, 227
umountall command, 162–63
umount command, 160, 162
uname command, 138
Unexport function, 161
UNI. *See* User-network interface
unix file, 23
UNIX-Macintosh integration
   AppleTalk addressing, 311–12
   AppleTalk and OSI/RM, 311
   AppleTalk environment, 310–11
   AppleTalk network types, 312–13
   AppleTalk protocols, 312
   internetworking services, 313–14
   internetworking software, 315–16
UNIX network
   arp command, 135–36
   bootptab file, 112–13
   domainname command, 137
   ethers file, 111–12
   flavors of, 4–12
   ftp command, 139–41
   history and growth, 2–3
   hostname command, 137
   hosts file, 107–8
   ifconfig command, 124–25
   inetd.conf file, 114–18
   netmasks, 113–14
   netstat command, 125–35
   nslookup command, 136–37
   operating system, 13–14
   processes, 118–19
      automount, 122
      biod, 122
      bootpd, 121–22
      DNS-related, 123
      inetd, 120–21
      named, 123
      nfsd, 122
      NFS-related, 122
      NIS-related, 122–23
      portmap, 123–24
      rarpd, 121
      routed, 121

rpcbind, 123
ypbind, 123
ypserv, 123
ypxfrd, 123
protocols file, 108–9
services, 109–11
rcp command, 141
rlogin command, 139
rpcinfo command, 137–38
rsh command, 141–42
snoop command, 142–44
telnet command, 139
uname command, 138
See also Security, UNIX
UnixWare, 12, 307
Unmarshalling, 268
unmountall command, 160
unshare command, 161
unshareall command, 160
Urgent pointer field, 74
User data field, 49
User datagram protocol, 32, 37
    client/server application, 289–91
    MIB-II group, 354, 369
    packet report, 93
    ports, 269–74
    and transport layer, 92–93
User/group checks, 237
User information commands, 145, 147
User mode, 326
User-network interface, 53–54, 59
User plane, 58
User's encryption key, 251
usrgrp.rpt command, 237
utmp file, 225–226

VCC. *See* Virtual channel connection
VCI. *See* Virtual circuit identifier
VC switch. *See* Virtual channel switch
Vector distance algorithm, 344
Version field, 69
vfstab file, 158–59
Virtual channel connection, 61
Virtual channel identifier, 61
Virtual channel switch, 62
Virtual circuit identifier, 56–57, 59
Virtual circuit status messages, 51
Virtual local area network, 102–3
Virtual machine interactive executive, 8
Virtual path connection, 61
Virtual path identifier, 56–57, 59, 61
Virtual path switch, 62
Visual systems management, 8

VM/ix. *See* Virtual machine interactive executive
vmunix file, 23
v option, 168
VPC. *See* Virtual path connection
VPI. *See* Virtual path identifier
VP switch. *See* Virtual path switch
VSM. *See* Visual systems management
Vulnerability, 213

WAN. *See* Wide area network
who command, 147
Wide area network, 3, 25
Window field, 74
Window manager, 318–19
Windows Internet name service, 329–30
Windows NT, 12–13, 326–35
WINS. *See* Windows Internet Name Service
Workgroup switch, 104
Workstations. *See* Dataless workstation; Diskless workstation; Hybrid workstation
wtmp file, 225–26

X client, 315, 319
xclock application, 324–25
X display manager control protocol, 322
XDMCP. *See* X display manager control protocol
xdm process, 322
XDR. *See* External data representation
XENIX, 11
xhost command, 324
xinit command, 324
Xlib, 318, 320
X/Open, 24
Xremote, 322
X server, 318
xtab file, 155
xterm command, 319, 324
X terminals, 66, 94
X Window, 315
    commands and applications, 323–25
    display manager control protocol, 322
    and PCs and UNIX, 325
    Project Athena, 316–17
    protocol, 319–21
    serial line protocols, 322–23
    servers and clients, 319
    standard, 317–18
    terminology, 318–19

Yellow pages, 122–23
    See also Network Information Service

YP. *See* Yellow pages
ypbind command, 123, 175–77
ypcat command, 179–80
ypinit command, 174, 176
yppasswd command, 180
ypserv command, 123, 175–76

ypwhich command, 179
ypxfr command, 173
ypxfrd command, 123

Zephyr, 317
Zones, 202

The Artech House Telecommunications Library

Vinton G. Cerf, Series Editor

Advanced Technology for Road Transport: IVHS and ATT, Ian Catling, editor

Advances in Computer Communications and Networking, Wesley W. Chu, editor

Advances in Computer Systems Security, Rein Turn, editor

Advances in Telecommunications Networks, William S. Lee and Derrick C. Brown

Analysis and Synthesis of Logic Systems, Daniel Mange

Asynchronous Transfer Mode Networks: Performance Issues, Second edition, Raif O. Onvural

ATM Switching Systems, Thomas M. Chen and Stephen S. Liu

A Bibliography of Telecommunications and Socio-Economic Development, Heather E. Hudson

Broadband: Business Services, Technologies, and Strategic Impact, David Wright

Broadband Network Analysis and Design, Daniel Minoli

Broadband Telecommunications Technology, Byeong Lee, Minho Kang, and Jonghee Lee

Cellular Radio: Analog and Digital Systems, Asha Mehrotra

Cellular Radio Systems, D. M. Balston and R. C. V. Macario, editors

Client/Server Computing: Architecture, Applications, and Distributed Systems Management, Bruce Elbert and Bobby Martyna

Codes for Error Control and Synchronization, Djimitri Wiggert

Communications Directory, Manus Egan, editor

The Complete Guide to Buying a Telephone System, Paul Daubitz

Computer-Mediated Communications: Multimedia Applications, Rob Walters

Computer Telephone Integration, Rob Walters

The Corporate Cabling Guide, Mark W. McElroy

Corporate Networks: The Strategic Use of Telecommunications, Thomas Valovic

Current Advances in LANs, MANs, and ISDN, B. G. Kim, editor

Digital Cellular Radio, George Calhoun

Digital Hardware Testing: Transistor-Level Fault Modeling and Testing, Rochit Rajsuman, editor

Digital Signal Processing, Murat Kunt

Digital Switching Control Architectures, Giuseppe Fantauzzi

Distributed Multimedia Through Broadband Communications Services, Daniel Minoli and Robert Keinath

Disaster Recovery Planning for Telecommunications, Leo A. Wrobel

Document Imaging Systems: Technology and Applications, Nathan J. Muller

EDI Security, Control, and Audit, Albert J. Marcella and Sally Chen

Electronic Mail, Jacob Palme

Enterprise Networking: Fractional T1 to SONET, Frame Relay to BISDN, Daniel Minoli

Expert Systems Applications in Integrated Network Management, E. C. Ericson, L. T. Ericson, and D. Minoli, editors

FAX: Digital Facsimile Technology and Applications, Second Edition, Dennis Bodson, Kenneth McConnell, and Richard Schaphorst

FDDI and FDDI-II: Architecture, Protocols, and Performance, Bernhard Albert and Anura P. Jayasumana

Fiber Network Service Survivability, Tsong-Ho Wu

Fiber Optics and CATV Business Strategy, Robert K. Yates et al.

A Guide to Fractional T1, J. E. Trulove

A Guide to the TCP/IP Protocol Suite, Floyd Wilder

Implementing EDI, Mike Hendry

Implementing X.400 and X.500: The PP and QUIPU Systems, Steve Kille

Inbound Call Centers: Design, Implementation, and Management, Robert A. Gable

Information Superhighways: The Economics of Advanced Public Communication Networks, Bruce Egan

Integrated Broadband Networks, Amit Bhargava

Intelcom '94: The Outlook for Mediterranean Communications, Stephen McClelland, editor

International Telecommunications Management, Bruce R. Elbert

International Telecommunication Standards Organizations, Andrew Macpherson

Internetworking LANs: Operation, Design, and Management, Robert Davidson and Nathan Muller

Introduction to Document Image Processing Techniques, Ronald G. Matteson

Introduction to Error-Correcting Codes, Michael Purser

Introduction to Satellite Communication, Bruce R. Elbert

Introduction to T1/T3 Networking, Regis J. (Bud) Bates

Introduction to Telecommunication Electronics, Second Edition, A. Michael Noll

Introduction to Telephones and Telephones Systems, Second Edition,
   A. Michael Noll

Introduction to X.400, Cemil Betanov

Land-Mobile Radio System Engineering, Garry C. Hess

LAN/WAN Optimization Techniques, Harrell Van Norman

LANs to WANs: Network Management in the 1990s, Nathan J. Muller and
   Robert P. Davidson

Long Distance Services: A Buyer's Guide, Daniel D. Briere

Managing Computer Networks: A Case-Based Reasoning Approach,
   Lundy Lewis

Measurement of Optical Fibers and Devices, G. Cancellieri and U. Ravaioli

Meteor Burst Communication, Jacob Z. Schanker

*Minimum Risk Strategy for Acquiring Communications Equipment and
   Services*, Nathan J. Muller

*Mobile Communications in the U.S. and Europe: Regulation, Technology, and
   Markets*, Michael Paetsch

Mobile Information Systems, John Walker

Narrowband Land-Mobile Radio Networks, Jean-Paul Linnartz

Networking Strategies for Information Technology, Bruce Elbert

Numerical Analysis of Linear Networks and Systems, Hermann Kremer et al.

Optimization of Digital Transmission Systems, K. Trondle and Gunter Soder

Packet Switching Evolution from Narrowband to Broadband ISDN, M. Smouts

Packet Video: Modeling and Signal Processing, Naohisa Ohta

Personal Communication Systems and Technologies, John Gardiner and
   Barry West, editors

The PP and QUIPU Implementation of X.400 and X.500, Stephen Kille

Practical Computer Network Security, Mike Hendry

Principles of Secure Communication Systems, Second Edition, Don J. Torrieri

Principles of Signaling for Cell Relay and Frame Relay, Daniel Minoli and
   George Dobrowski

Principles of Signals and Systems: Deterministic Signals, B. Picinbono

Private Telecommunication Networks, Bruce Elbert

Radio-Relay Systems, Anton A. Huurdeman

Radiodetermination Satellite Services and Standards, Martin Rothblatt

Residential Fiber Optic Networks: An Engineering and Economic Analysis,
   David Reed

Secure Data Networking, Michael Purser

Service Management in Computing and Telecommunications, Richard Hallows

Setting Global Telecommunication Standards: The Stakes, The Players, and The Process, Gerd Wallenstein

Smart Cards, José Manuel Otón and José Luis Zoreda

Super-High-Definition Images: Beyond HDTV, Naohisa Ohta, Sadayasu Ono, and Tomonori Aoyama

Television Technology: Fundamentals and Future Prospects, A. Michael Noll

Telecommunications Technology Handbook, Daniel Minoli

Telecommuting, Osman Eldib and Daniel Minoli

Telemetry Systems Design, Frank Carden

Telephone Company and Cable Television Competition, Stuart N. Brotman

Teletraffic Technologies in ATM Networks, Hiroshi Saito

Terrestrial Digital Microwave Communications, Ferdo Ivanek, editor

Toll-Free Services: A Complete Guide to Design, Implementation, and Management, Robert A. Gable

Transmission Networking: SONET and the SDH, Mike Sexton and Andy Reid

Transmission Performance of Evolving Telecommunications Networks, John Gruber and Godfrey Williams

Troposcatter Radio Links, G. Roda

Understanding Emerging Network Services, Pricing, and Regulation, Leo A. Wrobel and Eddie M. Pope

UNIX Internetworking, Second Edition, Uday O. Pabrai

Virtual Networks: A Buyer's Guide, Daniel D. Briere

Voice Processing, Second Edition, Walt Tetschner

Voice Teletraffic System Engineering, James R. Boucher

Wireless Access and the Local Telephone Network, George Calhoun

Wireless Data Networking, Nathan J. Muller

Wireless LAN Systems, A. Santamaría and F. J. López-Hernández

Wireless: The Revolution in Personal Telecommunications, Ira Brodsky

Writing Disaster Recovery Plans for Telecommunications Networks and LANs, Leo A. Wrobel

X Window System User's Guide, Uday O. Pabrai

For further information on these and other Artech House titles, contact:

Artech House
685 Canton Street
Norwood, MA 02062
617-769-9750
Fax: 617-769-6334
Telex: 951-659
email: artech@world.std.com

Artech House
 Portland House, Stag Place
London SW1E 5XA England
+44 (0) 171-973-8077
 Fax: +44 (0) 171-630-0166
Telex: 951-659
email: bookco@artech.demon.co.uk